Journalism

Recent titles in the
Reference Sources in the Humanity Series

Journalism

A Guide to the Reference Literature
3rd Edition

Jo A. Cates

Foreword by James W. Carey

Reference Sources in the Humanities
James Rettig, Series Editor

LIBRARIES
UNLIMITED

A Member of the Greenwood Publishing Group

Westport, Connecticut • London

Ref.

32/450

Library of Congress Cataloging-in-Publication Data

Cates, Jo A.
  Journalism : a guide to the reference literature / by Jo A. Cates ; foreword by
James W. Carey—3rd ed.
    p. cm.—(Reference sources in the humanities)
  Includes bibliographical references and indexes.
  ISBN 1–59158–061–7 (alk. paper)
    1. Journalism—Reference books—Bibliography. 2. Journalism—
  Bibliography. I. Title. II. Reference sources in the humanities series.
  Z6940.C38   2004
  [PN4731]
  016.0704—dc22   2003069491

British Library Cataloguing in Publication Data is available.

Library of Congress Catalog Card Number: 2003069491

ISBN: 1–59158–061–7

First published in 2004

Libraries Unlimited, 88 Post Road West, Westport, CT 06881
A Member of the Greenwood Publishing Group, Inc.
www.lu.com

Printed in the United States of America

The paper used in this book complies with the
Permanent Paper Standard issued by the National
Information Standards Organization (Z39.48–1984).

10   9   8   7   6   5   4   3   2   1

Contents

Foreword

When the first edition of Jo Cates's *Journalism: A Guide to the Reference Literature* fell into my hands, it was as if I had come upon a miracle. Journalism is one of the oldest of the literary arts, tracing a history, alongside that of the novel, as one of the characteristic inventions of the modern era. Journalism is certainly the oldest of the popular arts, a symbol of the democratic spirit taking up residence in the world of letters. However, some four hundred years after its birth, journalism had not been honored with its own reference book until Jo Cates came along with her elegant, exhaustive guide. Therefore, the original publication of this guide in 1990 was a matter of some moment in the history of journalism. Reference guides had existed for all the professions and for virtually every junction of human knowledge, including the media and communication. However, the resources of journalism never had been exhaustively catalogued for those who pursue the craft as well as those who teach and study it. This is a matter of some importance. In recent years, journalism has been threatened with absorption into the entertainment, communications, and electronics industries. Therefore, to insist on the distinctive nature of journalism as a practice is an act of courageous preservation as well as of publishing. At a time in history when journalism, the literary art, is threatened by technology, media, and bureaucracy, Jo Cates has rescued its prominence as a social, cultural, and political force. Moreover, and so much the better, she has done so with the wit, charm, and grace of great journalism: a reference book that authoritatively teaches, but in a rich, accessible language. I called that first edition an ideal collaboration of the arts of journalism and librarianship. The third edition updates, magnifies, and extends those virtues further into the new world of electronics and the Internet.

Libraries and journalism are tied together in a lively and paradoxical history. Prior to the invention of the printing press and the newspaper, the most important records and documents of community life were kept on parchment. Libraries were the keepers of those manuscripts, and librarians were charged with preserving them against wear, loss, and destruction from the hazards of promiscuous use. Parchment was expensive, manuscripts few, the art of copying tedious and time-consuming. As a result, parchment manuscripts were precious, even sacred. Parchment was durable, but manuscripts were so scarce that fire, vandalism, or the carnage of war could cause a cultural stroke: the loss of collective memory, of history, of the fundamental documents of community life. The library was, as a result, a fortress, a protection against loss, and the librarian a preserver against the forces of destruction and change.

Journalism, the printing press, and the newspaper changed all that. Journalism derives its name from the French word for *day*. Journalism is a diary, a day-book, a record of the significant happenings, occurrences, events, and sayings during a day in the life of a community. Journalism preserves not only the exotic, rare, and sacred but also the common, ordinary, and repetitive events of life. Printing on paper recommended itself because it overcame the rarity and fragility of parchment manuscripts. Paradoxically, placing writing on a cheaper and flimsier material made the collective memory of the community more secure, and permitted the recording of the commonplace. Cheap and easy reproduction of material in large numbers guaranteed that nothing of significance would ever be lost again. Thomas Jefferson early recognized the great advantage of printing, and, in one of his letters, provided not only the basic justification of freedom of the press but underlined the central value of printing and the newspaper:

> Our experience has proved to us that a single copy, or a few, deposited... in the public offices cannot be relied on for any great length of time. The ravages of fire and of ferocious enemies have had but too much part in producing the very loss we now deplore. How many of the precious works of antiquity were lost while they existed only in manuscript? Has there ever been one lost since the art of printing has rendered it practicable to multiply and disperse copies? This leads us then to the only means of preserving those remains of our laws now under consideration, that is, a multiplication of printed copies."

Early newspapers were underwritten by government grants to print the laws and records of the community. This was more than patronage. Freedom of the press guaranteed the records of the community against loss, made them easily accessible for research, and assured that the basic documents of the community would not disappear through the errant habits of county clerks. Because printing and the newspaper preserved this record of the community against loss, documents could be safely circulated. As a result, the library changed its function and librarians their role. Rather than simply preserving records, libraries disseminated them and made them widely available. The librarian oversaw a circulation system rather than simply a preservation system. The newspaper, above all, became the "paper of record": the unofficial but indispensable transcript of the community. The library, in turn, became a central depository accessible not just to scholars but to every citizen of the community.

The amount of paper produced has grown to Everest-like proportions. As Walter Bagehot said over a century ago, "The newspaper is like the city: everything is there and everything is disconnected." The task of the library, through its reference section, is to connect the disconnected. Through bibliographies and bibliographic guides, directories, yearbooks, records of archives and collections and, in our day, databases and other computerized sources, the library references, integrates, and makes systematically available the holdings of the community. However, this record of the record—the materials that actually index what is out there and held—has never been itself, at least as concerns journalism, brought together in one convenient form. Until this reference guide appeared, that is.

Jo Cates's *Journalism: A Guide to the Reference Literature* is an absolutely unique source and book. It is strictly a reference guide and it is strictly devoted to journalism—print, broadcast, and Internet. It is a thorough, exhaustive accumulation of nearly 800 sources in print and databases that collectively constitutes the records of journalism. Jo Cates is a first-class researcher rescuing obscure, often ephemeral, but always useful material from a thousand hidden niches in the archive, computer, and library.

She is ideally qualified to undertake this task. A superbly trained librarian, she created and directed the library at The Poynter Institute for Media Studies for a number of years. There she served students, faculty, and countless journalists and scholars who sought her advice and guidance to the literature and archive of journalism. Attuned to the needs of journalists and educators, sensitive to journalism as a craft and calling, she brought the polished skills of a librarian to very high-level detective work. This reference book makes widely available the generous advice and wide learning heretofore accessible only to the patrons of The Poynter Institute. Later, she served as library director of the Transportation Library at Northwestern University, tribute to the fact that once words are put on paper or in machines they must be distributed, a fact that has led to a lively intertwined history of journalism and transportation. She is now library director at Columbia College in Chicago where she continues to serve students and faculty, and through this guide, the wider world of journalism.

To one's immense pleasure, this is a reference book that is a delight to read. The annotated entries are mini-essays that are artfully crafted and critically acute. They are composed with grace and clarity, a steady and discerning intelligence, and great wit and good humor. The book disguises in its graceful effortlessness the immense and difficult work required to put it together. Everything is here and everything is now connected. Journalism has a reference guide worthy of its calling. You have some happy reading herein and, even more, it will set you onto some happy hunting.

James W. Carey
CBS Professor of International Journalism
Graduate School of Journalism
Columbia University

Acknowledgments

I owe thanks to many people.

To Calder Pickett and the late William Price, along with Eleanor Blum and Frances Wilhoit, who have set the high standards in journalism and mass communications bibliography.

To my friends at Columbia College Chicago, particularly my colleagues in the journalism department, who understand what I am trying to do here.

To the Columbia College library staff, and especially Michelle Ferguson. They were patient and understanding as I struggled to meet a final deadline.

To Steve Kapelke, Columbia College provost, for his interest in and support of this project.

To my friend and editor Jim Rettig, who simplified my job. He is sharp and intelligent, and never draws blood.

To Jim Carey, who offered wise words on journalism education and life.

To my former colleagues at The Poynter Institute for Media Studies, especially David Shedden, director of Poynter's Eugene Patterson Library. David is the penultimate bibliographer. Not only does he have a vast knowledge of journalism resources, he shares it.

To Gene Patterson, whose body of work and passion for doing the right thing bring me to tears.

To A. J. Anderson, professor of library science at Simmons College, mentor and lifelong friend, who encouraged me to write again. I'll never forget that.

To Jim Sulski, for everything.

To Hannah, Jake, and Emma. I love you more, hang up.

To Mom. She actually read the first two editions cover to cover. I wish she were here to enjoy this one.

Finally, this book is dedicated to Jacob Frank and Mabel Frank, who always asked how my day went and "how's your book going, how long have you been working on it, and when is it going to be done?"

Introduction

Way back in another lifetime before the first edition of *Journalism: A Guide to the Reference Literature* was even conceived and when I was the fledgling library director of The Poynter Institute for Media Studies, I remember thinking I needed a book like this. I sat on a packing box, surveying those empty library shelves, and wished for just one volume that would spell out what I needed to build a state-of-the-art journalism reference collection.

I had the classics in hand: Eleanor Blum's *Basic Books in the Mass Media* (University of Illinois Press, 1980); Warren C. Price's *The Literature of Journalism: An Annotated Bibliography* (University of Minnesota Press, 1959); and Price and Calder Pickett's *An Annotated Journalism Bibliography, 1958–1968* (University of Minnesota Press, 1970), to name a few. But Blum's book was showing its age, it focused on the mass media, and contained both general and reference works. Likewise, Price and Pickett listed both general and reference sources, but only in print journalism.

Journalism: A Guide to the Reference Literature was first published in 1990, and aimed to complement these important sources in addition to finding a niche as the first reference source focusing exclusively on journalism reference sources.

A lot has changed since the publication of the first edition, and even since the second edition was published in 1997. I am obviously not sitting on a packing box at The Poynter Institute and there has been a whirlwind of activity in journalism reference publishing, requiring a thorough second revision of this book.

With the publication of the third edition of Eleanor Blum and Frances Wilhoit's seminal *Mass Media Bibliography* (University of Illinois Press, 1990) and notable communications and mass communications bibliographies such as Eleanor Block and James Bracken's *Communication and the Mass Media* (Libraries Unlimited, 1991) and Christopher Sterling, James Bracken, and Susan Hill's *Mass Communications Research Resources* (Lawrence Erlbaum, 1998), a huge gap was filled. As a result, this edition of *Journalism: A Guide to the Reference Literature* is a far more discrete journalism reference source.

For librarians in search of a reference collection development tool, students and others beginning research in journalism, and print and broadcast journalists who want to know more about their field, here is the third edition. It is a selected, annotated bibliography and reference guide to the English-language reference literature of print, broadcast, and online journalism. It covers sources from the late 1960s through mid-2003. A small number of earlier classics also are included. I chose titles to include in this guide by examining bibliographic guides, catalogs, standard book review sources, and special library collections.

This is truly a new edition. The third edition has 784 entries. Of those, 155 are completely new and 420 have been substantially revised. In addition, to make way for the new, 127 entries included in previous editions were cut. I have also included a new chapter on Internet sources, with additional references to selected listservs, portals, weblogs, and a collection of interesting online resources.

Entries are numbered and arranged according to type of reference work. In addition to the chapter on Internet sources, there are chapters on bibliographies and bibliographic guides; encyclopedias; dictionaries; indexes and abstracts; commercial databases; biographical sources; directories and yearbooks; handbooks, manuals, and career guides; stylebooks and books of English language usage; catalogs; core periodicals; and miscellaneous sources, as well as chapters listing professional organizations and research centers. Detailed subject and author/title indexes are provided so that no title gets buried in a chapter.

Entries typically include author(s), title, place of publication, pagination, copyright date, annotation, URL (when appropriate), and, when available, Library of Congress and ISSN or ISBN information.

Annotations are descriptive and evaluative, and contain exhaustive cross-references. Most read like critical mini-reviews, aimed at librarians, educators, students, and others interested in beginning research in journalism. This book also will be useful in the newsroom and important to those writing about the media.

This book is not a reference guide to book publishing or advertising or telecommunications or public relations or film or television programming; books on these topics are not even included here unless they specifically address journalism. For example, a bibliography on television network news would be listed here. A guide to *The Andy Griffith Show* would not. [Actually, such publications exist: *Mayberry, My Hometown* (Popular Culture, 1991 reprint) is an encyclopedic chronicle of the show; *The Definitive Andy Griffith Show Reference* (McFarland, 1996) describes all 249 episodes and includes a "Guide to Collectibles."] This also is not a guide to general reference sources, so users should remember that for every specialized who's who or other type of source, there probably is a general reference counterpart.

So what does journalism encompass? For the purpose of this book, titles included passed the "journalism test." That is, the entries focus in some way on gathering, evaluating, displaying, or disseminating news, opinion, or information in print, broadcast, and digital or online formats. But it is so much more than that sterile definition.

I was reminded of what good journalism looks like when I recently read *The Changing South of Gene Patterson: Journalism and Civil Rights, 1960–1968* (University Press of Florida, 2002). I was fortunate enough to work with Patterson when I was at The Poynter Institute and he was editor and president of the *St. Petersburg Times* and later chairman and CEO of the Times Publishing Company. The library at Poynter is named for him.

Patterson was editor of the *Atlanta Constitution* during those early years and wrote daily, producing more than 3,000 columns. Roy Peter Clark writes in the introduction, "This collection passes on the enduring legacy of Patterson's work. For journalists working their craft, Patterson is an exemplar of courage, hard work, literary excellence, and endurance." He continues, "Patterson used the language the way only a lover could, with hope, care, and passion, and for the higher purposes of democracy and justice."

That passion and his pain were evident on September 16, 1963, when Patterson wrote "A Flower for the Graves."

"A Negro mother wept in the street Sunday morning in front of a Baptist Church in Birmingham. In her hand she held a shoe, one shoe, from the foot of her dead child. We hold that shoe with her.

"Every one of us in the white South holds that small shoe in his hand."

"It is too late to blame the sick criminal who handled the dynamite. The FBI and the police can deal with that kind. The charge against them is simple. They killed four children.

"Only we can trace the truth, Southerner—you and I. We broke those children's bodies.

"We watched the stage set without staying it. We listened to the prologue unbestirred. We saw the curtain opening with disinterest. We have heard the play."

That is journalism, at its very best and bravest.

Once again, I hope this book helps.

1
Bibliographies and Bibliographic Guides

1.   Adams, Julian, ed. **Journalism Bibliography.** Blue Springs, MO: Journalism Education Association, Inc., 1984. 16p.

This excellent bibliography of scholastic journalism is packed with several hundred book citations with brief annotations. Entries are arranged alphabetically by author within sections on high school journalism textbooks; advising school publications; yearbooks; history; freedom of the press, radio, and television; style; editorial and opinion writing; photojournalism; careers; and so on. Most entries were published from 1975 through 1983.

2.   Alali, A. Odasuo, and Gary W. Byrd. **Terrorism and the News Media: A Selected, Annotated Bibliography.** Jefferson, NC: McFarland, 1994. 213p. index. LC 94-2923. ISBN 0-89950-904-5.

If users of this source can wade through several pages of what appear to be apologist arguments for Arab terrorists (see specifically page 11) and decipher an occasional unintelligible statement ("We feel strongly that the studies in this volume are the illuminators of the belief system that permeates analysis of media coverage of terrorism"), they will discover some useful annotated listings of books, chapters, journal articles, and conference papers "that show how media operatives report terrorism in news programs." The introduction also contains other interesting and potentially controversial statements ("Terrorists are no different from any other group that uses the media to its advantage") and some direct hits on perceived newsroom politics ("Media conceptions of 'terrorism' and the labels assigned to perpetrators of political violence seem to reflect the anti-Muslim, anti-Islamic feelings that permeate American newsrooms"). In the wake of September 11, 2001, an updated edition would be a timely and significant addition to the literature. Organization is unwieldy, so be prepared to rely on the author, title, and subject indexes. Chapters, for example, are titled "Understanding Terrorism," which contains the first 325 citations, "Terrorism in the Electronic Media," and "Terrorism in the Print Media." Many citations belong in both print and electronic chapters; as a result, there are so many "see" references (nearly 200) that the total number of 738 citations is misleading. Media coverage of terrorism is a topic of great current interest; this source lists some relevant items, but use with care. Alali also is editor of *Mass Media Sex and Adolescent Values: An Annotated Bibliography and Directory of Organizations* (McFarland, 1991), and coeditor (with Kenoye Kelvin Eke) of *Media Coverage of Terrorism: Methods of Diffusion* (Sage, 1991). See also *Violence and Terror in the Mass Media: An Annotated Bibliography* (entry 111), which focuses primarily on scholarly studies through 1987.

3.   Alkire, Leland G. Jr., comp. **The Writer's Adviser.** Detroit: Gale, 1985. 452p. index. LC 84-24715. ISBN 0-8103-2093-2.

More than 800 books and 3,000 articles are cited in this popular guide to writing. Although it is most useful to fiction writers, the journalist may find an item or two of value. The 34 chapters include Television, Radio, and Film, Realism, Book Reviewing (a surprisingly scanty section—only 15 entries), Style Manuals, General Advice and Inspiration, and Freelancing. This is not a scholarly work and we are reminded in the introduction that it is for working writers "seeking advice and direction." Entries for books contain critical annotations. Article entries are not annotated at all. Even though this is not a comprehensive guide, there are some surprising omissions. Two articles written by Donald Murray, a writing coach, English professor, and Pulitzer Prize winner, are included, but none of his well-read books on writing such as *Writing for Your Readers* (Globe Pequot Press, 1983) are listed. Numerous articles are culled from *The Writer* and *Writer's Digest.*

4.   Anderson, Peter J. **Research Guide in Journalism.** Morristown, NJ: General Learning Press, 1974. 229p. index. LC 73-84662.

Less of a journalism research guide than a historical guide for journalism students, "this guide, if used correctly, will direct the reader to source material, and it will explain how to organize and document a paper in a style that is guaranteed to satisfy either a professor or an editor." It includes an annotated list of general reference sources arranged by subject, then alphabetically by title. Chapters on "How to Write and Research a Topic in Journalism," "The Library Card System," and "Form of the Paper" are provided, as well as a section on "Journalistic Instructions" that lists "top" instructors and schools of journalism. There is a subject and title index.

5.   Asante, Clement E. **Press Freedom and Development: A Research Guide and Selected Bibliography.** Westport, CT: Greenwood Press, 1997. 216p. index. bibliog. (Bibliographies and Indexes in Mass Media and Communications, no. 11). LC 97-021983. ISBN 0-3132-9994-3.

Asante writes that "to study communication and development is mostly to study a relationship between the media and government." This scholarly, annotated bibliography of more than 500 sources offers a unique glimpse into the interdependence between communications and freedom of the press. The volume, however, is divided into two "camps." Part 1 is press freedom and media government connections, subdivided into chapters on world press systems, media ownership and control, and the "new world information and communication order debate." The bibliography is geographically subdivided into Eastern Europe, Asia/Pacific, Africa, Latin America/Caribbean, and Middle East. Part 2 is communications and development, with chapters on the "mass media and development debate," media imperialism, the "contribution of communication to national development," and a "reassessment of the old and new media." Again, the separate bibliography is geographically arranged by Asia/Pacific, Latin America/Caribbean, and Africa/Middle East. This unusual arrangement makes it a bit of a challenge to use, and users will find it necessary to consult the index, which also is a challenge to use (specifically, subject indexing is selected and limited). Included are citations to books, theses, dissertations, periodicals, and scholarly or professional journal articles. Annotations are straightforward, but spare and formulaic (most entries begin with a statement such as "this book discusses," "this book defines," "this book examines," "this book provides," etc.) The author explains this by stating, "the style and approach used in this study is metaphorically that of an independent, unobtrusive referee in a boxing match who steps in only when it is absolutely necessary to do so to explain the rules of the game to both fighters." Asante, playing the referee who "steps in," provides not a critical assessment, but, in his own words a "descriptive review of some of the major studies or works done in the general areas of political communication and development communication. . . ."

6. Asian Mass Communication Bibliography Series. Singapore: Asian Mass Communication Research and Information Centre, 1975–1983.

Included in this series of mass media bibliographies are the following: *Mass Communication in Malaysia* (1975), *Mass Communication in India* (1976), *Mass Communication in Hong Kong and Macao* (1976), *Mass Communication in the Philippines* (1976), *Mass Communication in Taiwan* (1977), *Mass Communication in Nepal* (1977), *Mass Communication in Singapore* (1977), *Mass Communication in the Republic of Korea* (1977), *Mass Communication in Sri Lanka* (1978), *Mass Communication in Indonesia* (1978), and *Mass Communication in Thailand* (1983). They range in length from 34 pages (Nepal) to 335 pages (Philippines).

7. Association for Education in Journalism and Mass Communication, Mass Communication Bibliographers. **First Amendment Issues and the Mass Media: A Bibliography of Recent Works.** Presented by the MCB First Amendment Project Committee at the Annual Meeting of the Association for Education in Journalism and Mass Communication, Boston, 1991. 30p.

The First Amendment Project Committee, consisting of Ralph Lowenthal, David Shedden, and Dolores Jenkins, compiled a first-rate annotated bibliography of 109 books and monographs focusing on freedom of the press, freedom of speech, and censorship from the late 1970s to 1991. The committee wisely limited its scope as "the two McCoy bibliographies cited (entries 75–76) are so exhaustive for matter prior to 1977 that we saw no great virtue in reinventing that wheel." (For the record, the second McCoy supplement covering 1978–1992 was published in 1993. See entry 77.) Entries are arranged alphabetically by author; annotations are descriptive and critical. The foreword states that "one of the target audiences will always be the youth of this country; we have developed this bibliography with a view to faculty use with senior high and undergraduate students." There will be other users as well. Although the MCB group has disbanded, an updated version would be most welcome.

8. Barnhart, Thomas F. **The Weekly Newspaper: A Bibliography—1925–1941.** Minneapolis, MN: Burgess, 1941. 107p. LC 41-13300

This bibliography is useful only as a historical guide to weeklies, but is valued because it is written by an authority. Barnhart is also the author of *Weekly Newspaper Makeup and Typography* (University of Minnesota Press, 1949), *Weekly Newspaper Management* (Appleton-Century-Crofts, 1952), and *Weekly Newspaper Writing and Editing* (Drayed Press, 1949). Part of a Works Progress Administration project (later the Works Projects Administration), this annotated bibliography lists 1,200 articles, theses, books, and pamphlets by subject. Apparently, most of the articles included here were read and annotated by WPA workers. There is no index.

9.   Bennett, James R. **Control of Information in the United States: An Annotated Bibliography.** Westport, CT: Meckler, 1987. 587p. index. (Meckler Corporation's Bibliographies on Communications and First Amendment Law, no. 1). LC 87-16475. ISBN 0-88736-082-3.

Bennett has good control of his information, although the general introduction is fuzzy in parts. He states that "the process of creating and sustaining a national consensus in the United States is the subject of this bibliography." Assembling this guide was an ambitious undertaking, and he admits that the "compilation offers the tip of the iceberg." Information control is a central theme in journalism, and many entries relate to that topic. There are almost 3,000 descriptively annotated book and periodical entries on censorship and "primary sources of power," most published after 1945. Included is a list of periodicals cited, and it is an impressive selection of some lesser-known but invaluable publications. Sections are labeled broadly (anticommunism and anti-Sovietism, corporations, government, the Pentagon, intelligence agencies, and global control) but are further broken down into more accessible subjects. A section on "The Complex" is a strange mix of the military-industrial, government regulation, media, education, and "secrecy, censorship, disinformation and deceit." There are almost 200 entries in the media section, although the excellent subject index indicates other entries on that subject are scattered throughout the book. There also is a contributor index.

10.   Bennett, James R. **Control of the Media in the United States: An Annotated Bibliography.** Garland, 1992. 819p. index. (Garland Reference Library of Social Science, v. 456). LC 91-26064. ISBN 0-8240-4438-X.

Wading through the introductory material to discover just what lurks beyond is a daunting task, which is unfortunate, because this is an important source in censorship and general communications policy. The general introduction is an occasionally incoherent discussion subdivided into sections on "Media Research," "The Way Things Are and Might Be," "Arrangement," "Bibliographical Methods," and "Works Cited." Following is the first part of the book, entitled "The Structures of the Corporate State," which offers the user another opaque introduction. It is further subdivided into chapters on "The Master Institutions" and "The Secondary Institutions." The second section on "The Media Complex" is comprised of chapters on "The Media," Advertising and Public Relations," "Electronic Media," "Print Media," and "Art and Music." Section three is "Alternatives." On page xv, the author finally states that "Part II encompasses the specific subject of this bibliography, the role of all discourses and media in the big business/big government symbiotic relationship." Many potential users, unfortunately, still will not know what he is addressing. In addition, the small typewriter font on which Garland relies does not help the user navigate through the unwieldy text. In part because of these complexities, it is important for the user to be aware of Bennett's search methods. In "Bibliographical Methods," he indicates he "did not depend upon the mainstream indexes because they tend to survey mainstream journals, which means they are part of the phenomena of discourse control under study by this bibliography." He continues, "For example, after ten years of publication, *Mother Jones* was still not indexed by one of the most often-consulted library reference books in the US, the *Reader's [sic] Guide to Periodical Literature*." As in his earlier work (entry 9), he states that this source represents "only the tip of the iceberg," but, at 5,000 annotated entries "emphasizing post-World War II events and scholarship," it is a sizable tip. Users will rely heavily on the author index (pp. 649–83) and extensive subject index (pp. 684–819).

11.   Block, Eleanor S., and James K. Bracken. **Communication and the Mass Media: A Guide to the Reference Literature.** Englewood, CO: Libraries Unlimited, 1991. 198p. index. (Reference Sources in the Humanities Series). LC 91-19866. ISBN 0-87287-810-4.

A solid and welcome addition to the literature of mass media reference, this annotated bibliography "aimed at the upper division undergraduate or beginning graduate communication student" focuses on nearly 500 English-language sources in communication published from 1970–1990. The authors, the Ohio State University communications librarians, speak "academese" well ("Coverage includes sources relevant to the various areas that constitute the curricula offered by departments of communication in colleges and universities throughout the United States") but also offer succinct, critical, and occasionally blunt descriptions of specific sources. Producing this bibliography was no small undertaking. Included here is information on communication theory, interpersonal and small-group communication, organizational communication, mass communication, rhetoric, speech, applied linguistics, international and intercultural communication, telecommunication, and new communication technologies. Furthermore, Block and Bracken indicate that public relations, advertising, technical writing and business communication, and journalism are "closely affiliated with the communication curricula." They go on to say that this publication should complement guides such as Jean Ward and Kathleen Hansen's *Search Strategies in Mass Communication* (entry 430); Rebecca Rubin, Alan Rubin, and Linda Piele's *Communication Research: Strategies and Sources*; Kim N. Fisher's *On the Screen: A Film, Television, and Video Research Guide* (entry 30); Jo Cates's *Journalism: A Guide to the Reference Literature*; and Anne B. Passarelli's *Public Relations in Business, Government, and Society: A Bibliographic Guide*. There are chapters on bibliographies; dictionaries, encyclopedias and handbooks; indexes and abstracts; biographical sources; catalogs; directories and yearbooks; online and CD-ROM databases; core periodicals, research centers, and archives; and societies and associations as well as author/title and subject indexes.

12.   Blum, Eleanor. **Basic Books in the Mass Media.** 2d ed. Urbana: University of Illinois Press, 1980. 426p. index. LC 80-11289. ISBN 0-252-00814-6.

This is a classic work. Until the third edition was published in 1990 (entry 13), this was the source a journalism librarian would choose to take to a desert island library. Do not toss this edition, as it contains titles (albeit dated) that are not included in the third. Blum, formerly communications librarian at the University of Illinois, published in 1980 this second edition of her selected booklist of reference and general mass communications literature. It evolved from the first edition, *Reference Books in the Mass Media*. Even though it is "selected," it contains 1,179 entries and was, until the third edition, the most comprehensive and current bibliography available on mass communication. Chapters are broken down into such topics as general communications, books and book publishing, broadcasting, editorial journalism, film, magazines, and advertising and public relations. A chapter by Frances Wilhoit, then head of the journalism library at Indiana University, is devoted to mass communication indexes. The author-title and subject indexes are comprehensive and usable. Annotations are well-written and generally descriptive.

13.   Blum, Eleanor, and Frances Goins Wilhoit. **Mass Media Bibliography: An Annotated Guide to Books and Journals for Research and Reference.** 3d ed. Urbana: University of Illinois Press, 1990. 344p. index. LC 89-39705. ISBN 0-252-01706-4.

The new classic. Containing 1,947 annotated entries, with most of the new titles published between 1980 and 1987, this is no longer a "basic" bibliography as the authors felt the previous title was too "constricting." Blum was professor emeritus of library science at the University of Illinois at Urbana-Champaign and recipient of the Association of Journalism and Mass Communications' first Eleanor Blum Distinguished Service to Research Award. Wilhoit, a former editor of *Journalism Abstracts,* directed the Journalism Library at Indiana University. Their preface notes that the bibliography has three primary purposes: it is a reference source, research and reading list, and a collection management and buying guide. "All entries have one common factor: they treat the subject in broad general terms." Chapters include General Communications, Broadcasting Media, Print Media, Film, Advertising and Public Relations, Bibliographies, Directories and Handbooks, Journals, and Indexes to the Mass Communication Literature. Topics not covered (unless connected with broader mass communications subjects) are censorship, law, copyright, printing, post office, instructional broadcasting, and telephone and telegraph. Entries are descriptive and detailed. In the citation to Douglass Cater's *The Fourth Branch of Government* (no. 59), for example, it is revealed that Cater

was one of the early writers to realize the importance of the reporter's role in government, as exemplified by the Washington journalist. As a Washington reporter himself who was working at the time for *The Reporter,* an analytical fortnightly, he observed and participated, so that his book is written from firsthand knowledge.

It is this attention to detail that makes *Mass Media Bibliography* so indispensable. When used as a buying guide, the only problem one might encounter is the lack of purchase price and ISBN numbers. Author, title, and subject indexes are exhaustive. So is everything else.

14. Brown, Charles H., comp. **Reader's Guide to the Literature of Journalism.** University Park, PA: Pennsylvania State University, School of Journalism, 1961. 87p. LC 62-09665.

The audience for this selected, annotated, but outdated bibliography focusing on the historical and biographical literature of journalism is the "general reader" and student. Although it is not a scholarly work, it is worth browsing through. Be prepared to skim, however, as there is no index. Entries are listed alphabetically by author in sections on history, major figures, special fields of journalism, women in journalism, government and the press, advertising, broadcasting, magazines, and public opinion, among others.

15. Canadian Radio-Television Commission. **Bibliographie, Etudes Canadiennes sur les Mass Media: Bibliography, Some Writings on the Canadian Mass Media.** Ottawa: The Commission, 1974. 99p. index.

The journalism department at Universite Laval, Quebec, and the Canadian Radio-Television Commission list in French and English more than 1,000 books, government documents, dissertations, and journal articles focusing on most aspects of mass media in Canada. Works are either written by Canadians or published by authors living in Canada. Also included are "works published by American firms with Canadian branches (on the advice of the National Library) if they were published in Canada as well as in the States." Items are numbered and arranged alphabetically by author. There are no annotations. An unusual subject index is divided into sections on references (bibliographies, biographies, statistics), media and society, areas of research, and so on, and further subdivided.

16. Cannon, Carl Leslie, comp. **Journalism: A Bibliography.** Detroit, MI: Gale, 1967 (Reprint of 1924 edition). 360p. LC 66-25646.

In the preface, Cannon states he has emphasized the present rather than the historical; thus, this list includes references useful to the "American newspaperman actively engaged in his profession or to the student of journalism." One of the first bibliographies of journalism, it is now an excellent historical study of the newspaper press in the United States and Great Britain from the 1800s to 1923. This partially annotated list contains the New York Public Library's journalism holdings as well as material outside that library, and includes books, magazine articles, pamphlets, and other materials. There are more than 30 topical chapters, including the Negro press, the morgue, paragraphing, sensational journalism, and the country press.

17. Carothers, Diane Foxhill. **Radio Broadcasting from 1920 to 1990: An Annotated Bibliography.** New York: Garland, 1991. 564p. index. (Garland Reference Library of the Humanities, v.967). LC 90-24352. ISBN 0-8240-1209-7.

Covering "almost the entire range of radio broadcasting," this is a comprehensive, well-organized, and essential guide to the field. Carothers, then the Communications Librarian at the University of Illinois at Urbana-Champaign, writes in her succinct one-page introduction that "it is not intended to exhaust the subject but to provide a more extensive source of material than previously published." That it does. When used with *Radio: A Reference Guide* (entry 40), users have access to a wide range of bibliographical information previously scattered. More than 1,700 annotated book citations (with a few trade journals and periodical titles thrown in) are included in chapters on Background of Radio Programming, Economic Aspects, Production Aspects, Programming, International Broadcasting, Public Broadcasting, Regulation and Legal Aspects, Amateur/Ham Radio, Women and Minorities, Careers in Broadcasting, and Reference Sources. Entries are arranged alphabetically by author within each chapter. Radio engineering is not included. Also not included, unfortunately, is a subject index, which given the breadth of material covered, would have been a real time-saver for researchers. Users will have to scan and skim and be content with author and title indexes and table of contents. Researchers might also wish to consult Mitchell E. Shapiro's *Radio Prime Time Programming, 1926–1967* (McFarland, 2002), which offers schedules and tables.

18. Cassata, Mary, and Thomas Skill. **Television: A Guide to the Literature.** Phoenix, AZ: Oryx Press, 1985. 148p. index. LC 83-43236. ISBN 0-89774-140-4.

The three main parts of this book—"Test Patterns," "The Environment," and "Directions"—defy definition. This is not a traditional guide, but a collection of bibliographic essays on various aspects of television and television research. A bibliography is included at the end of each chapter. Originally published in three parts in *Choice* (January, February, April 1982), this guide was expanded to include more than 400 entries. "Test Patterns" includes chapters on the mass communication process, television history, and reference sources. "The Environment" covers television and children and contains good introductory essays on television news and television and politics. "Directions" gives an overview of the television industry, programming, and policy, and skims sources in television criticism. An expanded section on ethics would be very helpful. There is no mention of online sources. It includes author, title, and subject indexes. Users interested in information on cable television should consult Ronald Garay's *Cable Television: A Reference Guide to Information* (entry 34).

19.   Caswell, Lucy Shelton, ed. and comp. **Guide to Sources in American Journalism History.** Westport, CT: Greenwood Press, 1989. 319p. index. (Bibliographies and Indexes in Mass Media and Communications, no. 2). LC 89-11857. ISBN 0-313-26178-4.

Aimed at both scholars and students, this impressive and ambitious bibliographic guide and catalog to archival and manuscript collections in journalism is the first of its kind devoted exclusively to journalism history. Approximately two-thirds of the publication is a state-by-state assessment of archival sources. Entries are further arranged by institution and collection. Addresses, hours of operation, and name of archivist or curator are included. In the essay portions, Kathleen A. Hansen and Jean Ward (authors of *Search Strategies in Mass Communication,* entry 430) contribute two bibliographic essays on "Databases for Historical Research" and "Bibliographies for Journalism History: A Selection." Maurine Beasley offers a discussion of oral history, and Gary Charbonneau outlines the United States Newspaper Program. Caswell, associate professor and curator of the Library of Communication and Graphic Arts at Ohio State University, offers little introductory material (a one-half page preface), leaving that to Michael D. Murray in "Laying a Foundation for the Study of Journalism History: The Organization of the American Journalism Historians Association," Wm. David Sloan in "The History of Historical Writing," and John J. Pauly in "New Directions for Research in Journalism History." The index, although immensely helpful, is not comprehensive, omitting some named references quoted extensively in the essays (e.g., James W. Carey). It lists personal names and collections, but it is not a subject index and should not be used as a complete gauge of contents.

20.   Chaveau, Agnes, and Geoffrey Hare. **Media Studies in France: A Guide to Sources of Information.** Kingston-upon-Thames, Surrey: Apex Centre, Kingston Polytechnic, 1991. 34p. ISBN 1-873152-11-6.

Aimed at English-speaking researchers seeking information on French broadcasting and media, this specialized volume focuses on materials published in France in the 1980s. Annotations are spare, and, as the authors indicate, "brevity of comment inevitably brings with it the danger of caricature." Nevertheless, this is a valuable, if somewhat dated, thumbnail guide that includes sections on research centers, guides, periodicals, general works, media regulation, programs, and new technology.

21.   Chin, Felix. **Cable Television: A Comprehensive Bibliography.** New York: IFI/Plenum, 1978. index. 285p. LC 78-1526. ISBN 0-306-65172-6.

Chin says he has "attempted to provide the reader with all the best material ever published on any topic related to one of the most active areas of broadcasting, cable television." Annotations of 650 books, journal articles, and pamphlets are organized by subject. The "Chronology of Major Decisions and Actions Affecting Cable Television" through the mid-1970s might prove useful, even if the information is a little dated. There is a subject and name index as well as appendixes on CATV systems, associations, and FCC rules.

See Ronald Garay's *Cable Television: A Reference Guide to Information* (entry 34) for more current citations.

22.   Christians, Clifford, and Vernon Jensen **Two Bibliographies on Ethics.** 2d ed. Minneapolis, MN: Silha Center for the Study of Media Ethics and Law, School of Journalism and Mass Communication, University of Minnesota, 1988. 49p. (No. 86093).

Two separate bibliographies by media ethics experts are included in this brief volume. Christians's nine-page "Books on Media Ethics" is arranged chronologically beginning with Nelson Crawford's *The Ethics of Journalism* (1924). A brief introduction describes the scope of the publication and offers some background information on the author. Jensen's 36-page "Ethics in Speech Communication" is divided into sections on books and dissertations, chapters of books, journal articles, and bibliographic aids, and is arranged alphabetically by author. As would be expected, there is some overlap. Of 41 titles in Christians's list, 26 appear in Jensen's. Jensen, however, has not noted, as Christians does, later editions of at least four titles. Christians also is coauthor, with Mark Fackler and Kim B. Rotzoll, of *Media Ethics: Cases and Moral Reasoning* (Longman, 1995) and *Communication Ethics and Universal Values,* with Michael Traber (Sage, 1997).

23.   Cooper, Thomas W., comp. **Television and Ethics: An Annotated Bibliography.** Boston, MA: G. K. Hall, 1988. 203p. index. LC 88-7206. ISBN 0-8161-8966-8.

"Designed to assist readers and researchers interested in the relationships between television and ethics," this selectively annotated bibliography was compiled by Cooper, with the reference and research aid of other staffers at Emerson College (and inspired, no doubt, by Emerson's annual Television and Ethics Conference). It lists 1,170 titles, 473 of which are annotated. A lengthy introduction and methodology section prepare the user for what lies ahead. For example, when describing the book's audience, Cooper writes: "Hence, a balance among general, academic, professional, and trade publications has been sought. One finding, however, is that such a balance does not exist naturally within the field...Consequently, the small proportion of titles from trade and industry journals represents an imbalance discovered during our searches."

Fortunately, author and subject indexes allow relatively easy access to these important citations. Some introductory notes require second and third readings for clarity, such as the following:

> At the conclusion of each abstract, authorship and editing are ascribed in chronological order of the writing and adaptation of each abstract. For example, if the original abstract submitted by the author was ideal for his bibliography, the citation conclusion of the abstract reads <AU>. "author." If however, the Journal of Dissertation Abstracts in Journalism and Mass Communications (fictitious title) edited the author's abstract, which was rewritten by us for this bibliography, the final citation conclusion would read "author/JODAJMC/editor," or in our abbreviated terms <AU/JOD/ED>.

The first section of the bibliography focuses on ethical contexts and contains chapters on classical ethics, professional ethics, communication and mass media ethics, journalism ethics, and teaching media ethics. Part 2, television and ethics, includes advertising, children and television, television news, entertainment, public and educational television, and so on. Cooper offers a star-studded list of advisory editors (Clifford G. Christians, Eugene

Goodwin, J. Michael Kittross, Donald L. McBride, Robert Roberts, and Christopher Sterling) and contributors (Christians, Goodwin, Kittross, McBride, Roberts, Sterling, Deni Elliott, Edmund B. Lambeth, John Merrill, Robert Picard, and Robert Schmuhl, to name a few). In addition, Peter Medaglia acted as managing editor, Robert Sullivan as research editor, and Christopher Weir as business editor.

24.   Danielson, Wayne A., and G. C. Wilhoit Jr., comps. **A Computerized Bibliography of Mass Communication Research, 1944–1964.** New York: Magazine Publishers Association, Inc., 1967. 399p. index.

The Education Committee of the Magazine Publishers Association supported this study, and that may explain the emphasis on magazines in the 2,287 entries. It was published in the late 1960s, and the compilers and publisher were proud of their computer printout bibliography, as emphasized by the title. Its purpose is to "provide magazine executives and others with a comprehensive introduction to the social science journal literature on mass communication." Almost 50 social science journals were searched for mass communication–related articles published from 1944–1964, and this is the result. Numerous citations focus on broadcasting. Entries are arranged alphabetically by author, but the bibliography does not begin until page 192 because of a massive 191-page key word index.

25.   De Mott, John, and Robert Roberts. **White Racism, Blacks, and Mass Communications: An Instruction Source Bibliography.** Paper presented at the Annual Meeting of the Association for Education in Journalism, Houston, TX, 5–8 August 1979. 35p. ERIC, ED 176 315.

Without a table of contents, index, and annotations, how useful can this be? It all depends on the purpose of the guide, and the authors believe that this listing of about 500 books and periodical and magazine articles is sufficient "for the construction of not only a full complement of instructional units in a conventional program but also for creation of a comprehensive course in blacks and the media." Chapters include general listings on race relations, black history, and black mass media but chapters most useful for the stated purpose of this bibliography are "Minorities and the Mass Media: Effects, Criticism, Portrayals" and "Employment of Blacks in the Mass Media." Entries are dated from the 1940s to the mid-1970s. If this bibliography is used in the classroom, it should be updated.

26.   Du Charme, Rita, comp. **Bibliography of Media Management and Economics.** 2d ed. Minneapolis, MN: Media Management and Economics Resource Center, University of Minnesota, 1988. 131p. ISBN 0-944866-01-8.

Approximately 400 books on media management are listed here. Unfortunately, it is not annotated, and the author admits that, "in an effort to be complete," all books listed have not necessarily been read. The subject categories are broad and include sections on broadcasting, cable, journalists, newspaper management, and newspapers. Books are arranged alphabetically by author within the subject areas. The 54-page index (authors only) includes the authors' indexed works but no corresponding text page numbers. The compiler states that this bibliography will be issued annually, but this edition is still the most current one available. (The first edition appeared in 1986.) A form of this bibliography is included in John M. Lavine and Daniel B. Wackman's *Managing Media Organizations* (Longman, 1988).

27. Dunn, M. Gilbert, and Douglas W. Cooper. **"A Guide to Mass Communications Sources."** Journalism Monographs 74, 1981. 42p.

This handy bibliographic essay of reference sources in mass communications is aimed at the social scientist. The authors say that "in the absence of any comprehensive guide to these data sources, many scholars are unaware of the available resources," then fail to mention Eleanor Blum's *Basic Books in the Mass Media* (entry 12) in the introductory comments. (Blum is, however, listed in the appendix, "A Selected List of Directories, Bibliographies and Indexes Useful in Mass Communications Research.") There are separate sections on print and electronic media and each contains discussions of indexes, union lists, catalogs, archives, and so on. Cable television, book publishing, and advertising are excluded.

28. Einstein, Daniel. **Special Edition: A Guide to Network Television Documentary Series and Special News Reports, 1955–1979.** Metuchen, NJ: Scarecrow Press, 1987. 1,051p. index. LC 86-6599. ISBN 0-8108-1898-1. **Special Edition: A Guide to Network Television Documentary Series and Special News Reports, 1980–1989.** Lanham, MD: Scarecrow Press, 1997. 870p. index. LC 96-17904. ISBN 0-8108-3220-8.

More than 7,000 major network documentary programs, specials, and major series are listed and annotated in the first volume. In the introduction, Einstein touches on the history and evolution of the documentary, and talks about television as a "tool for actuality reportage." By the mid-1980s, the magazine format and docudrama had all but snuffed out the long-form documentary. He relies on *TV Guide, Television Index,* and network and production company files for data. Part 1 consists of documentary series programming from 1955 to 1979. Part 2 includes documentaries produced by David L. Wolper, and Part 3 lists television specials and special reports. For the most part, Einstein excludes presidential press conferences, space-shot coverage, and nonfiction public television broadcasts. Entries are numbered and arranged by date of telecast. There are indexes to personalities and production/technical personnel. Title and subject indexes would make this a far more accessible source, but at least (and at last) the information is under one cover. The second volume, encompassing major commercial network documentary and magazine series programs and news special reports broadcast from January 1980 through the end of 1989, is similar in scope and arrangement. Nearly 2,500 programs and 38 series are included here, in detail similar to the sample entry below:

139. 7/29/87 "The Battle for Afghanistan"

Report on the bloody war in Afghanistan that continues eight years after the Soviet invasion. Based on film dispatches shot by cameraman Mike Hoover during eighteen trips to eastern Afghanistan, the program summarizes key battles waged during the past three years, including the battle for the town of Khost and a rebel attack on a Soviet-protected power plant in the Sorubi valley. Also, a look at how the war has affected Afghanistan's children. Emmy winner. E:P-W: Perry Wolff. P-D-DP: Mike Hoover. N: Dan Rather.

Einstein has included in this latest volume an index of program and segment titles as well as subjects/places. Researchers should already be clamoring for a third installment, which would, by necessity, feature America at war, both in the Gulf and at home.

29.   Fejes, Fred. **Gays, Lesbians and the Media: A Selected Bibliography.** Boca Raton, FL: Department of Communication, Florida Atlantic University, 1987. 23p.

Media coverage of the gay and lesbian community is the concern of this brief but important listing, which is now showing its age. Fejes is concerned that most gay publications are not included in basic indexes he searched (*Business Periodicals Index, Communication Abstracts, Readers' Guide to Periodical Literature, Sociological Abstracts*), but fails to note that many of the journalism trade journals also are not indexed. It is in those journals and newsletters, most of which are not cited here, that a wealth of information can be found on this topic. This selected listing of more than 200 citations to newspaper and periodical articles, chapters in books, some dissertations, and books published primarily in the 1970s and 1980s is arranged alphabetically by author. There is no index, no table of contents, and no subject subdivision. A separate section on AIDS and the media would be most helpful. There is always a need for specialized bibliographies such as this, but annotations and indexes are usually advised. (For example, one must search out a 1981 issue of *Jump Cut* to find out what B. Zimmerman has to say about "Lesbian Vampires.") This list is a good starting point for historical research, but do not stop the search here.

30.   Fisher, Kim N. **On the Screen: A Film, Television, and Video Research Guide.** Littleton, CO: Libraries Unlimited, 1986. 209p. index. (Reference Sources in the Humanities Series). LC 86-20965. ISBN 0-87287-448-6.

Fisher has produced a well-written and nicely organized beginner's guide to the reference literature of television and motion pictures, but it is now dated; a second edition is overdue. Its value is the substantial number of entries focused on radio, television news, broadcast journalism, and other subjects relevant to journalism research. Annotations are both descriptive and evaluative, giving the reader a sense of the usefulness of each and every source. For example, it is good to know that some "browsing and digging is required" or that a particular source is "out of date but still respected" or that "a number of entries oddly conclude with a reference to the performer's sign in the zodiac." Most entries encompass the time period from the early 1960s through 1985, and focus on English-language works. Chapters are divided into broad categories based on type of reference work, and then further subdivided into film and television video sections. Entries are arranged alphabetically within chapters. Chapters on core periodicals, research centers, and societies and associations are included. The author/title and subject indexes are detailed.

31.   Ford, Edwin H. **History of Journalism in the United States: A Bibliography of Books and Annotated Articles.** Minneapolis, MN: Burgess, 1938. 42p.

According to Ford, "It is hoped that the references set down hereafter will serve to start students of the history of American journalism on a quest for precise and enlightening information." Of course, this is a dated source but an excellent listing of earlier works in American journalism history. Also included are brief sections on the British press. This bibliography is a Works Progress Administration project.

32.   Friedman, Leslie J. **Sex Role Stereotyping in the Mass Media: An Annotated Bibliography.** New York: Garland, 1977. 324p. index. (Reference Library of Social Science, vol. 47). LC 76-52685. ISBN 0-8240-9865-X.

Although in need of updating, Friedman's bibliography still offers a rich historical perspective. There are more than 1,000 references to books and book chapters, government documents, magazine and journal articles, theses, speeches, and other studies, and perhaps 200 of them touch on sex roles, stereotyping, and the news media, mass media and print media. Articles from *Journalism Quarterly, Editor & Publisher, ASNE Bulletin, Columbia Journalism Review,* and the defunct *Chicago Journalism Review* are included. The numbered entries are arranged alphabetically by author within subject categories. Author and subject indexes are included.

33. Gandy, Oscar H. Jr., Susan Miller, William L. Rivers, and Gail Ann Rivers. **Media and Government: An Annotated Bibliography.** Stanford, CA: Stanford University Institute for Communication Research, 1975. 93p LC 80-456075.

This now historical bibliography on government and the media "consists primarily of prototype studies which are, in the opinion of experts, outstanding or representative examples of research." According to the introduction, "this bibliography is ambitious." Included are books, book chapters, and journal articles (many of them from *Journalism Quarterly* and *Public Opinion Quarterly*). Entries are arranged alphabetically by author and include bibliographic citation, methodology, and a description of findings or conclusions. Unfortunately, there is no table of contents or index, so those less familiar with names of experts will have to scan. The book is divided into sections on the nature of news media, the impact of government on media, and the impact of media on government. Many familiar names turn up here—Altschull, Bagdikian, Argyris, Bogart, Wilhoit, Weaver, Polich, Nimmo, Guback, Emery, Schiller, Rivers, and Schramm—to name a few.

34. Garay, Ronald. **Cable Television: A Reference Guide to Information.** New York: Greenwood Press, 1988. 177p. LC 87-24955. ISBN 0-313-24751-X.

Garay's survey bibliography offers a clear picture of America's cable industry. In five well-organized chapters on general sources, business and economics, programming, law and regulations, and videotex he includes more than 400 book, government document, periodical, and periodical article citations to items published from 1980 to 1987. Excluded are newspaper articles. Garay also outlines succinctly his selection factors (substance, application to current and future needs, content utility, timeliness, lasting value, and accessibility). A general sources section provides overview material; other chapters include overview essays, bibliographical essays, and bibliographical listings. This is an essential source in broadcasting and cable. See also Felix Chin's *Cable Television: A Comprehensive Bibliography* (entry 21), which chronicles information on cable prior to 1978.

35. Genther, Fred L., comp. **Guide to News and Information Sources for Journalists.** Rev. ed. San Luis Obispo, CA: California Polytechnic State University, 1981. 58p.

Although now dated, Genther's guide can still serve as a skeletal introduction to the reference literature of journalism. Genther, who was a reference librarian at the Kennedy Library at California Polytechnic State University, selected about 100 sources he felt were most useful to journalism students and beginning reporters. Most entries are descriptively annotated, and parts of the guide center on holdings at the Cal Poly Library. Chapters are arranged according to subject matter or type of reference book. For example, there are sections on directories and dictionaries as well as chapters on marketing, advertising, and journalism law. There is no mention of online sources and there is no index. A journalism professor at the university writes in the introduction: "Familiarity with the GUIDE won't turn young reporters into amateur librarians. Nor will its use make more advanced news people able to solve all research problems without professional assistance." It is instead a "useful entente."

36. Gillmor, Donald M., Theodore L. Glasser, and Victoria Smith. **Mass Media Law: A Selected Bibliography.** Minneapolis, MN: Silha Center for the Study of Media Ethics and Law, University of Minnesota, School of Journalism and Mass Communication, 1987. 31p.

An unannotated listing of books and periodical articles on media law, this bibliography is arranged by subject, then author. It contains sections on casebooks and general texts, the First Amendment, libel, privacy, courts, obscenity and pornography, broadcast and cable regulation, commercial speech, student press, and legal research. Gillmor also is the author of *Power, Publicity, and the Abuse of Libel Law* (Oxford University Press, 1992) and wrote (with Jerome A. Barron) *Mass Communication Law: Cases and Comments,* 5th ed. (West, 1989).

37. Gitter, A. George, and Robert Grunin, eds. **Communication: A Guide to Information Sources.** Detroit: Gale, 1980. 157p. index. (Psychology Information Guide Series, vol. 3, Gale Information Guide Library). LC 79-26527. ISBN 0-8103-1443-6.

Almost half of the 723 references in this annotated guide are mass communications articles (many from *Journalism Quarterly*) or books, and they are divided into general subjects such as broadcasting, radio, television, and journalism. Most entries are from the 1970s and are numbered and arranged alphabetically by author. As the editors indicate, they are "extending the work of previously published bibliographies in the areas that cover the literature through the late 1960s." As such, this source should be used in tandem with more comprehensive and current book bibliographies such as Blum and Wilhoit's *Mass Media Bibliography* (entry 13). One chapter is devoted to reference works. Author, title, and subject indexes are included.

38. Gordon, Thomas F., and Mary Ellen Verna, comps. **Mass Communication Effects and Processes: A Comprehensive Bibliography, 1950–1975.** Beverly Hills, CA: Sage, 1978. 227p. LC 77-26094. ISBN 0-8039-0903-9.

This comprehensive research bibliography lists references to psychological and social effects of the media from 1950–1975. The Literature Overview section is rather tedious, but a necessary evil in using this source. There are 2,704 entries with very few annotations; the body of the bibliography is arranged alphabetically by author. The subject index is detailed and cross-referenced, but not designed for quick and easy access. Useful entries can be found indexed under magazines, newspapers, credibility, journalism, minorities, news, radio, and television. Gordon and Verna also wrote *Mass Media and Socialization: A Selected Bibliography* (Temple University, 1973).

39. Greenberg, Gerald S. **Tabloid Journalism: An Annotated Bibliography of English-Language Sources.** Westport, CT: Greenwood Press, 1996. 187p. index. (Bibliographies and Indexes in Mass Media and Communications, no. 10). LC 96-8942. ISBN 0-313-29544-1.

Focusing on scholarly publications, popular magazine articles, theses and dissertations, and books published between 1975–1994, this unique source examines not only historical aspects of tabloid journalism, but also sensational aspects of television broadcasting. Print journalism in the United States comprises the bulk of the volume, and is further subdivided into general works; historical overviews of the penny press, yellow journalism, jazz journalism and exposes; and Modern Practice. The table of contents reflects none of this, however, and users should expect to rely heavily on the useful author and subject indexes (users will not be surprised to discover several entries listed under "Aliens"). It also offers a section on legal implications as well as an international perspective, with citations arranged geographically by more than a dozen countries. Greenberg states that "whenever a nation's press has been able to break free from the control of government and political parties, a popular press aimed at mass readership has developed. England pioneered such newspapers in the nineteenth century, and produced the first tabloid early in the twentieth. Emerging nations are finding that commercialization of news reporting entails adoption of many tabloid-type features so popular in the west." Annotations are uniformly brief and descriptive. The author also notes that collections of yellow and penny press publications are found in many libraries, but he discovered only three libraries that collect the supermarket tabloids and phototabloids of the 1920s—the Library of Congress, the Bowling Green State University Popular Culture Collection, and the NYPL Research Library.

40.   Greenfield, Thomas Allen. **Radio: A Reference Guide.** Westport, CT: Greenwood Press, 1989. 172p. index. LC 88-24647. ISBN 0-313-22276-2.

"The giant shadow that television cast over radio in the 1940s and 1950s had its parallel in the production of copy on radio," Greenfield writes. He continues:

> One of the sobering lessons I was to learn in the preparation of this book is that sources on broadcasting written after 1950 tend to focus upon television at the considerable expense of radio. I chose to include here broadcasting sources that showed at least a reasonable balance in their treatment of the two media. This occurred far less frequently than I might have wished.

Thus, the tone is set in this narrative bibliographical guide to research materials on radio and radio programming in America. Greenfield makes numerous references to doctoral dissertations, and notes that "although dissertations are maligned as research sources in some areas of study, in the radio field they often hold some of the best available information on certain subjects (such as the history and development of National Public Radio)." Textbooks and how-to books are generally not included. There are chapters on Radio Networks and Station Histories, Drama, News Music, Comedy and Variety, Sports, Short Waves (offering brief sections on Women in Radio, Radio Advertising, Religious Radio Broadcasting, and Armed Forces Radio), and Organizations, Collections, Journals and Indexes. The Radio News chapter is subdivided into sections on General Works, The Press-Radio War, The Commentators, Edward R. Murrow, Miscellaneous Subjects, and a Bibliography for Radio News; the five-page bibliography has complete citations for works mentioned in the narrative, with titles ranging from "A Descriptive Study: Edward R. Murrow's Contributions to Electronic Journalism," a 1971 dissertation, to Mitchell V. Charnley's *News By Radio,* published in 1948. For further information and a more traditional bibliographic style, consult Diane Carothers's *Radio Broadcasting from 1920–1990: An Annotated Bibliography* (entry 17). Researchers might also wish to consult Mitchell E. Shapiro's *Radio Network Prime Time Programming, 1926–1967* (McFarland, 2002), which includes tables and schedules.

41.   Hansen, Donald A., and J. Herschel Parsons. **Mass Communication: A Research Bibliography.** Santa Barbara, CA: Glendessary Press, 1968. 144p.

The authors offer their opinions on existing mass communication research and say that numerous books and reports "range in quality from the profound to the trivial, but—compared to at least some other fields—a disturbing majority must be categorized near the latter end of such a continuum. That disturbing majority has for the most part been omitted from this bibliography. This is not to say that each of the studies listed here is of unquestionable quality, but rather that the unquestionably valueless have been excluded."

Entries for nearly 3,000 scholarly journal articles, reports, and monographs from 1945 to the mid-1960s are divided into sections on bibliographies and reference materials, research and methods, social contexts of media, audience and diffusion, and so on. Entries are further subdivided into such sections as general theory and content, and arranged alphabetically by author. There is, unfortunately, no subject index, nor are annotations provided. Scholarly research for the "social theorist" is emphasized, so users searching for *Editor & Publisher*–type citations are advised to look further.

42.   Hausman, Linda Weiner. **"Criticism of the Press in U.S. Periodicals: 1900–1939."** Journalism Monographs, No. 4, 1967. 49p. LC 68-06952. ISSN 0022-5525.

Hausman culled some 500 articles on press criticism from the trusty *Readers' Guide to Periodical Literature* and concentrated on the time period starting at the turn of the century to the beginning of World War II. It is not the definitive listing, but a good starting point for students researching the time period.

43.   Higgens, Gavin, ed. **British Broadcasting 1922–1982: A Selected and Annotated Bibliography.** London: British Broadcasting Corporation Data Publications, 1983. 279p. ISBN 0-563-12137-8.

Annotated references to English-language books, periodical articles, and pamphlets from the 1920s to the early 1980s are listed in this bibliography of radio and television broadcasting. Brief and descriptive annotations emphasize the BBC. Researchers might also wish to consult Andrew Crisell's *An Introductory History of British Broadcasting* (Routledge, 1997), which includes eight pages of useful bibliographical references.

44.   Hill, George H. **Black Media in America: A Resource Guide.** Boston, MA: G. K. Hall, 1984. 333p. index. (Reference Publication in Black Studies). LC 84-15672. ISBN 0-8161-8610-3.

In his preface, Hill, vice president of a television production company and public relations firm, states that "this annotated bibliography seeks to be the most comprehensive and exhaustive bibliography ever compiled on black media." This partially annotated bibliography of books and periodical and magazine articles is not exhaustive. A Communications/Media Works sections is divided into Books and Monographs, Dissertations and

Theses. These are not arranged according to subject, and, unfortunately, the index is scanty. *Journalism Quarterly* is cited in both Journal References and the Newspaper and Magazine Articles section. Nowhere are *Presstime, ASNE Bulletin,* or smaller journalism reviews and the like mentioned. This is not a scholarly work, but because few reference sources have dealt with this topic, it should be consulted initially.

45. Hill, George H., and Sylvia Saverson Hill. **Blacks on Television: A Selectively Annotated Bibliography.** Metuchen, NJ: Scarecrow, 1985. 223p. index. LC 84-23639. ISBN 0-8108-1774-8.

"Selectively annotated" is an understatement. The authors cover 45 years of black involvement in television and list more than 2,800 entries, but only books, dissertations, and theses (fewer than 60) are annotated. A surprisingly small section of journal article citations are taken from communications periodicals, and a search in *Social Sciences Index,* for example, reveals that relevant entries are absent. More than 2,600 popular magazine article entries are divided into 40 sections, but the table of contents and subject/author index do not reflect it. Because of its limitations, this bibliography is best used as a source for popular literature on blacks in broadcasting, religious broadcasting, broadcast management and ownership, news, and news/talk programs. See also George H. Hill's *Black Women in Television: An Illustrated History and Bibliography* (Garland, 1990), an unannotated bibliography offering a small section on black women in television news and sports.

46. Hill, Susan M., ed. **Broadcasting Bibliography: A Guide to the Literature of Radio & Television.** 3d ed. Compiled by the National Association of Broadcasters Library and Information Center Staff. Washington, D.C.: NAB, 1989. 74p. index. ISBN 0-89324-076-1.

A short, selective, and easy-to-follow listing of more than 500 current books in broadcasting, this updated bibliography (second edition published in 1984) was compiled by the people who ought to know. The brief introduction indicates that it is "intended to suggest titles which will help broadcasters, students, and observers of the broadcasting industry develop reading lists." Entries are divided into categories on reference sources, business, law, technology, broadcasting and society, comparative broadcasting, and telecommunications, and arranged alphabetically by author. There are no annotations. A bonus is a listing of more than 100 trade journals with one-sentence descriptions. Most recently, Hill was an editor of *Mass Communication Research Resources* (entry 120).

47. Hoerder, Dirk, ed. (Christine Harzig, asst. ed.) **The Immigrant Labor Press in North America, 1840s–1970s: An Annotated Bibliography.** Westport, CT: Greenwood Press, 1987. index. (Bibliographies and Indexes in American History, no. 4, 7–8). LC 87-168. Volume 1: Migrants from Northern Europe. 278p. ISBN 0-313-24638-6. Volume 2: Labor Migrants from Eastern and Southeastern Europe. 725p. ISBN 0-313-26077-X. Volume 3: Migrants from Southern and Western Europe. 583p. ISBN 0-313-26078-8.

According to the editors, "the idea of compiling this bibliography was born when it became obvious that the detailed studies of the role of individual ethnic groups in the North American working classes already available needed to be supplemented by a broad comparative approach taking into account the cultures of origin, migration processes, and specific forms of acculturation in the United States or Canada."

Each volume provides a lengthy introduction and user's guide, a discussion of the immigrant labor (not union) press, and descriptions of individual newspapers and periodicals. From Lithuanians to Dutch-speaking peoples, chapters are arranged primarily by language group, are written by experts, and include an introduction, bibliography, and title, place, and chronological indexes. Entries include translated titles, editors, publishers, dates, and depositories. These three volumes grew out of a 1978 symposium, "American Labor and Immigration History, 1877–1920s: Recent European Research" held at the University of Bremen, Federal Republic of Germany, where a project entitled "Bibliography and Archival Presentation of Non-English Language Labor and Radical Newspapers and Periodicals in North America, 1840s–1970s" was proposed. Hoerder and Harzig also edited *The Press of Labor Migrants in Europe and North America, 1880s to 1930s* (Bremen, 1985). Other useful sources on the ethnic press include Sally Miller's *The Ethnic Press in the United States* (entry 549) and Lubomyr R. and Anna Wynar's *Encyclopedic Directory of Ethnic Newspapers and Periodicals in the United States* (entry 376).

48.   Hoffmann, Frank W. **Intellectual Freedom and Censorship: An Annotated Bibliography.** Metuchen, NJ: Scarecrow Press, 1989. 244p. LC 88-18811. ISBN 0-8108-2145-1.

Aimed at "students in high schools and institutions of higher learning," this collection of 900 citations to book and periodical articles is very general but useful as a starting point for research on intellectual freedom issues. It is divided into sections on theoretical foundations, court cases, professions concerned with intellectual freedom (education, journalism, librarianship, and politics and government service), pro-censorship and anti-censorship, and cases of censorship in the mass media. The subsection on journalism, containing more than 50 citations, is divided into three parts: "The Role of the Press in American Society," "History of the Press," and "Notable Journalistic Issues Related to the First Amendment," which is further subdivided into categories on free press versus fair trial/gag orders, libel/invasion of privacy, right of access to information and the media, and the right to know (Freedom of Information Act, The Pentagon Papers). The journalism listings are a disappointing collection of titles, with almost one-third of them culled from Robert B. Downs and Ralph E. McCoy's *The First Freedom Today: Critical Issues Relating to Censorship and Intellectual Freedom* (ALA, 1984). This particular chapter seems dated; the two most current citations are dated 1986. In the mid to late 1980s, there was a watershed of reporting on FOIA (the Freedom of Information Act), Sunshine Laws, and legal and ethical issues in computer assisted reporting. This is simply not reflected here. There is no title index; the subject index includes titles of censored works but not titles cited in the main bibliography. The definitive work on the topic continues to be McCoy's *Freedom of the Press: An Annotated Bibliography* and supplements (entries 75–77). See also the following periodicals for current information, decisions, and related material: *IRE Journal* (entry 611), *Media Law Reporter* (entry 622), and *News Media and the Law* (entry 624).

49.   Hoffman, Frederick J., Charles Allen, and Carolyn F. Ulrich. **The Little Magazine: A History and Bibliography.** 2d ed. Princeton, NJ: Princeton University Press, 1947. 450p.

The little magazine is an "important source of information about twentieth century writing," according to the authors. The first half of the book defines little magazines and places them in historical perspective. The second half is a listing of magazines by year, then alphabetically. Most magazines listed began after 1910. Publication history and editorial information are provided and the length of the annotation is a good indication of the magazine's overall importance. There also is a supplementary list of about 100 magazines that influenced the little-magazine movement.

50. Howell, John Bruce. **Style Manuals of the English-Speaking World: A Guide.** Phoenix, AZ: Oryx Press, 1983. 138p. index. LC 82-42916. ISBN 0-89774-089-0.

Manuals from the United States, Canada, and Great Britain are included, as well as a sampling of style manuals from the "English language publishing communities" of Australia, India, New Zealand, and Nigeria. Most of the manuals were published between 1970 and 1983, or are older and considered "classic." To be included, the manual must be at least five pages long and in English. The "General Manual" section contains 124 entries arranged alphabetically and further subdivided into commercial publishers, government printing, term papers and theses, and university presses. Notes on bibliographic style are included. More than 100 entries are arranged alphabetically by compiler in the "Subject Manual" section. Subjects range from agriculture to zoology. Most of the stylebooks under the "News and News Magazines" heading are included in the stylebook chapter of this text. An appendix describes three handbooks on nonsexist language. The index includes compilers, titles, and general subjects.

51. Jackson, Fleda Brown, W. David Sloan, and James R. Bennett. **Journalism as Art: A Selective Annotated Bibliography.** Style 15 (1982): 466–487.

This small and selective journalism bibliography is included here because its topic is widely discussed in the classroom and the newsroom. What is the difference between journalism and literature? Is there a difference? Should there be? Books, journal articles, masters' theses, and other sources are examined, and the bibliography is divided into three parts. The first section includes historical studies of journalism and studies of individual writers. Part 2 is entitled "Journalism as Literary Art," and the last section concerns journalistic prose style. Entries are arranged alphabetically within the three sections. The authors surveyed basic journalism bibliographies and 30 communications, mass communications, and journalism magazines and periodicals. This is a broad overview of an even broader subject, but it works, making it a useful starting point.

52. Jenkins, Dolores, and Rosalie Sanderson. **The State Media Law Sourcebook.** Gainesville, FL: Brechner Center for Freedom of Information, University of Florida College of Journalism and Communications, 1992. 85p.

Both a handbook and bibliography, this is an ambitious effort to list sources on media law available in each state. The focus: "printed resource materials about media law written for journalists." The purpose: "to prepare a bibliography of media law materials for each state with information about their availability. We also hope to encourage journalists and/or attorneys in states that do not have such materials to prepare them." According to the preface, information about the following types of laws are included: laws regulating access (freedom of information, sunshine laws or open government laws, etc.), laws regulating media actions when legal proceedings begin, and libel and defamation law. This is the first published project of the Freedom Forum's National Freedom of Information Coalition. There are small but invaluable sections on sources covering all states, general sources, and textbooks, but the bulk of the handbook focuses on materials listed by state. Reference sources, hotlines, organizations, and newsletters are included; entries contain title and order information, format, and description. The entry for Massachusetts, for example, includes two publications: *Massachusetts Journalists' Court and Legal Handbook* and *Tapping Officials' Secrets: A State Open Government Compendium* (see entry 428), as well as a listing of two organizations: the Massachusetts Public Records Division and the Massachusetts Newspaper Publishers Association.

53.　　Kaid, Lynda Lee, Keith R. Sanders, and Robert O. Hirsch. **Political Campaign Communication: A Bibliography and Guide to the Literature.** Metuchen, NJ: Scarecrow Press, 1974. 206p. index. LC 73-22492. ISBN 0-8108-0704-1.

More than 1,500 books, pamphlets, journal articles, public documents, theses, and dissertations on political campaign communication in the United States from 1950–1972 are included in this bibliography. The authors carefully explain scope and methodology, and indicate that "its major purpose is to offer suggestions as to how the user may stay abreast of this burgeoning literature, using the bibliographic entries provided here as a point of departure." Included is an annotated list of 50 books "we believe to be seminal to the study of political campaign communication" and a list in German and French of books and periodical articles with foreign perspectives. Entries are numbered and arranged alphabetically by author. There are no annotations. See also *Political Campaign Communication: A Bibliography and Guide to the Literature 1973–1982* (entry 54).

54.　　Kaid, Lynda Lee, and Anne Johnston Wadsworth. **Political Campaign Communication: A Bibliography and Guide to the Literature 1973–1982.** Metuchen, NJ: Scarecrow Press, 1985. 217p. LC 84-23508. ISBN 0-8108-1764-0.

Political communication embraces many fields and disciplines, and researching this general subject can sometimes be an overwhelming task. The authors are to be congratulated for this update of *Political Campaign Communication: A Bibliography and Guide to the Literature* (entry 53). This bibliography lists 2,461 English-language books, pamphlets, journal articles, and dissertations and theses. Popular magazine and newspaper articles, unpublished papers, and government documents are not included; neither do the authors mention in the introduction whether they conducted computer searches of the literature. Publications on the role and effects of the communications media, credibility of the mass media, and media use in political campaigns are covered, in addition to general works on political campaigns. One must rely on the subject index to gain entry to the bibliography. Citations are in alphabetical order and numbered consecutively. This guide is the starting point for most scholarly research on this subject. Kaid coauthored (with Kathleen J. M. Haynes) the *Political Commercial Archive, A Catalog and Guide to the Collection* (University of Oklahoma, Political Communication Center, 1991), and *Of Civic Dialogue in the 1996 Presidential Campaign: Candidates, Media and Public Voices* (Hampton Press, 2000), with Mitchell S. McKinney and John C. Tedesco.

55.　　Kittross, John M., comp. **A Bibliography of Theses and Dissertations in Broadcasting: 1920–1973.** Washington, D.C.: Broadcast Education Association, 1978. 238p.

Kittross reminds the user that "much of what we know about mass communication was the product of graduate-level research." He continues, "Often, a thesis or dissertation effects more people than any other single piece of work in a person's career." On that note, Kittross goes on to highlight more than 4,300 dissertations and theses from American universities. All aspects of broadcasting are covered. In a section entitled, "How This Project Came About," Kittross offers details on other bibliographies upon which this publication is built: "Doctoral Dissertations in Radio and Television, 1920–1957," and "Graduate Theses and Dissertation in Broadcasting: A Topical Index," both appearing in the *Journal of Broadcasting* in the late 1950s. Some statistical analyses are included as well as subject, key word, and chronological indexes. A table of contents refers the user to page numbers, but the pages are not numbered. The numbered entries are arranged alphabetically by author and include title of thesis or dissertation, college or university, year degree awarded and, when available, last name of thesis adviser. See also Donald McBride's *Doctoral Dissertations on Broadcast Journalism: A Bibliography* (entry 73), with listings through the late 1980s. Kittross coauthored, with Christopher Sterling, *Stay Tuned: A Concise History of American Broadcasting* (Erlbaum. 2002).

56. La Brie, Henry G., III. **The Black Press: A Bibliography.** Kennebunkport, ME: Mercer Press, 1973. 39p.

A simple one-page preface introduces 400 entries on the black press, subdivided into sections on books, periodicals and monographs, unpublished theses and papers, and newspaper articles. Entries range from I. Garland Penn's *The Afro-American Press and Its Editors* (Ayer, 1969, reprint of 1891 ed.) to Lawrence D. Reddick's unpublished dissertation "The Negro and the New Orleans Press, 1850–1860." There is no index. La Brie also wrote *A Survey of Black Newspapers in America* (entry 363).

57. Langham, Josephine, and Janine Chrichley, comps. **Radio Research: An Annotated Bibliography, 1975–1988.** 2d ed. Aldershot, England: Avebury, 1989. 357p. ISBN 0-566-07130-4.

Radio research and audience data with a British bent are the focus of this very specialized "project commissioned by the Radio Academy and funded by the IBA" (Independent Broadcasting Authority). The second edition offers nearly 1,000 citations. Parts 1 and 2 deal with BBC and IBA research and are arranged in chronological order. The compilers note that "inclusion in the Bibliography does not imply availability. Individual researchers will still have to negotiate with the institutions for access to the material." Part 3 is "Other British Research," subdivided into sections on advertising, local radio, community radio, academic research, educational research, and general research. Entries are arranged alphabetically by author within each section. Part 4 is "Foreign Research," which contains citations to books, journal articles, and documents; it is arranged by continent and country, then author. Australia and New Zealand, Europe, and the Americas merit their own sections. The "Rest of the World" section contains a curious geographic mix: African nations, Arab World and Middle East, Asia, Canary Islands, Cape Verde, Cayman Islands, China, Pakistan, and Third World. The compilers note that "while every effort has been made to paraphrase the research correctly, no attempt has been made to evaluate either the results or the methodology." Annotations are frequently long-winded, and there are typographical errors in the table of contents and introductory material; one has to wonder if every effort was made to edit and proofread.

58. Lasswell, Harold D., Ralph D. Casey, and Bruce Lannes Smith. **Propaganda and Promotional Activities: An Annotated Bibliography.** Chicago: University of Chicago Press, c1935, 1969. 450p. LC 75-77979.

In his *Freedom of the Press: An Annotated Bibliography* (entries 75–77), Ralph McCoy does not include a great deal about propaganda but suggests that those searching for studies of propaganda turn to this bibliography. That is fine advice. This volume was more than 30 years old when it was reissued, and it is still valid today. (It was updated by Smith, Lasswell, and Casey in 1946 in *Propaganda, Communication, and Public Opinion: A Comprehensive Reference Guide*, entry 113). The authors indicate that this is a "research tool for use of specialists in the social sciences, as well as for a more general public." Descriptive annotations are, according to the authors, "terse." Divided into several subject sections, the most useful ones might be the channels of propaganda, and censorship and propaganda. Author and subject indexes are included, as well as cross-references.

59. Lent, John A. **Animation, Caricature, and Gag and Political Cartoons in the United States and Canada: An International Bibliography.** Westport, CT: Greenwood Press, 1994. 415p. index. (Bibliographies and Indexes in Popular Culture, no. 3.) LC 94-14433. ISBN 0-313-28681-7.

This bibliography is included here because it provides pertinent information on political cartoons. The title may be misleading, however. Lent writes that "most of the work in this volume deals with the United States, although Canada is mentioned." Per usual, Lent writes in his preface that "no item was too small or insignificant to be listed; if it dealt with comic art, it could become a citation," and "the search for literature was mostly manual, since that is the way the compiler works, and because much of the literature, being journalistic, anecdotal, or brief, is not in computerized databases." Keeping these limitations in mind, users should be prepared to plow through the subject index and massive table of contents to find unannotated citations. There are chapters on Global and Comparative Perspectives; Canada (20 pages); and (all U.S. sources) Resources; Comic Art; Gag, Illustrative, and Magazine Cartoons; Animation; Caricature; and Political Cartoons. Chapters are further subdivided (i.e., general studies, historical aspects, comic art and war); citations are arranged alphabetically by author. For example, in the U.S.: Resources chapter, Randall W. Scott's *Comics Librarianship: A Handbook* is listed on the same page as "Blackbeard Preserves Comics Culture in Newspaper Archive," a 1972 article published in *Newspaper Collector's Gazette*. There are author and subject indexes. For even more information on comic art, consult Lent's *Comic Art of Europe: An International, Comprehensive Bibliography* and *Comic Books and Comic Strips in the United States: An International Bibliography* (both published in 1994 by Greenwood Press), and *Animation in Asia and the Pacific* (Indiana University Press, 2001), in addition to Randall Scott's well-respected *Comic Books and Strips: An Information Sourcebook* (Oryx Press, 1988) and Paul P. Somers's *Editorial Cartooning and Caricature: A Reference Guide* (Greenwood, 1998).

60. Lent, John A. **Asian Mass Communications: A Comprehensive Bibliography.** Philadelphia, PA: Temple University School of Communications and Theater, 1975. 708p. LC 76-621167. Supplement, 1978. 619p.

This massive bibliography embraces all aspects of mass communications in Asia. It includes literally thousands of entries on such subjects as advertising, public relations, film, freedom of the press, government information, history, news agencies, printed media, radio, and television. The supplement alone includes more than 8,000 entries found since 1974 and new material on Mongolia, Nepal, and other Asian countries. Journal, periodical, and newspaper articles as well as books, speeches, theses, dissertations, and conference proceedings are listed, but not annotated. Arrangement is by region (Asia, East Asia, Southeast Asia, and South Asia), country, then subject. It is unfortunate to find a volume of this size and scope with no index.

61. Lent, John A. **Bibliographic Guide to Caribbean Mass Communication.** Westport, CT: Greenwood Press, 1992. 301p. index. (Bibliographies and Indexes in Mass Media and Communications, no. 5.) LC 92-19373. ISBN 0-313-28210-2.

English language sources dominate this bibliography, unlike Lent's *Caribbean Mass Communications: A Comprehensive Bibliography* (entry 63). There are 3,695 unannotated items arranged in chapters on comparative studies and regions—Commonwealth Caribbean, Dominican Republic, French Caribbean, Haiti, Netherlands Caribbean, and U.S. Caribbean—and further subdivided into subject areas (e.g., broadcasting, press freedom). Books, conference papers, dissertations, and periodical and newspaper citations are included. There are author and subject indexes but no title index. Lent's preface states that "A serious effort was made to compile a comprehensive and usable bibliography. No item was too small or insignificant to be listed; if it dealt with mass communications in the Caribbean region, it became a citation."

62. Lent, John A. **Bibliography of Cuban Mass Communications.** Westport, CT: Greenwood Press, 1992. 357p. index. (Bibliographies and Indexes in Mass Media and Communications, no. 6.) LC 92-24462. ISBN 0-313-28455-5.

This massive, unannotated bibliography contains 4,315 entries in English or Spanish from the nineteenth century to the early 1990s. It is divided into sections on resources, contemporary perspectives, and historical perspectives, including a useful section on Cuban journalists; sections are further subdivided by subject. An informative introductory essay examines Cuban mass media history. Lent again claims that "a serious effort was made to compile a comprehensive and usable bibliography. No item was too small or insignificant to be listed; if it dealt with mass communications in Cuba, it became a citation." He states that the "search for literature was manual because that is the way this compiler works and because much of the literature, being journalistic, anecdotal, or otherwise brief, would not be expected to be in computerized databases." Users are nonetheless advised to consult computerized databases in addition to Lent's listings. Author and subject indexes (no title index) make this unwieldy source more accessible. Scholars and students of Cuban journalism will find this a logical starting point for further research.

63. Lent, John A. **Caribbean Mass Communications: A Comprehensive Bibliography.** Waltham, MA: Crossroads Press, 1981. 152p. (Archival and Bibliographical Series). ISBN 0-918456-39-8.

Even though many of the 2,653 entries are not in English, this is important as an overview of and a historical and bibliographical reference point to the mass communication literature of the Caribbean. Books, journal articles, and working papers are included. Chapters are divided by region and country, and then arranged alphabetically within subject sections such as general mass communications, freedom of the press, history, print media, broadcasting, and advertising. There is a section on the U.S. Caribbean. With the addendum, the bibliography includes mass communication literature from the eighteenth century up to mid-1980. Unfortunately, only a few items are annotated. The author index is adequate, but a subject index would be very helpful. Lent also is the author of *Mass Communications in the Caribbean* (Iowa State University Press, 1990).

64.　　Lent, John A. **Comic Art: An International Bibliography.** Drexel Hill, PA: published by author. 1986. 156p. index.

Almost 2,000 books and periodical articles are included in this self-published, selected, international bibliography focusing on political and editorial cartoons, comic strips, and comic books. There are no annotations. Entries are arranged geographically by continent, then country, and range from a *Journalism History* article entitled "Museum of Cartoon Art Offers Possibilities for Research" to "Exposure to Comics-Magazines and Knowledge/Attitude Toward Family Planning of Rural Residents," AB Thesis, University of Philippines. The contents of *Target* magazine from spring 1982 to 1986 are included in a general section. Subject, author, title, and cartoonist indexes also are provided. For further information, consult Lent's *Animation, Caricature, and Gag and Political Cartoons in the United States and Canada* (entry 59), *Comic Art in Africa, Asia, Australia and Latin America: A Comprehensive, International Bibliography* (Greenwood Press, 1996), and Randall Scott's *Comic Books and Strips: An Information Sourcebook* (Oryx Press, 1988).

65.　　Lent, John A. **Global Guide to Media and Communications.** Munich, New York: K. G. Saur, 1987. 145p. ISBN 3-598-10746-3.

This "global guide" does not include the United States, but nowhere does Lent indicate why. Eleven compilers (including Jim Richstad, Robert Roberts, and Hamid Mowlana) contributed to this uneven and occasionally annotated collection of citations to books, dissertations and theses, monographs, serials, and periodical articles published through 1984. Entries are arranged geographically and focus on media systems and communications. There is no index.

66.　　Lent, John A. **Women and Mass Communications: An International Annotated Bibliography.** Westport, CT: Greenwood Press, 1991. 481p. (Bibliographies and Indexes in Women's Studies, no. 11). LC 90-23780. ISBN 0-313-26579-8.

An exceptional bibliographic guide, both for its content and scope, *Women and Mass Communications* should be a first stop for anyone researching "the most important literature on women in mass communications" from the early 1960s to December 1989. The preface offers a rich historical perspective and describes in detail the objectives and organization of the book. There is a chapter on "Women and Mass Communications: Global and Comparative Perspectives," further subdivided into sections on general studies, historical studies, images of women, women as audience, women practitioners, and women's media. Other chapters are arranged geographically and include Africa and the Middle East; Asia, Australia, and Oceania; Europe; Latin America and the Caribbean; and North America. These are further subdivided and arranged alphabetically by author. Books, periodicals, dissertations, conference papers, and "fugitive" materials such as theses, pamphlets, and conference papers are included. Lent indicates that "most of the search was manual because much of the literature is not in computerized databases" and states he searched the Sociofile database and ERIC. In fact, there are numerous databases in the social sciences, humanities, mass media, business and women's studies that could, and should, be tapped for further information. Users are cautioned that most of the annotations are lean (i.e., annotation for article on "Janet Chusmir and the Miami Herald" in the *Washington Journalism Review* is as follows: "The power of editor Chusmir"). Regardless, this is one of Lent's most valuable contributions to mass media bibliography, which is updated in *Women and Mass Communications in the 1990's* (entry 67). He also compiled *Women and the Mass Media in Asia: An Annotated Bibliography* (Asian Mass Communication Research and Information Centre, 1985). Also of possible interest is Carol A. Mills's "Women in Communication: Annotated Bibliography" (ERIC ED 361767), a brief but useful listing covering 1949–1990 and published by the Speech Communication Association in 1992.

67.   Lent, John A. **Women and Mass Communications in the 1990's: An International, Annotated Bibliography.** Westport, CT: Greenwood Press, 1999. 510p. index. (Bibliographies and Indexes in Women's Studies, no. 29). LC 99-21787. ISBN 0-313-30209-X.

This volume picks up where Lent's *Women and Mass Communications* (entry 66) leaves off in late 1989. It is arranged geographically, by continent and region, then topically (general studies, historical studies, images of women, women as audience, women practitioners, and women's media), and then, in some instances, further subdivided, and arranged alphabetically by author. The table of contents does not reflect this arrangement, which can be confusing, so users are strongly advised to read all introductory material and rely on the author and subject indexes to guide them through the 3,787 sparely annotated citations. Mass communications is defined broadly to include publishing, radio, television, film, newspapers, magazines, video, advertising, public relations, and so on. Lent's search process was similar to that used in the first volume and he has again been comprehensive in his inclusion of what he terms "fugitive" materials. In addition to books, periodicals, dissertations, and theses, he also includes dissertations that have not been indexed, conference papers, pamphlets, and other ephemeral materials. For example, AEJMC (Association for Education in Journalism and Mass Communication) annual meeting papers and panel discussions focusing on women and mass media are listed here.

68.   Lichty, Lawrence W., comp. **World and International Broadcasting: A Bibliography.** Washington, D.C.: Association for Professional Broadcasting Education, 1971. Various pagings.

This bibliography has a table of contents made in the twilight zone. Sure enough, there is a number for each entry, but it refers to number of pages in the chapter. In addition, Lichty writes, "For the most part I have depended on other bibliographies, indices, and listings. If these contained mistakes, I am repeating them; as well as adding my own mistakes." He began work on this nearly 10 years before it was finally published, but apparently did not consider verification important. He intended to compile a "rough, working bibliography" of radio and television broadcasting. In that he succeeds. Entries are divided by geographic area and arranged chronologically by year. The United States, Canada, and Great Britain are not included.

69.   Linton, David. **The Twentieth-Century Newspaper Press in Britain: An Annotated Bibliography.** London: Mansell, 1994. 386p. index. LC 93-42784. ISBN 0-7201-2159-0.

In 1987, Linton and Ray Boston published *The Newspaper Press in Britain: An Annotated Bibliography* (entry 70), but according to Linton, this new title is "not only a revision, an updating and a re-packaging, but also a thorough re-assessment of the twentieth century with a new line of readers in mind." Thus, users are advised to retain the earlier title because "virtually all traces of previous centuries" have been removed in this publication. With broader definitions of "news" and "journalist," the authors now covered in this alphabetically arranged source include sports reporters, critics, essayists, and media scholars. There are 3,728 numbered and briefly annotated entries for books, articles, theses, and even ships' newspapers, as well as a chronology of British newspaper history, 1900–1994. A section on "Reference Works" precedes the main bibliography and includes references to some seminal reference and historical titles. Boston, no longer a coeditor, does contribute a lengthy introduction. As before, the index provides the only subject access point.

70. Linton, David, and Ray Boston, eds. **The Newspaper Press in Britain: An Annotated Bibliography.** London: Mansell, 1987. 361p. index. LC 86-23837. ISBN 0-7201-1792-5.

The 2,909 briefly annotated entries chronicle British newspaper history. The periodical press is excluded. The detailed subject index provides the only subject access point but should be sufficient for the user. There is no title index. All periodical, book, and thesis citations are arranged alphabetically by author and numbered consecutively. The introduction provides a fine overview of the history of the newspaper industry in the United Kingdom, but ends with a curious thought: "It was no accident that the first newspaper revolution in modern times—the linotype machine—in itself did nothing for journalism. It was not intended to do so. Will the same be said of the second revolution—computerization? We think that it will; and would simply add this warning: those who today live by the market must expect also to die by the market."

71. MacDonald, Barrie. **Broadcasting in the United Kingdom: A Guide to Information Sources.** 2d ed. New York, London: Mansell/Cassell, 1993. 316p. index. LC 92-30097. ISBN 0- 7201-2086-1.

MacDonald, librarian of the Independent Television Commission, offers his second edition of a multidimensional and invaluable annotated bibliography, reference guide, handbook, and historical guide to radio and television broadcasting in the United Kingdom. The introduction covers changes in commercial broadcasting in the United Kingdom due to technological developments and the Broadcasting Act of 1990; the first chapter is a narrative chronology of broadcasting from 1886–1992. Chapter 2 "outlines the structure, and the legislative and constitutional framework of British broadcasting," including a discussion of the differences between broadcasting in the United Kingdom and the United States. Chapter 3 contains detailed information on primary sources while chapter 4 is a comprehensive, annotated listing of print and electronic sources subdivided into sections on histories; directories and yearbooks; company information; statistical sources; legal guides; dictionaries; production manuals; biographical information; periodicals; abstracts and indexes; bibliographies; and online services, among other subjects. Entries are then arranged alphabetically by author. The final chapter is a directory of archives, libraries, and museums. MacDonald states that this guide is aimed at students, researchers, journalists, librarians, "and the general enquirer." An ambitious undertaking, but one fulfilled; this is required reading for anyone beginning research on any aspect of commercial broadcasting in the United Kingdom or elsewhere.

72. Madden, Lionel, and Diana Dixon. **The Nineteenth Century Periodical Press in Britain: A Bibliography of Modern Studies, 1901–1971.** New York: Garland, 1976.

280p. index. (Garland Reference Library of the Humanities, vol. 53). LC 76-21872. ISBN 0-8240-9945-1.

Focusing on general studies and studies of general periodicals and newspapers, this annotated bibliography of the British press in the nineteenth century covers books, pamphlets, periodical articles, and theses published from 1901 to1971. Entries are numbered and arranged by date of publication under general sections. An alphabetical listing of individual periodicals and newspapers is included. See also the update to this source, *The Nineteenth Century Periodical Press in Britain: A Bibliography of Modern Studies, 1972–1987,* by Uffelman, Madden, and Dixon (Bowker, 1992). Alvin Sullivan's multivolume *British Literary Magazines* (Greenwood, 1983–1986) would be a useful additional resource.

73. McBride, Donald L., comp. **Doctoral Dissertations on Broadcast Journalism: A Bibliography.** Carbondale: Southern Illinois University, Department of Radio and Television, 1990. 31p.

Primarily useful as a "who's doing what and what should I do" resource for doctoral students, this listing is now dated, but offers a glimpse into broadcast research issues through the late 1980s. Entries, arranged alphabetically by author, are not annotated. According to the introduction, "this bibliography lists all of the dissertations on broadcast journalism approved by institutions of higher learning up to early 1989." McBride indicates he took a close look at the 1979–1988 period and discovered that many critical topics had not been treated, including the following: studies of television news anchors, quantitative studies of broadcast commentary or editorials, study of the Cable News Network, broadcast news in Central or South America, impact of computers on broadcast news, broadcast journalism ethics, and so on. Ideally, this resource should be updated every few years. See also Kittross's *A Bibliography of Theses and Dissertations in Broadcasting: 1920–1973* (entry 55).

74. McCavitt, William E., comp. **Radio and Television: A Selected, Annotated Bibliography.** Metuchen, NJ: Scarecrow Press, 1978. 229p. LC 77-28665. ISBN 0-8108-1113-8. **Supplement One, 1977–1981.** 1982. 155p. LC 82-5743. ISBN 0-8108-1556-7. **Supplement Two, 1982–1986.** 1989. ISBN 0-8108-2158-3. (Compiled by Peter Pringle and Helen Clinton).

If the purpose of the first volume is, as the author indicates, to provide a guide for purchasing broadcasting books and to indicate what is still needed by showing what exists now, why did he not give us a subject index? It would have been immensely helpful. Fortunately, the table of contents is useful in searching the 1,100 selected and descriptively annotated listings of books and other publications covering the years 1920 to1976. Topics such as history, public broadcasting, research, surveys, and criticism are further subdivided. The programming section, for example, is broken down into such topics as news, public affairs, and documentaries. In the first supplement of 566 entries, the stated purpose is still the same, as is bibliographical arrangement, but coverage has been expanded to include video, videotext, and satellites. See also the second supplement by Pringle and Clinton covering 1982–1986 (entry 100). Researchers might also consult *Early Television: A Bibliographic Guide to 1940* (Garland, 1997).

75. McCoy, Ralph E. **Freedom of the Press: An Annotated Bibliography.** Carbondale: Southern Illinois University Press, 1968. 576p. index. LC 76-10032. ISBN 0-8093-0335-3.

Press freedom and free expression in English-speaking countries is bibliographically chronicled, and any student of the topic will want to read this work from cover to cover. The press is defined broadly to include books, periodicals and newspapers, films, records, radio, and television; and all time periods since the beginning of printing are covered. This bibliography contains more than 8,000 citations to books, pamphlets, journal articles, and films. Newspaper, news magazine articles, and texts of laws are not included. The subject and title index is detailed and there are major subject headings for blasphemy, libel, censorship, First Amendment, fair trial, obscenity, broadcasting, sedition laws, and even library book selection policies. For further information on propaganda, McCoy refers to Lasswell, Casey, and Smith's contributions (entries 58 and 113). Annotations are primarily descriptive and concise. Entries are arranged alphabetically by author. Also of interest might be Frank Hoffman's *Intellectual Freedom and Censorship: An Annotated Bibliography* (entry 48).

76.   McCoy, Ralph E. **Freedom of the Press: A Bibliocyclopedia.** 10-year supplement, 1967–1977. Carbondale, IL: Southern Illinois University Press, 1979. 544p. index. LC 78-16573. ISBN 0-8093-0844-4.

More than 6,000 books, pamphlets, journal articles, dissertations, films, and other items are included in this annotated supplement, as well as some pre-1967 titles not in the earlier bibliography. There are far fewer entries for heresy, blasphemy, and sedition, McCoy notes, but more for government and the media and free press/fair trial.

77.   McCoy, Ralph E. **Freedom of the Press: An Annotated Bibliography.** Second Supplement, 1978–1992. Carbondale, IL: Southern Illinois University Press, 1993. 441p. index. LC 92-8395. ISBN 0-8093-1583-1.

According to McCoy, "the present volume is somewhat more selective than the original and first supplement." Nonetheless, this is a valuable addition to press freedom literature. As in the first supplement, this second supplement is an annotated bibliography of books, pamphlets, journal articles, dissertations, films, and other materials arranged alphabetically by author. Press still includes "all media of mass communications: books, newspapers, and other printed matter, but also motion pictures, recordings, radio and television broadcasting, and to a limited extent, stage plays." McCoy informs users that the "long-established printed periodical indexes proved more useful than the more recent electronic information services, which often carried an inordinate amount of trivia or failed to include sufficient bibliographic information. An exception was the useful and comprehensive computerized index to United States government documents." Franklyn S. Haiman's foreword outlines changes in freedom of speech, interpretation of the First Amendment, and press law since the publication of the first supplement. McCoy ends his preface on a melancholy note:

> Although new issues, facets, and concepts in press freedom are likely to appear in the future, there will also be a certain amount of repetition in the content of books and articles, already evident in this and earlier compilations. This fact plus the increased difficulty and expense of producing periodic supplements will probably mean that this is the last such bibliographic effort—at least the last for this compiler.

Thanks to McCoy for his seminal bibliographic "effort."

78. McGoings, Michael C. **Newsmen's Privilege, 1970–1974.** Washington, D.C.: Library of Congress, Law Library, 1976. 19p. LC 77-601676.

McGoings focused on the early 1970s because that was the "period which may be considered the height of the newsmen's privilege controversy." Books, periodical articles, and U.S. congressional hearings are listed in this annotated bibliography; entries range from Dale R. Spencer's *Law for the Newsman* (Lucas Brothers, 1973) to "Reporters and Their Sources: The Constitutional Right to a Confidential Relationship" in a 1970 issue of *Yale Law Review.* Lisa Epstein's "Newsman's Privilege, An Annotated Bibliography, 1967–1973" (California State Library, Law Library, 1973) also might provide some useful references.

79. McKerns, Joseph P. **News Media and Public Policy: An Annotated Bibliography.** New York: Garland, 1985. 171p. (Public Affairs and Administration, vol. 11. Garland Reference Library of Social Science, vol. 219). LC 83-049290. ISBN 0-8240-9004-7.

Pity the scholar who is trying to grasp, document, or dissect the relationship between the news media and the United States government. However, that is precisely the audience McKerns aims for, and he has done a superb job with this selective, annotated bibliography. He dismisses most of the literature of the popular press as superficial and therefore focuses on books, monographs, theses, and dissertations published from the late 1960s to 1984. His criteria for selection are rigid: subjects must deal with at least one aspect of news media and public policy, the publication must follow "commonly accepted standards of research," and the work must be "significant beyond its time of publication." The bibliography is divided into chapters such as newsmaking and the conventions of journalism (which includes an important section on ethics and values), the executive branch of government, legislative, judicial, and their bureaucracies. The 731 entries are consecutively numbered and arranged alphabetically by author within chapters. The subject index is spare and somewhat difficult to use. Since much has been written on this topic since 1984, a supplement would be desirable. McKerns also edited the *Biographical Dictionary of American Journalism* (entry 327).

80. **Media After 9/11.** IWantMedia.

Available on the IWantMedia Web site (www.iwantmedia.com), this collection of about 150 unannotated citations provides direct links to published articles on media coverage of September 11, 2001. Included are newspaper and journal articles and editorials, arranged by month, in reverse chronological order from the present to September 11, 2001. The introduction stated in 2002: "9/11 had a profound impact on the media world. This archive . . . traces significant events across the media landscape following last year's terrorist attacks. The stories cover a variety of issues still open to debate—from the repeated televising of the planes hitting the World Trade Center to the purchasing of al-Qaeda videotapes by TV news networks." Articles from the *New York Times* are featured, as well as items from the Associated Press, Cyberjournalist.net, *Columbia Journalism Review,* and *Online Journalism Review.* In "Views of Sept. 11, Through the Web's Sharpest Eyes," Jason Anders, in *The Wall Street Journal Online,* writes, "The terror attacks were among the most covered news events in history," but "some pieces stood out." He describes what he considers the most effective, and by the nature of the event, "shocking and heart-wrenching" articles, photos, and images published on the Web. This is a powerful and graphic compilation of American journalism, providing a snapshot of news coverage during the initial tragic moments, and in the months to follow. Researchers also should consult Shedden's bibliography "Remembering September 11, 2001" (entry 109).

81. Miles, William, comp. **The People's Voice: An Annotated Bibliography of American Campaign Newspapers, 1828–1984.** Westport, CT: Greenwood Press, 1987. 210p. index. (Bibliographies and Indexes in American History, no. 6). LC 87-11969. ISBN 0-313-23976-2.

Most presidential campaign newspapers are issued only during the campaign to promote the party and ticket, and then die a natural death. Miles has resurrected 733 of them, dating from 1828 to 1984, including Jesse Jackson's *Rainbow News*. Fewer than 100 newspapers can be counted after 1900. Excluded are general party-supported and partisan sheets, press releases, and mimeographed newsletters. The lengthy introduction gives a historical overview of campaign literature and political parties. The bibliography is arranged chronologically according to campaign. Within each campaign, the successful candidate and papers are listed first, then those of the defeated candidate, official third-party candidates, and would-be candidates. Listings are numbered and include title, dates of publication, place, and (when available) editor, slogan, biographies, and library holdings. Indexing is ample with an editor, publisher and candidate index, and separate title and geographical indexes.

82. Mowlana, Hamid, ed. **International Flow of News: An Annotated Bibliography.** Paris: UNESCO, 1985. 272p. index.

International news and foreign correspondents are themes in this selected bibliography of 1,500 references. Part 1 defines news flow and offers an overview of research trends. Part 2 is a section on theories, methods, and policies with entries arranged alphabetically by author. Part 3 focuses on the regional and national flow of news, and is subdivided into sections on Africa, Arab states, Asia, Eastern Europe, Western Europe, North America, and South and Central America. Entries range from "The Flow of International Events, July–Dec. 1969," a World Event/Interaction Survey Interim Technical Report, to "The Perception of Foreign News" in a 1971 issue of the *Journal of Peace Research*. Mowlana also is the author of *International Communication: A Selected Bibliography* (Kendall/Hunt, 1971) and *Global Information and World Communication: New Frontiers in International Relations* (Sage, 1997). Jim Richstad and Jackie Bowen's *International Communication Policy and Flow: A Selected, Annotated Bibliography* (East-West Center, 1976) might also provide some useful references.

83. Nafziger, Ralph O., comp. **International News and the Press: Communications, Organization of News Gathering, International Affairs, and the Foreign Press— An Annotated Bibliography.** New York: Ayer, c1940, 1972. 223p. LC 72-04675. ISBN 0-405-04759-2.

A meticulous and well-organized source, this international bibliography has withstood the ravages of time. It now serves as a useful historical guide to international news from the early 1900s to the beginning of World War II. Documents, books, pamphlets, magazine articles, and studies are included in sections labeled either International News or Foreign Press, and then arranged in chapters such as Washington Correspondence, Foreign Correspondence, Censorship, Press Law, News Gathering Organizations, and Press and

Public Opinion. Descriptively annotated entries are listed alphabetically by author. Foreign press entries are arranged geographically by continent, then country. There is only an author index; fortunately the table of contents is detailed. In 1949, Nafziger also edited, with Marcus M. Wilkerson, an *Introduction to Journalism Research* (Louisiana State University Press).

84. Nelson, Marlan. **Free Press—Fair Trial: An Annotated Bibliography.** Logan, UT: Utah State University, 1971. 89p.

An exhaustive bibliography for its time, this listing of 600 books, periodical articles, theses, and dissertations needs an update. Still, it is useful as a historical resource, covering 1950–1969. Material was culled from legal and scholarly journals and trade and popular periodicals.

85. Nordquist, Joan. **Gender and Racial Images/Stereotypes in the Mass Media: A Bibliography.** Santa Cruz, CA: Reference and Research Services, 2001. 72p. (Contemporary Social Issues, no. 64.) ISBN 1-892068-26-5. ISSN 0887-3569.

This no-frills bibliography fulfills the intent of the Contemporary Social Issues series: "The material selected for inclusion in the bibliographies represents various social, political viewpoints, is current, and includes the authoritative work on the subject. Publications from small presses, alternative presses, feminist presses, and activist organizations are included." More than 700 unannotated citations are packed in a scant 72 pages. There are chapters on sex roles, women, sex, body image and eating disorders, gays, minorities, African Americans, Asian Americans, Latinos, and Native Americans, further subdivided into sections such as general literature, motion pictures, television, the press, and advertising. Entries are arranged by format (book, article, videotape), then alphabetically by author. This is an exceptional overview resource, and especially useful for a librarian or researcher seeking a current and "best" list of literature on the topic.

86. Noyes, Dan, ed. **Reporter's Reference Guide.** Beverly Hills, CA: Urban Policy Research Institute, 1976. 42p.

Noyes is straightforward in his introduction:

This guide is incomplete. It represents only a first step in compiling a thorough guide to reference materials for reporters and researchers. Some of the information included here is now outdated and should be replaced by more contemporary sources. Some annotations are too brief and deserve greater detail. Information on the cost and method of obtaining many of these sources is missing.

This is all true, especially years after the original publication date. For example, the National Faculty Directory is listed, but the ERIC indexes (entries 197 and 210) are omitted. The 190 annotated entries are arranged alphabetically by author within the following categories: business, consumer affairs, education, foundations, general, individuals, government/politics, health, law, labor, media, military, and real estate. The beginning reporter is better served by *The Investigative Reporter's Handbook* (entry 407).

87. Nuessel, Frank. **The Image of Older Adults in the Media: An Annotated Bibliography.** Westport, CT: Greenwood Press, 1992. 181p. index. (Bibliographies and Indexes in Gerontology, no. 18). LC 92-24259. ISEN 0-313-2801-5.

The author writes:

Two decades ago a reference manual such as this one would have been both impossible and unthinkable. In the first instance, the extant research would not have justified such as undertaking, hence its impossibility. In the second instance, the notion that an annotated bibliography devoted to the topic of the image of an older adult would be worthy of an entire book would have been just as incredible.

The 558 citations are arranged alphabetically by author in chapters on bibliographies; ageism, attitudes and stereotypes; communication; media guidelines; children's literature; adolescent literature; literature; art; humor; cartoons; greeting cards; advice to older adults; advertising; magazines; newspapers; history; film; music; oral history; and television. Coverage is somewhat uneven. The brief chapter on newspapers, for example, contains only four citations, two from *The Gerontologist* and two from *Educational Gerontology*. Nuessel explains that "some of the categories contain only a few entries, while other areas feature abundant citations. In this sense, this reference book points out areas for future study." It also reveals that the literature of journalism and mass communication was slighted, as there are numerous and current studies, especially in newspapers, on the image of older adults. This is a specialized and occasionally groundbreaking work, but a far more useful contribution to the literature of gerontology than that of mass communication.

88.   Oduko, Segun. **Guide to Students' Research: A Bibliography of Mass Communication.** Lagos, Nigeria: VDG Press, Ltd., 1992. 318p. ISBN 978-017-072-3.

In a short, perturbed, and self-righteous preface, Oduko writes, "After having continual battles with students for shoddy reporting of their research and professional projects year-in, year-out, I realised that the only way to enforce a permanent ceasefire was to put down in black-and-white a reference material." Unfortunately, distracting typographical errors also abound in black-and-white in the preface, contents, and listings. The first four chapters focus on research proposals and qualitative and quantitative research methods. Users are advised to skip to chapters 6–11, indexes to communication research studies at Nigerian universities, respectively, Bayero University, Kano (1981–1990); University of Nigeria, Nsukka (1980–1990); University of Maiduguri (1986–1990); University of Jos (1980–1990); and the University of Ibadan (1980–1990). Chapter 5 is a subject index of research. Samples of research projects range from "Press Freedom Under Military Regimes in Nigeria from 1966–1988" to "Appraisal of News Reporters' Dressing." In spite of its obvious and distracting drawbacks, this is a very rich source of information on the press in Africa. See also Chris Ogbondah's *The Press in Nigeria* (entry 89) and *Communication Studies in Africa: A Bibliography* (Nairobi, Kenya: African Council for Communication Education, 1994), an unannotated bibliography covering major issues in journalism in Africa from 1950 to 1990.

89.   Ogbondah, Chris W., comp. **The Press in Nigeria: An Annotated Bibliography.** Westport, CT: Greenwood Press, 1990. 127p. index. (African Special Bibliographic Series, no. 12). LC 90-3676. ISBN 0-313-26521-6.

This bibliography contains 501 annotated citations to journal articles, books, conference papers, and reports on the Nigerian press, arranged alphabetically by author. Joseph P. McKerns, editor of the *Biographical Dictionary of American Journalism* (entry 327) gives it high praise in his foreword: "Professor Ogbondah has given to the field of

Nigerian media studies what the benchmark works of Warren Price and Calder Pickett, *The Literature of Journalism* and *An Annotated Journalism Bibliography, 1958–1968,* gave to the field of American media studies." That may be, but the misspelling in the introduction and introduction notes of the name of a major journalism bibliographer (Wolseley) is disturbing. The introduction states that "Hitherto, researchers on Nigerian press must painfully search through several dry sources for what has been written or published about the press. Sometimes they search in vain and at other times, they are lucky to come across items scattered here and there like the seeds of oil bean trees of tropical Nigeria." Oil bean trees aside, users are advised to consult the author/title/subject index for easiest access. See also *Guide to Students' Research: A Bibliography of Mass Communication* (entry 88), which chronicles research studies, many focusing on critical issues in journalism, at five Nigerian universities.

90.   Paine, Fred K., and Nancy E. Paine. **Magazines: A Bibliography for Their Analysis, with Annotations and Study Guide.** Metuchen, NJ: Scarecrow Press, 1987. 690p. index. LC 86-29825. ISBN 0-8108-1975-9.

As the title plainly states, this is a guide for locating sources on magazines. It takes up where Schacht, in his *A Bibliography for the Study of Magazines* (entry 104), left off in 1978. In fact, the authors say they intentionally excluded most material in the Schacht book. They also say they examined more than 15,000 items and included a very selected list of 2,200 of those books, dissertations, and magazine, journal, and newspaper articles focusing mainly on journalistic and business aspects of the industry. Annotations are descriptive and short, sometimes just a sentence or two. Part 1 is a study guide listing journals, magazines, and newsletters that publish articles pertaining to the magazine industry in the United States. Also included is a chapter on reference books. Part 2 is a selected bibliography divided into 31 broad subject categories such as editing, audience, writing, production and design, history, business, advertising, and ethics. Indexing is sparse, limited to Part 2, with no author index. In the preface, the authors attempt to define magazine and distinguish the differences between magazines and newspapers. Some readers may, however, disagree with statements such as "Helping readers understand rather than simply presenting a 'laundry list of facts' is more important in magazines."

91.   Palmegiano, E. M. **The British Empire in the Victorian Press, 1832–1867: A Bibliography.** New York: Garland, 1987. 234p. index. (Themes in European Expansion, vol. 8; Garland Reference Library of Social Science, vol. 389). LC 86-29624. ISBN 0-8240-9802-1.

A painstaking work, the introduction alone takes up 56 pages, and offers a rich historical overview of the British Empire, the British people, and the writings of the press. Almost 3,000 articles from a sampling of 50 London-based magazines are listed. There are no annotations, but very short notes are included for articles that are not self-explanatory. The checklist is arranged alphabetically by magazine title, with article entries listed by date and numbered consecutively. Titles such as *Blackwood's Edinburgh Magazine, Chamber's Journal,* and *Household Words* are included. The first section lists 37 magazines dealing specifically with the empire, and gives publication history as well as location information. Most titles can be found in the British Library, but it is interesting to note that *The Anti-Slavery Reporter* can be found at the Newark Public Library. The preface states that "journals have been determined on the basis of their historical significance," and that those in the

Wellesley Index to Victorian Periodicals, and 16 in *Poole's Index* are included. There is an author index, but the subject index is a travesty. It is primarily geographic in nature and contains vast listings under Australia, Canada, China, and India. William S. Ward's *British Periodicals and Newspapers, 1789–1832: A Bibliography of Secondary Sources* (University Press of Kentucky, 1972) addresses the time period immediately before this and may be of some use. Palmegiano also is the author of *Health and British Magazines in the Nineteenth Century* (Scarecrow Press, 1998).

92. Parker, Elliott S., and Emelia M. Parker. **Asian Journalism: A Selected Bibliography of Sources on Journalism in China and Southeast Asia.** Metuchen, NJ: Scarecrow Press, 1979. index. LC 79-022785. ISBN 0-8108-1269-X.

The authors tell us that this volume was entirely computer processed, "a fact of little importance except to demonstrate the comparative ease with which a general purpose computer can be used to print a bibliography." It may have been easy to print, but it is difficult to use and read. More than 2,000 books, articles, essays, and theses on the "communication process" in China and Southeast Asia are listed in this printout. (No items on Korea can be found.) Most are English-language sources, published before 1960 and dealing with print journalism. Radio and television receive less attention. Parker and Parker say that Lent's *Asian Mass Communications* (entry 60), among other sources, should be consulted first.

93. Picard, Robert G., and Stephen Lacy, comps. **Newspaper Economics Bibliography.** Columbia, SC: Association for Education in Journalism and Mass Communication, Teaching Standards Committee of the Media Management and Economics Division, 1991. 17p.

Divided into two sections on books and serials and articles and monographs, this is a no-frills unannotated listing of scholarly and trade materials on newspaper management and economics. Entries are arranged alphabetically by author and range from *The Community Press in an Urban Setting* (Free Press, 1952) to Bagdikian's "The Myth of Newspaper Poverty" (*Columbia Journalism Review*, March/April 1973). It is useful primarily as a starting point in compiling a syllabus, preparing reading lists, and beginning research. Picard also has authored *Economics and Financing of Media Companies* (Fordham University Press, 2002).

94. Picard, Robert G., and Rhonda S. Sheets, comps. **Terrorism and the News Media Research Bibliography.** Columbia, SC: Association for Education in Journalism and Mass Communication, Mass Communication and Society Division, 1986. 33p.

A part of the Terrorism and the News Media Research Project, this selective bibliography contains more than 450 entries arranged in sections on books, articles, book chapters, government reports and documents, and unpublished material. Picard also is the author of *Media Portrayals of Terrorism: Functions and Meanings of News Coverage* (Iowa State University Press, 1993) and, with Yonah Alexander, *In the Camera's Eye: News Coverage of Terrorist Events* (Brassey's, 1991).

95. Picard, Robert G., and James P. Winter, comps. **Press Concentration and Monopoly: A Bibliography.** Columbia, SC: Association for Education in Journalism and Mass Communication, Mass Communication and Society Division, 1985. 23p.

More than 300 publications focusing on chain ownership, joint operating agreements, and local monopolies in North America are listed in this Press Council and Monopoly Research Project. Divided into sections on books, articles, government reports, and unpublished materials, entries are arranged alphabetically by author and focus on topics such as the effects of concentration and monopoly on news coverage, diversity of opinion, labor relations and management activities, and economic behavior. There are no annotations or indexes. Although not comprehensive, "the bibliography contains the most important literature in the field and is intended to provide researchers starting points at which to carry out further research in the areas in which they are most interested."

96. Pitts, Michael R. **Radio Soundtracks: A Reference Guide.** 2d ed. Metuchen, NJ: Scarecrow Press, 1986. 337p. index. LC 85-30409. ISBN 0-8108-1875-2.

This second edition is more than twice the size of the first, published in 1976, as many old shows have become available since then. Material from the late 1920s to the 1960s (the golden age of radio) is covered, and all entries are numbered consecutively. Part 1 consists of an alphabetical listing of radio programs available on tape; Part 2 is a sample listing of radio specials on tape; Part 3 contains radio programs available on LP records (no 45 rpm or 78 rpm recordings listed); Part 4 features performers' radio appearances on LP records; and Part 5 is a compilation of record albums not included in Parts 3 or 4. An appendix lists tape and record sources. Performers and shows are listed in the index. Pitts indicates that this is not a "complete guide to all the radio programs ever broadcast or a listing of every performer's radio appearances." It is, however, a very useful, well-constructed, and entertaining guide.

97. Price, Warren C. **The Literature of Journalism: An Annotated Bibliography.** Minneapolis: University of Minnesota Press, 1959. 489p. LC 59-013522. ISBN 0-317-10434-9.

An objective, complete, and well-organized jewel of an annotated bibliography. Price's definition of journalism is broad, and he lists 3,147 English-language books on newspapers, magazines, ethics, education, management, radio, television, and public opinion published through 1957. Annotations are mostly descriptive, though some are evaluative. The book contains 52 subject categories; perhaps the only ones Price intentionally skips are fiction and high school journalism. Historical and biographical works are emphasized. The "Bibliographies and Directories" section is especially useful for those who seek early-twentieth-century bibliographies on the press. The subject index has some nice features such as an entry for textbooks, subdivided by subject area. More than 200 bibliographies and directories are included, and should be of particular interest to the serious historical researcher. Price writes that "relatively few efforts have been made in journalistic research toward compiling general and descriptive bibliographies of the press as a whole." This is his answer and triumph.

98. Price, Warren C., and Calder M. Pickett. **An Annotated Journalism Bibliography, 1958–1968.** Minneapolis: University of Minnesota Press, 1970. 278p. index. LC 70-120810. ISBN 0-8166-0578-5.

When Warren Price died in 1967, Calder Pickett carried on and produced this supplement to *The Literature of Journalism* (entry 97). The 2,172 entries are numbered, arranged alphabetically by author, and cover the history of journalism, biography, narratives, anthologies, appraisals of the press, ethics, law, techniques of journalism, journalism education, magazines, periodicals, management, public opinion and propaganda, public relations, radio and television, foreign press, and bibliographies and directories. Fortunately, there is a detailed subject index. Annotations are brief and descriptive. Pickett says, "Worthy or not, here it is, this supplement, a volume almost as comprehensive as its predecessor, a fact that may seem strange but that somehow seems apt, for this is mainly a supplement of mass media titles of the busy 1960s." He also thanks Price and says, "Often I have wished for his help, knowing he would have been able to answer questions. I hope he would feel I have not done him a disservice in assembling a work that was so important to him." Price and Pickett's volumes constitute the very best of journalism bibliography. Pickett also compiled an anthology of articles entitled *Voices of the Past: Key Documents in the History of American Journalism* (Macmillan, 1977).

99.   Pride, Armistead S. **The Black Press; A Bibliography.** Jefferson City, MO: Chauma Department of Journalism, Lincoln University, 1968. ["The Black Press to 1968: A Bibliography." Journalism History 4 (Winter 1977–78): pp.148–53.]

This represents a first effort in documenting the history of the black press. Pride gathered these 386 references to books and magazine and journal articles in 1968 for what was then the Association for Education in Journalism. Contents include advertising and marketing, analysis and criticism, biography and history, competition, coverage of black community by non-black media, employment, magazines, radio and television. Entries are numbered and arranged alphabetically by author within chapters. There are no annotations. Pride coauthored with Clint C. Wilson *A History of the Black Press* (Howard University Press, 1997), which contains some more current citations. Lenwood Davis's *A History of Journalism in the Black Community: Preliminary Survey* (Council of Planning Librarians, 1975) might also provide some useful references.

100.   Pringle, Peter K., and Helen E. Clinton. **Radio and Television: A Selected, Annotated Bibliography.** Supplement Two, 1982–1986. Metuchen, NJ: Scarecrow Press, 1989. 237p. index. LC 88-23968. ISBN 0-8108-2158-3.

An update of the late William McCavitt's sources (entry 74), this collection of nearly 1,000 annotated references to books and reports on broadcasting covers English-language sources published from 1982–1986. Annotations are descriptive and frequently terse. The authors offer no introductory material except for a one-page preface, also terse. It is fortunate that the table of contents is exhaustive, for there is no subject index. There are, however, author and title indexes. The bibliography is divided into sections on broadcasting (covering items that focus on both radio and television), radio, television, cable, and new technologies. Entries are further subdivided by subject or geographical region and arranged alphabetically by author. A chapter listing broadcasting periodicals also is included. This book is best used as a research tool for students and scholars examining a critical time period in a burgeoning field. Its use as a buying guide, diminished even at time of publication by lack of LC and ISBN numbers, is fading fast with age. A third supplement, with a subject index, would be helpful. Researchers might also wish to consult *Early Television: A Bibliographic Guide to 1940* (Garland, 1997).

101.   Richstad, Jim, and Michael McMillan, comps. **Mass Communication and Journalism in the Pacific Islands: A Bibliography.** Honolulu, HI: published for the East-

West Center by the University of Hawaii Press, 1978. 333p. index. LC 77-020795. ISBN 0-8248-0497-X.

The compilers point out that little attention has been paid to mass communication in most Pacific islands, and their research proves them correct. There is one citation each for Easter Island and Midway Island. Hawaii has almost 2,000. This Center for Cultural and Technical Interchange Between East and West bibliography contains citations to 3,332 books, periodicals, articles, documents, pamphlets, and so on, and covers 1854–1975, with some entries from 1976. Topics include the press, newspapers, freedom of the press, broadcasting, news agencies, organizations, radio broadcasting, cinema, and television in the Pacific Islands. Entries are arranged alphabetically by more than 20 island groupings, and broken down into specific subject areas, numbered, and arranged chronologically within those subjects. Richstad also produced *The Pacific Islands Press: A Directory* (East-West Communication Institute, 1973).

102.   Rivers, William L. **Finding Facts: A Research Manual for Journalists.** New York: Magazine Publishers Association, 1966. 65p.

This basic but quite dated research guide contains chapters on general reference sources and specialized sources in the humanities, biological sciences, physical sciences, and social sciences. It also includes entries for sources in communication, broadcasting, film, newspapers, and magazines. Each entry offers general bibliographic information and a description of the source. As the title suggests, this is more useful as a beginning reference guide for journalists than as a beginning reference source in journalism.

103.   Rose, Oscar, ed. **Radio Broadcasting and Television: An Annotated Bibliography.** New York: H. W. Wilson, 1947. 120p. LC 47-3360.

It is old, but not yet dead. This descriptively annotated bibliography features books and pamphlets primarily on radio until 1945. This work attempts to be comprehensive, and it probably was in its time. Technical studies are not included. The index contains titles and authors.

104.   Schacht, John H. **A Bibliography for the Study of Magazines.** 4th ed. Urbana, IL: College of Journalism and Communications, University of Illinois, 1979. 95p.

The fourth edition (earlier editions were published in 1966, 1968, and 1972) contains 600 new listings and includes a section on foreign magazines and publishers. This selected and annotated bibliography of journal articles, reports, conference papers, and proceedings is divided into sections on bibliographies, directories, general sources, history, audiences, editorial research, magazine content, law, magazine advertising, circulation, editors and editing, and layout and production. Appendixes selectively list periodicals and indexes covering magazine journalism. See *Magazines: A Bibliography for Their Analysis, with Annotations and Study Guide* (entry 90) for materials on magazines published after 1978.

105.   Schreibman, Fay C., comp. **Television News Resources: A Guide to Collections.** Washington, D.C.: Television News Study Center, George Washington University, 1981. 27p. LC 82-146621.

Schreibman lists useful sources for the novice television researcher and includes information on news documentaries, network television news archives, and local stations' news archives. This is a guide to American television news sources in 20 collections in the United States. It's not a how-to guide, but a very brief listing of what is available. There is no index.

106. Schreibman, Fay C., comp. **Broadcast Television: A Research Guide.** Frederick, MD: University Publications of America, 1983. 62p. (American Film Institute Factfile 15). index. ISBN 0-89093-571-8.

In a mere 62 pages, Schreibman, coeditor of *Television Network News: Issues in Content Research* (George Washington University, 1978) and compiler of *Television News Resources: A Guide to Collections* (entry 105), gives a clear picture of domestic television broadcasting reference sources. This descriptively annotated, selected "factfile" is divided into three sections. Part 1 covers general reference works, historical sources, programming information, and economic and technological aspects of the field. Particularly useful is the short section on research, which is further subdivided into studies from academic sources, research methods, yearbooks, and rating services. Lists of television-related periodicals and indexes, catalogs of television archive collections, and news transcript and script sources are contained in Part 2. Part 3 identifies special libraries and academic and network archives. Biographies, memoirs, and material on general mass communications are not included. There are author and title indexes, but no subject index. Schreibman should get a thumbs-up from every librarian in the field for including a useful section on "How to Approach a Special Library or Archive."

107. Schwarzlose, Richard A. **Newspapers: A Reference Guide.** Westport, CT: Greenwood Press, 1987. 417p. index. (American Popular Culture). LC 87-246. ISBN 0-313-23613-5.

Although the author, of Northwestern's Medill School of Journalism, seems more knowledgeable when discussing the history of newspapers than when critiquing the profession, he has written a thoughtful and well-organized selective guide to the literature of American newspapers. This ambitious work refers to more than 1,700 books, and covers newspaper history, business, freedom of the press, technology, design, ethics, reporters, and reporting through the mid-1980s. Each chapter is an essay, and includes complete bibliographical references at the end. It does not replace Blum (entries 12–13) or Price (entries 97–98), but the author says this guide "offers a selective update of Price and Price-Pickett." This is debatable because Schwarzlose does not focus on radio or television broadcasting. Major research collections are discussed in an appendix. The chapter on references and periodicals about newspapers is concise and well done. Schwarzlose also is the author of *The Nation's Newsbrokers: The Formative Years: From Pretelegraph to 1865* (Northwestern University Press, 1989).

108. Shedden, David B., comp. Bibliography Series. St. Petersburg, FL: The Poynter Institute for Media Studies, 1994. Frequent updates. 14p.

Shedden, library director at The Poynter Institute for Media Studies, has compiled and meticulously maintained a series of approximately 20 bibliographies on selected journalism topics, and all are available on the Poynter Web site (www.poynter.org, see entry 774). Bibliographies are bare bones—very selective, unannotated listings of online resources and books. It is both the quality of content and quantity of seminal citations that make these modest publications indispensable for beginning researchers and journalism instructors seeking sources for undergraduate and graduate reading lists. Bibliographies available include Broadcast Journalism, Computer Assisted Reporting, Crime Coverage, Diversity, Interviewing, Investigative Reporting, Journalism History, Journalism Libraries, Media Credibility, Media Ethics, Media Leadership, New Media, Photojournalism, Politics and the Press, Presidential Debates, Public Journalism, Reporting, Writing and Editing, Visual Journalism, World Press, and Youth and the Media. Most are updated several times a year. The prolific Shedden also is the author of *Preserving a Newspaper's Past: A Guide to Developing a Newspaper Oral History Program,* a special report for the American Society of Newspaper Editors.

109.   Shedden, David. **Remembering September 11, 2001.** St. Petersburg, FL: The Poynter Institute for Media Studies, 2002. Updated frequently.

Media coverage of events related to September 11, 2001, will undoubtedly be a subject of numerous book-length bibliographic studies, especially over time. But for now, researchers must sift through the hundreds of listings produced by bibliographers and selectors at academic institutions, public libraries, and media and government organizations. Librarian/bibliographer Shedden, however, has tailored a no-frills, yet comprehensive and up-to-the-minute bibliography of online resources, and made it available on The Poynter Institute Web site (www.poynter.org, see entry 774). It is divided into sections on Poynter.org publications, archival pages, news coverage, resource pages, U.S. government sources, and additional resources. The Poynter.org citations include Jonathon Dube (MSNBC.com Technology Editor) and Sreenath Sreenivasan's (Columbia University journalism professor) Web Tips series columns, including one entitled "More Sept. 11 Resources." Especially valuable is Shedden's news section, with links to special coverage in more than 20 news organizations. Researchers also might want to consult "Media After 9/11" (entry 80). In addition, Terry Kiss, bibliographer at Maxwell Air Force Base, Air University Library in Alabama, produced and maintains a modest bibliography on "Coverage of 9/11 and Its Aftermath," available at www.au.af mil/au/aul/bibs/9-11/9-11.htm. It lists books, articles, and online resources, both pre- and post-September 11, focusing on media and the broader issues of terrorism.

110.   Shuman, R. Baird. **Resources for Writers: An Annotated Bibliography.** Pasadena, CA: Salem Press, 1992. 167p. index. (Magill Bibliographies). LC 91-36214. ISBN 0-89356-673-X.

Although Shuman stresses fiction writing, he presents an impressive selection of both timely and classic materials ranging from how-to guides to books of style and rhetoric. Chapters on "General Studies," "Writing Nonfiction for Commercial Publication," "Writing for Film and Television," and "Writing for Magazines and Journals" contain numerous journalism sources. Critically annotated entries are arranged by author within chapters; annotations are thoughtful and clearly written. Aspiring writers, freelancers, and creative writing and journalism students will find this an accessible introduction to sources readily available in the public library. A "Parting Words" chapter lists writing programs and writer's workshops. Another suggested source is *The Writer's Adviser* (entry 3).

111.   Signorielli, Nancy, and George Gerbner, comps. **Violence and Terror in the Mass Media: An Annotated Bibliography.** Westport, CT: Greenwood Press, 1988. 264p. index. (Bibliographies and Indexes in Sociology, no. 13). LC 87-29556. ISBN 0-313-26120-2.

Scholarly articles and books on violence and terror in the mass media comprise the bulk of this bibliography. The 784 entries are numbered, divided into sections on mass media content, mass media effects, pornography, and terrorism, then arranged alphabetically by author. Content and effects chapters are by far the largest, with 673 entries and 184 pages. Annotations are descriptive. The introduction lists several other useful bibliographic studies of terrorism and violence, including Richard L. Moreland and Michael L. Berbaum's "Terrorism and the Mass Media: A Researcher's Bibliography" in Abraham H. Miller's (ed.) *Terrorism: The Media and the Law* (Transnational, 1982) and *Violence and the Media: A Bibliography* (Toronto: The Royal Commission, 1977). This publication started as a UNESCO project in 1984 and includes, according to the compilers, most relevant publications through early 1987. Most works included were published in the United States although "an effort was made to obtain and include studies from all countries where relevant research has been conducted. Communications research in general and media violence studies in particular have had the widest reach in the United States." Author and subject indexes are provided. See also *Terrorism and the News Media: A Selected, Annotated Bibliography* (entry 2).

112. Sloan, William David, comp. **American Journalism History: An Annotated Bibliography.** Westport, CT: Greenwood Press, 1989. 344p. index. (Bibliographies and Indexes in Mass Media and Communications, no. 1). LC 88-35800. ISBN 0-313-26350-7.

The introduction provides a mini-course in journalism history and sets the stage for a bibliographical presentation designed primarily to "assist historians in their bibliographical searches...one will find the most important articles and books included in the following pages." This is not an exaggeration. Sloan writes that "no claim is made that this bibliography is exhaustive." It does, however, come very close to that, and is essential in any phase of research conducted in journalism and mass media history. More than 2,500 periodical articles and books published from 1810–1988 are included, arranged by historical period and general theme, then alphabetically by author. Chapters are entitled "General History of Journalism, 1690-Present," "The Colonial Press, 1690–1765," "The Revolutionary Press, 1765–1783," "The Party Press, 1783–1833," "Freedom of the Press, 1690–1800," "The Penny Press, 1833–1860," "The Antebellum and Civil War Press, 1820–1865," "The Press of the Industrial Age, 1865–1883," "The Age of New Journalism, 1883–1900," "Frontier and Regional Journalism, 1800–1900," "The Emergence of Modern Journalism, 1900–1945," "The Press and the Age of Reform, 1900–1917," "The Media and National Crises, 1917–1945," "Broadcasting, 1920–Present," "The Contemporary Media, 1945–Present," and "Research Guides and Reference Guides." Annotations are brief and descriptive. The index, unfortunately, does not contain authors or titles, but provides detailed subject listings. The prolific Sloan coedited (with James D. Startt) *The History of American Journalism* (Greenwood Press, 1994); *The Media in America* (Publishing Horizons, 1989); and *The Significance of the Media in American History* (Vision Press, 1994). He also edited *Makers of the Mind: Journalism Educators and Their Ideas* (L. Erlbaum, 1990) and *Media and Religion in American History* (Vision Press, 2000).

113. Smith, Bruce Lannes, Harold D. Lasswell, and Ralph D. Casey, comps. **Propaganda, Communication, and Public Opinion: A Comprehensive Reference Guide.** Princeton, NJ: Princeton University Press, c1946, 1966 index. 435p.

This update of Lasswell, Casey, and Smith's *Propaganda and Promotional Activities: An Annotated Bibliography* (entry 58) lists books and periodical articles published from 1934 through early 1946.

114. Smith, Bruce Lannes, and Chitra M. Smith, comps. **International Communication and Political Opinion: A Guide to the Literature.** Westport, CT: Greenwood Press c1956, 1972. 325p. index. LC 72-01108. ISBN 0-8371-007-3.

Although it purports to be a further update to *Propaganda and Promotional Activities: An Annotated Bibliography* (entry 58) and *Propaganda, Communication, and Public Opinion: A Comprehensive Reference Guide* (entry 113), this selected bibliography focuses more on international issues. The 2,563 entries are divided into sections on theoretical and general writings, political persuasion and propaganda, specialists in political persuasion, channels of international communication (from radio and television to rumor), audience characteristics, research methods, and bibliographies.

115. Smith, Myron J. Jr., comp. **U.S. Television Network News: A Guide to Sources in English.** Jefferson, NC: McFarland, 1984. 233p. LC 82-42885. ISBN 0-89950-080-3.

John Chancellor says in the foreword that "I find it ironic, but not totally surprising, that the best record of this immensely influential medium of television will be found in the printed word." This may not be the best record, but it is the first of its kind. This is a selected bibliography of 3,215 books, papers, periodical articles, government documents, dissertations, and theses published from the 1940s to 1982. All are English-language sources (mostly United States). Unfortunately, there is no mention of online sources or databases. Chapters are broadly labeled and further subdivided. Citations are numbered and arranged alphabetically within chapters. Subjects include reference works, histories, networks and programming, network news and collections, domestic and foreign affairs, and biography. Book titles and a few periodical entries are descriptively annotated, mostly in a sentence or two. There are subject and author indexes, but a title index would help. This is a useful but ugly guide, with entries crammed on pages single-spaced. Smith also compiled *Watergate: An Annotated Bibliography of Sources in English, 1972–1982* (Scarecrow Press, 1983).

116. Snorgrass, J. William, and Gloria T. Woody, eds. **Blacks and Media: A Selected, Annotated Bibliography, 1962–1982.** Tallahassee: Florida A&M University Press, 1985. 150p. LC 84-15296. ISBN 0-8130-0810-7.

The relationship between blacks and the media, especially coverage of the explosive civil rights years, is explored in 743 books, chapters, and magazine and journal articles. Chapters on print media, broadcast media, advertising and public relations, film and theater contain numbered entries arranged alphabetically by title, not author. Annotations are short and evaluative. Although Snorgrass and Woody limit themselves to a fairly short historical period, they do include books and other materials that were reprinted between 1962 and 1982. Indexing is curious: titles of books and magazine articles are listed, but there is no subject index. This source would benefit from some further subject arrangement. For example, in the magazine articles portion of broadcast media, an article entitled "Is Network News Slighting the Minorities?" is preceded by "Is Kunta Kinte the New Fonzie?" Numerous selected articles from *The Quill, Columbia Journalism Review, Journalism Quarterly,* and *Journal of Broadcasting* are mentioned.

117. Sotiron, Minko, ed. **An Annotated Bibliography of Works on Daily Newspapers in Canada 1914–1983.** Une Bibliographie Annotee des Ouvrages Portant sur les Quotidiens Canadiens. Montreal: Inkstain Publications, 1987. 288p. index. ISBN 0-9693102-0-X.

In addition to "works on daily newspapers," and the Canadian press, this annotated bibliography of 3,766 books, periodical articles, dissertations, and other materials also covers advertising and ethics. General works on Canada are listed first and other entries are arranged geographically by province. The 545 French entries, however, are grouped in a separate section, have a separate index, and are listed and annotated only in French. Sotiron also is the author of *From Politics to Profit: The Commercialization of Canadian Daily Newspapers, 1890–1920* (McGill–Queen's University Press, 1997).

118. Speck, Bruce W. **Editing: An Annotated Bibliography.** Westport, CT: Greenwood Press, 1991. 295p. index. (Bibliographies and Indexes in Mass Media and Communications, no. 4). LC 90-29290. ISBN 0-313-26860-6.

Reference sources on the art and craft of editing are a rarity. In fact, Speck reveals in his introduction that "I searched the literature on editing and found only one book-length bibliography that listed materials on editing, *An Annotated Bibliography on Technical Writing, Editing, Graphics, and Publishing 1966–1980* published by the Society for Technical Communication." Only a fraction of Speck's book, listing books and articles covering 1960–1988, touches on news editing and related topics in journalism, but entries in other categories raise peripheral issues and could be fruitful. There are separate sections on general and technical editing; a third section on "Editing, Types of Publications" is broken down by publication type (i.e., anthologies, books, journals, press releases, reports) and arranged alphabetically by author. The annotated entries in "Magazines," "Newsletters," and "Newspapers" will be most useful. A substantial subject index ensures the user easy access. Speck also is the author of *Managing the Publishing Process: An Annotated Bibliography* (Greenwood Press, 1995), which also might pinpoint some useful resources.

119. Sterling, Christopher H., ed. and publ. **Communication Booknotes Quarterly.** (Formerly Communication Booknotes,1980–1997; Mass Media Booknotes 1973–1980; Broadcasting Bibliophiles Booknotes, 1969–1972). Mahwah, NJ: Erlbaum, 1998 (v. 29)— ISSN 0748-657X.

This quarterly annotated booklist and review service, also available online, is an excellent collection development tool for librarians as well as an up-to-date guide to current communications, telecommunications, and media publications. Sterling covers it all; if a source deals with communications on any level, he locates and reports on it. This is truly an essential resource and core periodical in journalism bibliography. He indicates that "comments are mainly descriptive to allow users to make ordering decisions. Where possible, comparative and evaluative comments are included as well." These critical evaluations are invaluable, and they are sprinkled liberally throughout each issue. Regional contributors offer listings from Australia, Great Britain, Canada, France, Germany, and so on. Sterling also has created other useful revised bibliographies such as "Bibliography on Telecommunications Policy," "Bibliography on Mass Communication and Electronic Media," and "Bibliography on Foreign and International Communication," all available from the Center for Advanced Study in Telecommunications (CAST) at Ohio State University in Columbus. Sterling coauthored (with Sydney W. Head and Lemuel B. Schofield)

Broadcasting in America: A Survey of Electronic Media, 7th ed. (Houghton Mifflin, 1994) and (with John M. Kittross) *A Concise History of American Broadcasting,* 3d ed. (Erlbaum, 2002).

120. Sterling, Christopher H., James K. Bracken, and Susan M. Hill, eds. **Mass Communication Research Resources: An Annotated Guide.** Mahwah, NJ: Erlbaum, 1998. 208p. index. bibl. LC 97-28441. ISBN 0-8058-2024-8.

The authors describe this resource as a "road map for researchers." That it is, with more than 1,400 descriptively annotated entries ranging in length from one sentence to a substantial paragraph. *Mass Communication Research Resources* is a seminal mass media bibliography, and it joins the ranks of "must haves" in academic library collections. It bridges an important decade-long gap, from the materials covered in *Mass Media Bibliography* (entry 13) to the mid to late 1990s, with emphasis on materials published since 1980. The editors define mass media as including "print journalism and electronic media and the processes by which they communicate messages to their audiences. Included are newspapers, magazines, radio, television, cable, and newer electronic sources." Users will need to rely heavily on the author/title index because of the complicated arrangement of chapters on general reference, history, technology, industry and economics, content, research and audiences, policy and regulation, international, media periodicals, and audiovisual sources, all further subdivided, either topically or by source type. This means, for example, that users searching for topical bibliographies will need to look in nine different chapters. Further, there is no subject index, but, oddly, listings of Library of Congress and Dewey subject headings on mass communications. In spite of these speed bumps, this road map is unparalleled. According to the editors, this was modeled after Sterling and Haight's *The Mass Media: Aspen Institute Guide to Communications Industry Trends* (entry 557). Sterling's *Telecommunications, Electronic Media, and Global Communications: A Survey Bibliography* (Communication Booknotes, 1996) may also provide some useful references.

121. Swindler, William F. **A Bibliography of Law on Journalism.** New York: Columbia University Press, 1947. 191p.

Swindler says that "the researcher needs a catalogue to all that has gone before, which would seem to be of lasting value, as well as a guide to the selection of current and future materials. This has been the twofold aim of this bibliography." In this he succeeds. The listing includes more than 1,100 books, monographs, and periodical articles published from 1844 to the 1940s focusing on journalism law, although popular and ephemeral materials are excluded. A 20-page bibliographic essay precedes the bibliography and offers a historical overview of the subject. Entries are numbered and arranged alphabetically by author within the following sections: texts and general works, history, press freedom, censorship, public records, libel, privacy, contempt, confidences, copyright, advertising, communications, radio, and so on. A separate section on international and foreign law also is subdivided by subject. Author and subject indexes are provided. Consult this classic work when researching any aspect of journalism and the law. Swindler also is the author of *Problems of Law in Journalism* (Macmillan, 1955).

122. Thomson, Ellen Mazur, comp. **American Graphic Design: A Guide to the Literature.** Westport, CT: Greenwood Press, 1992. 282p. index. (Art Reference Collection, no. 15). LC 92-23786. ISBN 0-313-28728-7.

Aimed at a wide audience of students, professional designers, art historians, collectors, and librarians, this annotated bibliographic reference is destined to become a classic. Thomson modestly notes that "this is not the first bibliography to consider graphic design," and lists several seminal sources including Lois Swan Jones's *Art Information: Research Methods and Resources,* 3d ed. (Kendall/Hunt, 1990) and Bernard Karpel's four-volume *Arts in America* (Smithsonian Institution Press, 1979). This volume, however, covers it all, encompassing "material printed commercially for mass consumption during the last three hundred years of the American experience." Chapters focus on the following topics: general reference; theory and history of graphic design; business and legal issues; design education; production; printing and typography; color; computer technology; visual resources; illustration and illustration photography; comics and cartoons; advertising; publication design; information graphics; logos and trademarks; package design; posters; annuals; and periodicals. An appendix contains listings of professional organizations. Excluded are fine arts and book art, cartography, and stamp design. Chapters are further subdivided, with citations arranged alphabetically by author within each subdivision. Publication designers and journalism instructors will find this source invaluable, as both electronic and print resources are detailed. The periodicals section is especially useful as an introduction to this vast and burgeoning field.

123.   Vanden Heuvel, Jon. **Untapped Sources: America's Newspaper Archives and Histories.** Craig LaMay and Martha FitzSimon, eds. Prepared for the American Society of Newspaper Editors' Newspaper History Task Force. New York: Gannett Foundation Media Center, Columbia University, 1991. 101p.

This little volume is packed with critical information on American newspaper history, including narrative bibliographies and holdings of major newspaper archives. The introduction lists numerous classic histories and reference sources, and includes information on the National Endowment for the Humanities' United States Newspaper Project. The section on "Research on Newspapers" includes discussions of ethnic, frontier, underground, religious, and army newspapers; "Books About Journalists" is a century-by-century report (beginning with the eighteenth century) of journalists, editors, publishers, correspondents, essayists, and reporters. There is a small section on cartoonists and photographers.
     The conclusion states:

the history of American newspapering is a field ripe for consolidation. Many studies of individual papers and individual journalists stock our shelves, and rather than adding to their numbers scholars should look to producing more synthetic works, which would pose more overarching questions about the American press and deal with journalists and papers in groups rather than in isolation.

Point taken; the only quibble is the consistent use of the term "newspapering," which reduces the art and craft of journalism to a decidedly more utilitarian act than it is. Newspaper archives profiled include the Library of Congress, the largest collection available in the United States, and the impressive State Historical Society of Wisconsin, with the second-largest collection. Librarians, book collectors, journalism students, and working journalists will all find something of value here, and that is a rarity.

124.   Wall, Celia Jo, comp. **Newspaper Libraries: A Bibliography, 1933–1985.** Washington, D.C.: Special Libraries Association, 1986. 126p. index. LC 86-14604. ISBN 0-87111-319-8.

The literature of news libraries extends far beyond the standard library journals, and this is an attempt to gather a comprehensive listing of books, chapters, professional and trade journal articles, unpublished papers, and pamphlets on the subject. English-language material from 1933–1985 is numbered and arranged alphabetically in chapters such as history, organization and administration, reference materials in the newspaper library, newspaper indexing, automation, and newspaper librarianship. Articles from *Editor & Publisher, Presstime,* and *Journalism Quarterly* are included. Since there are few published volumes on news libraries and the like, this is a valuable source. Annotations and lists of journals consulted would make it even better.

125.   Walsh, Gretchen. **The Media in Africa and Africa in the Media: An Annotated Bibliography.** New Providence, NJ: Hans Zell, 1996. 291p. index. bibl. ISBN 1-873836813.

More than 1,700 citations spanning a 30-year period from the mid-1960s to the mid-1990s are included in this exhaustive, annotated bibliography of print materials. Divided into sections on the press, broadcasting, film, and general, it includes numerous journals from Africa as well as Western resources. Detailed author, subject, and geographic indexes allow easy access to this unique resource.

126.   Wedell, George, Georg-Michael Luyken, and Rosemary Leonard, eds. **Mass Communications in Western Europe: An Annotated Bibliography.** Manchester, England: European Institute for the Media, 1985. 327p. index. (Media Monograph, no. 6). ISBN 0-948195-04-5.

Mass communications includes press, radio, television, film, publishing, telecommunications, and informatics and information technology in this international, selected bibliography. More than 750 documents and books and some periodical articles are organized by country, then arranged alphabetically by author. According to the editors, "it is the intention of this work to give references to the most recent developments in the Western European communications scene, including legislation and official documents, as well as of scholarly and policy-oriented texts." The following countries are included: Austria, Belgium, Cyprus, Denmark, Federal Republic of Germany, Finland, France, Greece, Iceland, Italy, Luxembourg, Netherlands, Norway, Portugal, Republic of Ireland, Spain, Sweden, Switzerland, Turkey, and United Kingdom. There are subject and author indexes.

127.   Wolseley, Roland E., and Isabel Wolseley. **The Journalists' Bookshelf: An Annotated and Selected Bibliography of United States Print Journalism.** 8th ed. Indianapolis, IN: R. J. Berg, 1986. 400p. index. LC 84-070769. ISBN 0-89730-139-0.

This annotated booklist of print journalism in the United States includes more than 2,000 entries (the 7th edition published in 1961 had 1,324 entries). Unfortunately, it still contains some very dated material. There is little cross-referencing because the authors say it "would swell the size of the book too much"; thus, users are invited to "scan" other categories. There is no subject index, so scanning will indeed be necessary. The authors include an interesting section on "Journalism Fiction," but it has been reduced because "few if any of these books are of interest to scholars." Although their definition of journalism is narrow (broadcast journalism is not included), the authors do include sections on ethics, minority press, college journalism, and high school journalism. *The Journalist's Bookshelf* is more useful as a journalism history source than as a current bibliography of journalism.

128.   Zuckerman, Mary Ellen, comp. **Sources on the History of Women's Magazines, 1792–1960: An Annotated Bibliography.** Westport, CT: Greenwood Press, 1991. 297p. index. (Bibliographies and Indexes in Women's Studies, no. 12). LC 91-12151. ISBN 0-313-26378-7.

Popular women's magazines in the United States are chronicled in this exhaustive reference guide to historical sources. "Where does the truth about these publications lie?" Zuckerman asks. "Are women's magazines the narcotic, negative forces their critics have claimed? Or are they the indispensable trade magazines of housewives, providing unique assistance to women in the home? The answer, of course, stands somewhere in between, varying according to magazine title, editor and time period." A detailed introduction provides historical background and describes arrangement of citations. Books, journals, and magazine articles, theses and dissertations are included. Individual chapters focus on women's magazines from the eighteenth century through the Civil War; general studies of women's magazines from 1865 to 1960; the depiction of women in the media; content in women's magazines; individuals working for women's magazines; advertising; surveys, marketing research reports, and promotional materials; business issues; critiques of women's magazines; and archives and manuscript collections. Bibliographic entries are further subdivided, numbered, and arranged alphabetically by author. An additional section on "Individual Women's Magazine Titles" focuses exclusively on seminal women's publications and provides a closer bibliographic picture of 10 magazines, ranging from *Good Housekeeping* to *Vogue*. It is interesting to note that the first magazine for women in the United States was *The Lady's Magazine and Repository of Entertaining Knowledge*. With this bibliography, Zuckerman offers yet another "repository" of entertaining and skillfully researched material. She writes in her preface that "its primary purpose is to aid others interested in researching, reading and writing about women's magazines." It does this and much more. Zuckerman also wrote *Women's Magazines and the American Woman* (Columbia University Press, 1992), *History of Popular Women's Magazines in the United States, 1792–1995* (Greenwood Press, 1998), and coauthored with John Tebbel *The Magazine in America, 1741–1990* (Oxford University Press, 1991). See also Nancy K. Humphrey's *American Women's Magazines* (Garland, 1989), which provides information on women's pages in newspapers and confession and romance magazines.

2
Encyclopedias

129.   Barnouw, Erik, ed. in chief, et al. **International Encyclopedia of Communications.** New York: Oxford University Press, 1989. 4 vols. illus. bibliog. index. LC 88-18132. ISBN 0-19-504994-2 (set).

This is one of the most important publications in the field of communications, and is the first of its kind. It addresses a broad range of topics in communications, with numerous references to subjects in journalism and mass communication. More than 450 scholars and professionals contributed to this four-volume collection of signed articles on animal communication, arts, communications research, computers, education, folklore, government regulation, international communication, journalism, language and linguistics, literature, media, motion pictures, music, nonverbal communication, photography, political communication, print media, radio, religion, speech, television, communication theories and theorists, and so on. There are more than 550 alphabetically arranged articles, a comprehensive index, topical guide, cross-references, and illustrations. Each entry also contains a brief bibliography, listing basic bibliographic information but, unfortunately, no publishers (place of publication, however, is included). In all, 9 editorial board members, 25 section editors, and 170 editorial advisers were involved in this project. Another useful and more current resource that overlaps some of the mass media covered here is *History of the Mass Media in the United States: An Encyclopedia* (entry 130). Researchers might also want to scan *From Talking Drums to the Internet: An Encyclopedia of Communications Technology* (ABC-CLIO, 1997), the *Encyclopedia of International Media and Communications* (entry 143), and the *Encyclopedia of Communication and Information* (Macmillan Reference, 2002).

130.   Blanchard, Margaret A., ed. **History of the Mass Media in the United States: An Encyclopedia.** Chicago: Fitzroy Dearborn, 1998. 752p. illus. bibliog. index. LC ISBN 1-57958-012-2.

"Readers of this encyclopedia will find background on how the media reached their positions of authority, influence, and controversy in American society today," the editor writes. "The authors who contributed to this work illustrate the development of media forms and the evolution of their practices; they show how media efforts have succeeded and how they have failed; and they illustrate the manner in which media cope with a changing world and changing demands on them." The list of authors is impressive—more than 260 individuals who contributed their scholarly perspectives on media events, concepts, and developments occurring over a 300-year span of time, roughly 1690–1990. Blanchard also writes that the contributors had a "single goal in accepting an assignment to write for this volume: to make the history of the media more accessible and understandable for those not expert in this field." In this, they have surely succeeded. The media represented here are advertising, books, broadcasting, cable, magazine, motion pictures, newspapers, photography and photojournalism, public relations, radio, and television. Thankfully, this meticulous resource is largely thematic, and arranged alphabetically. It is purposely light on biographical entries, acknowledging that an adequate body of knowledge on mass media personalities is available. Some entries are no more than a quarter of a page (classified advertising); others such as the Civil War Press take up several pages, and include see also references, illustrations, newspaper accounts, and brief bibliographies. Users of this source might also wish to consult the *International Encyclopedia of Communications* (entry 129) and *The ABC-CLIO Companion to the Media in America* (entry 544).

131. Boyd, Amanda et al., eds. **Writer's Encyclopedia.** 3d ed. Cincinnati, OH: Writer's Digest, F & W Publications, 1996. 499p. bibliog. LC 95-53299. ISBN 0-89879-749-7.

First entitled the *Writer's Encyclopedia* (1983), then *Writing A to Z* (1990), the third edition retains the encyclopedic format but returns to the original title. Aimed at the professional writer, this book does not masquerade as a reader's encyclopedia. The brief preface informs us that "this reference work brings together in one volume all the terms, techniques, procedures and trade expressions you'll need to know, whether your interest is publishing, broadcasting, films, lecturing, the theater, advertising or public relations." Its use as a current journalism reference, however, is limited, in part, by the broad spectrum of topics covered. The 1,300 entries are arranged alphabetically, but there is no index.

132. Brown, Les. **Les Brown's Encyclopedia of Television.** 3d ed. Detroit, MI: Gale, 1992. 496p. index. LC 91-48157. ISBN 0-8103-8871-5.

Brown, author of books such as *Television: The Business Behind the Box* (Harcourt Brace Jovanovich, 1971), states that the 900 new entries and other rewritten and updated articles in this third edition represent "the changes wrought by the tempests of the 1980s." The scope is broad. On one page, for example, there are entries for "F-Troop," "Face the Nation," facsimile, and Fairness Doctrine. On another page one finds "Night Gallery," "Nightline," and Leonard Nimoy. Arrangement is alphabetical and includes terminology, programs, and biographical entries. There is solid information on the networks, some international information, and a smattering of entries on documentaries, broadcast personalities, correspondents, and anchors. Entries are frequently quite brief, which is a disappointing feature in an encyclopedic source, but it is nonetheless a useful one-volume resource. For a British perspective on television, users may wish to consult Halliwell's *Television Companion* (Grafton, 1986); be forewarned, however, that Halliwell excludes news and current affairs programming.

133. Capa, Cornell, Jerry Mason, and William L. Broeker, eds. **International Center of Photography Encyclopedia of Photography.** New York: Crown Publishers, 1984. 607p. illus. bibliog. LC 84-1856. ISBN 0-517-55271-X.

The ICP encyclopedia is one of the most handsome and high-toned one-volume reference sources in print today. Capa states that "all concerned sought to produce a volume light enough to hold in hand, beautiful to look at, and inexpensive enough for wide public use, one that would cover the range from the aesthetic and historical to the technical and practical aspects of the medium." It succeeds, except, weighing in at more than five pounds, it is more than a handful. More than 1,300 alphabetically arranged entries describe, according to the introduction, the aesthetic, communicative, scientific, technical, and commercial applications of photography. Of special interest are entries for documentary and social documentary photography, photojournalism, and satire in photography. More than 250 biographical entries for inventors and photographers born between 1840 and 1940 and examples of their photography, as well as a biographical supplement of more than 2,000 photographers, are included. An excellent subject bibliography is the final feature. Photography receives some scholarly treatment here, but both the general reader and professional photographer will find their own particular uses for this rich source.

134. Drost, Harry, ed. **The World's News Media: A Comprehensive Reference Guide.** Harlow, Essex, United Kingdom: Longman Current Affairs, 1991. Detroit, MI: Gale, distr. 604p. ISBN 0-582-08554-3.

Nearly 200 countries are surveyed in this alphabetical, international guide to print and broadcast media. Each country profile contains a brief historical and political overview and sections focusing on news sources, the press, broadcasting, and a directory of major newspapers, broadcast organizations, agencies, and press associations. Most entries are two to four pages in length, although a few (Japan, United Kingdom, United States) are 10 pages or longer. Drost passively states in his spare one-page introduction that

A few words should perhaps be said on terminology: "owned by" is used loosely to cover a maze of ownership patterns; "independent" is used as a description of ownership, not political or editorial stance; a "daily" is published on at least four days per week; and "tabloid" refers to paper size not content.

For further information, consult *The World Media Handbook* (entry 153), *World Communication and Transportation Data* (ABC-CLIO), and the *World Press Encyclopedia* (entry 150).

135. Green, Jonathon. **The Encyclopedia of Censorship.** New York: Facts on File, 1990. 388p. bibliog. LC 89-1210. ISBN 0-8160-1594-5.

"Censorship takes the least flattering view of humanity. Underpinning its rules and regulations is the assumption that people are stupid, gullible, weak and corrupt." So says Green in his introduction to this international encyclopedic account of political, moral, and cultural censorship, past and present. Alphabetical entries range from The Pentagon Papers to Germany's Rubbish and Smut Bill. Press censorship is covered extensively in this provocative, one-volume ready-reference source on political, moral, and cultural censorship. Users also will be interested in the *Historical Dictionary of Censorship in the United States* (entry 140) and *Banned in the Media* (Greenwood Press, 1998).

136. Griffiths, Dennis, ed. **The Encyclopedia of the British Press 1422–1992.** New York: St. Martin's Press, 1992. bibliog. 694p. LC 92-29118. ISBN 0-312-08633-4.

Griffiths indicates this is "the first reference book of its kind" and concludes in his foreword that "For more than a century there has been an urgent need for a widely-available, convenient and authoritative first source of reference" on the British press. This encyclopedia is just that. It offers introductory essays on the early newspaper press in England, and the British press in the eighteenth century, 1800–1860, 1861–1918, 1919–1945, and postwar. The 3,000 alphabetical entries make up the bulk of this work, with emphasis on British publishers, editors, and newspapers. There are some surprises as well; one would expect to find the likes of Robert Maxwell and Alastair Cooke here, but one also unearths an entry for the Rev. J. P. Bacon-Phillips (1857–1938), described simply as "letter writer extraordinary." Apparently, his claim to fame was penning more than 8,000 letters to the editor in his lifetime. There is, unfortunately, no index, but entries are enhanced by useful cross-references. Also included is a brief chronology of the British press compiled by David Linton, coeditor of *The Newspaper Press in Britain: An Annotated Bibliography* (entry 70) and editor of *The Twentieth Century Newspaper Press in Britain: An Annotated Bibliography* (entry 69). Twenty-five brief articles on a range of topics, from newspaper design to ombudsmen, round out this source. News historians and students will use this rich source as a starting point for discussion and research. Reference librarians will use this as a companion volume to *The Encyclopedia of American Journalism* (entry 149), which, in comparison, is dated.

137.   Griffiths, Dennis, ed. **Encyclopedia of the World Press.** Chicago: Fitzroy Dearborn, 2004. ISBN 1579582346.

The *Encyclopedia of the World Press* will be released after *Journalism: A Guide to the Reference Literature* has gone to press.

138.   Hixson, Richard F. **Mass Media and the Constitution: An Encyclopedia of Supreme Court Decisions.** New York: Garland, 1989. 529p. index. (American Law and Society, vol. 1; Garland Reference Library of Social Science, vol. 421). LC 99-25069. ISBN 0-8240-7947-7.

Librarians, researchers, and students who do not speak legalese will be relieved to find straightforward explanations and brief descriptions of Supreme Court cases focusing on a myriad of issues in mass communication. More than 200 entries are arranged chronologically in the following broad categories: broadcasting, business, censorship, commercial speech, copyright, fair trial, Freedom of Information Act, free speech, libel, newsgathering, obscenity, and privacy. For those who need further assistance, Hixson provides an ample subject index, an index of decisions, and bibliographies. Each mercifully succinct entry pinpoints dates and title, case summary, abstract of opinion (including supporting and dissenting jurists), and case citations. Some landmark decisions, such as those dealing with copyright, date back to the early nineteenth century. Users might also be interested in Douglas S. Campbell's *The Supreme Court and the Mass Media: Selected Cases, Summaries, and Analyses* (Praeger, 1990).

139.   Hudson, Robert V. **Mass Media: A Chronological Encyclopedia of Television, Radio, Motion Pictures, Magazines, Newspapers, and Books in the United States.** New York: Garland, 1987. 435p. bibliog. index. (Garland Reference Library of Social Science, vol. 310). LC 85-45153. ISBN 0-8240-8695-3.

"Information in a Hurry" could be the subtitle of this useful source for students and those searching for a fact or two. Keep in mind, though, that this chronological list of mass media events in the United States through 1985 is not a scholarly tool. Chapters such as "The Great Depression, 1930–1941" and "The American Revolution, 1765–1783" are subdivided into sections on books and pamphlets, newspapers, and magazines. (Motion picture, radio, and television categories are included from 1878 on.) Entries are arranged chronologically within these subdivisions. There is a name and subject index. A shortcoming of this work is the existence of factual errors and some surprising omissions. The Janet Cooke scandal in 1981 was a major media event, but neither she nor the Pulitzer Prize she forfeited is mentioned. In fact, the only Pulitzers mentioned are the prizes awarded in literature.

140. Hurwitz, Leon. **Historical Dictionary of Censorship in the United States.** Westport, CT; Greenwood Press, 1985. 584p. bibliog. index. LC 84-15796. ISBN 0-313-23878-2.

Why are they called the Pentagon Papers? What were the issues in *Cox Broadcasting Corporation v. Cohn*? This source is designed to answer such questions, but the criteria for selection and inclusion of items are unclear. Although only a portion of the book covers constitutional censorship and First Amendment rights, "it attempts to present an overview of the types of speech and press that have been subjected to censorship, repression, and punishment" (preface). The lengthy introduction identifies four categories of governmental censorship: political, community, constitutional, and moral. Entries are arranged alphabetically and cross-referenced. The index includes subjects and titles. The list of almost 500 legal cases may be the strongest feature. Appendixes include a chronology of events from 1644 to 1984, a table of cases, and a selected bibliography. Users also will be interested in *The Encyclopedia of Censorship* (entry 135) and *Banned in the Media* (Greenwood, 1998).

141. Ingelhart, Louis E. **Press Freedoms: A Descriptive Calendar of Concepts, Interpretations, Events, and Court Actions, from 4000 B.C. to the Present.** New York: Greenwood Press, 1987. 430p. bibliog. index. LC 85-31834. ISBN 0-313-25636-5.

No mere calendar, this encyclopedic chronology of freedom of the press covers all time periods from prehistory to the present. Although the arrangement is chronological, with chapters such as "Printing in a World of Irreverence, 1500 through 1599," a detailed subject and name index makes it fully accessible. Brief entries describe pivotal events and court decisions in North America, South America, Europe, Asia, Africa, and Australia. A selected bibliography presents about 200 important books on press freedom. Aimed at teachers and students, this volume is a valuable ready reference source and highlights other areas ripe for research. Users should also consult Ingelhart's updated press and speech freedom volumes (entry 142). See also McCoy's *Freedom of the Press: An Annotated Bibliography* (entry 75) and *Freedom of the Press: A Bibliocyclopedia* (entry 76). Ingelhart also authored *Freedom for the College Student Press* (Greenwood Press, 1985) and *Press Law and Press Freedom for High School Publications* (Greenwood Press, 1986).

142. Ingelhart, Louis E., ed. **Press and Speech Freedoms in America, 1619–1995: A Chronology.** Greenwood Press, 1997. 367p. index. LC 96-41287. ISBN 0-313-30174-3. Press and Speech Freedoms in the World, from Antiquity Until 1998: A Chronology. Greenwood Press, 1998. 320p. ISBN 0313308519.

Ingelhart has adapted his earlier *Press Freedoms* chronology (entry 141), broadening its scope to include press and speech, and separating the American press from the world press. The arrangement is chronological and is valuable as a ready reference source and snapshot of the vocabulary of press and speech freedom worldwide through the ages. Librarians are quoted extensively and offer some rousing sentiments. For example, one learns that in 1970, Martha Boaz, librarian, stated: "The student has a right to read; he has a right to free access to books. He has a right to a wide variety and to an extensive selection of materials. He has a right to examine all ideas, to explore all forms of learning, to investigate all cultures. He has a right to investigate every medium of art and every model of expression of it. He has a right to search for truth wherever it may be found." And in 1838, James Fenimore Cooper, who was not a librarian and "who hated American newspapers," said: "The entire nation breathes an atmosphere of falsehoods. The country cannot much longer exist in safety under the malign influence that now over-shadows it; the press as a whole owes its existence to the schemes of interested political adventurers." Entries are arranged chronologically by year, and subject and name indexes provide easy access. Not included in these volumes are court decisions and statements by judges; in the preface the editor lists other resources to consult when researching those areas. It is alarming, however, to also read in the preface that "there are computer data sources also available such as Nexus-Lexus." Those who go in search of that won't find it—the correct title is LexisNexis.

143. Johnston, Donald H., ed. **Encyclopedia of International Media and Communications.** 4 vols. San Diego, CA: Academic Press, 2003. index. LC 20-03100764. ISBN 0-12-387670-2.

This impressive and exhaustive collection of more than 200 articles written by more than 200 specialists fills a huge gap in current mass media scholarship (Barnouw's the *International Encyclopedia of Communications,* entry 129, was published in 1989). Each article provides a lengthy exploration of one aspect of international communications, with essays ranging from "Internet as Political Advocacy Forum" to "Ethnic and Gender Stereotyping." Broad subjects covered include media types, media formats, media outlets, media genres, media interrelationships, media issues, media concepts, geopolitical studies, historic views, and future projections. Articles uniformly contain an outline, glossary, defining paragraph, essay, cross-references, and bibliography and range from 10 to 15 pages in length. "Women in the Media," for example, by Marilyn Greenwald, is divided into sections on print media, broadcast media, the women's movement, and women's representation and the glass ceiling, all further subdivided. "See also" references guide the user to other relevant articles such as "Cultural Values and Mass Communications" and "Daytime Television, Culture of," and the glossary defines terms such as glass ceiling, Title VII, and muckrakers. A detailed index makes this resource highly accessible. Researchers might also wish to consult the *World Press Encyclopedia* (entry 150).

144. Lackmann, Ronald W. **The Encyclopedia of American Radio: An A–Z Guide to Radio from Jack Benny to Howard Stern.** New York: Facts on File, 2000. 370p. index. LC 99-35263. ISBN 0-8160-4137-7.

This revised edition of *Same Time, Same Station* is an encyclopedic guide to radio programs and broadcasters in the United States and Canada from the 1920s to the present. It supplements the reference literature on old-time radio, fills a gap in current sources, and is especially useful when researching lesser-known radio personalities. One page, for example, offers information on Frank Nelson, Ozzie Nelson, the New York Philharmonic, and Newscasters. Appendixes include chronologies of radio events; sponsors; personalities; and vintage radio show clubs, conventions, museums, newsletters, and organizations. The index, frequently an element given short shrift in encyclopedias, is detailed and well constructed. Users also will be interested in *Radio's Golden Years* (entry 151), Buxton's *The Big Broadcast* (Scarecrow, 1997), and to a lesser extent, Luther Sies's *Ency-*

clopedia of American Radio, 1920–1960 (McFarland, 2000), which is less of an encyclopedia than a catalog of programs.

145.   Lackmann, Ronald W. **The Encyclopedia of 20th-Century American Television.** New York: Facts on File, 2002. 528p. index. LC 20-01056856. ISBN 0-8160-4554-2.

From "All My Children" to "Newsradio," this alphabetically arranged ready reference source offers a snapshot of television broadcast programming from 1947 to 2000. According to Lackmann, "only programs originally produced by or for the national broadcast TV networks (CBS, NBC, ABC, Fox, WB) and syndicated shows that were seen on these networks" are included. In addition, only series that lasted at least one season will be found here. Entries contain broadcast history and air times as well as brief descriptions and story lines. Special programs and biographies of major performers and producers also are included. Lackmann also authored *The Encyclopedia of American Radio* (entry 144).

146.   Lowe, Denise. **Women and American Television: An Encyclopedia.** Santa Barbara, CA: ABC-CLIO, 1999. 513p. index. LC 99-050178. ISBN 0-87436-970-3.

From Linda Ellerbee to Lucy, this popular account of women in television profiles those who have had an impact on popular culture and the media. Included are more than 400 individual biographies and thematic entries such as Black Female Roles, Talk Shows, Screwball Wives, and Female Impersonators. There is a strong focus on contributions that minority women have made to television. Beyond that, the criteria for inclusion loses focus. For example, Lowe includes "every series that featured a female character in a lead role that lasted at least six months," but also says that "if a series was controversial, groundbreaking, or vastly popular—with or without a prominent female character—it was included." Entries are brief, generally one page or less, and arranged alphabetically. The author writes, "While I was gathering my research I was struck by the lack of information about women who worked in television. Men of less repute were readily covered, but women who made real contributions were left out of so-called comprehensive references." The indexes (more than 100 pages) are dense and amazingly comprehensive. While not scholarly in nature, this resource provides an entertaining and wide-ranging snapshot of women's contributions to television. Lowe writes, "I have tried to include individuals who were trendsetters or groundbreakers or cultural icons. So although Farah Fawcett and Loni Anderson did not make a lasting impact on the medium, while they were popular, they were the medium to many viewers." Students of popular culture and cultural studies, however, might beg to differ.

147.   Murray, Michael D., ed. **Encyclopedia of Television News.** Phoenix, AZ: Oryx, 1999. 315p. index. LC 98-36705. ISBN 1-57356-108-8.

While this might be more aptly titled *Encyclopedia of Television News People,* it is still a comprehensive and current glimpse into television news. More than 100 researchers and experts authored 309 alphabetically arranged entries on the people and issues associated with television news, from Edward R. Murrow and Stone Phillips to documentary television and covering Clinton/Lewinsky. Ed Bliss writes in the foreword, that "In covering the whole range of broadcast journalism—issues, programs, personalities—the scope of this work is, I believe, unparalleled, The inquiring reader will find here a vast storehouse of biography and history." The editor states that his goal is to "provide a beginning, a tool useful to students of the television, journalism, and broadcast fields; television journalists; and the general public—anyone interested in information gathering for television, its achievements, and its many challenges." He continues, "Television news is still in the early stages of development. The field as a whole remains at a critical juncture in which additional resources are sorely needed." While this volume is heavy in biography and lighter in topical issues, it is nonetheless a first stop for students and researchers exploring issues and personalities in television news. It also is highly accessible, with a detailed index signed by author Linda Webster.

148. Newcomb, Horace, ed. **Encyclopedia of Television.** Chicago: Fitzroy Dearborn, 1997. 3 vols. index. LC. ISBN 1-884964-26-5.

A project of the publisher and the Museum of Broadcast Communications, this is an important, wide-ranging, comprehensive publication. Nearly 300 contributors offer their perspectives on more than 1,000 topics related to the history, significance, and influence of television, from "60 Minutes" to "Starsky and Hutch." These three volumes are packed with relevant information on subjects such as activist television, documentary, local news, network news, the civil rights movement, and is an excellent source on television in the U.S., Canada, Australia, and Great Britain. The editor writes that this source "offers no definition of its own for 'television.' Instead, it offers a multitude of beginning points from which to trace the intersections, conflicts, struggles, and convergences that can be applied, used as partial explanations for particular events, policies, developments, even for the existence of particular television 'shows.' " This is a particularly relevant resource for students exploring vocabulary, history, and genres, and for reference librarians searching for ready reference information. A second edition of the *Encyclopedia of Television* will be published by CRC/Routledge in 2004.

149. Paneth, Donald. **The Encyclopedia of American Journalism.** New York: Facts on File, 1983. 548p. index. LC 81-12575. ISBN 0-87196-427-9.

This encyclopedia of newspapers, magazines, radio, television, photography, newsreels, and documentaries lists more than 1,000 entries, some dictionary-length, some essays. The most influential educators, columnists, editors, black journalists, reporters, women journalists, and foreign correspondents also are surveyed. A special feature is "Legendary Figures," of which, according to Paneth's subject index, there are only 13. (Legendary names range from A. J. Liebling to the fictional Hildy Johnson, star reporter in "The Front Page.") Legal cases, broadcasting and broadcasting networks, news agencies, journalism periodicals, and military terms are some of the subjects covered in this well-designed and crisply written reference source. Entries are alphabetical and cover the field of journalism through 1982. Major entries provide bibliographical references. Journalism students will use this as a source for research topics, journalism librarians may bolt it to the reference desk, and newsrooms might get some use out of it also.

150. Quick, Amanda C., ed. **World Press Encyclopedia: A Survey of Press Systems Worldwide.** 2 vols. Farmington Hills, MI: Gale, 2003. bibliog. index. ISBN 0-78765-582-1.

According to the introduction written by George Thomas Kurian, editor of the first edition, this second edition has been "100 percent revised" and is a "magisterial survey of the state of the press at the beginning of the twenty-first century." Quick and 80 contributors have examined print and electronic media in 232 countries (up from 180 in the first edition published in 1982). Each signed essay is arranged alphabetically and covers economic framework, press laws, censorship, state-press relations, attitude toward foreign media, news agencies, broadcast media, electronic media, education and training, summary, important dates, and a current bibliography. Profiles range in length from one page (Christmas Island) to a few pages (Azerbaijan) to more than 30 pages (United States). Appendixes include tables of newspaper statistics, a listing of news agencies, press associations, and media rankings, and regional maps. An author and subject index allows easy access to this seminal resource. See also the *Encyclopedia of International Media and Communications* (entry 143) and the *International Encyclopedia of Communications* (entry 129).

151. Terrace, Vincent. **Radio's Golden Years: The Encyclopedia of Radio Programs, 1930–1960.** San Diego, CA: A.S. Barnes, 1981. 308p. index. LC 79-87791. ISBN 0-498-02393-1.

This browsing tool chronicles old-time radio, listing alphabetically about 1,500 national broadcast show and syndicated entertainment programs from 1930 to 1960. A few new programs from the 1970s also are included, along with documentaries and talk-interview shows. (John Dunning's *Tune in Yesterday: The Ultimate Encyclopedia of Old-Time Radio, 1925–1976* [Prentice-Hall, 1976] might also be consulted, but its use is limited as it excludes news and documentaries.) Information is spotty in parts, but entries usually include a story line, cast lists, and some credits. Buxton's *The Big Broadcast, 1920–1950* (Scarecrow, 1997) obviously overlaps this material, but he includes names you wish Terrace had—writers and directors. The entry for "Hear It Now" tells us that Edward R. Murrow narrated this documentary-type program, that "this series replayed famous events previously heard on the air," and that this hour-long show was first broadcast on CBS in 1950. Unfortunately, not even a sampling of these famous events is offered, but we do learn that Alfredo Antonini conducted the orchestra. Researchers might also want to consult Lackmann's *Encyclopedia of American Radio* (entry 144).

152. Terrace, Vincent. **Encyclopedia of Television: Series, Pilots and Specials, 1937–1973.** New York: New York Zoetrope, 1986. 480p. LC 85-043428. ISBN 0-918432-69-3. **Encyclopedia of Television: Series, Pilots and Specials, 1974–1984.** New York: New York Zoetrope, 1985. 458p. LC 84-061786. ISBN 0-918432-61-8. **Encyclopedia of Television: Series, Pilots and Specials, The Index: Who's Who in Television, 1937–1984.** New York: New York Zoetrope, 1986. 662p. LC 86-43211. ISBN 0-918432-71-5.

This three-volume set is a limited source for journalistic endeavors. Terrace sets us up for disappointment with this statement from volume 1: "Many obscure feature films, as well as live coverage of sporting and news events, were broadcast on an experimental basis to the few television sets existing at the time." He then tells us that news and sports are not within this encyclopedia's range. Entertainment programming is the focus, although talk shows and documentaries are covered. Entries are numbered and arranged alphabetically in volumes 1 and 2. Volume 1, covering the years 1937–1973, describes 4,982 programs, including cast lists and credits. Volume 2 encompasses the years 1974–1984 and contains 2,878 programs. The index, volume 3, is divided into four sections covering performers, producers, directors, and writers. Names are arranged alphabetically within those sections, and refer the user to volume and entry number. Terrace says it contains the names of more than 18,000 performers, 5,000 producers, 5,000 writers, and 3,500 directors.

153.   The World Media Handbook 1992–94. New York: United Nations Department of Public Information, 1990– . Biennial. ISSN 1014-871X.

Although its audience is described as the United Nations Department of Public Information and "other media professionals within the UN-system," this is a timely and accessible ready reference source for public and university libraries as well as individuals seeking general information and numbers on international mass media systems. Limitations are spelled out in the brief introduction. Perhaps the biggest drawback of this source is the "limited space" issue, which, in the 1992–94 handbook, "allowed the inclusion of a maximum of 16 newspapers and 20 magazines and other periodicals per country." This is not a problem with small countries such as Bhutan and Samoa, but definitely limiting with entries for the United States, United Kingdom, Germany, Japan, and other larger countries. Entries for more than 150 countries are arranged alphabetically by country and also include information in the following categories: basic (population, per capita income, life expectancy); cultural (official languages, student population, illiteracy rates); print and electronic media (daily newspapers, newsprint, broadcasting, including, for example, number of television sets); telecommunications (telephones, telex, data transmission, etc.). A 1995 edition was published, but that appears to be the latest in what was supposed to be a biennial publication. See also *The World's News Media: A Comprehensive Reference Guide* (entry 134) and *World Communication and Transportation Data* (ABC-CLIO, 1989).

154.   World Press Trends. Paris: Federation Internationale des Editeurs de Journaux, International Federation of Newspaper Publishers, 1990– . Annual.

This international survey of trends in the newspaper industry also contains an impressive amount of current factual information and statistical data and is thus included in this chapter. In addition, it can serve as a selected annual update to the seminal *World Press Encyclopedia* (entry 150) published in 1982. The 1995 edition surveys 46 countries, from Estonia to the United States; the 2000 edition covers 64 countries, from Azerbaijan to Kyrgyzstan. Global circulation figures, market penetration and advertising revenues, ownership, and subsidies also are reviewed.

3
Dictionaries

155.   Bollard, John K., ed., Frank R. Abate and Katherine M. Isaacs, assoc. eds. **Pronouncing Dictionary of Proper Names.** 2d ed. Detroit, MI: Omnigraphics, Inc., 1997. 1,100p. ISBN 0-78080-098-2.

Although not designed specifically with the journalist in mind, this is an invaluable source for all communications specialists, especially radio and television broadcasters. Subtitled "Pronunciations for more than 28,000 Proper Names, Selected for Currency, Frequency, or Difficulty of Pronunciation," this 1,100-page tome is too massive to be considered a pocket guide to pronunciation, but journalists who have embarrassed themselves on the air (or elsewhere) by mispronouncing names of countries or dinosaurs will consult this regularly. This updated edition contains approximately 5,000 more entries than the previous one. Categories covered include given names and surnames, geographic names, geographical features, people, nature and environment history, politics and current affairs, literature, religion, philosophy, culture and the arts, company and product names, popular culture, food and drink, and science and technology. Two pronunciation systems are used—simplified English spelling and, for the linguist, the alphabet of the International Phonetic Association. Eugene H. Ehrlich and Raymond Hand's *NBC Handbook of Pronunciation*, 4th ed. (Harper & Row, 1984) is useful, but not as current or comprehensive. *The BBC Pronouncing Dictionary of British Names* (Oxford University Press, 1983) might be consulted as well.

156.   Brown, Timothy G. **International Communications Glossary.** Washington, D.C.: Media Institute, 1984. 97p. index. LC 84-62298. ISBN 0-937790-27-3.

It appears the author intended this to be far more than a dictionary of international communications. In actuality, it is a Media Institute indictment in glossary format of UNESCO and the New World Information Order. According to the introduction, "the glossary explores how the advocates of a New World Information Order use language to mask their real intentions." As long as the user keeps this bias in mind, this can be a useful additional reference source. Almost 50 terms and phrases are arranged alphabetically in chapter 1, with some entries extending to more than a page. Included are alternative media, censorship, correct and factual information, national communications policies, and (a personal favorite) progressive incorporation of communications technology. Some definitions deserve more detailed treatment, as in the case of propaganda: "This is not an easy one. According to the West, propaganda is what most of the Second and Third World governments and government-run news services put out. According to those entities, propaganda is what Western governments and news services put out. It all depends whose ox is being gored." Chapter 2 describes more than 40 organizations involved in international communications. Appendixes include a short bibliography, a chronological description of "Government Actions and Press Freedom 1981–82," and an explanation of the United States International Communications Policy. See the *Glossary for International Communications: Communications in a Changing World* (entry 179) for a similar treatment.

157. Brown, William P., and Kathryn Sederberg. **The Complete Dictionary of Media Terms.** Chicago, IL: Commerce Communications, 1986. 151p. LC 86-70712. ISBN 0-913247-01-4.

Although the emphasis is on advertising media terms, this dictionary is useful in defining some broadcasting terms. According to the authors, "In the media world, a bad break isn't poor luck but awkward typesetting; a band isn't necessarily a musical group but a range of broadcast frequencies; and carts aren't used for transportation but as video tape containers. Dummies are suggested magazine layouts. Gutters become inside margins in magazines. *The Complete Dictionary of Media Terms* is intended to help you through this word maze."

158. Connors, Tracy Daniel. **Longman Dictionary of Mass Media and Communication.** New York: Longman, 1982. 255p. (Longman Series in Public Communication). LC 82-92. ISBN 0-582-28337-X.

This dictionary was designed to bridge the communication gap between professionals in advertising, television and radio broadcasting, film, graphic arts, journalism, photography, and publishing. Several thousand entries are arranged alphabetically and name the field of communication in which the term or phrase is used. There are some surprising omissions; for example, a journalism "lead" is defined here as a news tip or inside information. While that is not incorrect, the lead can also be defined as the first paragraph in or the main idea of a story. Both ought to be included. Still, this is an ambitious and well-organized sourcebook. Fourteen contributing editors selected and compiled terms. Consult *Webster's New World Dictionary of Media and Communications* (entry 181) and *NTC's Mass Media Dictionary* (entry 162) for useful and more current information.

159. Devito, Joseph A. **The Communication Handbook: A Dictionary.** New York: Harper & Row, 1986. 337p. LC 85-17547. ISBN 0-06-041638-6.

Essay-length entries aim at nonexperts—students, professionals, and researchers in search of definitions to the basic vocabulary used in communication. Theoretical and practical terms are included in the areas of literature, art, television, speech, and science. Entries are arranged alphabetically. This is not an adequate substitute for a good journalism dictionary, and it is not designed to be.

160. Diamant, Lincoln, ed. **Dictionary of Broadcast Communications.** 3d ed. Lincolnwood, IL: NTC Business Books, 1991. (Reprint of Broadcast Communications Dictionary, 3d ed., Westport, CT: Greenwood Press, 1989). 255p. LC 90-24791. ISBN 0-8442-3325-0.

The second edition was published in 1978, so this third edition, which "provides an indispensable guide to the most frequently used terms in every area of contemporary electronic communications," is a welcome update. More than 6,000 technical, nontechnical, and slang terms—from "cattle call" to "reaction shot"—used in radio, television, film, video, and audio, are arranged alphabetically. Terms in programming, production, and network and station operations are addressed, along with engineering terms. Diamant's introduction states that "in short, the *Dictionary of Broadcast Communications* is comprehensive, sensible, accurate, and indispensable." That it is.

161. Ellmore, R. Terry. **The Illustrated Dictionary of Broadcast-CATV-Telecommunications.** Blue Ridge Summit, PA: TAB Books, 1977. 396p. LC 77-008529. ISBN 0-8306-7950-2.

A broad source for the beginner, this dictionary stresses theoretical and technical terminology used by the broadcast and cable professional. Several thousand brief entries are arranged alphabetically. In spite of its age, this dictionary is still a recommended resource.

162. Ellmore, R. Terry. **NTC's Mass Media Dictionary.** Lincolnwood, IL: National Textbook, 1991. 668p. LC 89-63861. ISBN 0-8442-3185-1.

More than 20,000 terms and phrases in radio, television, cable, film, newspapers, magazines, book publishing, direct mail, and outdoor advertising are included in this ambitious and comprehensive work. Ellmore writes that this dictionary "was written to aid writers, broadcasters, publishers, film and video makers, printers, advertisers, and other industry professionals, as well as teachers, students and others interested in the vocabulary of the mass media." Entries are brief, and, according to Ellmore, are "descriptive rather than proscriptive." There are numerous cross-references and entries for current jargon. With entries ranging from "fairy godmother" ("a derogatory term for an uncreative musical director") to "Farmer's reducer" ("a chemical used to reduce the amount of silver in a film print"), this is an authoritative source. See also *Webster's New World Dictionary of Media and Communications* (entry 181) and the *Longman Dictionary of Mass Media and Communication* (entry 158).

163. Ensign, Lynne Naylor, and Robyn Eileen Knapton. **The Complete Dictionary of Television and Film.** Briarcliff Manor, NY: Stein and Day, 1985. 256p. LC 83-42634. ISBN 0-8128-2922-0.

This may not be the first book "to compile, define, and standardize the language of television and film," but it is among the most thorough. More than 2,500 terms and phrases, including jargon and slang, from the early silent picture days to the present are included. Most important, common definitions as well as other meanings are given. Alphabetically arranged and easy to use, it should appeal to both the professional and student. Users might also be interested in Harvey Rachlin's *The TV and Movie Business: An Encyclopedia of Careers, Technologies, and Practices* (Harmony Books, 1991).

164. Fletcher, James E., ed. **Broadcast Research Definitions.** 3d ed. Washington, D.C.: National Association of Broadcasters, 1988. 75p. index. ISBN 0-8058-1046-3.

Considering the size of this book, it offers great detail in terminology used in broadcast audience measurements. Sections focus on terminology and jargon, statistical measures, sampling, and survey methods. This is useful for the scholar in search of standard definitions of more than 100 terms.

165. Godfrey, Donald G., and Frederic A. Leigh, eds. **Historical Dictionary of American Radio.** Westport, CT: Greenwood Press, 1998. 485p. bibliog. index. LC 97-33140. ISBN 0-31329-636-7.

According to the preface, "In accordance with the dictionary definition of a 'dictionary,' this alphabetical listing of terms comprehensively treats the various branches of knowledge relating to the specific subject of American radio history. Readers will find entries on almost every subject related to the topic of radio." Signed entries, ranging from Public Radio to Sequencing, are uniformly written in a "just the facts" style; the editors, in fact, "requested a purely factual writing." Most include a brief narrative and references. This is a well-designed ready reference resource for librarians and a useful topical introduction to radio history for students. Researchers might also wish to consult *The Encyclopedia of American Radio* (entry 144) and *Radio's Golden Years* (entry 151).

166. Jacobson, Howard B., ed. **Mass Communications Dictionary.** New York: Philosophical Library, 1961. 393p. LC 60-053157. ISBN 0-8022-0785-5.

As a source for current terminology in mass communications, this is obviously a very dated book. It proves useful, however, as a historical study of common terminologies by the press and in printing, broadcasting, film, advertising, and communication research in the late 1950s and early 1960s. Arrangement is alphabetical, and many definitions, even those that are one sentence in length, are signed.

167. Kent, Ruth Kimball. **The Language of Journalism.** Kent State University Press, 1970. 186p. bibliog. LC 71-100624. ISBN 0-87338-091-6.

In her introduction, Kent writes, "Does the world of journalism need the up-to-date glossary of terms here presented? The answer is yes, for there is not a comparable book readily available to the journalism student." The answer is still yes because, as useful as this was and is, it is in dire need of updating. Also, it is out of print. *The Longman Dictionary of Mass Media and Communication* (entry 158), *Webster's New World Dictionary of Media and Communications* (entry 181), and the *Encyclopedia of American Journalism* (entry 149) should be consulted as well. Alphabetically arranged entries focus on print journalism, but include jargon, technical terms, and selected terms in graphic arts, photography, book production, and the electronic press. Computer terms are excluded. This is best used as a historical resource.

168. Knowles, Elizabeth, ed., with Julia Elliott. **The Oxford Dictionary of New Words: The Intriguing Stories Behind 2,000 New Words in the News.** New ed. Oxford, England; New York: Oxford University Press, 1997. 357p. ISBN 0-19-863152-9.

Originally compiled by Sara Tulloch in 1991, this new edition targets approximately 2,000 words that were "in the news" from the 1980s to the mid-1990s. Users should note that a "minority of items covered in the first edition claim a place here because their stories have continued to develop," that is, do not toss the first edition. According to the editor, a new word is "any word, phrase, or sense that came into popular use or enjoyed a vogue in the given period." The alphabetically arranged entries contain definition, etymology, history and usage, and "illustrative quotations" from "works of fiction, newspapers, and popular magazines." There are numerous cross-references. Subject icons (some are obvious, others are less so), follow each headword. New words include "Lambada: So popular did the dance become that the word has entered the language in a metaphorical sense: if your nerves or feelings are doing the lambada it means that you are very agitated." The illustrative quotation is from a 1993 issue of the Fort Collins Coloradoan: "I'm trying to act and sound calm...but my nerves are doing the lambada as I frantically work to come up with some kind of an answer." Examples of other entertaining new words and phrases are awesome, bad hair day, Joe Sixpack, road rage (not to be confused with roid rage—a "heightened aggression toward others as a side-effect of taking anabolic steroids") and, of course, power breakfast, power dressing, power lunch, power nap, power user, and Power Ranger. Mouse potato also met the criteria for inclusion. Students, copy editors, stylists, and wordsmiths looking to be "sussed" (well informed) will use this "stonking" (impressive) and unique reference.

169. Maggio, Rosalie. **The Bias-Free Word Finder: A Dictionary of Nondiscriminatory Language.** Boston: Beacon Press, 1992. 293p. LC 92-004694. ISBN 0-80706-003-8.

The Bias-Free Word Finder was originally published as *The Dictionary of Bias-Free Usage* (Oryx, 1991), which was an update to *The Nonsexist Word Finder* (1988). Maggio states that "those of you who have used the first edition will notice that in addition to terms that are prejudicial to women this edition also includes terms that are prejudicial to men as well as words and phrases that are biased against people because of their race, age, sexual orientation, disability, ethnic origin, or belief system." According to the book's User's Guide, there are 5,000 entries and 15,000 alternatives. A section on writing guidelines discusses definitions of terms, sex and gender, the "pseudogeneric 'he'" and the "pseudogeneric 'man/men/mankind.'" Entries are arranged alphabetically in the dictionary and range from "Adam's Apple" ("there is no good substitute for this term other than a lengthy description") to "unwomanly" ("see 'unfeminine' for an explanation of the subjective cultural meanings attached to this word"). The entry for "good old boy/good ole boy" is as follows: "Loyal Southerner, Southern supporter, supporter, sidekick, crony, pal, goombah. These terms were particularly popular in the mid-1960s when they referred to the Texas cronies of President Lyndon B. Johnson. Women don't often choose to play a 'good ole boy' role. Sometimes this might be the appropriate term for a particular man. See also old boys' network; old girls' network." Maggio writes that "you will not agree with everything in this book" and there is "imperfect consensus today on which words are biased." She also says that "this is nothing more than a collection of the ways people have found to deal with the bias in our language. Unbiased language is not being legislated somehow 'from above.' Ordinary people have chosen to replace linguistic pejoration and disrespect with words that grant full humanity and equality to all of us." Maggio occasionally overstates her case; nonetheless, just a glance at this source will force journalists to think twice before they write, and that, in itself, is not a bad thing. She also is the author of the *How to Say It Style Guide* (Prentice-Hall, 2002).

170. McDonald, James R. **The Broadcaster's Dictionary.** Rev. ed. Denver, CO: Wind River Books, 1987. 198p. LC 86-9215. ISBN 0-938023-04-7.

Broadcasting terms, many dealing with broadcast electronics, are listed alphabetically. The author writes, "It is hoped that this book will prove useful in training entry-level personnel in all station departments to speak and understand the same language." Appendixes include lists of associations, organizations, and societies; preventive maintenance routines; and problem-solvers such as "A Painless Filter Tutorial" and "Cooling Your Equipment." Definitions are short and to the point.

171. Murray, John. **The Media Law Dictionary.** Washington, D.C.; University Press of America, 1978. 139p. LC 78-63257. ISBN 0-8191-0616-X.

Murray is stingy with prefatory and introductory material, leaving users to their own resources. More than 400 standard and mass media law terms and phrases are defined, some in great detail, with references to cases and historical background. Definitions are, on the whole, very well-written and easy to understand. Tables of cases and a short bibliography make up the appendixes. Murray suggests that his dictionary is appropriate for students and "news handlers and editorialists." Never chatty, he offers the "news handler" just enough information with which to engage in intelligent conversation on neutral reportage, a lively debate on access to information, or an argument over fighting words.

172. Oakey, Virginia. **Dictionary of Film and Television Terms.** New York: Barnes and Noble, 1982. 206p. LC 82-48254. ISBN 0-06-463566-X.

A typical entry reads: "Announcement. A commercial. 'We'll be back after the following announcement.' " Isn't it comforting to see some terms used in a complete sentence? More than 3,000 briefly-defined words and phrases are listed alphabetically and address the technical and nontechnical, informal, business, and artistic aspects of film and television. There are cross-references, and terms capitalized within a definition have separate entries. Oakey has compiled a serviceable, although now a bit dated, reference for industry professionals and students.

173. Penney, Edmund F. **A Dictionary of Media Terms.** New York: Putnam, 1984. 158p. LC 83-27051. ISBN 0-399-12958-8.

Ray Bradbury provides an appropriate commentary in the introduction: "Well, enough of kicking the dead horse alive. Here is the talk, here are the words that encompass the ideas that lubricate an Industry to help make of it an Art. Jump in. But be careful not to trip over the clapper board, the Green-Man, or the Release Negative." This listing of the "workaday vocabulary"—more than 1,000 terms, phrases, jargon, and slang used in television, radio, and film—is an adequate source for the beginner, but others are urged to look elsewhere for more thorough definitions. *The Complete Dictionary of Television and Film* (entry 163) and the *Webster's New World Dictionary of Media and Communications* (entry 181) offer more terms, more details, and less superficiality. See also Penney's *The Facts on File Dictionary of Film and Broadcast Terms* (entry 174).

174. Penney, Edmund F. **The Facts on File Dictionary of Film and Broadcast Terms.** New York: Facts on File, 1991. 251p. LC 88-7023. ISBN 0-8160-1923-1; 0-8160-2782-X (pbk).

According to Penney, a screenwriter, director, and author of *A Dictionary of Media Terms* (entry 173), this dictionary focuses on the performing arts in mass media and is designed to "help you make your way through the verbal undergrowth of the media jungle." The user is urged to "unsheathe your machete, don your khaki fatigues and pith helmet, and start cutting your way through." Fortunately, the only undergrowth to "cut through" here is the blessedly brief but metaphor-ridden introductory material. Penney uses an effective quote from Ralph Waldo Emerson in the introduction: "The language of the street is always strong…I confess to some pleasure from the stinging rhetoric of the rattling oath in the mouths of truckmen and teamsters…Moreover they who speak them have this elegancy, that they do not trip in their speech. It is a shower of bullets, whilst Cambridge men and Yale men correct themselves and begin again every half sentence." The author then goes on to ask if "Mr. Know-it-all Emerson really did know something more about language than the linguists." Penney did not intend this to be a scholarly work, and it is not. It is, however, a useful dictionary of trade terms and working language with a variety of alphabetically arranged entries ranging from "crutch tips" to "off-the-record." It contains some current words and phrases not included in other subject dictionaries, but offers little context and background. Users with more scholarly intentions are still advised to consult important sources such as *Webster's New World Dictionary of Media and Communications* (entry 181), Diamant's *Dictionary of Broadcast Communications* (entry 160), and *The Complete Dictionary of Television and Film* (entry 163), to name a few.

175. Reed, Robert M., and Maxine K. Reed. **The Facts on File Dictionary of Television, Cable, and Video.** New York: Facts on File, 1994. 226p. LC 94-1221. ISBN 0-8160-2947-4.

According to the authors, this electronic media dictionary covers advertising; agencies, associations, companies, and unions; broadcasting and cablecasting; educational and corporate communications; engineering; general terms; government and legal terms; home video; production; and programming. The definitions "are considered current as of 1993." Entries are arranged alphabetically and include acronyms, abbreviations, detailed definitions, and, in many cases, helpful background information. In addition, there are numerous cross-references. Entries range from "A.C. Nielsen Company" and "ABCD counties" to "off-network programs" and "off the air." This is a straightforward, well-organized, and tightly edited reference to the language of electronic media.

176. Shilling, Lilless McPherson, and Linda K. Fuller, comps. **Dictionary of Quotations in Communications.** Westport, CT: Greenwood Press, 1997. 315p. index. LC 97-5599. ISBN 0-313-30430-0.

Communications is broadly defined in this collection of more than 3,000 quotations from ancient to modern times. According to the compilers, "Almost everyone has said something quotable about communications. Children are particularly observant." As evidence of this, several quotations from Shilling's daughter also are included. Quotations are arranged by communications topic, then alphabetically by author. Included, as one might expect, are entries focusing on journalism, editing, newspapers, opinions, interviewing, and the like. But also included are topics such as clothing, advice, eloquence, flattery, lying, teamwork, and speaking anxiety. This is most useful as a ready reference source for librarians and as a source for students and others in need of quotations for papers and speeches. It also is an entertaining volume, and readers may find themselves nodding in empathy to quotations such as H. G. Wells's on editing: "No passion in the world, no love or hate, is equal to the passion to alter someone else's draft."

177. Silverblatt, Art, and Ellen M. Enright Eiceiri. **Dictionary of Media Literacy.** Westport, CT: Greenwood Press, 1997. 234p. bibliog. illus. LC 96-35023. ISBN 0-313-29743-6.

The scanty preface indicates this is a "compilation of significant concepts, issues, organizations, people, and international developments in the field of media literacy," and that media literacy is a "broad-based movement, originating from a number of different sectors: education, community based, media arts, professional, and public policy," but, oddly, media literacy is not actually defined for the layperson here. Hint: Researchers skimming the text for a definition will not find it under Media Literacy; it is filed instead under "Definition, Media Literacy." In short, media literacy is a "critical-thinking skill that enables audiences to decipher the information that they receive through the channels of mass communications and empowers them to develop independent judgments about media content." Explanations of media literacy concepts, significant scholars and figures, international issues, and organizations, from Audience Interpretation Perspectives to Romantic Ideal, are arranged alphabetically. Entries also contain references, with Silverblatt's *Media Literacy: Keys to Interpreting Media Messages* (Praeger, 1995) frequently cited.

178.   Slide, Anthony. **The Television Industry: A Historical Dictionary.** Westport, CT: Greenwood Press, 1991. 374p. index. LC 91-4363. ISBN 0-313-25634-9.

The prolific and witty Slide states in his preface that "While the book answers a good many questions, two that remain unexplained are why on Steve Allen's "Meeting of the Minds" (PBS, 1976–1981) every female figure in history looked like Allen's wife, Jayne Meadows, and why has Lawrence Welk, one of the most enduring of television stars, not been inducted into the Television Academy Hall of Fame? These questions notwithstanding, the present volume should serve as an essential reference tool for any scholar, student, or librarian involved in the study of the television industry." It focuses on all aspects of American television industry, but also offers a wide spectrum of information on television in the United Kingdom. More than 1,000 entries, ranging in length from a few lines to a few pages, cover companies, organizations, distributors, genres, and technical terms. There is even an entry for "A Vast Wasteland" (see "Vast," not "A"), a phrase coined by Newt Minow when he became chairman of the FCC in 1961; sadly, he was describing American television. Some of the more substantive entries include bibliographies. There are also name and program indexes with a brief television reference bibliography. According to Slide, this is the first "what's what" of television and is not a guide to television programming. He also is the author of *The International Film Industry: A Historical Dictionary* (Greenwood, 1989) and *The American Film Industry: A Historical Dictionary* (Greenwood, 1986).

179.   Sussman, Leonard R. **Glossary for International Communications: Communications in a Changing World.** Volume III. Washington, D.C.: Media Institute, 1983. unpaged. LC 83-62432. ISBN 0-937790-18-4.

In his introduction, Sussman mentions George Orwell and Newspeak, and talks at length about UNESCO and its relationship with the press. Finally, he addresses the glossary: "This glossary seeks to demonstrate the varied uses of a single word or term in the decade-long debates." Included are 50 terms and phrases in communications, each with four definitions: first world, second world (or Marxist), third world, and UNESCO. Entries include equitable news flow, freedom of the press, journalistic code, New World Information Order, right to communicate, source of information, and human rights. Sussman says the glossary is aimed at students, reporters, lawyers, and public policymakers in international discussion. "It will be possible to understand the aims of the participants and the intent of the drafters." See also the *International Communications Glossary* (entry 156).

180. Watson, James, and Anne Hill. **A Dictionary of Media and Communication Studies.** 5th ed. New York: Oxford; London: Arnold, 2000. 364p. ISBN 0-340-73205-9.

A dictionary with a British slant, terms and phrases are listed alphabetically, defined in great detail, and cross-referenced. Formerly the *Dictionary of Communication and Media Studies,* the authors decided to emphasize the term "media" in this fifth edition, "to acknowledge both the dominance of media in studies, and of media in our lives...." Mediasphere, information blizzards, hyperreality, pretty good privacy, and balance sheet culture are examples of the newest entries. A Chronology of Media Events timeline also is introduced. This is an impressive scholarly source for students of journalism and mass communications. Entries on broadcasting, media commissions, communication models, communication theories, film, interpersonal communication, language, news, the press, radio, media technology, television, and violence and the media are included, with an expanded area of coverage including the Internet. For a less scholarly approach to British broadcasting, consult *Teletalk: A Dictionary of Broadcasting Terms* (BBC Television Training, 1991).

181. Weiner, Richard. **Webster's New World Dictionary of Media and Communications.** New York: Simon & Schuster, 1996. rev. ed. 676p. LC 96-12949. ISBN 0-02-860611-6.

A weighty dictionary of more than 30,000 media terms, this is a basic source for communications scholars, students, and practitioners. It covers jargon and slang as well as historical and technical terms, and includes it all—marketing, journalism, broadcasting, book publishing, graphic arts, advertising, newspaper, radio, television, photography, and printing. Weiner's humor and originality are still evident in this revised edition, although some of his descriptions have been toned down a bit. In the first edition, a "dingbat," for example, is "a typographic decoration. No kidding. That's what they're called, except when they're called flubdub." In the revised edition "dingbat" is simply a "typographic decoration; also called a flubdub." "Frisky furniture" is still "*Wall Street Journal* jargon for a dull article that was made a bit more sprightly with anecdotes and pithy quotations." Users seeking to identify the differences betwixt news butchers, news doctors, news dealers, news hawks, newsmongers, and newsies will find their answers here. Weiner writes, "Whether you are a professional in the media and communications fields or a lay person, you will find this dictionary all up, big time, a blockbuster, boffo, on the button, a keep, a magnum opus, socko, and whammo. So take it away, this is a wrap" He continues, "The primary goal is for the reader to understand a definition, even if it is outside his or her field." In this he succeeds. Definitions are straightforward, frequently humorous, and vivid in detail. See also *NTC's Mass Media Dictionary* (entry 162) and the *Longman Dictionary of Mass Media and Communication* (entry 158).

4
Indexes and Abstracts

The following indexes and abstracts focus on various aspects of journalism. Unfortunately, only a few indexes are devoted solely to journalism and none is comprehensive. Some have ceased publication in recent years. More and more, publishers are offering online versions of indexes and abstracts; some, such as Wilson, continue to offer print, CD-ROM, and online access. Some libraries, however, when faced with budget cuts and other reductions, and in weighing the value and convenience of an online product versus a print index, have opted to cancel subscriptions to the print indexes.

For the most part, indexes to individual newspapers are not included in this chapter. (UMI's Serials in Microform lists numerous newspaper indexes, and Milner's Newspaper Indexes [entry 511] provides a union list.) For updates on indexes available on compact disc, users are advised to check the latest edition of CD-ROMs in Print: An International Guide to CD-ROM, CD-1, 3DO, MMCD, CD32, Multimedia, Laserdisc, and Electronic Products (Gale). Commercial databases are covered in chapter 5; Internet sources in chapter 6.

182.   ABC News Index. Woodbridge, CT: Primary Source Microfilm, 1969– . Quarterly, with annual cumulation. ISSN 0891-8775.

"Nightline," "ABC News Closeup," "ABC News Special," "Business World," "20/20," "This Week with David Brinkley," "World News Tonight," and "Viewpoint" are included in this index, available on microfiche and on CD-ROM, which provides access to complete transcripts of 11 network news programs. Users can search the index for subject, program title, or names of personalities. A brief abstract, date, and fiche number accompany each entry. Users also will be interested in the *ABC News Moving Image* collection, a film and video catalog of important news events covered by ABC News from 1960–1991. See also the *ABC News Transcripts* (entry 217) online, the ABC Television home page (entry 251), and ABC News Radio (entry 252).

183.   Alternative Press Index: Access to Movements, News, Policy, and Theory. Baltimore, MD: Alternative Press Center, Inc. 1969– . Quarterly, with annual cumulation. LC 76-24027. ISSN 0002-662X.

Clearly a by-product of the sixties, this index pays tribute to nearly 200 "radical" and less known journals of the alternative press. Excluded are ultraconservative publications. Periodicals ranging from the *Journal of Palestine Studies* to *Phoenix Rising* (an "anti-psychiatry" journal) are indexed along with other alternative, ethnic, Marxist, feminist, and gay publications. Even *SJR: The St. Louis Journalism Review* (entry 635) has found a home here, along with the *Community Media Review, In These Times, Jump Cut, Utne Reader,* and the *Index on Censorship*. This is a no-frills resource that takes its time with indexing: it may take a year or so for an article citation to appear. Still, this is a very important resource in journalism research. Obviously, it is a useful guide for identifying and delving into the alternative press publications. But it also is a vehicle by which one can study how the alternative press covers the press. Subject headings on journalism, television reporters and reporting, newspaper reporters and reporting, photojournalism, newspapers and politics, and even the alternative press make this possible. It also is available electronically via OCLC's First Search.

184.   Art Index. New York: H. W. Wilson, 1929– . Quarterly, with annual cumulation. LC 31-7513. ISSN 0004-3222.

Although there are a few citations under "Newspaper Layout and Photography," "Journalism," and "Editing," this index excels in domestic and foreign coverage of photojournalism and photography. Articles appear under the headings "Photography, Journalistic," "Television Programs—News," "Photography, Documentary," and "War Photography." Entries to the periodical literature of art, architecture, fine and graphic arts, design, and photography are arranged alphabetically by subject and author. References to yearbooks and museum bulletins are scattered. It is also available online and on CD-ROM.

185.   Barnett, Tracy, and Andrew Scott, eds. The Investigative Journalist's Morgue. Columbia, MO: Investigative Reporters & Editors, 1993. 226p.

In an earlier edition of *The Investigative Journalist's Morgue* (1986, Steve Weinberg and Jan Colbert, eds.), the IRE story is described as follows: "Investigative Reporters and Editors, Inc., was established by journalists who were weary of starting at ground zero every time they began an investigation. The founders knew that sharing ideas and information was the cornerstone of IRE. They began compiling stories that had been done by investigative journalists around the country, and envisioned a research center with easy access for all members."

This shared information assumes the form of an index of investigative newspaper articles. According to this introduction, "The Morgue draws from the past 10 years of IRE's Resource Center, which contains more than 9,000 stories that have been collected since IRE's beginning 18 years ago." Entries are arranged by subject and contain an identification number, name of newspaper, brief description of the article or series, and date of publication. Headlines and page numbers are excluded, but that is not a problem if you order the piece directly from IRE (www.ire.org.; there is a fee). Subjects cover the usual muckraking range (handguns, toxic waste, migrant labor, pornography, etc.), with numerous computer-assisted projects detailed as well, but there also are daily stories from lower-profile beats. A wide range of newspapers and television stations is represented. Further, the editors write, "If you don't find what you want, give us a call. The Morgue index is in a computer database, so we can search on keywords to come up with a more inclusive collection of entries. We'll also find more recent stories—we're constantly adding to our collection—and stories that were published before 1982."

This unique "morgue," although now dated, is the most comprehensive source available for solid examples of researching, interviewing, reporting, and writing. There is nothing else like it. See entry 682 for more information on IRE and its resource center, which includes access to a database of nearly 20,000 print and broadcast articles.

186. **Black Newspaper Index.** Ann Arbor, MI: UMI, 1977– . Quarterly, with annual cumulation. ISSN 0149-7502.

Formerly the Index to Black Newspapers, this quarterly abstracting source provides access to the *Black Newspaper Collection* on microfilm (entry 567), and indexes the following newspapers: *Afro-American, Amsterdam, Call & Post, Chicago Defender, Journal & Guide, Los Angeles Sentinel, Michigan Chronicle,* and *Muslim Journal.* Entries are arranged alphabetically by subject and name. It is now available online in Proquest Newspaper Abstract and Index (entry 241).

187. Blassingame, John W., Mae G. Henderson, and Jessica M. Dunn, eds. **Antislavery Newspapers and Periodicals.** Boston: G. K. Hall, 1980. 5 vols. LC 79-20230. ISBN 0-8161-8163-2 (vol. 1); 0-8161-8434-8 (vol. 2); 0-8161-8558-1 (vol. 3); 0-8161-8559-X (vol. 4); 0-8161-8560-3 (vol. 5).

According to the editors of this index, only letters are included in this multivolume annotated index of various nineteenth-century abolitionist and reform newspapers "because we felt they contained more of the personal details of history than did editorials, signed articles, book reviews, advertisements, and the like." Annotations are arranged chronologically in each journal. Volume 1 includes the *Philanthropist* (Mount Pleasant, OH), *Emancipator* (Tennessee), *Abolition Intelligencer* (Shelbyville, KY), *Genius of Universal Emancipation, African Observer,* and the first 15 years of the *Liberator* (Boston). Volume 2 contains the second part of the *Liberator, Anti-Slavery Record* (New York), *Human Rights* (New York), and the *Observer* (Alton, IL). Volume 3 holds the *Friend of Man* (Utica, NY), *Pennsylvania Freeman, Advocate of Freedom* (Hallowell, ME), and the *American & Foreign Anti-Slavery Reporter* (New York). Volume 4 contains the first 20 years of the *National Anti-Slavery Standard,* and volume 5 contains the final 11 years. This is an unusual collection, and provides another avenue in the study of black and Southern history, editors and editing, and publishing practices.

188. **British Humanities Index.** London: Library Assoc., 1962– . Quarterly, with annual cumulation. ISSN 0007-0815.

This source is essential in searching, for example, periodical literature on the newspaper industry in Great Britain; it indexes articles in the humanities as well as the social sciences. Entries are arranged alphabetically by subject, include abstracts, and focus on all aspects of the humanities including journalism, mass media, political journalism, newspapers and editors, television news, and television documentaries in the United Kingdom. Consult the *Subject Index to Periodicals* for articles published prior to 1961.

189. **Business Periodicals Index.** New York: H. W. Wilson, 1958– . Monthly, with bimonthly, semiannual, and annual cumulations. ISSN 0007-6961.

Journalism is a business, and this index is easy to overlook if one forgets that. *Business Periodicals Index,* a subject index to all aspects of business and management, is brimming with subject headings relevant to journalism and media management: "Freedom of the Press," "Journalism Awards," "Journalism Schools," "Journalistic Ethics," "Minorities in Journalism," "Newspaper Editors," "Newspaper Publishers and Publishing," "Reporting," and "Television Broadcasting—News," to name a few. In addition, journals such as *Editor & Publisher, Folio,* and *Mediaweek* are selectively indexed. This also is available online (entry 247) and on CD-ROM.

190.   Canadian Index. Toronto: Micromedia, 1993– . Monthly, with semiannual cumulation. ISSN 1192-4160.

The Canadian Index was formed when the *Canadian News Index, Canadian Business Index,* and the *Canadian Magazine Index* merged. A wide range of general interest and specialized periodicals and newspapers is included here, with titles ranging from *Canadian Nurse* to *Parliamentary Government.* Of special interest are titles such as the *Ryerson Review of Journalism, Canadian Journal of Communication,* and *Media West.* Articles on journalism are arranged under such broad subject headings as "Journalism," "Media Coverage," "Newspapers and Newspaper Industry," "Television Broadcasting," and "Journalistic Ethics." There are separate corporate and personal name indexes. This index is available online (entry 224) and on CD-ROM. See also the *Canadian Periodical Index* (entry 191).

191.   Canadian Periodical Index. Index de Periodiques Canadiens. Ontario: Gale Canada, 1938– . Monthly, with annual cumulation. LC 49-2133. ISSN 0008-4719.

More than 400 Canadian and 25 American magazines are included in this index of general-interest periodicals. Citations are arranged alphabetically by author and subject. Subject headings are in English, although there are French cross-references. Business, the arts, humanities, social sciences, education, and science and technology are all covered. In addition, numerous subject headings such as "Radio Broadcasting," "Television Broadcasting," "Journalistic Ethics," "Press and Politics," and "Reporters and Reporting" make this a valuable source to be used in addition to the *Readers' Guide to Periodical Literature* (entry 209). It is available online and on CD-ROM. See also the *Canadian Index* (entry 190).

192.   CBS News Index. Ann Arbor, MI: University Microfilms International Research Collections, 1975–1987. LC 76-648172. ISSN 0362-3238.

CBS News broadcasts from 1975 to 1987 are indexed in this resource, which is no longer updated. Citations are arranged alphabetically by subject and name. Full-text transcripts of the broadcasts are available on microfiche (entry 568) and CD-ROM, and also are available via Burrelle's sources (entry 223) and the *Vanderbilt Television News Archive* (entry 781). See also the *Television News Index and Abstracts* (entry 212).

193.   ComAbstracts. Rotterdam Junction, NY: Communication Institute for Online Scholarship (CIOS). Updated "at intervals."

"No other electronic resource on the world wide web provides more comprehensive coverage of the communication discipline's scholarship," according to the CIOS Web site. Nearly 60 scholarly communication titles are abstracted and made available through individual or institutional membership in CIOS. For the most part, coverage begins in the late 1980s or early 1990s, depending on the publication. In addition to standard communication and journalism titles, publications such as *Convergence* and the *International Journal on Listening* are included. The sample entry provided includes a complete bibliographic citation, a very brief abstract, author affiliation, and a list of keywords. "Synonyms are available for many clusters of terms and are automatically included in searches unless they are explicitly overridden in the user's search specification. All the synonym sets have been designed with the conceptual realm of the communications scholar and student in mind." For those who have "conceptual realm" issues, the keyword searching feature will be useful. *ComAbstracts* is produced and edited by Timothy Stephen, Associate Professor of Communication at the Rensselaer Polytechnic Institute and also the president of CIOS. Users will also be interested in its sister publication, *ComIndex* (entry 194).

194.   ComIndex. Rotterdam Junction, NY: Communication Institute for Online Scholarship. 1992– . Annual updates.

Contents of more than 70 international communication, mass communication, rhetoric, journalism, and speech journals, from the 1970s to the present, appear in this menu-driven electronic index (watch out for those "pop-up" keyword dictionaries). Relevant titles include *American Journalism, Australian Studies in Journalism, Journal of Mass Media Ethics, Journalism and Mass Communication Quarterly,* and *Nordicom Review*; other titles range from *Operant Subjectivity* to *Discourse Processes.* Entries consist of skeletal citations—author, title, volume number, pages, and date. Users can, however, search by author, title, and subject. For those in need of more comprehensive information, consult CIOS's *ComAbstracts* (entry 193), not to be confused with *Communication Abstracts* (entry 195).

195.   Communication Abstracts. Thousand Oaks, CA: Sage Publications, 1978– . Six issues/year. LC 78-645162. ISSN 0162-2811.

The major communication abstracting source, *Communication Abstracts* also touches on numerous mass communications and journalism-related items. Abstracts are numbered and subdivided into sections of articles, then books and book chapters. Each issue contains approximately 300 abstracts from nearly 100 journals and 30–40 books. A complete list of periodicals abstracted in *Communication Abstracts* (around 250 titles) is published in the fifth issue (October) of each volume. In addition, *Communication Abstracts* indexes all articles in *Journalism and Mass Communication Quarterly* and the *Journal of Mass Media Ethics.* Subject indexes in random issues have included topics such as media ownership, media stereotypes, First Amendment, freedom of the press, government and the media, journalism history, libel, news selection, news gathering, and television news. Abstracted articles range from "Information, Storytelling and Attractions: TV Journalism is Three Modes of Communication" in *Media, Culture and Society* to "Voices of Homeless People in Street Newspapers: A Cross-Cultural Exploration" in *Discourse and Society.* Subject and author indexes cumulate annually. Communication is broadly defined, thus this source should not be overlooked. It is now available online and updated bimonthly.

196.   The Cumulated Magazine Subject Index, 1907–1949. Boston, MA: G. K. Hall, 1964. 2 vols. LC 65-98.

Of great historical value, this index complements the *Readers' Guide to Periodical Literature* (entry 209) and offers subject and author access to the general periodical literature of its time. Regional magazines receive emphasis. Subject headings such as "Army Newspapers," "Negro Newspapers," "Reporters and Reporting," allow access to articles entitled "Newspapers—How They Annihilate Time" in *Munsey's Magazine* and "Ethics of

Newsboys" in the *Westminster Review.* Consult Pooles' *Index or Nineteenth Century Readers' Guide to Periodical Literature* for pre-1907 writings.

197. **Current Index to Journals in Education (CIJE).** Educational Resources Information Center. Westport, CT: Greenwood, 1969– . Monthly, with semiannual cumulations.

In addition to serving as an index to almost 800 education periodicals, *CIJE* also allows easy access to the journalism education–related literature in periodicals one might normally overlook. For example, an issue of *Omega: The Journal of Death and Dying* contains "Death As a Measure of Life: A Research Note on the Kastenbaum-Spilka Strategy of Obituary Analyses." *CIJE'*s sibling, *Resources in Education* (entry 210), indexes and abstracts unpublished material and documents in education. Both are part of the ERIC family and available online (entry 229) and on CD-ROM. This is a source not to be overlooked, as it indexes *Critical Studies in Mass Communication, English Journal, Journalism and Mass Communication Educator, C: JET, Quill & Scroll, Newspaper Research Journal, College Media Review, Journal of Broadcasting & Electronic Media,* and *Journalism and Mass Communication Quarterly. Education Index,* available in printed indexes, on CD-ROM, and online might also be useful, but it relies quite heavily on *Journalism and Mass Communication Educator.*

198. **Essay and General Literature Index.** New York: H. W. Wilson, 1900– . Semiannual, with annual and five-year cumulations. LC 34-14581. ISSN 0014-083X.

When a newspaper editor was searching for an essay that Henry J. Smith, managing editor of the *Chicago Daily News,* wrote more than 50 years ago, *Essay and General Literature Index* provided the missing pieces—the title and the collection in which the essay was located. Sometimes overlooked, this dependable old standby, which allows access by author, title, and subject to collections of essays, presents the researcher with an alternative to periodical literature. Fruitful subject headings include "Newspaper Publishing," "Freedom of the Press," "Television Broadcasting of News," and "Press and Politics." This also is available online and on CD-ROM.

199. **Humanities Index.** New York: H. W. Wilson, June 1974– . Quarterly. LC 75-648836. ISSN 0095-5981.

This index to the arts, history, language, and literature includes a wide range of English-language print and broadcast journalism–oriented periodicals. (To locate pre-1974 articles, use the *Social Sciences and Humanities Index* [1965–1974] and the *International Index* [1907–1965]. See also the sibling of *Humanities Index,* the *Social Sciences Index* [entry 211]). *American Journalism Review, Columbia Journalism Review, Communication Quarterly, Journalism and Mass Communication Quarterly, Journalism History,* and even *Quill* are selectively indexed. Consult this index for articles on current research trends as well as news and views on journalism. Especially useful are subject headings labeled "Newspaper Publishing," "Journalistic Ethics," "Radio Broadcasting," "Television Broadcasting," "Journalism and Politics," "Hidden Cameras in Journalism," and "Photojournalism." *Humanities Index* is indispensable. It is available online (entry 248) and on CD-ROM.

200. **Index to Journalism Periodicals.** London, Ontario: Resource Center, Graduate School of Journalism, University of Western Ontario, 1986–1997. ISSN 1181-3202.

This microfiche source, which ceased publication in 1997, indexed regularly more than 40 journalism periodicals and indexed "selectively" a dozen more journals. Entries are arranged by broad subject such as censorship, reporting, women and media, and so on, and include citations to articles from the mid-1960s to the present. Entries are cumulative, listing title, volume, month, and year but not authors or page numbers. There is a separate "Subject Headings" list. Journals indexed regularly included the following: *American Journalism Review, American Editor, APME News, Columbia Journalism Review, Content, IPI Report, Nieman Reports, Journalism and Mass Communication Quarterly, Masthead, Newspaper Research Journal, Presstime,* and *Quill.* Although this index is not comprehensive and can be cumbersome to use, the University of Western Ontario is to be commended for being a pioneer in journalism periodical indexing. It is now best used as a historical resource.

201.   Index to Journals in Mass Communication. Riverside, CA: Carpelan, 1988–1995. Annual. ISSN 1058-4242.

In this subject and author index, which ceased publication in 1995, mass communication covers the fields of advertising and public relations as well as print media, broadcasting, and visual communication. The introduction states that "articles from the most important journals in the field" are included, but scholarly publications are emphasized. More than 40 periodicals, including *Journalism and Mass Communication Quarterly, Newspaper Research Journal, American Journalism, Journal of Broadcasting and Electronic Media,* and the *Journal of Mass Media Ethics* were included. Titles such as *Columbia Journalism Review, Design,* and *Presstime,* unfortunately, were not covered. Available only in print format, it is most useful now as a historical resource for a limited time frame. Subjects are broad, and there are no abstracts. Most users seeking current journalism references will obviously be better served by *Communication Abstracts* (entry 195) and, depending on subject matter, *Current Index to Journals in Education* (entry 197), and *Humanities Index* (entry 199), to name just a few.

202.   Index to Legal Periodicals and Books. New York: H. W. Wilson, 1908– . Monthly. LC 41-21689. ISSN 1079-4719.

To locate articles such as "The Installation Commander Versus an Aggressive News Media in an On-Post Terrorist Incident: Avoiding the Constitutional Collision," in *Army Law,* and "Death TV? Is There a Press Right of Access to News that Allows Television of Executions?" in the *Tulsa Law Journal,* reach for this resource. Indexed are legal periodicals, yearbooks, and reviews published in the United States, Canada, Great Britain, Ireland, Australia, and New Zealand. This is one of the best sources for searching communications law, and subject headings such as "Freedom of the Press," "Censorship," and "Libel and Slander" provide easy access. The index also is available online and on CD-ROM. See also *Legal Resource Index,* available on Gale Group Newsearch (entry 234), an online database offering abstracts of legal periodicals, and *Media Law Reporter* (entry 622).

203.   Jacobs, Donald M., ed. Antebellum Black Newspapers. Westport, CT: Greenwood Press, 1976. 587p. index. LC 76-002119. ISBN 0-8371-8824-5.

Freedom's Journal, The Rights of All, The Weekly Advocate, and the *Colored American* are indexed separately in this index of pre–Civil War black newspapers. Entries are listed chronologically under alphabetically arranged subject headings. Biographical material for editors is included, along with newspaper background and publishing information. This is a valuable source on newspaper publishing history and black journalism. The entire contents are indexed, unlike *Antislavery Newspapers and Periodicals* (entry 187), which indexes letters only.

204.   Jodziewicz, Thomas W. **Birth of America: The Year in Review, 1763–1783; A Chronological Guide and Index to the Contemporary and Colonial Press.** Glen Rock, NJ: Microfilming Corporation of America. 152p. LC 76-50542. ISBN 0-667-00288-X.

This selected index of 52 colonial and revolutionary newspapers on microfilm is arranged chronologically and provides a year-by-year account of the colonial press. According to the introduction, "during the era of the American Revolution, the colonial press served to convey patriot and, for a time, non-patriot sentiments within the colonies from New Hampshire to Georgia, as well as to instruct colonists in how to dress and what to buy." Descriptive and topical chronologies for each year, as well as citations to newspaper articles "that are consciously selected to illustrate the chronological text" are included. Newspapers range from the *Boston Evening Post* to the *Gazette* of the State of Georgia. A subject index rounds out the volume.

205.   **Journalism and Mass Communication Abstracts (JMCA).** Columbia, SC: Association for Education in Journalism and Mass Communication. 1963– . Annual.

Now published electronically and searchable online from 1996 to the present, *JMCA* remains a unique resource for graduate students researching thesis and dissertation topics. Doctoral dissertations and masters' theses in journalism and mass communications from nearly 50 universities in the United States and Canada are indexed and abstracted. A detailed subject index and separate author and institution indexes allow thorough access to this important source, formerly entitled *Journalism Abstracts*. Research subjects range from the alternative press to the Associated Press. Students write their own abstracts, so the quality, style, and readability vary. An average of 250 to 300 abstracts appear in each issue; each is numbered and arranged alphabetically by author name. Also included is a section on "Other Dissertations," citations of mass communication dissertations that have appeared in *Dissertation Abstracts International* but have not been included in *Journalism and Mass Communication Abstracts*.

206.   Matlon, Ronald J., and Sylvia P. Ortiz, eds. **Index to Journals in Communication Studies Through 1990.** Annandale, VA: Speech Communication Association, 1992. 2 vols. 819p. LC 87-061400. ISBN 0-944811-08-6.

In this fourth edition, "communication studies" is a mix of communication, mass communication, journalism, and speech. Volume 1 includes tables of contents through 1990 of the following journals: *Quarterly Journal of Speech* (1915–), *Communication Monographs* (1934–), *Communication Education* (1952–), *Critical Studies in Mass Communication* (1984–), *Southern Communication Journal* (1935–), *Western Journal of Speech Communication* (1937–), *Communication Studies* (1949–), *Communication Quarterly* (1953–), *Association for Communication Administration Bulletin* (1972–), *Philosophy and Rhetoric* (1968–), *Journal of Communication* (1951–), *Human Communication Research* (1974–), *Journalism Quarterly* (1924–), *Journal of Broadcasting and Electronic Media* (1956–), *Argumentation and Advocacy* (1964–), *Text and Performance Quarterly*

(1980–), *Communication Research* (1974–), *Journal of Applied Communication Research* (1973–), and *Women's Studies in Communication* (1977–). All entries are numbered. Volume 2 comprises indexes: contributors, coded subject classification, and keyword subject index. There is no introductory or explanatory material except for a terse rundown of the coded classifications. Most of these journals are indexed in *Communication Abstracts*. It is convenient, however, to have the entire contents of these 19 journals reproduced and indexed in one volume even though one has to deal with coded classifications. The arrangement is still confusing, but users can now consult the keyword index and turn immediately to articles cited in the contents pages.

COMMSEARCH95 is the CD-ROM version of this resource and includes the full text of articles in Speech Communication Association journals such as *Critical Studies in Mass Communication*. It was released in 1995 and includes a keyword index for the 19 journals through 1990.

207.   The New York Times Index. New York: The New York Times Co., First Series, 15 volumes, 1851–1912; Second Series, 68 volumes, 1913–1929; Third Series, 1930– . distr. Ann Arbor, MI: UMI. Semimonthly, with quarterly and annual cumulations. LC 13-13458. ISSN 0147-538X.

This newspaper index earns a separate entry because, as the subtitle modestly informs us, it is "a book of record." *The New York Times Index* is an amazing subject, geographical name, and personal name reference source as it "can be used by itself for a basic chronological overview of the news, or it can be used as a guide to the location of the full articles in the original newspapers." A search in a late 2001 index, for example, provided a stark and exhaustive timeline of terrorism and world events, beginning with the first entries for September 11, 2001. Abstracts of all significant news articles, features, and editorials are included. It cumulates annually. Also available is a *Guide to the Incomparable New York Times Index* (entry 414), a 71-page treatise complete with index. Consult Milner's *Newspaper Indexes: A Location and Subject Guide for Researchers* (entry 511) for other printed newspaper indexes. The *New York Times* newspaper is available online, on microfilm, on CD-ROM, and indexed in numerous online resources.

208.   PAIS International in Print. New York: Public Affairs Information Service, 1914– . Monthly, with quarterly and annual cumulations. LC 16-920. ISSN 1051-4015.

The *PAIS Bulletin* and *PAIS Foreign Language Index* merged in 1991 and formed *PAIS International in Print*. This subject index lists periodical articles, books, government documents, and reports focusing on all aspects of contemporary public issues or public policy. It includes numerous sources in German, French, Italian, Portuguese, and Spanish, as well as those in English. Articles such as "El Salvador: A Comparative Study of Canadian and American Press Reporting, 1981–1983" (in the *Canadian Journal of Latin American and Caribbean Studies*) can be found here. Numerous citations appear under general broadcasting, journalism, radio, television, and press headings. It also is available online and on CD-ROM.

209.   Readers' Guide to Periodical Literature. New York: H. W. Wilson, 1900– . Monthly. LC 06-8232. ISSN 0034-0464.

Readers' Guide, the deity of popular periodical indexes, offers a wealth of information to anyone willing to dig a little. Certainly, in searching the literature of journalism, one will run into the " 'Don Johnson Made Me Cry (Almost)' and Other Confessions of a Celebrity Reporter" articles. But there also are articles such as "The $19,000 Press Pass: A Former Journalism School Dean Asks Is It Worth It?" from *The Washington Monthly*. All major news and current affairs magazines are also included in this author and subject index. Subject headings such as "Black Journalists," "Terrorism and the Press," "Information Systems—Journalistic Use," "Editors and Editing," "Police-Press Relations," "Journalistic Ethics," "Bioterrorism and the Press," and "Television Broadcasting—News" can yield useful articles. *Readers' Guide* also can be used to trace societal developments; for example, articles from "Is the Newspaper Office the Place for a Girl?" (1901) to "The Girls on the Bus" (1992) trace the evolution of the female journalist. *Readers' Guide* is available online (entry 249) and on CD-ROM; *Readers' Guide Abstracts* also is available from 1984 on. Also of use is *Nineteenth Century Readers' Guide to Periodical Literature and Access: The Supplementary Index to Periodicals,* another general-interest index, which makes it a point not to duplicate any periodicals indexed in the *Readers' Guide.*

210.   Resources in Education (RIE). Bethesda, MD: Educational Resources Information Center, 1966– . Monthly, with semiannual index and annual cumulation. (Subscriptions to Superintendent of Documents, U.S. Government Printing Office, Washington, D.C.). ISSN 0197-9973.

Part of the ERIC family of publications, this monthly subject and author abstracting service attempts to harness the reports, documents, papers, and other materials that so easily get buried and lost. Among these are the Association for Education in Journalism and Mass Communication (AEJMC) papers presented at annual meetings. *Journalism and Communication Monographs,* formerly *Journalism and Mass Communication Monographs,* (entry 615) also is included. Subject headings such as "Journalism History," "Television News," "Press Opinion," and "News Sources" provide numerous entry points and make using this abstracting source fairly painless. Publications are available on microfiche, arranged according to ERIC Document number. Paper copies also are available from ERIC Document Reproduction Service. *RIE* can be searched online in the ERIC database (entry 229), which includes *RIE*'s sister publication, *Current Index to Journals in Education* (*CIJE,* entry 197).

211.   Social Sciences Index. New York: H. W. Wilson, June 1974– . Quarterly. LC 75-649443. ISSN 0094-4920.

Among the more than 450 social sciences periodicals focusing on political science, psychology, economics, law, geography, and so on are useful articles on print and broadcast journalism. Articles on journalism and politics, freedom of the press, news agencies, reporters and reporting, and news programs on television are located in English-language periodicals ranging from the *Journal of Adolescence* to the *Far Eastern Economic Review.* A subject and author index makes locating such articles easier. *Social Sciences Index* is available online on WILSONLINE, CDP Online, OCLC EPIC, and OCLC First-Search, and on CD-ROM. For pre-1974 articles, use the *Social Sciences and Humanities Index* (1965–1974) or the *International Index* (1907–1965). See also the *Social Sciences Index* humanities counterpart, *Humanities Index* (entry 199).

212.   Television News Index and Abstracts: A Guide to the Videotape Collection of News Programs in the Vanderbilt Television News Archive. Nashville, TN: Vanderbilt Television News Archive, 1968–1995. LC 74-646462. ISSN 0085-7157.

Network news from mid-1968 to 1995 is abstracted thoroughly in this detailed index to ABC, CBS, and NBC evening news reports. (Reports are available on videotape in the *Vanderbilt Television News Archive,* entry 781, along with videotapes of special newscasts not included in the indexes.) Abstracts for each day's news are arranged according to network, date, and time, and include reporters' names, time code information, and commercials. The index is arranged alphabetically according to name and subject, and there is a separate index to reporters. There was usually a three- or four-month time lag, not surprising considering the detail involved in creating such an index. An excerpt from the November 1994 index (November 7) reads:

5:43:30 LOS ANGELES, CA/SIMPSON MURDER CASE
(Studio: Tom Brokaw) Judge Lance Ito reported deciding to allow cameras in the courtroom for the O. J. Simpson murder trial.
5:44:00 UPCOMING ITEMS
(Studio: Tom Brokaw)
5:44:10 (COMMERCIAL: Kellogg's Bran Flakes, The Olive Garden Restaurant, Harvest Crisps, Robitussin.)
5:45:40 NAVY/SEX FOR GRADES
(Studio: Tom Brokaw) Report introduced.
(Pentagon: Ed Rabel) Accusation by women attending a Navy communications school in San Diego that male instructors demanded sex for passing grades examined. [Naval training center commander Capt. John ENSCH—says harassment will not be tolerated.] The 1991 Tailhook scandal & the recent incident at West Point recalled. [Representative Pat SCHROEDER—comments.]

This is one of the most important historical print resources available in researching the growth and development, the rise and fall, of television news. Researchers may now access the *Vanderbilt Television News Archive* by using TV-NewsSearch online (entry 243). Not only are ABC, CBS, and NBC covered, but CNN and PBS as well.

213.   The Times Index. Reading, England: Primary Source Microfilm, 1973– . Monthly, with annual cumulation. ISSN 0260-0668.

The Times, as well as *The Sunday Times, The Times Literary Supplement, The Times Educational Supplement,* and *The Times Higher Education Supplement* are now indexed, and one of its best uses is as a book of record. Annual cumulations begin in 1977. *The Times* and *Sunday Times* also are accessible online and all *Times* indexes from 1990 to the present are available on *British Newspaper Index* on CD-ROM (Primary Source). See also the following: *Index to the Times* (1906–1972 *Times*), Palmer's *Index to the Times Newspaper* (1790–June 1941, Palmer), and *The Times Index* (1785–1790, Newspaper Archive Developments).

214.   Transcript/Video Index. Denver, CO: Journal Graphics. 1968– . Annual. ISSN 1057-0764.

"Television Good Enough to Read," proclaims the cover of this index, published monthly in 1993, quarterly in 1994, semiannually in 1995, and now annually. The index lists and abstracts transcripts from television and radio news and public affairs programs on ABC, CBS, NBC, CNN, PBS, and National Public Radio. Syndicated programs are included as well as tabloid television shows. *Transcript/Video Index* is described in the introduction as the "only comprehensive guide to broadcast information that includes complete abstracts," but those seeking network news through 1995 will continue to be well-served by Vanderbilt's *Television News Index and Abstracts* (entry 212). Entries are arranged by broad subject, listed chronologically by air date, and contain program name, network or producer, date of broadcast, summary, show number, and show date. There are some interesting "see also" references: "Marriage and Couples" refers users to "Love and Romance," "Domestic Violence," "Adultery," and "Divorce." In addition, some occasional filing glitches might prove confusing. For example, a 1995 index lists 55 pages of O. J. Simpson story transcripts under "O" instead of "S." Users may order transcripts directly from *Journal Graphics,* but prices are not included with abstracts. This source also is available online. Users might also be interested in Burrelle's broadcast transcript resources (entry 223).

215.   **The Wall Street Journal Index.** Ann Arbor, MI: UMI, 1957– . Monthly, with annual cumulations. LC 59-35162. ISSN 0083-7075.

The *Wall Street Journal,* available on microform, online, and on CD-ROM, is the newspaper of record for business and finance. This index, containing abstracts, is divided into two volumes. Volume 1 contains *The Wall Street Journal* corporate news and *Barron's Index.* Volume 2 comprises *The Wall Street Journal* general news and special reports. The abstracts provide as much ready reference material as indexing information.

216.   **The Washington Post Index.** Ann Arbor, MI: UMI, 1971– . Eight times/year, with quarterly and annual cumulations. ISSN 1041-1534.

If *The New York Times Index* is "a book of record," then *The Washington Post Index* is a record of government. Formerly *The Official Washington Post Index* (through 1988), this subject and name index contains abstracts of all news and feature stories, editorials, reviews, obituaries, editorial cartoons, and photographs and maps, with information of "permanent value." The newspaper is available on CD-ROM and online.

5
Selected Commercial Databases

While there are numerous resources available on the Web for free or nominal fees (see chapter 6, "Selected Internet Sources"), some information is still only available on commercial databases. Many of these databases are accessible via the Web through fee-based vendors such as First Search, Dialog, ERL, InfoTrec Searchbank, LexisNexis, Internet Database Service, and Ovid. Researchers should consult the Gale Directory of Databases (Gale Research, available via Dialog or DataStar) for further listings and subject-specific databases.

217.   ABC News Transcripts. Publisher: The Transcription Company. transcripts.net/. Coverage from: 1980. Update frequency: Daily.

This full text database offers more than 20,000 transcripts of the following ABC news programs: "This Week," "World News This Morning," "20/20," "Good Morning America," "Nightline," "World News Now," "World News Saturday," "World News Sunday," and "World News Tonight." Archived transcripts, such as reports from Peter Jennings, also are available .

218.   ABI/Inform. Producer: ProQuest Information and Learning, proquest.com/. Coverage from: 1971. Update frequency: Weekly. CD-ROM versions available.

Abstracts of principal business and management articles in more than 1,000 professional, academic, and trade journals are included, with full text versions of some articles. Newspaper, magazine, and broadcast management are covered. There is no printed version.

219.   Agence France-Presse. Producer: Agence France Presse. afp.com/. Coverage from: 1991. Update frequency: Continuous.

Full text versions of French and international news stories transmitted over Agence France Presse newswire are included in this English-language database. Founded in 1835, AFP is one of the world's largest and oldest news agencies. It also maintains a photo service.

220.   Alt-PressWatch. Producer: ProQuest Information and Learning. proquest.com/. Coverage from: 1995. Update frequency: Monthly.

More than 100 journals, magazines, and newspapers of the alternative and independent press are covered in this full text resource. Titles included range from *Social Anarchism* to the *Progressive Librarian*.

221. **Associated Press.** Producer: The Associated Press. ap.org. Coverage from: Varies. Update frequency: Continuous.

United States and international news and feature, business, sports, and political stories from the Associated Press. Founded in 1848, the AP is one of the most important suppliers of news to the media. Consult the AP's Web site (ap.org/) for a complete listing and description of online services such as AP Online, The WIRE, and AP Photo Archive (containing more than 500,000 images from the mid-1800s to the present).

222. **BBC Monitoring Online.** Producer: British Broadcasting Corporation. monitor.bbc.co.uk/database.shtml/. Printed version: *Summary of World Broadcasts Daily.* Coverage from: 1979. Update frequency: Daily.

BBC Monitoring was "created on the eve of World War II to help Britain track foreign propaganda." Television and radio news broadcasts from more than 150 countries (mostly Eastern Europe and developing nations) are translated into English by BBC linguists and are filed in this full text database. It does not cover the United States, Canada, or the United Kingdom.

223. **Burrelle's Transcripts.** Producer: Burrelle's Information Services. burrelles.com/. Coverage from: Varies. Update frequency: Daily.

More than 150,000 news and public affairs programs on radio and television are transcribed, including CBS News, NBC News, CNBC, C-SPAN, Christian Broadcasting Network, Discovery Channel, Fox News, MSNBC, MTV, PBS, and WNBC-TV. The following syndicated programs also are transcribed, some with videotapes available: "Geraldo," "Jerry Springer," "Maury Povich," "Montel Williams," "NewsWorthy," and "Rush Limbaugh." Researchers interested in ABC News should consult the ABC News Transcripts (entry 217); those searching for CNN coverage should review transcripts available at cnn.com (entry 259). Burrelle's also offers a Media Directory and Media Database Online (entry 350).

224. **Canadian Business and Current Affairs Fulltext.** Producer: Micromedia ProQuest. mmltd.com/. Printed version: Canadian Index (entry 190). Coverage from: 1980. Update frequency: Semimonthly. CD-ROM version available.

The *Canadian Business Index, Canadian News Index,* and *Canadian Magazine Index* are merged in this database of article citations and full text articles in more than 500 Canadian business periodicals, popular magazines, and newspapers. This is an exceptional source for Canadian business and industry information as well as current affairs. Abstracts are provided for articles published 1991–1994; full text articles for approximately 100 publications are included from 1994 to the present.

225. **Canadian Newsstand.** Producer: Micromedia ProQuest. mmltd.com/. Coverage from: 1985. Update frequency: Daily. CD-ROM version available.

Full text articles published in a dozen major Canadian daily newspapers are available. Included are the *Calgary Herald, Edmonton Journal, Montreal Gazette, Ottawa Citizen,* and *Vancouver Sun.*

226.   Canadian Press Command News. Producer: The Canadian Press. Coverage from: Varies. Update frequency: Continuous.

Full texts of local, national, and international English-language news reports from the Canadian Press newswire service comprise this database. The Associated Press, Reuters, and Broadcast News (a Canadian news service for private radio and television stations) also contribute to Command News, now an interactive Web-based service.

227.   ComAbstracts. See entry 193.

228.   Current Digest of the Post-Soviet Press. Producer: Current Digest of the Post-Soviet Press. currentdigest.org/. Coverage from: 1982. Update frequency: Weekly. CD-ROM version available.

Selected full text articles in Russian-language newspapers and periodicals from Russia and former Soviet republics comprise this English-language database, formerly the *Current Digest of the Soviet Press.* Political news and current affairs are emphasized.

229.   ERIC (Educational Resources Information Center). Producer: ERIC Processing and Reference Facility, Computer Sciences Corp. ericfac.piccard.csc.com/. Printed version: *Current Index to Journals in Education (CIJE,* entry 197); *Resources in Education (RIE,* entry 210). Coverage from: 1966. Update frequency: Monthly. CD-ROM version available.

Sponsored by the U.S. Department of Education Office of Educational Research and Improvement, ERIC contains more than a million citations and is the largest education database in the world. The Resources in Education subfile consists of documents, technical reports, conference papers, open papers, bibliographies proceedings, and so on, which can be located by ERIC Document number on microfiche. The *Current Index to Journals in Education* contains citations to more than 750 education-related journals and serial publications. In addition, the ERIC Document Reproduction Service (EDRS) now provides full text of documents though its e-subscribe service (edrs.com/logon.cfm/). This is an important resource for information on journalism education. Researchers might also wish to consult *Wilson's Education Abstracts, Education Index,* and *Education Full Text* (www.hwwilson.com/).

230.   Ethnic NewsWatch. Producer: ProQuest Information and Learning. il.pro quest.com/. SoftLine Information. Coverage from: Varies. Update frequency: Monthly. CD-ROM version available.

This full text database, available in English and Spanish, offers news articles and editorials in more than 200 ethnic and minority publications published in the United States. *Ethnic NewsWatch: A History,* also available through ProQuest, is a full text database covering the minority, ethnic, and native press from 1960 to 1989.

231.   Gale Database of Publications and Broadcast Media. Producer: Gale Group. galegroup.com/. Printed version: *Directories in Print; Gale Directory of Publications and Broadcast Media* (entry 356); *Newsletters in Print.* Coverage from: Current. Update frequency: Semiannual.

Nearly 70,000 newspapers, magazines, newsletters, radio, and television stations in the United States and Canada are briefly described in this important online directory.

232.   Gale Group Magazine Database. Producer: Gale Group. galegroup.com/. Coverage from: 1959–1970, 1973. Update frequency: Daily.

Citations and abstracts to more than 400 general-interest magazines (full text for 250 of those titles) on business, current affairs, media trends, regional news, arts, and literature are included; it also covers print and broadcast journalism. It is updated daily on Gale Group Newsearch.

233.   Gale   Group   National   Newspaper   Index. Producer: Gale   Group. galegroup.com/. Coverage from: 1979. Update frequency: Weekly.

The Christian Science Monitor, The Wall Street Journal, The New York Times, Reuters Financial Report, and *PR Newswire* are indexed comprehensively; citations to national and international news stories from the *Los Angeles Times* and *The Washington Post* also are included.

234.   Gale Group Newsearch. Producer: Gale Group. galegroup.com/. Coverage from: Current 45 days. Update frequency: Daily.

This is a daily update of full text, indexing, and abstracts for Gale Group databases such as Computer Database, Magazine Database, Legal Resource Index, Management Contents, National Newspaper Index, and Newswire ASAP.

235.   Historical Abstracts. Producer: ABC-CLIO. serials. abc-clio.com/. Printed version: *Historical Abstracts: Part A, Modern History Abstracts (1450–1914), Part B: Twentieth Century Abstracts (1914 to the Present).* Coverage from: 1954. Update frequency: six times/year. CD/ROM versions available.

Abstracts of articles from 2,100 social science and humanities journals covering world history (United States and Canada are excluded) comprise this file, where researchers will likely find citations not duplicated in other resources. A quick search of journalism ethics, for example, turned up the following article: "The Medical Pundits: Doctors and Indirect Advertising in the Lay Press, 1922–1927" in a 1994 issue of *Medical History.* Dissertations and books have been included since 1980. For American history, see *America: History and Life,* also produced by ABC-CLIO.

236.   Inter Press Service International Database. Producer: IPS-USA. ips.org/. Coverage from: 1984. Update frequency: Daily. CD-ROM version available.

This international news wire service covers foreign events and developing countries in Latin America, Africa, the Caribbean, and Europe. Full text stories are selected from daily IPS newscasts.

237.   NewsBank. Producer: NewsBank, Inc. newsbank.com/. Coverage from: Varies. Update frequency: Varies.

NewsBank is a massive database, the NewsFile Collection alone providing access to full text articles in more than 500 newspapers, wire services, and broadcasts. Also available through NewsBank is Global NewsBank, Foreign Broadcast Information Service Daily Reports, and NewsBank Newspapers, to name a few.

238.   PAIS International. Producer: Public Affairs Information Service, Inc. pais.org/. Printed version: PAIS International in Print (entry 208). Coverage from: 1972. Update frequency: Monthly. CD-ROM version available.

Brief abstracts are attached to citations to articles, pamphlets, directories, reports, government documents, and yearbooks focusing on political, social, and economic issues. PAIS indexes non-English-language sources as well.

239.   ProQuest Historical Newspapers. Producer: ProQuest Information and Learning. proquest.com/. Coverage from: Varies.

This remarkable digital archive with full text and full image articles is a work in progress. *The New York Times* (1851–1999) and *The Wall Street Journal* (1889–1985) digitization are complete and *The Washington Post* (beginning with the first issue in 1877) underway. *The Christian Science Monitor* will also be part of this series. The newspapers are digitized from cover to cover, including all graphics and advertisements. Researchers might also be interested in Micromedia ProQuest's Paper of Record database (mmltd.com/CIRC/PoR/htm/), which is an online historic newspaper archive of numerous Canadian newspapers such as *Toronto Star* and *The Globe and Mail.*

240.   ProQuest International Newswires. Producer: ProQuest Information and Learning. proquest.com/. Coverage from: 1998. Update frequency: Daily.

Reports from more than 25 international wire services such as BBC Monitoring, Africa News Service, and TASS are covered in this full text database.

241.   ProQuest Newspaper Abstract and Index. Producer: ProQuest Information and Learning. proquest.com/. Coverage from: 1986. Update frequency: Daily. CD-ROM version available.

Nearly 30 regional, national, and international newspapers, ranging from *The Wall Street Journal* to the *Times-Picayune,* are indexed and abstracted. Also included is the Black Newspaper collection, which abstracts titles such as the *American Muslim Journal, Chicago Defender,* and the *Afro-American.* Users might also be interested in the *ProQuest Periodical Index.*

242.   TASS. Producer: ITAR-TASS News Agency. itar-tass.com/. Coverage from: 1987. Update frequency: Daily.

This database contains the full text of English-language news from TASS, the official Soviet news agency.

243.   TV-News Search. Producer: Vanderbilt University Television News Archive. tvnews.vanderbilt.edu/database.shtml/. Coverage from: 1968.

This seminal database of nearly 700,000 records provides information about and access to ABC, CBS, NBC, CNN, and PBS television evening news programs and more than 8,000 hours of special news broadcasts located in the *Vanderbilt Television News Archive* (entry 781). Users may search for commercials as well.

244. **United States Newspaper Program (USNP) Database.** Producer: National Endowment for the Humanities, Library of Congress. oclc.org/oclc/usnp.htm/. Coverage from: 1690. Update frequency: Continuously.

This ambitious project database contains bibliographic and holdings information for newspapers published in the United States from 1690 to the present. Bibliographic and holdings records are accessible using WorldCat (OCLC's online union catalog) service. More than 200,000 titles should be included by 2006, when the project is expected to be completed.

245. **UPI.** Producer: United Press International, Inc. upi.com/. Coverage from: 1980. Update frequency: Continuous.

Full text of national and international news stories, columns, features, and commentaries transmitted over the United Press newswire is available.

246. **U.S. Newswire.** Producer: U.S. Newswire Corp. usnewswire.com/. Coverage from: 1989. Update frequency: Continuous.

This full text database files press releases from the U.S. federal government and other sources.

247. **Wilson Business Abstracts; Wilson Business Full Text; Business Periodicals Index.** Producer: H. W. Wilson Company. www.hwwilson.com/. Printed version: *Business Periodicals Index* (entry 189). Coverage from: 1982 (abstracts and indexes); 1995 (full text). Update frequency: Varies. CD-ROM versions available.

Approximately 350 English-language business and management journals are indexed, abstracted, or available full text, depending on the subscription. Numerous mass media and communications titles are covered. Subjects covered include communications, and printing and publishing.

248. **Wilson Humanities Abstracts; Wilson Humanities Full Text. Humanities Index.** Producer: H. W. Wilson Company. www.hwwilson.com/. Printed version: *Humanities Index* (entry 199). Coverage from: 1984 (abstracts and indexes); 1995 (full text). Update frequency: Varies. CD-ROM versions available.

These services offer citations or abstracts to articles, book reviews, obituaries, bibliographies, interviews, and reviews in almost 350 English-language humanities periodicals. Subjects covered include journalism, art, film, communications, philosophy, photography, and world literature. These are important sources for researching general topics in journalism. Researchers might also wish to consult the Wilson Social Sciences indexes and abstracts.

249. **Wilson Readers' Guide Abstracts; Wilson Readers' Guide Full Text; Readers' Guide to Periodical Literature.** Producer: H. W. Wilson Company. hwwilson.com/. Printed version: *Readers' Guide to Periodical Literature* (entry 209). Coverage from: 1983 (abstracts and indexes); 1994 (full text). Update frequency: Varies. CD-ROM versions available.

An indispensable general index, *Readers' Guide* offers citations, abstracts, and full text articles in 250 popular periodicals. Areas covered include journalism, news and current events, advertising and public relations, photography, politics, television, and education.

250.   **Xinhua General News Service.** xinhuanet.com/. Producer: Xinhua News Agency. Coverage from: 1977. Update frequency: Daily.

Full text English-language news stories from the People's Republic of China national news agency comprise this file. Emphasis is on current events and politics.

6
Selected Internet Sources

Internet sources covered include bulletin board services available on commercial databases, weblogs, listservs, and many Web sites Individual newspaper home pages or services are not included. Webzines are considered in chapter 13, "Core Periodicals." There are hundreds of sites focusing on journalism or aimed at journalists. Included here are a selected few, some bibliographic in nature, but all are primarily usable as reference resources. Internet sources are cited and cross-referenced throughout Journalism: A Guide to the Reference Literature, *notably in the chapters "Societies and Associations"; "Core Periodicals"; "Selected Research Centers, Archives, and Media Institutes"; and "Selected Commercial Databases." Researchers also should consult "A List of Journalism Websites," produced by the AEJMC Mass Communication Bibliographers Group, 2002, and surf the News and Media listings on Yahoo—A Guide to WWW Resources (yahoo.com/News_and_Media/Journalism/). Other excellent Internet resource listings include John A. Olson and Patience L. Simmonds's "Internet Resources for Journalism/Communications" (College & Research Libraries News, February 1997) and Paul Cammarata and Clo Cammarata's "Photojournalism on the Web" (College & Research Libraries News, July/August 2003).*

INTERNET SOURCES

251.   ABC News. abcnews.com/

Press the ABC News on Demand button and gain immediate access (with your paid subscription) to live news and selected ABC news radio and television programs and summaries such as "World News Tonight," "Nightline," "20/20," "Primetime," and "Good Morning America." This site also provides a link to Transcripts, TV, which provides access to more than 20,000 ABC News transcripts from 1980 to the present. Users also may be interested in *ABC News Transcripts* (entry 217).

252.   ABC News Radio. abcradio.com/

For audio access to news and talk programs such as Paul Harvey, Moneytalk, Business Week, Sam Donaldson, and Larry Elder.

253.   AJR. ajr.org/

Published by the Philip Merrill College of Journalism at the University of Maryland, *American Journalism Review*'s impressive site offers links to nearly 10,000 newspapers, magazines, television networks, television affiliates, radio stations, news and wire services, and media companies throughout the world. It also lists journalism awards and journalism organizations. Users can freely search the *AJR* archives as well, from 1991 to the present. See also *NewsLink* (entry 273).

254.   The Backhaul. backhaul.com/

Local television news stories are selectively indexed and profiled in this unique site whose subscribers are "national and local television news directors, producers, assignment editors, reporters and photographers each looking for story ideas to supplement their daily news budget."

255.   BBC News. news.bbc.co.uk/

The British Broadcasting Corporation offers details on BBC programming and services, such as program listings and annual reports.

256.   Broadcasters: WWW Virtual Library. comlab.ox.ac.uk/archive/publishers/broadcast.html/

This exhaustive site offers links to national and international lists of broadcasters, satellite information, newsgroups, museums, and other resources related to broadcasting.

257.   CBC (Canadian Broadcasting Corporation). cbc.ca/

This site provides access, in French and English, to radio and television programming in Canada, as well as the CBC radio and television archives.

258.   CBS News. cbsnews.com/

News, opinion, and entertainment stories are provided on this site as well as i-videos—"interactive, individual, when I want it" news clips. There also are pages devoted to "The Early Show," "CBS Evening News," "48 Hours," "60 Minutes," and "Face the Nation," to name a few.

259.   CNN Online. cnn.com/

This impressive site produced by the Cable News Network provides full text of all CNN stories and offers links to useful related information as well as video clips. A Breaking News page provides transcripts of up-to-the-minute news reports. In addition, there is a searchable archive.

260.   College News Online. collegenews.com/

This no-frills site offers links to hundreds of college newspapers. Users might also wish to use the NewsDirectory: College Locator at newsdirectory.com/college/press/.

261.   Computer-Assisted-Reporting. computerAssistedReporting.com/

Aimed at journalists, journalism students, and journalism educators in English-speaking countries outside the United States, this resource assembled by Stephen Lamble,

University of Queensland, Australia, offers links to more than 500 resources on computer-assisted reporting. Also of interest is CARparkUK, computer-assisted reporting resources for journalists in the United Kingdom, www.rawlinson.co.uk/CARparkUK/.

262.   C-SPAN (Cable-Satellite Public Affairs Network). c-span.org/

This full text "public affairs on the web" database offers current network program schedules, C-SPAN in the classroom, and a searchable video archive. On a typical news day, users would be able to view a "Report on Intelligence Recommendations" on C-SPAN; "Enron Financial Transaction" on C-SPAN2; and "Saudi Child Custody Cases" on C-SPAN3. C-SPAN Radio offers public affairs programming 24/7.

263.   dotJournalism. journalism.co.uk/

Subtitled "online news for online journalists," this Web site emphasizes international news and resources. Especially useful is the news and research page, offering links to and brief descriptions of news sites and research resources. There also is a large Jobs for Journalists section.

264.   European Journalism Page. demon.co uk/eurojournalism/media.html/

Focusing on the needs of journalists working in or covering Europe, the site is packed with useful links to international, regional, and special interest newspapers; radio and television resources (such as Radio TWIST from Slovakia); news agencies; magazine publishers; Web publications; and media gateways. It was "created as a reference tool for journalists covering aspects of politics, business, culture and the Internet in Europe in response to suggestions by members of the CARR-L mailing list."

265.   1stHeadlines. 1stheadlines.com/

This is an exceptional online ready reference source for breaking news and current events. 1stHeadline's goal is to "provide a one-stop location where readers can view the latest 'breaking news' headlines from top online news sources around the world in a fast, easy-to-read format." News is divided into categories such as U.S. and world, business, health, lifestyles, sports, technology, and weather, and includes source and dateline.

266.   Investigative Reporters and Editors, Inc. See entry 682.

267.   JournalismNet. journalismnet.com/

J-Net is described as a "working journalist's guide to the Net—300 different web pages with over 6,000 links designed to help journalists (and anyone else) find useful information fast." Maintained by Julian Sher, this well-organized site has grown immensely in the last decade. There are links for international, U.S., and Canadian media, news archives, and breaking news, as well as links focusing on how to find people and facts. Working journalists are advised to bookmark this one.

268.   The Journalist's Toolbox. journaliststoolbox.com/

More than 17,000 links to Web sites focusing on the media and journalism, as well as sites useful to journalists and researchers are included in this comprehensive resource. Users also might be interested in the Journalist's Toolbox E-Newsletter, featuring search strategies, tips and information on new resources.

269.   Megasources. www.ryerson.ca/~dtudor/megasources.htm

Dean Tudor, Emeritus Professor at Ryerson University's School of Journalism, has aptly named his file "mega." It is arranged by broad subject in sections labeled "gateways"—Search Indexes/Massive Gateways, Information/Journalism/Canadiana, Computer-Assisted Reporting and Research, Beats/Breaking News, Business and Finance, to name a few. Users should be prepared to spend a good amount of time in this massive listing, for it is just that—a compilation of hundreds and hundreds of sources in no apparent order other than that described above.

270.   National Public Radio. npr.org/

This site, established in late 1994 and updated daily, offers brief descriptions of individual news programs and content, and provides information for ordering tapes and transcripts. The NPR Hourly newscast is updated every hour.

271.   NBC Television. nbc.com/

Featured here is background information on each NBC news program, including data on staff, and anchor and reporter biographies. It also provides links to CNBC and MSNBC. (Dow Jones provides business news content to CNBC.)

272.   NewPages. newpages.com/

NewPages.com, subtitled "alternatives in print & media," is described as "the portal of independents." It includes links to Web sites focusing on independent publishers, alternative periodicals, literary periodicals, alternative newsweeklies, and alternative online magazines, to name a few. It also offers a weblog.

273.   NewsLink. newslink.org/mag.html/

This organization provides access to home pages of magazines, newspapers, and radio and television stations. See also *AJR* (entry 253), NewsDirectory: Newspapers and Media at newsdirectory.com/, and Online Newspapers at onlinenewspapers.com/.

274.   Newspaper Design: Design With Reason. ronreason.com/.

Described as the "first online site for news design ideas and advice," this is a nice resource for tips, samples of redesigns, case studies, and conversations about visual journalism. Other resources such as the News Page Designer (newspagedesigner.com) might also be useful.

275.   NewsTrawler. newstrawler.com/

NewsTrawler is described as a "parallel processing search engine" capable of searching more than 300 sites. "Most of the current meta search engines on the Internet limit themselves to around half a dozen sites and basically they search the search engines. Whilst NewsTrawler can do this too, the current application of NewsTrawler's parallel search technology has been confined to trawling through the archives of news, magazine, and journal resources as this was felt to be one area on the Internet where there is a distinct lack of service." Users may search by country or category, across countries or categories, or by subject. In searching English News, for example, the user may "trawl" through 40 news publications ranging from *Pakistan Press International* to *Newsweek*.

276.   The Power of Words. projo.com/words/

In addition to offering weekly tips on newspaper writing, *The Providence Journal* also provides links to journalism and beat-related Web sites.

277.   Power Reporting. powerreporting.com/

The incomparable Bill Dedman offers "thousands of free research tools for journalists. And no ads." Bless him and bookmark this site. It is meticulously organized and searchable by beat, company research, reference sources, government information, people finders, and so on. Journalism Shoptalk is an impressive collection of links to associations, books, cartooning, editing, education, ethics, graphics, jobs, and management. Journalism educators will be impressed with the CAR bookshelf and syllabi, and may wish to recommend this site to their students.

278.   Poynter Online. poynter.org/

Poynter Online ("everything you need to be a better journalist") is essentially a one-stop shopping experience for anyone seeking timely information, background, links, and wisdom on journalism. It is crammed with useful and well-written columns, briefs, and news tips, such as Al's Morning Meeting (Al Tompkins shares his story ideas) as well as exhaustive resource files offering links to journalism organizations, news sites, centers, and publications. The journalism jobs page offers links to sites such as the National Diversity Newspaper Job Bank and Planetmedia. Users also can check out the Institute's class offerings, faculty line-up, and publications. Reporters, librarians, and researchers will find using this well-organized and newly redesigned site to be a real timesaver.

279.   The Pulitzer Prizes. pulitzer.org/

A current record of Pulitzer Prize winners in journalism as well as the Pulitzer Prize archives are located here. Full text articles, cartoons, and photographs are available from 1995 on. Users may click on a timeline on the home page and retrieve names of all winners in all categories from 1917 to the present. Researchers might also wish to consult *Who's Who of Pulitzer Prize Winners* (entry 315).

280.   Reporter's Internet Guide (RIG). www.crl.com/

Described as a "guidebook for news professionals needing to use the Internet as a tool for daily reporting," RIG sources are arranged according to beat. (Note: This resource may no longer be available. A recent search resulted in a "page not found" message.)

281.   The Reporters Network. reporters.net/

Formed in the mid-1990s by a *Houston Chronicle* reporter, this resource is designed to "promote the Internet as a research and communication medium for working journalists."

282.   SLA News Division. ibiblio.org/slanews/sland.htm/

The Special Libraries Association News Division is a leader in enterprising online projects, and its Web site is no exception. It contains links to Internet sites and Intranet resources, such as U.S. News Archives on the Web, with links to U.S. papers and information on Newsbank's News Library, reference tools, organizations, and jobs and internships. See also *NewsLib* (entry 302).

283.   The Slot. theslot.com/

For copy editors, by a copy editor. *The Washington Post*'s Bill Walsh, author of *Lapsing into a Comma,* maintains this well-written and tightly edited site.

284.   U-Wire. uwire.com/

This daily college media newswire is produced by students and includes contributions from more than 550 student publications. It also contains CopyBoy, a comprehensive online story archive.

285.   WWWVirtual Library: Journalism. 209.8.151.142/vlj.html/

Developed and maintained by John Makulowich, this is one of the most comprehensive bibliographic tools on journalism available on the Internet. Featured are sections on virtual library subfields and specialized fields; associations and societies; awards, grants, and scholarships; higher education; courses, papers, studies, and surveys; Internet alert and news and research services; news bureaus and organizations; other resources and services; and an interesting section called "Not Elsewhere Classified," (not to be confused with "Other Resources and Services") which recently contained a link to the Ancient Thespians One-Minute Web Guide. Internet initiates are advised to start their searching here for topics on journalism.

286.   Zap2It. tv.zap2it.com/

In addition to television listings and information on television news, the resources page provides links to broadcast, cable, and satellite networks and television stations throughout the world.

WEBLOGS

Weblogs, or blogs, according to Steve Outing, senior editor at Poynter.org., are "regularly updated online journals—websites where commentary, original reporting, links to other content on the Web, etc., are sorted in reverse chronological order (newest items up top). Items posted to weblogs typically are very short. Most weblogs are a quick read" (18 July 2002). The Chicago Tribune's Ellen Warren defines a weblog as a "personal Web site where anybody with the energy and/or ego can comment on anything, anytime, anywhere" (Tribune, 7 January 2003). In light of this, only a selected "very best of the blogs" list is included here.

287. **Barbara's News Researcher Page.** gate net/~barbara/

Journalists and librarians seeking an expert news librarian's Internet choices will be intrigued by Shapiro's listing. She also includes a link to her journalism and research resources webring called "HACKS," which "focuses on gathering the hundreds of thousands of bookmarks posted on the websites of professional journalists, researchers, government agencies, news agencies, and others." As of this writing the ring boasted 24 active sites and more than 4,000 total page views. See http://s.webring.com.

288. **Behind the News. Liz Donovan's weblog.** newsresearch.blogspot.com/

Donovan, longtime news research editor at the *Miami Herald*, offers a wealth of links on weblog resources ranging from "Blogbib," an annotated bibliography on weblogs, to Dave Winer's "How to Start a Weblog for Professional Journalists." Most every aspect of news research is covered on this impressive site.

289. **Cyberjournalist.net.** cyberjournalist.net/

Subtitled "tips and talk for the wired world," this online journalism site offers tips and links to resources as well a section on convergence, a wealth of journalists' weblogs or "J-Bloggers" ("The Internet's most complete directory of J-Blogs") and a Weblog Blog or "reports on Weblogging as journalism."

290. **Liblog.** csmonitor.com/linkslibrary/liblog html/

The Christian Science Monitor's meticulous blog is maintained by the library staff.

291. **Lost Remote.** lostremote.com/

This daily television broadcasting weblog is the brainchild of Cory Bergman, KING-TV's executive producer, Seattle. According to Bergman, "Today, we've grown into a respected source of trends and practical tips on the rapidly-changing world of TV news, technology, sales and marketing. TV convergence is more than cool; it's a matter of survival."

292. **Thescoop.org.** thescoop.org/

A weblog compiled by Derek Willis, a Washington D.C. reporter, who states that "this site is primarily a weblog about my interests and opinions, especially as they relate to reporting and technology." Users are advised to skip over the photo of his cats and go directly to the portal page, which contains links to useful resources for journalists as well as other well-developed blogs.

293. **Top Journalist Weblogs.** epnworld-reporter.com/

Described as a "round-up of the best journalist weblogs, and the debate on whether or not blogging is doomed to last week's soggy fishwrap" (6 May 2002).

294. **Weblogs and the News: Where News, Journalism and Weblogs Intersect.** well.com/user/jd/weblog/roundup.html/

A nice primer of weblogs and blogging, this resource offers links to background reading on blogging, weblog directories and search engines, collaborative news sites, and alternative online news sites. It also includes a weblogs "Sampler" of some of the better blogs such as Netrunner (weblog from the *Providence Journal*) and *eJournal*, Dan Gillmor's daily weblog.

LISTSERVS

295.   Association of UK Media Librarians. aukml.org.uk/lists2.htm/

This specialized listserv focuses on topics of interest to news librarians in the United Kingdom. See also *NewsLib* (entry 302).

296.   Canadian Association of Journalists listservs. caj.ca/services/list-serves.html/

The CAJ maintains several listservs for Canadian journalists: CAJ-list is the general, moderated listserv; WIM-list is the listserv for the Women in Media caucus; CANCAR-list is a forum for the Canadian Computer Assisted Reporting caucus; and CAJE-list supports discussion among the CAJ Educators' caucus.

297.   CARR-L (Computer Assisted Research and Reporting List). louisville.edu/it/listserv/archives/carr-l.html/

This listserv on computer-assisted reporting is supported by journalism educators, professional journalists, and news researchers and librarians. See also NICAR-L (entry 303).

298.   COMLIB-L. listserv.uiuc.edu/

Communications Librarians Discussion List

299.   Copyediting-1. listserv.indiana.edu/archives/copyediting-1.html/

The unique challenges encountered by copy editors are discussed here.

300.   IRE-L. ire.org/resources/ire-l/

The Investigative Reporters and Editors listserv is a popular Internet meeting ground for reporters, librarians, and researchers seeking tips, background, and support covering current and public affairs.

301.   Journet. lsoft.com/scripts/wl.exe?SL1 = JOURNET&H = LISTSERV.CMICH.EDU/

This unmoderated, international list is reserved for journalism educators.

302.   NewsLib. listserv.unc.edu/chi-bin/lyris.pl?enter = newslib&textmode = 0&lang = english/

NewsLib, the listserv of the Special Libraries Association News Division, was set up in the fall of 1993 and has developed into an important resource for news librarians and media bibliographers. Barbara Semonche, University of North Carolina Journalism

Library, continues to maintain this list. See also *SLA News Division* (entry 716) and *Association of UK Media Librarians* (entry 295).

303.   NICAR-L. nicar.org/nicarl.html/

The National Institute for Computer Assisted Reporting (entry 766) supports this listserv. See also CARR-L (entry 297).

304.   NPPA-L. journalism.sfsu.edu/www/internet/mail/nppa.htm/

This listserv of the National Press Photographers Association (entry 698) includes contributions from news photographers, graphic artists, photo editors, and others involved in visual communication.

305.   SPJ-L. lsoft.com/scripts/wl.exe?SL1 = SPJ-L&H = LISTS.PSU.EDU/

Maintained by the Society of Professional Journalists, this unmoderated general journalism discussion list welcomes professional journalists, journalism educators, and students.

306.   STUMEDIA. journalism.sfsu.edu/www/internet/mail/stumedia.htm/

This student journalism discussion list is aimed at students involved in newspaper and yearbook publishing as well as broadcasting.

307.   WriterL. writerl.com/

Jon Franklin, author of *Writing for Story,* cofounded this subscription-only literary and explanatory journalism listserv with Lynn Franklin. According to the Web site, "It has been said that the atmosphere of WriterL is reminiscent of Paris of the 1920s—those heady days when Hemingway, Fitzgerald, Gertrude Stein, and their contemporaries gathered in cafes to discuss writing." Additionally, "Our club includes mostly nonfiction writers at all levels from wantabes to the most consummate of professionals. The Pulitzer Prizes for feature writing in 2001 and 2002 were both won by Writer L members." Those interested in narrative journalism might also wish to examine The Narrative Newspaper, inkstain.net/narrative/.

7
Biographical Sources

308.   Abrams, Alan E., ed. **Journalist Biographies Master Index.** Detroit, MI: Gale Research Company, 1979. 380p. (Gale Biographical Index Series, no. 4). LC 77-9144. ISBN 0-8103-1086-4.

This ambitious index is an offspring of (and now superseded by) *Biography and Genealogy Master Index* (entry 314), and is a useful, albeit aged, single-volume source to biographical information on journalists. Sam Donaldson and Linda Ellerbee are considered "unidentified persons" here, and next to their names are the letters "NF" for "Not Found." (If this is confusing, it might help to know that the editor first identified the journalists to be included, then located biographical sketches in approximately 200 biographical directories, major journalism texts, and historical sources.) The subtitle states that this is a "guide to 90,000 references to historical and contemporary journalists." Entries are arranged alphabetically, and list only year of birth/death and title codes for book references. Among the sources indexed are *Who Was Who in Journalism* (entry 338); *American Journalism: A History, 1690–1960* (entry 550); *The American Radical Press, 1880–1960; Authors in the News; Biography Index; Blacks in Communications, Journalism, Public Relations, and Advertising; Contemporary Authors* (entry 317); *Famous War Correspondents; The Foreign Press: A Survey of the World's Journalism; Foremost Women in Communications* (entry 326); *A History of American Magazines; The Investigative Journalist: Folk Heroes of a New Era; Lords and Laborers of the Press: Men Who Fashioned the Modern British Newspaper; The New Muckrakers; Overseas Press Club of America and American Correspondents Overseas 1975 Membership Directory; Reporting the News: Selections from Nieman Reports;* and *Who's Who in Graphic Art.*

309.   Applegate, Edd. **Journalistic Advocates and Muckrakers: Three Centuries of Crusading Writers.** Jefferson, NC: McFarland & Co., 1997. 219p. index. LC 97-11662. ISBN 0-7864-0365-9.

In the introduction, Applegate pulls together dozens of definitions of new journalism, literary journalism, muckraking, advocacy journalism, and alternative journalism, but boils it down to this: In advocacy journalism, "the writer presents his or her opinion when discussing a specific topic" and muckraking journalism "occurs when a reporter or writer suspects that there may be a potential problem in some field, investigates to determine if the problem actually exists, and then reports about the problem." Biographical sketches of 100 journalists are arranged alphabetically and run two to three pages in length. They are typically straightforward and formulaic, include birth and death dates, basic background information, and major publications or works. Crusaders include the likes of Elizabeth Cochrane (aka Nellie Bly), Nat Hentoff, Seymour Hersh, Robert Sherrill, Upton

Sinclair, I. F. Stone, and Ida Tarbell, to name a few. This is best used as a ready reference source or by students seeking basic encyclopedia information and ideas for research project topics.

310. Applegate, Edd. **Literary Journalism: A Biographical Dictionary of Writers and Editors.** Westport, CT: Greenwood Press, 1996. 326p. index. LC 96-7142. ISBN 0-313-29949-8.

Students of journalism will appreciate the lengthy introduction in *Literary Journalism,* which sets new or literary journalism in historical context and includes a discussion of the differences between literary journalism and other forms of journalism. Biographical sketches are arranged alphabetically, contain listings of published works, and run from two to four pages in length. While this resource does not offer the detail and evaluative components of essays included in DLB's *American Literary Journalists, 1945–1995* (entry 325), for example, it does offer more writers who practiced literary journalism over the course of two centuries. In addition to Greil Marcus and Tracy Kidder, the literary lives of authors such as Charles Dickens, Daniel Defoe, and Mark Twain are explored. Researchers might also wish to consult *A Sourcebook of American Literary Journalism* (entry 316).

311. Ashley, Perry J., ed. **American Newspaper Journalists, 1690–1872.** Detroit, MI: Gale Research Company, 1985. 527p. illus. index. (*Dictionary of Literary Biography,* vol. 43). LC 85-20575. ISBN 0-8103-1721-4. **American Newspaper Journalists, 1873–1900.** Detroit, MI: Gale Research Company, 1983. 392p. (*Dictionary of Literary Biography,* vol. 23). LC 83-20582. ISBN 0-8103-1145-3. **American Newspaper Journalists, 1901–1925.** Detroit, MI: Gale Research Company, 1984. 385p. (*Dictionary of Literary Biography,* vol. 25). LC 83-25395. ISBN 0-8103-1704-4. **American Newspaper Journalists, 1926–1950.** Detroit, MI: Gale Research Company, 1984. 410p. (*Dictionary of Literary Biography,* vol. 29). LC 84-8182. ISBN 0-8103-1707-9.

"The most important thing about a writer is his writing," according to the *Dictionary of Literary Biography* Advisory Board, and that is the tone set in these four volumes delineating four distinct periods in journalism history and in journalistic writing and reporting. Experts and scholars contributed critical and biographical essays, ranging in length from one and one-half pages to twenty pages. Again, the emphasis is on writing, and each entry contains the essay and usual sketch data along with books written and periodical publications. At the end of each essay is a list of biographies, bibliographies, letters, recordings, references, and locations of papers.

Volume 43 (1690–1872) showcases 66 pioneers of the American press, with some emphasis on the penny press. Among those included are Samuel Adams, Benjamin Henry Day, Frederick Douglass, Joseph Medill, and Sara Payson Willis Parton (aka Fanny Fern). Volume 23 (1873–1900) covers the age of New Journalism and, later, yellow journalism, and investigates the lives of 46 journalists such as James Gordon Bennett, Ida B. Wells-Barnett, Henry W. Grady, and Joseph Pulitzer. The years 1901–1925 are chronicled in volume 25, with 47 essays examining the rise of yellow journalism, jazz journalism, and a new interest in public and community service. "In all," the editor writes, "the first fourth of the twentieth century was a transitional period from the highly personalized journalism of the nineteenth century to the corporate journalism of today." Names such as Elizabeth Cochrane (Nellie Bly), E. W. Howe, W. Randolph Hearst, Adolph S. Ochs, E. W. Scripps, William Allen White, and Melville Stone appear here. Finally, volume 29 (1926–1950) looks at the growth of mass circulation magazines, radio, and television, and the rise of interpretive journalism through the lives of 54 journalists such as Walter Lippmann, Ralph McGill, H .L. Mencken, Dorothy Day, Red Smith, Ernie Pyle, and Joseph Pulitzer Jr.

These volumes provide a starting point in the search for basic biographical information on star journalists, fashioned into an attractive, well-illustrated, and highly readable package. Ashley's American Newspaper Publishers (entry 312) and Sam Riley's American Magazine Journalists (entry 331) also are part of the *Dictionary of Literary Biography* series.

312. Ashley, Perry J., ed. **American Newspaper Publishers, 1950–1990.** Detroit, MI: Gale Research Company, 1993. 424p. bibliog. index. (*Dictionary of Literary Biography*, vol. 127). LC 92-42531. ISBN 0-8103-5386-5.

Ashley writes in his preface: "In 1990 American journalism celebrated its tricentennial—three hundred years of newspaper publishing in this country. Therefore, it seems fitting that this volume—with the four previous DLB volumes on American journalists—completes the story of the leaders in American newspaper journalism during those three centuries. It also seems fitting to present the readers of this volume with not only the last forty years in this history, but also an overview of the entire history of U.S. newspaper publishing." Ashley proceeds to do just that. Twenty-two pages later, Ashley and his contributors begin to pay homage to "those individuals who have published major newspapers with regional and national reputations and have put together newspaper chains, multimedia corporations, and media conglomerates." Forty-six essays chronicle the lives of 55 individuals who influenced how American newspapers were published, perceived, and defined. The names are familiar—Katherine Channing, Otis Chandler, Philip Graham and Katharine Graham, William Loeb, Rupert Murdoch, Eugene Patterson, Nelson Poynter, John Sengstacke, Arthur Hays Sulzberger, and Arthur Ochs Sulzberger. The contributors list reads like a who's who as well: John De Mott, Alf Pratte David Coulson, Maurine Beasley, and Jean Folkerts. Essays generally are five to eight pages in length and are well written and documented. A typical entry includes positions held, a lengthy biographical essay, references, and locations of papers. Per usual, the beastly DLB cumulative index of names and titles is the only entry into this source. Regardless of indexing shortcomings, the names included are the big guns, and anyone researching these legends in newspaper publishing should begin here.

313. **ASJA Membership Directory.** New York: American Society of Journalists and Authors. 1952– . Annual. ISSN 0278-8829.

Brief biographical sketches of members of The American Society of Journalists and Authors, an organization of freelance writers, are included here. Entries are arranged alphabetically and include such information as address, telephone, areas of expertise, publications, and so on. Geographical and subject specialty indexes are provided.

314. **Biography and Genealogy Master Index.** Detroit, MI: Gale Group, 1980– . Annual. LC 82-15700. ISSN 0730-1316.

A first stop for anyone researching biographical information on anyone in any field, especially in the United States, this is indeed a "master index." The subtitle to the 1991–95 Cumulation reads: "A consolidated index to more than 2,270,000 biographical sketches in 320 current and retrospective biographical dictionaries." First published as *Bio-*

graphical Dictionaries Master Index in 1975, it acquired its current title with the second edition in 1980. Annual supplements began in 1981, as well as five-year supplements. *Journalists Biographies Master Index* (entry 308) is an important by-product of this index. Useful indexed sources include *Contemporary Authors* (entry 317); *Biography Index* (New York: H. W. Wilson); *Newsmakers* (Detroit, MI: Gale Research Company); *Biographical Dictionary of American Journalism* (entry 327); *International Who's Who of Authors and Writers* (entry 323); *Journalists of the United States* (entry 318); *Sourcebook of American Literary Journalism* (entry 316); *American Magazine Journalists* (entry 331); *American Newspaper Journalists* (entry 311); and all Marquis *Who's Who* sources. Even very specialized sources such as *American Peace Writers, Editors and Periodicals* (entry 333) have been indexed. It is useful to note that "there is no need to consult the work itself if the name being researched is not found, since it is editorial policy to index every name in a particular book." This source also is available on CD-ROM and online. Researchers might also wish to consult H. W. Wilson's massive online *Biography Reference Bank.*

315.   Brennan, Elizabeth A. **Who's Who of Pulitzer Prize Winners.** Phoenix, AZ: Oryx, 1999. 666p. index. LC 98-44979. ISBN 1-57356-111-8.

Pulitzer Prize Winners from 1917 to 1998 are profiled in this specialized resource. Entries are arranged alphabetically by category, then chronologically. (If this arrangement is confusing, consult the Index of Individual Winners.) Biographical entries typically contain birth and death dates, education, prize information, career background, selected works, other awards, references, and a brief commentary. Researchers might also wish to consult The Pulitzer Prizes, pulitzer.org (entry 279), which lists winners from 1917 to the present along with the full text of prize-winning stories from 1995 to the present.

316.   Connery, Thomas B., ed. **A Sourcebook of American Literary Journalism: Representative Writers in an Emerging Genre.** Westport, CT: Greenwood Press, 1992. 408p. index. LC 91-17127. ISBN 0-313-26594-1.

"Some diehards still insist on using the term 'new journalism,' " Connery writes in the lengthy and intriguing introduction, "but literary nonfiction, artistic nonfiction, the nonfiction novel, the nonfiction story, and new reportage are a few of the names used to describe what is here being called literary journalism." He goes on to say that "literary journalism informs at a level common to fiction." Specific examples of literary journalism that users might identify with are Truman Capote's *In Cold Blood* (Random House, 1965) and Joe McGinniss's *Fatal Vision* (G. P. Putnam's Sons, 1983). Connery profiles 35 writers in this unique and important collection of essays on literary journalism or "nonfiction printed prose whose verifiable content is shaped and transformed into a story or sketch by use of narrative and rhetorical techniques generally associated with fiction." Entries are arranged in "roughly chronological order from Mark Twain to Tracy Kidder." Essays on Stephen Crane, Lincoln Steffens, Theodore Dreiser, Ring Lardner, Dorothy Day, Ernest Hemingway, James Agee, John Steinbeck, Lillian Ross, Tom Wolfe, Hunter Thompson, Richard Ben Cramer, John McPhee, and Joan Didion are included, and contain 8–12 pages of critical comments on the author's works, biographical information, notes, primary sources and secondary sources. Most of the essays are engaging and thoughtful, and, in themselves, exemplify the best of literary journalism. Users also will be interested in *Literary Journalism: A Biographical Dictionary of Writers and Editors* (entry 310) and *American Literary Journalists, 1945–1995* (entry 325).

317. **Contemporary Authors; New Revision Series: A Bio-Bibliographical Guide to Current Writers in Fiction, General Nonfiction, Poetry, Journalism, Drama, Motion Pictures, Television, and Other Fields.** Detroit, MI: Gale Group, 1980– . illus. index. ISSN 0275-7176.

This multivolume *Contemporary Authors* (1962–) still doesn't seem comfortable with its inclusion of journalists. There are "authors" and there are "media people" and though the twain have met, it is still an uneasy alliance. Broadcast journalists, cartoonists, communications theorists, essayists, film critics, gossip columnists, magazine and newspaper editors, music critics, publishers, radio personalities, television writers, and the stars of print journalism are included, though criteria for selection are a bit hazy. Entries offer more than your standard biographical fare. Besides date of birth, address, awards, honors, and education, there are complete lists of writings, works in progress, "sidelights," and a section for avocational interests. The cumulative index (in even-numbered original volumes) provides complete access to all *Contemporary Authors* volumes (Permanent Series, First Revision, etc.).

318. Downs, Robert B., and Jane B. Downs **Journalists of the United States: Biographical Sketches of Print and Broadcast News Shapers from the Late 17th Century to the Present.** Jefferson, NC: McFarland, 1991. 391p. index. LC 91-52634. ISBN 0-89950-549-X.

The comprehensive title is an annotation in itself. Invaluable as a ready reference source, this is a collection of well-written and informative biographical sketches of nearly 600 print and broadcast journalists practicing journalism from the 1600s to the present. Narrative entries are arranged alphabetically by author and range in length from a few lines to two pages. It is important to note that only the most prominent journalists of the "present" are included, and, even then, very selectively. Janet Chusmir and Katherine Fanning, for example, are mentioned only in the introduction, and names such as John Sengstacke are omitted entirely. This title is best used as a biographical source emphasizing eighteenth- and nineteenth-century journalists ranging from Winifred Sweet Black (1863–1936) to William Trotter Porter (1809–1858). The brief introduction offers observations on some of journalism history's high and low points in censorship, muckraking, journalism education, and the electronic age. This will supplement the *Dictionary of Literary Biography*'s highly selective *American Newspaper Journalists* (entry 311), *American Newspaper Publishers* (entry 312), and *American Magazine Journalists* (entry 331) volumes in addition to the *Encyclopedia of Twentieth Century Journalists* (entry 337).

319. Dziki, Sylwester, Janina Maczuga, and Walery Pisarek, eds. **Who's Who in Mass Communication.** 2d rev. ed. Munich and New York: K. G. Saur, 1990. 191p. index. ISBN 3-598-10884-2.

This revised edition of the *World Directory of Mass Communication Researchers* (Krakow: Press Research, 1984) is an improved version with an index and more copious editing. It is still, however, a dated, problematic, and rough source. For example, most of the 1,124 listed names are those attending a biennial conference of the International Association for Mass Communication Research; this is hardly "who's who" criteria. In addition, the foreword states that communications experts ("not just IAMCR members") are urged to "apply" for inclusion in this directory. There is little introductory material, and users are left to decipher sometimes cryptic entries. Names are arranged alphabetically and include educational background, current position, address, publications, and research interests (ranging from the "cultural domination of the West upon Arabic press in practice and in the theory" to the "effects of TV on children"). In the first edition, signs of the zodiac accompanied each biographical entry (e.g., Elie Abel was listed as a Libra). This second edition offers no such trivia.

320.   Gale, Steven H., ed. **Encyclopedia of American Humorists.** New York: Garland, 1988. 557p. index. LC 87-8642. ISBN 0-8240-8644-9.

More than 70 contributors profile 135 humorists from America's colonial period to the present in this alphabetically arranged encyclopedia. There are essays on Roy Blount, Art Buchwald, Jules Feiffer, A. J. Liebling, E. B. White, Ogden Nash, S. J. Perelman, and even Davy Crockett. Each signed essay contains general biographical information, a biographical essay, a lengthy literary analysis, a summary, and a selected bibliography. This work "is intended to be the most comprehensive and up-to-date reference text on American and Canadian humorists ever published." It is indeed that, but perhaps a second edition will include Dave Barry. There is a subject and name index. Users might also wish to consult the *Encyclopedia of British Humorists* (Garland, 1996).

321.   Havlice, Patricia Pate. **Index to Literary Biography.** Metuchen, NJ: Scarecrow Press, 1975. 2 vols. 1,300p. LC 74-8315. ISBN 0-8108-0745-9. **First Supplement,** 1983. 2 vols. 1,193p. LC 82-25051. ISBN 0-8108-1613-X.

Numerous journalists are involved in literary pursuits, and their names, from Hemingway to Rather, are included here. The original index lists references to biographical information of 68,000 authors from the earliest times to the 1970s. The supplement lists 53,000 authors in more than 50 reference sources between 1969 and 1981. Each alphabetical entry contains the author's name, pseudonym (if any), birth and death dates, nationality, type of writing, and a letter code to reference sources. This is no replacement for *Biography and Genealogy Master Index* (entry 314), but it is an excellent, easy-to-use additional, albeit dated, source.

322.   Inman, David. **The TV Encyclopedia.** New York: Perigee/Putnam, 1991. LC 90-24917. ISBN 0-399-51718-9; 0-399-51704-0 (pbk).

Glib, flip, and frequently subjective, this biographical source will disappoint those seeking "who's who" information; it will appeal primarily to browsers and persons seeking supplemental information on television personalities. The introduction sets the tone and Inman confides in the first sentence, "Being a guy, I like to switch channels as I watch TV. Incessantly." He goes on to describe Kathie Lee Gifford as a "TV personality whose picture should be next to 'perky' in the dictionary; adoring wife of Frank Gifford." Geraldo Rivera is the "grandstanding, self-important reporter-talk show host who never hesitates to make himself more important than whatever story he's covering." Entries on performers, directors, and writers, including news personalities, are arranged alphabetically and include birth and death dates, thumbnail description of career and/or personality (see above), regular appearances on television series, and guest appearances on other television shows. According to Inman, this book "tells you more than the easy stuff." It does not, however, offer address, educational background, and other standard personal information found in mainstream biographical sources.

323.   International Who's Who of Authors and Writers. 18th ed. Cambridge, England: Europa, 2003. ISBN 1-857431-58-8.

This latest edition offers nearly 8,000 entries and includes biographical information on editors, journalists, critics, and columnists. The scope is worldwide, although there is a definite British slant, and the emphasis is placed on poets, novelists, essayists, and critics. Entries are arranged alphabetically, and include date of birth, address, education, publications, appointments, memberships, and honors. Appendixes include literary agents, literary organizations, and literary awards and prizes. Its use is limited, but at least it is updated frequently (usually every two to three years).

324.   Johnson, Ben, and Mary Bullard-Johnson. Who's What and Where: A Directory and Reference Book on America's Minority Journalists. 2d ed. Columbia, MO: Who's What and Where, 1988. 735p. index. LC 88-50602. ISBN 0-9614418-2-8.

More than 4,000 black, Hispanic, Asian American, and Native American journalists are listed in this dated alphabetical guide of "thumbnail biographies." Each entry contains minority status, current position, address, and telephone number; some entries list educational background and career history. Chapters examine affirmative action, hiring minority journalists, language, multiculturalism, internships, and other topics, and one section discusses the history of minority journalism. An appendix lists local minority organizations (no addresses), and minority Nieman Fellows, Knight Fellowships, MMP Fellows, and columnists. This was an important source which, considering high turnover, needs to be updated.

325.   Kaul, Arthur J., ed. American Literary Journalists, 1945–1995: First Series. Detroit: Gale Research, 1997. 417p. index. illus. (*Dictionary of Literary Biography*, vol. 185). LC 97-40240. ISBN 0-7876-1119-0.

Kaul writes that "In the past fifty years literary journalists and novelists-turned-journalists have produced masterful nonfiction writing of enduring aesthetic, cultural, and political significance; they have, in fact, reshaped the contours of contemporary American letters." The 36 literary journalists profiled in this DLB volume (the first of two on the subject) are indeed the big guns of what was once called "new journalism." Truman Capote, Richard Ben Cramer, Joan Didion, Tracy Kidder, Norman Mailer, John McPhee, P. J. O'Rourke, Hunter Thompson, Calvin Trillin, and, of course, Tom Wolfe, are profiled in this rich biographical resource. Scholarly essays are 8 to 15 pages in length and include a listing of the writer's works, a detailed and critical biographical sketch, and references. For example, on McPhee, Norman Sims writes, "In his literary journalism McPhee proves the value of what is often considered ordinary life, using writing techniques and a style that are far from ordinary. Organizing his material and structuring his narratives before he starts writing, McPhee uses this tightly controlled method to treat an unprecedented variety of subjects including basketball and tennis, art and airplanes, the New Jersey Pine Barrens and the wilderness of Alaska, atomic energy and birchbark canoes, oranges and farmers, the Swiss Army and United States Army Corps of Engineers, and the control of nature and the scientific revolution in plate tectonics that created modern geology." Besides the table of contents, the convoluted DLB cumulative index of names and titles is the only entry into this source. Researchers also will be interested in *A Sourcebook of American Literary Journalism* (entry 316) and *Literary Journalism* (entry 310).

326.   Love, Barbara J., ed. **Foremost Women in Communications: A Biographical Reference Work on Accomplished Women in Broadcasting, Publishing, Advertising, Public Relations, and Allied Professions.** New York: Foremost Americans Publishing Company, 1970. 788p. index. LC 79-125936. ISBN 08352-0414-6.

Reference sources that address high-turnover professions require almost continual updating. Published in 1970 and exceedingly important in its time, this book now serves as more of a "where was she then" or "who was who" source. For example, the entry for the late Jessica Beth Savitch informs us that she has just been hired as an administrative assistant at CBS. Biographical profiles of almost 8,000 women in communications, broadcasting, advertising, public relations, and "allied professions" include date of birth, career information, education, awards and honors, and other "who's-who" data. Arrangement is alphabetical, with the geographical and subject cross-indexes providing a way to track down names associated with a specific industry (television, radio, newspapers) or profession (management, editing, writing). Some things have changed a bit, albeit slowly, in the 30-plus years since this was published. The editor writes, "Still, few women are city editors, newscasters of world events, political and editorial writers, officers in publishing firms or radio and television stations." Users also will be interested in *Women In Communication: A Biographical Source* (entry 336), published in 1996.

327.   McKerns, Joseph P., ed. **Biographical Dictionary of American Journalism.** Westport, CT: Greenwood Press, 1989. 820p. index. LC 88-25098. ISBN 0-313-23818-9.

Biographical sketches of nearly 500 reporters, editors, columnists, editorial cartoonists, photographers, and correspondents from 1690 to the present are included in this alphabetical guide to significant names in print and broadcast journalism. Criteria for inclusion are a bit confusing; McKerns writes that "the decision to include living subjects prevented the kind of closure possible when the selection of subjects is limited to those who are dead. Therefore, I decided to weight the selection of subjects who are living in favor of those who have retired, thus achieving closure to an extent." McKerns goes on to describe criteria for selection in detail in the introduction. A typical signed entry of one to four pages includes birth and death dates, a summary of the journalist's contributions and significance, other important dates, career information, other interests, and a brief bibliography. Listed are more than 130 contributors, a veritable "who's who" in journalism education: Ashley, Beasley, Kobre, McBride, Riley, Teel. The list goes on and on. Other important sources in journalism biography include the Dictionary of Literary Biography's *American Magazine Journalists* (entry 331), *American Newspaper Journalists* (entry 311), and *American Newspaper Publishers* (entry 312).

328.   Nimmo, Dan, and Chevelle Newsome. **Political Commentators in the United States in the Twentieth Century: A Bio-Critical Sourcebook.** Westport, CT: Greenwood Press, 1997. 424p. index. LC 96-28069. ISBN 0-313-29585-9.

The title aptly describes the focus of the book. More than 40 print and broadcast journalists, columnists, and other news personalities are chronicled in this well-written and -organized volume, which aspires to document the "careers of key political commentators of the era and, through their lives and works, to illustrate the rise and decline of political commentary across the century." Further, "each bio-critical essay in this volume situates the selected political commentator in the communication environment of the commentator's life, describes the commentator's background and career, and analyzes the com-

mentators' contributions to the development of the art in twentieth-century America."
Alphabetically arranged essays include references and a frequently entertaining one-
sentence description of the commentator's communication style and/or political leanings:
Noam Chomsky's style is "Propaganda Analysis and Analysis as Propaganda"; Paul Harvey, "Bardic Political Commentary"; Mike Wallace, "The Political Commentator as Grand
Inquisitor"; and Eric Sevareid, "Political Commentary to Elucidate Not Advocate." A few
female commentators are included (Georgie Anne Geyer, Cokie Roberts) but this is a political arena where women have yet to make their mark.

329.   Orodenker, Richard, ed. **American Sportswriters and Writers on Sport.**
Detroit, MI: Gale Group, 2001. 421p. illus. index. (*Dictionary of Literary Biography*, vol.
241). LC 20-01023165. ISBN 0-7876-4658-X.

According to the editor, "As the entries in this volume try to show, on the one
hand, sportswriters have written with much originality and variety, even when they are not
gifted stylists and sometimes when they stray far from the field. They cannot be defined by
a single adjective, even when they seem to fall into one of the three schools of sportswriters and whether or not they are classified as reporters, columnists or feature writers." He
continues, "Finally, contemporary sportswriting has shed itself of certain antediluvian
fashions, although it has lost some of its zing because of political correctness and tenden-
tiousness." Antediluvian issues aside, this collection of 40 well-written and entertaining
biographical essays on high-profile sportswriters has plenty of zing. Written by scholars of
sport, each critical article is arranged alphabetically and contains a listing of major writings, positions held, and a brief bibliography. On Blackie Sherrod, Kevin Kerrane writes
that "Sherrod's own game stories often use verse epigraphs in the form of rhyming couplets
that identify the key play or players, in a style familiar to readers of Grantland Rice or
Shirley Povich. He occasionally wrote whole poems, or parodies of poems, as offbeat commentaries on the world of sport; in 1955, for example, he recast Edgar Allan Poe's 'The
Raven' as 'The Raving,' recounting in seven stanzas an imaginary interview with a football
coach who, instead of spouting the cliches of false modesty and pregame caution, says what
he really thinks."

Researchers might also wish to consult *Twentieth Century American Sportswriters* (DLB vol. 171).

330.   Page, James A., and Jae Min Roh, comps. **Selected Black American, African,
and Caribbean Authors: A Bio-Bibliography.** Littleton, CO: Libraries Unlimited, 1985.
388p. index. LC 85-5225. ISBN 0-87287-430-3.

An expanded version of *Selected Black American Authors: An Illustrated Bio-Bibliography* (Boston, MA: G. K. Hall, 1977), this selective publication of African American
literature covers more than 600 authors, many of whom are "publishers or editors of newspapers and magazines that have an impact on writing." Included are both fiction and nonfiction writers as well as writers outside the United States, provided they have "lived, studied,
or been published in the continental United States." Entries are arranged alphabetically
and include basic biographical information, comments, sources, and a "Writings" section
listing the author's works. More than 80 magazine and newspaper editors, journalists,
and columnists such as Robert Sengstacke Abbott, Ida Bell Barnett-Wells, John Herman
Henry Sengstacke, Alice Dunbar Nelson, Carl Rowan, John B. Russwurm, Louis E.
Martin, and William C. Matney Jr. are listed in this important source on "what is being

thought about, written, and spoken of in that vast, diverse world known as Black America." With four indexes (African Writers, Caribbean Writers, Occupational, and Title), it also is immensely accessible.

331.   Riley, Sam G., ed. **American Magazine Journalists, 1741–1850.** Detroit, MI: Gale Research Company, 1988. 430p. index. (Dictionary of Literary Biography, vol. 73). LC 88-17586. ISBN 0-8103-4551-X. **American Magazine Journalists, 1850–1900.** Detroit, MI: Gale Research Company, 1989. 387p. index. (Dictionary of Literary Biography, vol. 79). LC ISBN 8103-4557-9. **American Magazine Journalists, 1900–1960.** First series. Detroit, MI: Gale Research Company, 1990. 416. illus. index. (Dictionary of Literary Biography, vol. 91). LC 89-48356. ISBN 0-8103-4571-4. **American Magazine Journalists, 1900–1960.** Second series. Detroit, MI: Gale Research Company, 1994. 411p. illus. index. (Dictionary of Literary Biography, vol. 137). LC 93-81176. ISBN 0-8103-5396-2.

This is a logical starting point for those researching any historical aspect of magazine publishing. Coverage is broad, however, and only the best-known and most influential journalists are included in these four volumes profiling magazine editors and publishers from 1741–1960. Riley offers a historical minicourse in the foreword to each volume, linking them all with discussions of economic concerns, social issues, and publishing trends. As with most *Dictionary of Literary Biography* titles, this series will appeal to the masses and fit comfortably in most reference collections. Per usual, there is no subject index (except for the huge DLB cumulative index), so using these well-organized and well-written volumes is more unwieldy than it should be. Entries are arranged alphabetically and include positions held; publications; essays, ranging in length from a few pages to 12 pages; references; location of papers; and black-and-white photographs and illustrations. Contributors are listed at the end of each volume.

"The first American magazines were received indifferently by colonial readers," writes Riley in volume 73 (1741–1850). "By the mid-1700s most Americans were too busy taking care of their basic needs to devote much time to reading, and even if they had the time, they were unable to afford the cost of a magazine subscription." Nearly 50 journalism pioneers are profiled in this eclectic collection, including Washington Irving, Edgar Allan Poe, Ralph Waldo Emerson, William Bradford III, Sarah Josepha Hale, Isaiah Thomas, and Noah Webster. Volume 79 details the years 1850–1900, with the proliferation of political periodicals and religious magazines. According to Riley, "the American magazine was a changed creature. It was already in the process of becoming a large industry led by national magazines of enormous circulation, and overall it informed, as opposed to entertained, more than it had been able to do in the mid 1800s." Names such as Louisa May Alcott, Amelia Bloomer, Frederick Douglass, Bret Harte, Lyman Abbott, Frank Leslie, Edward I. Sears, William Sydney Porter (aka O. Henry), and Lucy Stone are included in this collection of 50 essays. Volume 91 is the first of two volumes focusing on journalists active from 1900 to1960, when the "most striking feature of the American magazine evolution during this period was the emergence of the magazine as a truly mass medium. In 1900 perhaps two hundred thousand households subscribed to one or more magazines; by 1950 the number had soared to around thirty million...." Robert S. Abbott, W.E.B. Du Bois, Henry R. Luce, and Conde Nast are among the 37 names profiled. The second volume covers 40 more journalists, including Theodore Dreiser, William F. Buckley Jr., Harold Ross, John H. Johnson, and Norman Cousins. An appendix contains a selection of editorial statements from initial issues of 12 magazines, including a pompous piece from *The American Mercury* (1924), which reveals a great deal about the magazine and perhaps more about editor

H. L. Mencken (also featured in the essay section). Perry Ashley's *American Newspaper Journalists* (entry 311) and *American Newspaper Publishers* (entry 312) also will provide useful information.

332. Riley, Sam G. **Biographical Dictionary of American Newspaper Columnists.** Westport, CT: Greenwood Press, 1995. 411p. index. LC 95-7185. ISBN 0-313-29192-6.

Riley focuses on an elite group of 600 American newspaper columnists from the Civil War to the present in this unique addition to journalism biography. Some names are familiar (Safire, Raspberry, Royko, Buckley, Quindlen, Bombeck, Goodman); others are local columnists. Riley offers some surprises by including such names as Ed Sullivan, Mikhail Gorbachev, and Lee Iacocca, who indeed wrote columns, but are notable for other achievements. The well-written profiles range in length from a few lines to two pages; many contain colorful background information and observations, occasionally subjective, regarding the influence or prominence of individuals. Pat Buchanan, for example, "delights in ruffling liberal feathers and in 1991 was given the Jesse Helms Defamer of the Year award by the Gay & Lesbian Alliance Against Defamation." Ernie Pyle was, at the time of his death in 1945, "his nation's favorite columnist." And Oliver North is "one of those politicians who make use of a syndicated newspaper column to further their political ends." Entries are arranged alphabetically and include birth and death dates, major accomplishments, education, career summary, column information, publications, and references. The general index includes names and news organizations. Riley writes that "A great many columnists have used their column as a stepping-stone to the literary world. The author hopes that the arrangement of this book will graphically demonstrate the considerable link between the spheres of the columnist and the book author. The column is a sort of intersection where journalism and literature sometimes meet, or at least brush by one another at close range." Keeping this in mind, users might be interested in *A Sourcebook of American Literary Journalism* (entry 316), *Literary Journalism* (entry 310), and *American Literary Journalists, 1945–1995* (entry 325). Riley also is the author of *The American Newspaper Columnist* (Praeger, 1998).

333. Roberts, Nancy L. **American Peace Writers, Editors and Periodicals: A Dictionary.** Westport, CT: Greenwood Press, 1991. 362p. index. LC 90-23469. ISBN 0-313-26842-8.

According to Roberts, this book "aims to shed light on the link between journalism, especially, and U.S. peace movements" and is aimed at "historians of journalism, communication, and peace movements—as well as anyone who wishes to understand the historical role of advocacy writing in the United States." This specialized source profiles 400 individuals from colonial times to the present who "proselytized for peace in a variety of ways." Roberts admits that the "relative obscurity of peace advocates has, in many cases, mandated some far-flung research, including consultation with state and local historical societies to ferret out biographical and bibliographical information not readily available." Entries are arranged in alphabetical order and include the likes of Noam Chomsky, Norman Cousins, Clarence Darrow, Eugene Debs, John Foster Dulles, Daniel Ellsberg, Ralph Waldo Emerson, Allen Ginsberg, Martin Luther King Jr., Linus Pauling, Ida B. Wells-Barnett, and E. B. White. Most names, however, will not be so familiar to those unacquainted with the literature. Roberts lists basic biographical information as well as views on war and peace, major journalistic contributions, selected works, bibliographies, and locations of papers. In addition, an informative introductory essay and a descriptive listing of more than 200 peace advocacy periodicals make this an invaluable source for anyone surveying the topic or seeking information on an individual. It is useful to note that this is indexed in *Biography and Genealogy Master Index* (entry 314).

334. Roth, Mitchel P. **Historical Dictionary of War Journalism.** Westport, CT; Greenwood Press, 1997. 482p. bibliog. index. LC 96-35024. ISBN 0-313-29171-3.

Roth writes, "the larger history of the war correspondent has not been thoroughly explored. A historical dictionary covering war correspondents has probably not been previously attempted due to the difficulties in identifying anonymous or pseudonymous journalists." This resource, he continues, "is designed to fill this existing gap in the history not only of war journalism, but military affairs, literature, imperialism, and the Victorian era as well. The war correspondent is a comparatively new phenomenon. Prior to the Mexican War, military commanders preferred to report their own victories and resented the presence of any civilian correspondents. But, with the introduction of the telegraph in the 1840s, a new urgency was given to news gathering." The author located references to thousands of war reporters, and so it was "necessary to be selective and choose reporters who covered significant events and left behind more than a trace of their presence at the frontlines." War correspondents, photojournalists, and artists working for newspapers, magazines, radio or television stations, or other legitimate news sources are featured in this alphabetically arranged resource. More than a dozen appendixes list correspondents according to the wars or conflicts they covered. The Mexican War list, for example, includes but nine names from papers such as the *New Orleans Delta, New Orleans Picayune, New York Sun,* and the *Philadelphia North American*; nearly 2,000 journalists are included in the World War II listing. Entries are well-written and succinct, generally one or two paragraphs, including references. Also covered are major war events, skirmishes, and terms, from "Rooftop Journalism" to the "Patton Slapping Incident."

335. Scheuer, Steven, ed. **Who's Who in Television and Cable.** New York: Facts on File, 1984. 579p. index. illus. LC 82-12045. ISBN 0-87196-747-2.

Prone to using such phrases as "delightfully wacky," and "unabashedly masculine," Scheuer (spelled "Sheuer" on the cover of one copy), lists approximately 2,000 persons involved in television, video, and cable, including network and public television executives, television journalists, and actors. This dated source addresses a range of personalities from communications professor Elie Abel to that late comedian/announcer/host Gene Rayburn. Entries are arranged alphabetically and occasionally are accompanied by mug shots. (Rayburn has one, Abel does not.) Date of birth is included (although the year often is not), as well as address, education, career highlights, and achievements and awards. The are numerous "NAs" in sections marked for personal information. We do learn, however, that Dan Rather is "known for his impeccable deportment and conservative but casual wardrobe." Corporation and job title indexes are included. Consult this source for initial and/or historical information, then search elsewhere.

336. Signorielli, Nancy, ed. **Women in Communication: A Biographical Sourcebook.** Westport, CT: Greenwood Press, 1996. Index. 497p. LC 95-52756. ISBN 0-313-29164-0.

Nearly 50 of the most notable women in broadcasting and journalism—many of them active in the field today—are profiled in this impeccably researched resource. Selection of names for inclusion involved a stringent peer review process described in detail in the introduction. Included as an appendix is a collection of short biographies of nearly 30 "notable women" who did not make the final cut but are nonetheless major players in communications. Essays are four to eight pages in length and contain notes and bibliographies. Signorielli writes that "Biographers were asked to focus on each woman's scientific and professional contributions to the field. Most also conducted personal interviews to gather all the information they needed to write a full account of the woman's life and work." On Helen Rogers Reid, Elizabeth Burt writes, "Although Reid was perhaps one of the most influential women in New York for more than four decades, little is written about her in history books, and she is barely mentioned in journalism histories. When she is mentioned, more often than not her name is linked with the names of women such as columnist Dorothy Thompson and war correspondent Marguerite Higgins. It is ironic that it is these women, who were mentored by Reid and perhaps achieved their fame as 'firsts' among women because of her sponsorship, who have captured the interest and attention of scholars and historians." Other profiles focus on Helen Gurley Brown, Peggy Charren, Dorothy Day, Nancy Dickerson, Pauline Frederick, Ellen Goodman, and Cokie Roberts. This volume, complete with comprehensive author and subject indexes, fills a huge gap in journalism biography.

337. Taft, William H. **Encyclopedia of Twentieth Century Journalists.** New York: Garland, 1986. 408p. index. LC 84-48011. ISBN 0-8240-8961-8.

This star-studded sketchbook of nearly 800 well-known, award-winning, and/or highly reputed print and broadcast journalists is invaluable for basic biographical information. Most of those chosen for inclusion were still alive at the time of publication with the exception of deceased journalists who played a major role in the formation of present-day journalism. Excluded are those in such fields as advertising, public relations, management, and production. Sketches are short, usually four to six paragraphs in length, but are loaded with pertinent information. Length of entry usually is an indication of the importance of the journalist and contributions he or she has made, but that is not always so; the entry for Geraldo Rivera (that "practitioner of advocacy journalism") is about as long as the one for the entire Pulitzer family. Names were culled from various *Who's Who* publications, *Contemporary Authors* (entry 317), journalism histories, trade journals, and journalism reviews. Arrangement is alphabetical and there is an excellent index of names, subjects, and organizations. Also included is a short essay on journalism awards, useful as a quick overview. See also the *Encyclopedia of American Journalism* (entry 149).

338. **Who Was Who in Journalism, 1925–1928.** Detroit, MI: Gale Research Co., c1925, c1928, 1978. 664p. (Gale Composite Biographical Dictionaries, no. 4).

Nearly 4,000 early-twentieth-century newspaper and magazine journalists are included in this biographical source comprising material from the 1925 and 1928 editions of *Who's Who in Journalism.* Every page places the reader squarely back in this period of journalism history, with biographical sketches of the American and Canadian publishers, editors, reporters, writers, and teachers who made journalism yellow or aimed for higher ground. Adolph S. Ochs, Joseph Medill Patterson, Eugene C. Pulliam, William Randolph Hearst, R. W. Bingham, and Henry Justin Smith are all listed here, with entries arranged alphabetically and reproduced as they appeared in the original volumes. Biographical information includes date of birth, home address, position and other career information, education, and published writings. Also included are lists of syndicates, foreign news agencies, clubs and associations, schools of journalism, and a bibliography. An eight-page "Codes of Ethics" section contains the Journalist's Creed ("I believe that no one should write as a journalist what he would not say as a gentleman") and "Commandments" for "desk men," such as "Boil it down. Reporters' jargon is always susceptible of condensation." This is an important historical source, and is included in *Journalist Biographies Master Index* (entry 308).

339.   Who's Who in the Media and Communications. New Providence, NJ: Marquis Who's Who. ISSN 1094-6985.

The first edition of this standard Marquis resource covers 1998–1999 and is slated to be a biennial publication. More than 18,000 executives, publishers, senior managers, and other top officials or high-profile professionals working in journalism, telecommunications, broadcasting, publishing, new media, and advertising are listed alphabetically. Profiles are brief and include basic biographical information, work history, awards and honors, education, publications, and address. This information also is available on *The Complete Marquis Who's Who* on CD-ROM.

340.   Who's Who in the Press: A Biographical Guide to British Journalism. 2d ed. London: Carrick Publishing Company, 1986. 133p. ISBN 0-946724-15-6.

Nearly 1,000 British journalists from daily, evening, and Sundays newspapers are profiled in this unique but dated source. Also included are some editors of leading trade and mass circulation magazines. From the motoring correspondent at the *Yorkshire Evening Post* to the industrial editor at the *Sunday Express,* names are arranged alphabetically and include title, birth date, education, career background, awards and prizes, publications, and address.

341.   Who's Who in Writers, Editors, and Poets: United States and Canada 1992–1993. 4th ed. Highland Park, IL: December Press, 1992. 547p. index. LC 87-648220. ISBN 0-913204-25-0. ISSN 1049-8621.

Biographies of approximately 9,000 poets, novelists, short story writers, journal and book editors, journalists, nonfiction writers, critics, playwrights, translators, and scriptwriters are included in this sourcebook, formerly titled *Who's Who in U.S. Writers, Editors and Poets.* (For the record, emphasis is still on writers in the United States.) Entries are alphabetically arranged and list general biographical information as well as a full publishing history. According to the preface, "Inclusion is considered to be a mark of literary/publishing distinction and achievement," but it is interesting to note that "to ensure accuracy, biographees were given the opportunity to proofread, amend, and update their sketches, which in most instances were prepared from data they themselves provided. If a biographee wished to exclude information that would normally appear in a sketch, that was done." Names range from John N. Berry III, editor in chief of *Library Journal,* to author Stephen King, with emphasis on novelists and the periodical press. This source has been indexed in *Biography and Genealogy Master Index* (entry 314) since 1988 and is an unusual and frequently curious collection of names, many lesser known. Users of this source might also be interested in *The Writers Directory* (St. James Press), a biennial publication focusing on writers who have published at least one book in English.

8
Directories, Yearbooks, and Collections

Directories of individual organizations are listed in the entries in chapter 14, "Societies and Associations."

DIRECTORIES AND YEARBOOKS

342. **Bacon's International Media Directory.** Chicago, IL: Bacon's, 1974– . Annual. ISSN 0161-4363.

343. **Bacon's Magazine Directory.** Chicago, IL: Bacon's, 1952– . Annual, with updates. index. ISSN 1088-9663.

344. **Bacon's Newspaper Directory.** Chicago, IL: Bacon's, 1952– . Annual, with updates. index. ISSN 1088-9639.

345. **Bacon's Radio Directory.** Chicago, IL: Bacon's, 1987– . Annual, with updates. index. ISSN 1088-9647.

346. **Bacon's TV/Cable Directory.** Chicago: Bacon's, 1987– . Annual, with updates. index. ISSN 1088-9655.

Aimed primarily at public relations professionals, these volumes nonetheless have a broader appeal as evidenced by several title changes. The *International Media Directory,* formerly *Bacon's International Publicity Checker,* is a directory of print media for Western Europe, listing nearly 15,000 business and trade publications and 1,200 newspapers. Arranged by country, then market classification, entries typically include publication title; address; telephone, fax, and telex numbers; editor, frequency, circulation, language, and profile. Radio and television volumes cover all U.S. broadcast media. Stations and systems are arranged by state, city, and call letters, and include frequency or channel, address, telephone and fax numbers, network affiliation, staff, station profile, and programs. The *Radio Directory* covers more than 13,000 national and regional radio networks, syndicators, and commercial and noncommercial radio stations in the United States and Canada. The *TV/Cable Directory* provides information on nearly 3,500 television and cable networks, syndicators, stations, and cable systems in the United States and Canada.

The *Newspaper/Magazine Directory,* formerly *Bacon's Publicity Checker,* has been split into separate newspaper and magazine volumes. The *Newspaper Directory,* arranged geographically, covers nearly 15,000 daily newspapers, community newspapers, news services, syndicates, and college newspapers published in the United States and Canada, with selected listings from Mexico and the Caribbean. The *Magazine Directory* is organized by market or subject and lists more than 14,000 business, trade, professional, and consumer magazines in the United States, Canada, Mexico, and the Caribbean. Both contain basic directory information found in other Bacon volumes. Users are urged to call Bacon's complimentary "research hotline" at 1-800-972-9252 with questions regarding any directory entries. Most users will be better served by the *Broadcasting & Cable Yearbook* (entry 349), *Television & Cable Factbook* (entry 370), and *Editor & Publisher International Yearbook* (entry 354), but the Bacon guides will supply a great deal of rudimentary directory information in a pinch. The directories also are available on CD-ROM. Users might also wish to consult Gebbie Press publications such as the *All-In-One Media Directory.*

347. Bjorner, Susanne, comp. and ed. **Newspapers Online: A Guide to Searching Daily Newspapers Whose Articles Are Online in Full Text.** 3d ed. Needham Heights, MA: BiblioData, 1995. various paging. index. ISBN 1-879258-12-9.

Nearly 200 daily newspapers, ranging from *Neue Zuercher Zeitung* to the *Dallas Morning News* are profiled in this source for librarians, journalists, and others who search newspaper literature online, either daily or sporadically. Although it offers 50 new newspaper entries since the second edition was published in 1993, it is, by now, a resource in need of updating. There is ample introductory material ("About This Book," "What's New in the 1995 Edition," "How To Use This Book," "About Newspapers Online," etc.), although it does not ease the first-time user into the contents; instead, it bombards with information. Arrangement and pagination are confusing as well, but users will be well served if they plow through the important advice, tips, and warnings, especially the sections on tips for using professional and consumer systems. Profiles are arranged geographically in sections on "Asia & Australia"; "Europe & Middle East"; "Canada"; and the "U.S. Newspaper"; titles appear alphabetically within each section. Entries typically consist of regional information; a "Newsmakers" list of significant names and businesses; online vendors and CD-ROM systems; background and historical information on the newspaper; and important search tips. If the newspaper prepares an electronic edition, this information also is noted. There are seven exhaustive indexes: newspapers providing same-day news; ownership groups; country; state; metropolitan statistical areas (MSAs); U.S. geographical names; and U.S. state/regional codes. Those who are seeking the most up-to-date information on newspapers will be better served by consulting *Fulltext Sources Online* (Information Today, Inc.), which includes newspapers, newsletters, newswires, and television and radio transcripts. It is published twice a year.

348. Brewer, Annie M. **Talk Shows and Hosts on Radio: A Directory Including Show Titles and Formats, Biographical Sketches on Hosts, and Topic/Subject Index.** 3d ed. Dearborn, MI: Whitefoord Press, 1995. 293p. index. LC 92-192492. ISBN 0-9632341-4-5.

"A radio talk show is considered one where conversation occurs between host and guest, host and listener, or guest and listener—or in any combination of these," according to the introduction. Whether or not this is journalism is debatable, but this title is included, even though it is a dated source, because of the proliferation of and media interest in talk shows. It identifies more than 1,500 live AM and FM radio talk shows and their hosts, and provides brief biographical information on 331 hosts. Section 1 is a geographic listing of stations, including name of show and hosts, format, power, frequency, topics addressed, and telephone and fax numbers. Section 2 identifies networks and syndicates, and includes names of hosts and shows. Section 3 offers biographical sketches. Section 4 is a show topic/subject index, which aids the user in identifying shows on, for example, consumer affairs, international news, current events, politics, and even pets and "nostalgia." Section 5 is a name index. Shows range from "Peppy Fields House Party," WKAT AM, North Miami, FL to the "Christine Craft Show," KFBK AM, Sacramento, CA. (Television news aficionados will remember Craft as the Kansas City news anchor who was demoted because she was "too old, too ugly, and not sufficiently deferential to men.")

349.   **Broadcasting & Cable Yearbook.** Newton, MA: Reed Elsevier, 1935– . Annual. LC 71-649524. ISSN 0000-1511.

Formerly *Broadcasting/Cablecasting Yearbook, Broadcasting & Cable Market Place,* and *Broadcasting Yearbook,* this important directory is crammed with up-to-date information on all aspects of the Fifth Estate in the United States and Canada. Introductory material includes a historical overview of the industry as well as current growth and developments. Radio station listings, arranged geographically, offer call letters, address, telephone number, and programming and personnel information. Also in this section are cross-referenced lists of AM and FM stations by call letters and frequencies. Most television station listings, also arranged geographically, include call letters, address, telephone number, personnel, and Arbitron circulation figures. Television and radio stations on the Internet also are included. Separate sections cover law and regulation; cable; satellites; programming services; technological services; brokers and professional services and suppliers; and associations, events, education, and awards. There is a table of contents for each section.

See also the annual *Television and Cable Factbook* (entry 370), an impressive annual source addressing only television and cable, and *World Radio TV Handbook* (Billboard).

350.   **Burrelle's Media Directory. Newspapers and Related Media. 2 vols. Magazines and Newsletters. 2 vols. Broadcast Media. 2 vols.** Livingston, NJ: Burrelle's Information Services. Annual, with quarterly updates. index. ISSN 1074-9446.

Burrelle's directories are remarkably comprehensive and used by both public relations professionals and journalists for up-to-date listings on approximately 60,000 media companies and snapshot information on print and broadcast media. *Newspapers and Related Media* focuses on daily and non-daily newspapers. Entries for both parts are arranged by state, then city and newspaper, and contain ADI (Areas of Dominant Influence), DMA (Dominant Market Area), and MSA (Metropolitan Statistical Area) codes, address, telephone and fax numbers, circulation, coverage, deadlines for news releases and advertising, ad rates, ownership, and bureau and staff information (mostly executives and editors). Canadian and Mexican newspapers are profiled in separate sections. In addition, there are listings of news syndicates, news services, and black, college, Hispanic, legal, and

Native American newspapers. Numerous indexes (including ownership groups, circulation groups, and daily newspapers online) make this one of the most accessible directories available.

Professional, consumer, and trade magazine and newsletter titles are featured in *Magazines and Newsletters*. Entries are arranged alphabetically by title within 300 areas ranging from building and construction to social activism. The section on journalism magazines, although not comprehensive, is solid, but one wonders why the *Journal of Court Reporting* is placed here. Entries contain directory information similar to that in the *Newspapers* volume.

Broadcast media is divided into parts on radio and television/cable. Entries in both volumes are arranged by state, then city and station. Separate sections cover Canada and Mexico. Entries typically contain ADI, DMA, and MSA, along with call letters, address, telephone and fax numbers, hours of broadcasting, format, network, coverage area, public service announcement policy (for radio), staff, programs, types of interviews used, and program descriptions. In addition there are sections on national radio, television and cable programming, and indexes.

This is a bulky set, but it also is available online (Burrelle's Media Database OnLine) and on CD-ROM.

351.   DWM: A Directory of Women's Media. Susan A. Hallgarth, ed. 17th ed. New York: National Council for Research on Women, 1994. 205p. index. ISBN 1-880547-17-1.

Formerly published by the Women's Institute for Freedom of the Press, this is an unparalleled collection of more than 1,600 international resource listings on all aspects of women's media, most of which are owned or run by women. From the Yokohama Women's Association for Communication and Networking to the International Women's Fishing Association, DWM lists it all in sections on periodicals; presses and publishers; news services; radio and television; film, video, and tape; music; theater, dance, and multimedia; arts and crafts; writer's groups; distributors; speakers' bureaus; media organizations; bookstores; libraries, archives, and museums; directories and catalogs; and electronic access. The periodicals section is by far the largest with nearly 1,000 alphabetical listings. Typical directory information such as address, telephone and fax numbers, contact names, and brief descriptions is included. This accessible source also offers adequate indexing—publications and organizations, individuals, and geographic. The preface notes that the 18th edition has an "anticipated publication date of 1996." A current *Directory of Women's Media,* however, is once again published by the Women's Institute for Freedom of the Press and is available on its Web site (entry 783).

352.   Dyer, Carolyn S., ed. The Iowa Guide: Scholarly Journals in Mass Communication and Related Fields. Iowa City, IA: Iowa Center for Communication Study, School of Journalism and Mass Communication, The University of Iowa, 1987– . ISSN 1099-310X.

"It began as a homely gray pamphlet to hand out at a convention session on academic publishing," writes Dyer. "That first edition reported submission requirements for about 25 U.S. communication journals. It is now broadly interdisciplinary and international in scope." Users are invited to review the most current information available about the Iowa Guide on the School of Journalism and Mass Communication's home page at uiowa.edu, where it is revealed that the 10th edition will be made available online.

The purpose of this guide is to "help researchers find appropriate academic journals in which to publish their work and offer advice on how to prepare manuscripts for publication." The introduction also lists criteria for journal selection and describes the directory format. Journal titles included encompass the broad disciplines of mass communications, speech communication, and journalism. In the directory portion, entries for 125 English-language journals are arranged alphabetically and include the following information: focus, affiliation, readership, editors, address, telephone, frequency, circulation, pages per issue, blind refereed, review period, acceptance rate, time to publication, abstract, style guide, length, number of copies, notes, illustrations, non-English usage, computer format, and additional notes. Titles included range from the *Journal of Computer-Mediated Communication* to *Newspaper Research Journal*. This is truly the *Writer's Market* (entry 374) for scholarly mass communication publishing.

353. Dziki, Sylwester. **World Directory of Mass Communication Periodicals.** Kraków, Poland: Press Research Centre, 1980. 218p.

According to Walery Pisarek, director of the Press Research Centre, "In its present version this Directory is beyond a doubt the most comprehensive and most complete annotated bibliography of mass communication periodicals." Since it has not been updated in more than 20 years, however, it is best used as a unique historical resource. More than 500 scientific and professional journals, periodicals, magazines, newsletters, and other publications from 55 countries are listed. A large number of these titles are published in the United States, Great Britain, France, Germany, Australia, and Czechoslovakia. Entries are numbered, arranged alphabetically by title, and include address, publisher, editor, brief description, target audience, circulation, and frequency of publication. Some entries are incomplete, such as the entry for *MORE: The Media Magazine*. Though an address and editor are still listed, it does not indicate that *MORE* ceased publication in 1978. Titles range from the familiar *Journal of Communication* to *Korrespondent,* a monthly journal published in the Soviet Union that focuses on sociopolitical issues of journalism. Excluded are film, theater, book publishing, photography, and advertising periodicals. Country, town, language, and other indexes are provided.

354. **Editor & Publisher International Yearbook.** New York: Editor & Publisher. 3 vols. 1924– . Annual. index. ISSN 0424-4923.

This yearbook, claiming to hold "hundreds of thousands of facts" about newspapers, touts itself as the encyclopedia of the newspaper industry. That is no misnomer, as it is possibly the single most important source on newspaper industry facts, numbers, and names in the United States and Canada. Part 1 makes up the bulk of the annual, a state-by-state listing of daily newspapers, arranged alphabetically by city and newspaper. Entries include information on address, telephone number, circulation, price, advertising and representatives, news services, politics, date established, special editions and sections, supplements, market information, mechanical specifications, commodity consumption, and equipment. A personnel list contains names in general management, advertising, circulation, finance, human resources, information services, marketing, news, and production, as well as news executives, editors, and managers.

College and university newspapers and newspaper groups are covered as well. In addition, the section entitled "Newspapers Published in Foreign Countries" offers an overview of the British press and a list of newspapers in the British Isles. Newspapers of

Europe, Africa, Asia and the Far East, Caribbean, Central America and Mexico, Middle East, South America, Australia and New Zealand, and Pacific Ocean territories are arranged by country, then alphabetically by newspaper. Brief entries contain address, circulation, editor in chief, and business manager.

Other sections list news and syndicate services; equipment and services; and organizations, associations, and press clubs; schools and departments of journalism (from the AEJMC's *Journalism and Mass Communication Directory,* entry 362).

The top 100 U.S. daily newspapers and the top 10 Canadian daily newspapers are two frequently consulted features. When searching for specific information, remember that the table of contents serves as a better index than the index.

In part 2, non-daily newspapers are arranged alphabetically by state, then by principal community or neighborhood served. Community and weekly newspapers, shopper publications, and specialty publications, including alternative, black, Hispanic, and Jewish newspapers, are also listed. Daily Canadian newspapers are listed by province.

Part 3 is Who's Where, an industry telephone directory. It is an alphabetical listing of all names included in the U.S. and Canadian daily and weekly newspaper sections in parts 1 and 2. Brief entries include telephone number, title, newspaper, and city and state. It is important to note that most names included are managers, editors, and publishers; if you are attempting to contact a reporter at a major daily, chances are you will still have to call the main switchboard or consult the newspaper's Web site.

Whether studying the newspaper business or figuring out where (and to whom) to send clips, one will, of necessity, consult this source. It now is conveniently available online and on CD-ROM. Researchers might also be interested in the *Editor & Publisher Market Guide,* an annual publication with detailed market data on United States and Canadian daily newspapers.

355. Elmore, Garland C. **CommuniQuest Interactive.** (The Communication Disciplines in Higher Education: A Guide to Academic Programs in the United States and Canada). Association for Communication Administration. aca.iupui.edu/cq-i/home.html/

Now available as an online publication and maintained by Indiana University and Purdue University Indianapolis, this update of Elmore's *Communication Media in Higher Education* (1993) details hundreds of undergraduate and graduate departments and programs in media studies. Communication "disciplines" include communication, speech, media studies, journalism, radio, television, film, advertising, public relations, and new technologies. It aims at scholars, educators, administrators, advisers, and students, but anyone, especially undergraduate students and counselors seeking in-depth information on communication and media programs in the United States and Canada, will find this guide accessible. Industry personnel with hiring responsibilities also will find some useful data here.

College and university listings are arranged alphabetically by state or province; the database also is searchable by program or institution name. Each entry lists program, department or school, address, telephone number, chief administrators, curriculum and instruction information, and facilities and services. Users may also tabulate data and create customized tables. Objectives and criteria for inclusion are clearly spelled out in the welcome and background information, and an impressive number of both renowned and lesser-known programs are included. Still, much of the material is now dated, some of it having been entered or updated in the mid-1990s. Elmore, however, reminds the user that "an edit option with a built-in authentication process encourages program deans and chairs to update information regularly."

356.   Gale Directory of Publications and Broadcast Media. 5 vols. Detroit, MI: Gale, 1869– . Annual. index. ISSN 1048-7972.

This granddaddy of periodical directories, known in its lifetime as the *American Newspaper Annual,* N. W. Ayer and Son's *Directory of Newspapers and Periodicals,* the *Ayer Directory of Publications,* and the *Gale Directory of Publications,* to name a few, is now a geographic guide to newspapers, magazines, journals, radio stations, television stations, and cable systems in the United States and Canada. Newsletters and directories are not included.

In the first two volumes, publications and stations are arranged by state or province. Entries are numbered and contain address, telephone number, and descriptive information such as advertising rates, local programming, and station statistics.

Most impressive is Gale's exhaustive indexing, and now Volume 3 is devoted almost exclusively to indexes, including master name and keywords and agricultural, Jewish, black, Hispanic, foreign-language, college, fraternal, religious, and women's magazines, daily periodicals, daily magazines, daily newspapers, free newspapers and shoppers, radio station formats, and trade publications. Broadcast and cable networks as well as news and feature syndicates are profiled here. Volume 4 is the *Regional Market Index,* with sections on newspapers, periodicals, cable, radio, and television.

Volume 5 is international in scope, with publications and stations arranged alphabetically by country, with 14 additional indexes included. Maps were recently eliminated from the directory to make room for the enhanced indexing. The *Gale Directory* is available online and on CD-ROM.

357.   Godfrey, Donald G., comp. Reruns on File: A Guide to Electronic Media Archives. Hillsdale, NJ: Lawrence Erlbaum Associates, 1992. 322p. index. LC 91-35707. ISBN 0-8058-1146-X; 0-8058-1147-8 (pbk).

Godfrey published in 1983 *A Directory of Broadcast Archives* (Broadcast Education Association), and his 1992 guide appears to update and expand on that source. Recordings available at the Pacifica Foundation, the Human Studies Film Archive, National Geographic Television, CNN Library, Vanderbilt Television News Archive, and even the Rod Serling Archives, to name a few, are listed in this directory of approximately 170 radio and television program archives located primarily in the United States. Organized alphabetically by state, entries offer addresses, telephone numbers, contacts, formats, program types, subject content description, and accessibility of the collection (catalogs, indexes, on-site facilities, tape availabilities, finding aids, appointments, and restrictions). Listings for Canada and the United Kingdom are spare; a total of eight collections are described. Still, it is an important and unique source, reflecting the difficulties and historical import of finding, collecting, maintaining, and researching the primary material Godfrey calls "reruns." Information was garnered from a survey "mailed to all known collections: institutional, private and commercial," and followed up with other mailings and telephone calls. Researchers might also wish to consult *The Researcher's Guide: Film, Television, Radio and Related Documentation Collections in the UK* (British Universities Film & Video Council, 2001).

358.   Grants and Awards Available to American Writers. New York: PEN American Center, 1969– . Biennial. index. ISSN 0092-5268.

For this publication's purposes, a writer is someone who pens fiction, poetry, drama, journalism, general nonfiction, children's literature, or translation. Only those grants or awards that involve $500 or more, publication of a manuscript, or carry special distinction are included. Nearly 100 journalism awards and scholarships are listed, such as the Courage in Journalism Award, Ernie Pyle Writing Award, Knight-Bagehot Fellowships, the Mike Wallace Fellowship in Investigative Reporting, and even the James T. Grady–James H. Stack Award for Interpreting Chemistry to the Public. Other journalism awards, such as the Pulitzer Prizes, are indexed in a "multiple listing" section. The section detailing awards and grants available to Canadian writers has been removed, and only those Canadian awards that are available to American writers are included. Each entry features a code to designate the subject area (journalism, drama, etc.), describes the award, and lists address, fax number, Web site, e-mail address, deadline, and restrictions. There are award, organization, and subject category indexes. For a wider selection of grants, see *The Journalist's Road to Success: A Career and Scholarship Guide* (entry 434).

359. **Hudson's Washington News Media Contacts Directory.** Rhinebeck, NY: Hudson's Directory, 1968– . Annual, with supplements. index. LC 68-22594. ISSN 0441-389X.

Arranged in 25 sections on news services, newspapers, foreign newspapers, radio and television, magazines, newsletters, syndicates, Canadian and foreign media, and freelance writers and photographers, this specialized source sets itself apart from other "current" directories with its new "round the clock" updates available (to subscribers only) on the Hudson Web site. This is a substantial publication—the 2003 directory contained more than 4,200 listings and names of 5,000 journalists—with basic directory information such as name and address of publication, service, or station; telephone and fax numbers; and correspondents or contact persons. In addition, the directory includes name, organization, and beat or assignment indexes. This title will appeal to journalists and others seeking names and telephone numbers of colleagues and to public relations professionals; lobbyists will also find some practical applications. Users may also be interested in the *Washington Blackbook: The Directory to the Washington Press Corps* (entry 365).

360. **International Television & Video Almanac.** New York: Quigley Publishing, 1955– . Annual. LC 56-2008. ISSN 0539-0761.

This is largely a source of lists, addresses, and a "who's who" in motion pictures and television, with alphabetical listings including persons such as Judith Crist and John Travolta. As such, it is indispensable in retrieving ready reference facts and figures; it will be a disappointment for those seeking criticism and context. The almanac lists Emmy Award winners, including awards for television journalism. An ample services section features everything from animals and trainers to government film bureaus and trailers. The section on television provides lists of companies, television stations (including channel allocation and personnel), advertising agencies, television programs, organizations, and the press (trade and newspaper), and includes basic address information. To make it truly an international almanac, the industry in Great Britain and Ireland, as well as the "world market" is profiled. The home video section details statistics, companies, publications, organizations, and retailers. It also is available on CD-ROM.

361. Ippolito, Andrew V., ed. **The International Directory of News Libraries Including Banners.** 5th ed. Bayside, NY: LDA Publishers, 1996. 225p. ISBN 0-935912-61-4. ISSN 0889-0919.

News libraries and librarians at newspapers and broadcast organizations through-out the world are identified in this comprehensive and specialized directory. Divided into sections on the United States, Canada, and International listings, entries are numbered, arranged by state, province or country, and further subdivided by city. A typical entry contains address, telephone and fax numbers, newspaper group, hours, circulation, publisher and editor, interlibrary loan information, access privileges for reporters and librarians, service to news libraries, online systems, computers, electronic library systems, resources, special collections, and personnel. An alphabetical list of libraries is provided as well as numerous indexes. This is invaluable to the news librarian and important to researchers seeking a new angle on media research, but it is important to note that most news libraries are not open to the public and offer the bulk of services to other news libraries. This directory will be best used by information professionals and enterprising reporters.

362.   Journalism and Mass Communication Directory. Columbia, SC: Association for Education in Journalism and Mass Communication, University of South Carolina, 1983– . Annual. LC 87-655726. ISSN 0735-3103.

A wealth of information on journalism education and educators is neatly arranged in this annual paperbound volume. Listed first are schools and departments of journalism and mass communication, arranged alphabetically by state. There also are some listings for Canada, Puerto Rico, Australia, Austria, England, France, Germany, Malaysia, Nova Scotia, Scotland, South Africa, and the United Kingdom. A special section on International Journalism Programs profiles journalism schools in countries such as Albania, Uganda, and Slovakia. The bulk of the directory is the annual AEJMC membership roster, arranged alphabetically and including addresses, e-mail addresses, telephone numbers, and brief biographical information. Also included are descriptions of journalism information centers, Web sites, collegiate and scholastic services, journalism education organizations, and other media organizations (these special directory sections are available online at aejmc.org/pubs/). It is the journalism education yellow pages, and it is indispensable.

363.   La Brie, Henry G., III. A Survey of Black Newspapers in America. Kennebunkport, ME: Mercer House Press, 1979. 72p.

Less useful as a directory than a record of black publishing, this is a guide to nearly 200 black newspapers in the United States. The third edition was published in 1973 as *The Black Newspaper in America: A Guide.* Entries are arranged by state, then newspaper, and list address, telephone number, circulation, advertising rate, publisher, editor, method of printing, size of paper, when published, total number of employees on staff, and number of white employees. So much time has elapsed since its publication, however, much of this information will not be accurate. Included are biweekly or monthly black newspapers, and a state-by-state list of black newspapers no longer published.

364.   Lane, Susan, and Elizabeth Hasten. The 1992–1993 Guide to Newspaper Syndication. Newspaper Syndication Specialists, 1992. 179p. LC 91-066481. ISBN 0-9615800-4-6.

More than 250 newspaper syndicates in the United States are included in this guide and directory, along with tips and advice from some syndicate executives. The directory portion is spare—a simple alphabetical listing with address, telephone number, and editor or contact person. Some entries contain information on number of employees, whether or not the syndicate is accepting submissions (this information is most likely dated), and number of features. Major syndicates are profiled in more depth in chapter 2, which features personal observations and sage advice from syndicate editors. In the entry for King Features, for example, Jay Kennedy, comics editor, defines the "perfect cartoon" in terms of artwork, humor, and characterization.

Other chapters focus on writers' and cartoonists' guidelines, newspaper markets, best-selling features, and submission packages. According to the authors, "We believe this directory is the most complete and up-to-date list of syndicates available." True, this source contains valuable advice and information for freelancers exploring the syndicate market. Users are advised, however, not to overlook the trusty and timely *Editor & Publisher Directory of Syndicated Services,* a special issue published annually by the magazine since 1925.

365.   Newmyer, Marina, ed. **Washington Blackbook: The Directory to the Washington Press Corps.** Lanham, MD: Madison Books, 1988. 565p. index. LC 88-5181. ISBN 0-8191-6878-5.

This book (which is literally black) offers the following observation in the introduction: "There is no single city in America with the concentration of journalists found in the Capital. And there is certainly no city in the country where journalists are more talented, more sophisticated or more powerful than those who work in the shadows of the Capital and the White House." Those who work in the shadows are listed in the personnel index. There is a media index as well. Divided into sections on newspapers, magazines and newsletters, electronic media, wire services (print and broadcast), television and radio programs, multi-title publishers, and freelancers, entries are spare (or, according to the introduction, arranged in a "highly streamlined format"). Names, titles, addresses, and contacts are included. Publicists searching for a media contact or journalism students considering the job market in D.C. will be better served by the more current *Hudson's Washington News Media Contacts Directory* (entry 359).

366.   **News Media Yellow Book.** New York: Leadership Directories, 1993– . Quarterly. ISSN 1071-8931.

Formerly the *News Media Yellow Book of Washington and New York* (1989–1993) and subtitled "Who's Who Among Reporters, Writers, Editors and Producers in the Leading National News Media," this does not contain standard "who's who" biographical information. Aimed at public relations professionals, it is simply a directory of newspapers, bureaus, television stations, radio stations, consumer and trade magazines; the executives and editors who run them; and some of the writers and reporters who work for them. The fall 2002 edition claims to list more than 33,000 journalists and more than 2,300 national media organizations. Entries are arranged by media type, then alphabetically by publication title or station. There is a small section on non-U.S. media and U.S. foreign-language media. The quality and quantity of listings in this directory have greatly improved over the years, and the indexing is superb. If a journalist's name has been included in this source, one should be able to find the listing—there are nearly 300 pages of indexes (e.g., assignment, program, geographic, personnel, media, online media). The *Yellow Book* also is available online as part of The Leadership Library on the Internet. Users may also be interested in *Power Media Selects,* which is similar in scope, but published semiannually.

367. Nordland, Rod. **Names and Numbers: A Journalist's Guide to the Most Needed Information Sources and Contacts.** New York: John Wiley & Sons, 1978. 560p. index. LC 78-18903. ISBN 0-471-03994-2.

Nordland says this "was developed as a professional tool for the working press, and it is intended to fulfill the serious need for a national directory of information sources and contacts" and that it would "take dozens of specialized directories to duplicate even a portion of this directory." It is now a historical document, and while still an excellent book of ideas and sources for the information gatherer, one must seek out all those specialized directories. More than 20,000 listings are organized into three main sections. "Useful logistics" provides information on "getting around," toll-free numbers, unpublished numbers, and information on automobile, airline, and hotel reservations. The information sources and contacts section is a directory of the federal government; regional state, city, and county governments; and also details police and emergency agencies; major American businesses; federal, state, and local consumer offices; labor unions; education organizations; arts and entertainment organizations; the National Weather Service; major international organizations; and the "Most Newsworthy Americans." A section on the media lists media organizations, daily newspapers, leading magazines, book publishers, wire services, broadcasting networks, all-news radio stations, television stations, public relations firms, national journalism awards, and press clubs. A more timely and focused source for working journalists is *The Investigative Reporter's Handbook* (entry 407).

368. Ross, Marilyn. **National Directory of Newspaper Op-Ed Pages.** Buena Vista, CO: Communication Creativity, 1994. 158p. LC 94-17060. ISBN 0-918880-17-3.

Ross defines op-ed pages in the introduction, stating that "it doesn't mean that articles oppose the editorial point of view of the paper, rather it literally denotes where these pieces are found: opposite the editorial page." Aimed primarily at media planners and freelance writers, this collection of U.S. and Canadian newspaper op-ed data lists more than 200 newspapers by state. Entries include name of op-ed page editor or editor responsible for the opinion page, address, telephone and fax numbers, copyright information, word lengths, and comments. Pay scales also are included, and in this category more than half the entries are marked "seldom," "0," or left blank. This is interesting to note as the directory is promoted on the cover as a "new, profitable tool." Perhaps the most revealing and entertaining information is found in comments supplied by editorial page editors: "I'm sorry—not in market at this time Aloha." *(Honolulu Advertiser)* and "The page is not a talk show where any idiot is entitled to sound off, we have Letters to the Editor for that." *(The Baltimore Sun).* Part 1 is "What It's All About," including information on "The Hows and Whys of Op-Ed Pages" and "Crafting Compelling Essays," in which Ross offers a judgmental observation: "While a medieval analogy might charm a well-read audience, a sports comparison could work better for less literate readers." In the section on "Using This Directory for Maximum Results," Ross advises, "Don't give up easily. Editors can be a quaint bunch; what one hates another may love." Part 2 focuses on U.S. newspapers; part 3 (actually "Art 3' on the contents page of one copy) examines Canadian papers. This dated source will appeal to fledgling writers eager to see their names in print and public relations practitioners in need of this specialized information.

369. Sova, Harry W., and Patricia L. Sova. **Communication Serials.** 1992/1993 ed. Virginia Beach, VA: SovaComm, 1992. 1,041p. index. ISBN 0-929976-00-2. ISSN 1041-7893.

Communications Serials is an impressive effort in harnessing the scattered and multidisciplinary periodical literature of communication. This massive volume is international in scope and covers it all—advertising, animation, comics, direct mail, film, graphic arts, journalism, publishing, radio, speech, telephone, television, theater, even vaudeville. More than 2,700 titles in 40 areas of communication and performing arts are arranged alphabetically in this annotated guide. Entries include address, description, regular features or departments, typical article titles, publishing schedule, and LC and ISSN numbers. The collection of titles in journalism, however, is not as comprehensive as one might expect. For example, some major publications such as *IRE Journal and Design* are excluded (*The National Enquirer,* however, is included). Journalism is not even a major subject heading in the subject heading guide index; it is a subheading, making the subject search for journalism periodicals a tedious process. Perhaps this is because the authors subscribe to a fairly narrow definition of journalism ("the creative process of writing for mass communication. Also see News and Scripts"). Still, this is a valiant effort, and although its use as a journalism reference may be limited, it remains a necessity for all communication collections.

370. **Television and Cable Factbook.** Washington, D.C.: Warren Publishing, Inc., 1945– . 3 vols. Annual. LC 83-647864. ISSN 0732-8648.

Television station, cable operators, and industry services volumes make up this directory and factbook. It is loaded with current information on the United States and Canadian markets, including lists of stations by call letters, television markets, a station directory with demographic data, foreign-language programming, translators, and sections on group and newspaper ownership of television stations. Entries are arranged primarily by state, then city. The services volume includes a section on associations and organizations, and information ranging from public and educational television networks, to cable construction and installation companies. See also the *Broadcasting & Cable Yearbook* (entry 349), which includes information on radio as well.

371. Veciana-Suarez, Ana. **Hispanic Media, USA.** Washington, D.C.: The Media Institute, 1987. 225p. index. LC 87-60208. ISBN 0-937790-35-4.

Divided into two major parts, the first is a narrative description of Hispanic newspapers, television, and radio in the United States. Spanish-language dailies in Los Angeles, New York, and Miami as well as the weekly Spanish-language newspapers of Texas are highlighted, with emphasis on advertising, news coverage, and editorial policy. The Spanish Language Communication Corporation, Univision, and Telemundo are described in the television section. The radio markets in Los Angeles, New York, South Florida, and Texas also are explored. There are sections on wire services and English-language media aimed at Hispanics. The directory is subdivided into print media, electronic media, and Hispanic media organizations, then further subdivided geographically (East, South, Midwest, West, Texas, California) and arranged alphabetically. Entries for newspapers contain address, telephone number, publisher, editor, circulation, language, frequency of publication, distribution, regularly published sections, and type of news. Station entries usually contain just the address, phone, news director, and assignment editor. The author indicates that this is not a comprehensive directory, and "only electronic outlets which devote at least one-half of their air time to Spanish-language broadcasting were surveyed...outlets which did not respond to the questionnaire were not included in this directory." There is a dearth of information available on the Hispanic media. Even though it is not comprehensive and has become dated, this book is still a useful and welcome source. Those researching Hispanic media also should consult Standard Rate and Datas *Hispanic Media & Market Source,* a quarterly publication aimed at media planners that provides current information on radio, television, newspapers, and other publications.

372. **Willing's Press Guide.** Farmington Hills, MI: Gale Group. 3 vols. 1874– . Annual. ISSN 0000-0213.

This three-volume guide describes the newspaper and periodical press in the United Kingdom, Europe (excluding the U.K.) and World (excluding the U.K. and Europe). Entries are arranged by country within these sections, and include title, address, e-mail, telephone, subscription information, circulation, publication date, publisher, editor, advertising manager, and circulation manager. It is now available online. Researchers might also wish to consult the *Pims UK Media Directories,* available in hard copy and online.

373. **Working Press of the Nation. Vol. 1: Newspaper Directory. Vol. 2: Magazines and Newsletter Directory. Vol. 3: TV and Radio Directory.** New Providence, NJ: Bowker, 1949– . Annual. indexes. LC 46-7041. ISSN 0084-1323.

Formerly a five-volume opus, this set has been trimmed down to three volumes, but still contains essential information on the media. Conspicuously absent is the *Feature Writer and Photographers Directory.* The contents of the slim fifth volume on internal publications were absorbed into the *Magazines and Internal Publications* volume, now titled *Magazines and Newsletters Directory.* Volume 1, similar to the *Editor & Publisher International Yearbook* (entry 354), is first and foremost, a directory of daily newspapers organized alphabetically by state and subdivided by city and newspaper. Entries include address, URL, e-mail address, telephone number, publishing company, circulation, wire services, deadlines, and management and editorial personnel. Weekly newspapers are given much the same treatment, with far more detailed information appearing here than in the *Editor & Publisher International Yearbook.* Other sections include weekly, special, religious, ethnic, foreign-language, and national newspapers. There also are listings of news and photo services and feature syndicates. One index lists newspapers by Area of Dominant Influence (ADI), another indexes editorial personnel by subject.

Volume 2 is a magazine and newsletter directory arranged by subject. Section 1 is the comprehensive index of subjects with assigned group numbers, section 2 is an alphabetical index of titles, and section 3 is an alphabetical cross-index of subjects and related subject groups. Publication descriptions are listed alphabetically by title within subject groups in sections 4–7; service, trade, professional, and industrial publications make up section 4. Other sections include farm and agricultural publications (from beekeeping to rural electricity), consumer publications, and newsletters.

The *TV and Radio Directory* is volume 3. Commercial radio and television are listed alphabetically by state, city, and call letters in a separate section, as are public/educational radio and television stations. There also are separate sections on local radio and television programming, organized by subject, and by state and city within subject. Listings include station name, call letters, program name, broadcast days and times, and names of host or announcer. Personnel and headquarters and division location are listed for the radio and television networks section. There are indexes of radio stations by Arbitron metro markets and television stations by Designated Market Area (DMA), listed alphabetically by state; there also are indexes of radio and television personnel, arranged by subject, then state.

374. **Writer's Market.** Cincinnati, OH: F&W Publications, 1921– . Annual. illus. index. LC 31-20772. ISSN 0084-2729.

The freelance or part-time writer in search of a market or in search of an idea to market will get some good leads from this annual publication. It does tell you, as its subtitle promises, where and how to sell what you write, be it scripts, greeting cards, business articles, or romance novels. This book also offers realistic advice on the writing profession and on working with publishers and editors. In addition, a WritersMarket.com is now available online and includes listings for newspapers and online publications.

The bulk of material here is on the markets, which are subdivided into sections on literary agents; book publishers; Canadian and international book publishers; small presses; book producers; consumer publications (further subdivided into almost 50 subject headings such as animal and inflight magazines); trade, technical, and professional journals (also subdivided by subject, including a section on journalism and writing); scriptwriting; syndicates; greeting card publishers; and contests and awards. Entries list address, e-mail, telephone number, publisher and/or editor, short description of the publication, circulation, response time, what kind of nonfiction and/or fiction needed, payment, photo needs, information on columns and departments, fillers, and advice.

The Tips sections offer practical, frequently blunt advice. Under "Journalism and Writing," for example, the following tip in the 2003 *Writer's Market* is offered for those seeking to publish in *Freelance Writer's Report*: "Write in a terse, newsletter style."

A book publishers subject index, subdivided by fiction and nonfiction, and general index allow easy access to subject areas and journal titles. Pickings are slim in the journalism section; for those seeking access to scholarly journals in journalism and mass communication, a better bet is *The Iowa Guide: Scholarly Journals in Mass Communications and Related Fields* (entry 352). Some users also will be interested in the *Canadian Writer's Market* (McClelland & Stewart), and photojournalists might wish to consult Writer's Digest's annual *Photographer's Market*.

375. Wynar, Lubomyr R. **Guide to the American Ethnic Press: Slavic and East European Newspapers and Periodicals.** Kent, OH: Center for the Study of Ethnic Publications, Kent State University, 1986. 280p. index. LC 86-18825.

Wynar narrows his subject matter in this detailed guide to include only Slavic and East European newspapers and periodicals published in the United States. Similar to *Encyclopedic Directory of Ethnic Newspapers and Periodicals in the United States* (entry 376) in scope and format, this guide enables researchers and scholars to locate information on 17 ethnic groups. Almost 700 of the 770 questionnaires sent to Slavic and East European presses were answered and returned; the 580 titles included here are numbered and arranged alphabetically within ethnic sections, and each section is usually subdivided into native-language and English titles. Entries contain address, sponsoring organization, date established, editor, language, frequency, circulation, subscription, and brief description. When available, library holdings are included. Wynar notes in his essay on the "Nature of the Slavic and East European Press" that "many ethnic serials are not deposited in the Library of Congress or other major American libraries" and "at the present time, there is no systematic approach to the preservation of all East European and Slavic serials published in this country." In view of that, his directory is al the more important, especially in the absence of more current sources.

376. Wynar, Lubomyr R., and Anna T. Wynar. **Encyclopedic Directory of Ethnic Newspapers and Periodicals in the United States.** 2d ed. Littleton, CO: Libraries Unlimited, 1976. 248p. index. LC 76-23317. ISBN 0-87287-154-1.

The ethnic press in the United States is defined, identified, and described in this scholarly guide emphasizing non-English-language newspapers and periodicals. Lubomyr Wynar, also the author of *American Ethnic Groups: A Guide to the Reference Sources* (Libraries Unlimited, 1987) and *Slavic Ethnic Libraries, Museums and Archives in the United States* (American Library Association, 1980), has revised his 1972 edition to include 63 ethnic groups, eight of which were not covered in the first edition: Argentinian (see Spanish press), East Indian (see Indian press), Egyptian and Pakistani (see Arabic press), Basque, Iranian, Irish, and Scottish. Black and American Indian presses are excluded, as each have been covered in numerous separate volumes.

The introduction explains methodology and scope, and introduces useful statistical data. An essay on the nature of the ethnic press addresses the history of the ethnic press as well as current role. Arrangement is primarily by individual ethnic group (except in the case of Arab, Spanish, and Jewish presses), then alphabetically by publication. Entries contain title and title translation, address, telephone number, year of origin, editor, languages used, sponsoring organization, circulation, frequency, subscription rate, and description. The authors offer a title index and indicate that the table of contents should be used as subject index. Slavic and East European newspapers and periodicals are awarded their own volume in Wynar's *Guide to the American Ethnic Press* (entry 375), but a third edition would be welcome. Users will be interested in Sandra Ireland's *Ethnic Periodicals in Contemporary America* (Greenwood Press, 1990), a directory identifying 86 ethnic-interest categories and nearly 300 periodicals (newspapers excluded).

SELECTED ANNUAL COLLECTIONS, REVIEWS, AND COMPETITIONS

377. **ASNE: Proceedings of the American Society of Newspaper Editors.** ASNE, 1923– .

Formerly *Problems of Journalism,* this is an account of the annual ASNE convention and major committee reports.

378. **Attacks on the Press.** New York: Committee to Protect Journalists, 1985– . ISSN 1078-3334.

The Committee to Protect Journalists documents physical attacks against journalists or news organizations in this annual source. Reports are arranged geographically, with separate chapters on journalists in jail and journalists killed in the line of duty. CPJ investigates more than 2,000 cases per year.

379. **Best Editorial Cartoons of the Year.** Gretna, LA: Pelican Publishing Company, 1973– . ISSN 0091-2220.

Spotlights newspaper cartoons by members of the Association of American Editorial Cartoonists.

380.   Best Newspaper Writing. St. Petersburg, FL: The Poynter Institute for Media Studies, 1979– . Chicago, IL: Bonus Books, distr. LC 80-646604. ISSN 0195-895X.

Presents winners of the American Society of Newspaper Editors Writing Awards sponsored by ASNE and The Poynter Institute. Includes winning articles as well as interviews with the winners, study questions, and comments by judges.

381.   Best of Newspaper Design. Rockport, MA: Rockport Publishers, 1979–80– . LC 83-641901. ISSN 0737-2612.

Presents annual winners of Society of Newspaper Design competition.

382.   Best of Photojournalism. Durham, NC: National Press Photographers Association, 1977– . LC 77-81586. ISSN 0161-4762.

Presents winners of "Picture of the Year" Competition sponsored by the NPPA. The NPPA also sponsors an annual Best of Television Photojournalism competition.

383.   Broadcast Designers' Association Annual International Design Competition. New York: Broadcast Designers' Association, 1980– .

Presents BDA Award–winning television and advertising graphics.

384.   Communication Yearbook. Thousand Oaks, CA: Sage, 1977– . LC 76-45943. ISSN 0147-4642.

This annual publication of the International Communication Association contains current reports and commissioned articles on issues in communication.

385.   Graphis Design Annual. New York: Graphis Press, 1952/53– . ISSN 1012-9340.

This resource includes sections on magazine covers, and newspaper and magazine illustrations. Text is in English, French, and German.

386.   Graphis Photo Annual. New York: Graphis Press, 1966– . LC 66-4571. ISSN 1016-0507.

This is an international collection of photographs used in advertising, newspapers, and magazines.

387.   Mass Communication Review Yearbook. Newbury Park, CA: Sage Publications, 1980–1988. ISSN 0196-8017.

Published in conjunction with Center for Research in Public Communication, this important anthology of published studies and original contributions in mass communication was discontinued in 1989.

388.   Publication Design Annual. New York: Society of Publication Designers. Rockport, MA: Rockport Publishers, 1965– .

Continues Best Magazine Design. Presents Society of Publication Designers Annual Competition award winners in editorial design, illustration, and photography.

9
Handbooks, Manuals, and Career Guides

This chapter emphasizes selected reference handbooks and manuals and research guides, and includes a separate section on career guides. Most journalism textbooks are excluded. Bibliographies and bibliographic guides are in chapter 1. Books of newspaper, publishing, and broadcast style, as well as English-language usage, are in chapter 10.

HANDBOOKS AND MANUALS

389.   Access to Electronic Records: A Guide to Reporting in the Computer Age. Arlington, VA: The Reporters Committee for Freedom of the Press, 1998.

The bulk of this concise guide, now available online at rcfp.org/elecres/, is a state-by-state summary of law on electronic access to computer records, with sections on statutes, cases and opinions, and fees. The introduction answers questions such as: "Is electronic information public?" "Can a requester choose the format?" "Is software a public record?" and "Can government pump up the price for useful systems?" All reporters and editors involved in computer-assisted reporting should consult this enlightening thumbnail guide.

390.   Adair, Sarah, ed., and Selwyn Eagle, consultant ed. Information Sources for the Press and Broadcast Media. 2d ed. London; New Providence, NJ: Bowker-Saur Ltd., 1999. 242p. (Guides to Information Sources). index. LC 99-039540. ISBN 1-85739-261-2.

Those seeking a broadly conceived annotated bibliography of print and broadcast journalism will be sorely disappointed. The second edition of this guide focuses primarily on British news library practices and reference sources, although Adair indicates that the "scope has been expanded to include the unexplored issues of media ethics, the underused resources of television written archives, and the innovations in the digitization of stills, film and video, and written archives." She also writes that this second edition is not meant to replace, "but to enhance the first and to be used in conjunction with it." Fourteen essays explore issues such as "A Journalist's View of the Changes in Information Access for Newspapers Over the Years" and "The Future of the BBC Archives." Nora Paul contributes "The Changing Role of the News Librarian" and Barbara Semonche writes about "Good News, Bad News: Credibility of Information and Data Gathered for the Internet and the World Wide Web." It is unclear exactly who the target audience is, but the introduction to the first edition written by Eagle states: "I hope the main purpose will be achieved if the book gives some understanding of how media librarianship and information work functions and of how it assists in the process of actually producing the media output on a day-to-day, hour-by-hour, minute-by-minute basis." In this second edition, Adair writes "Rather than being a Guide to the literature of a recognized subject field, it attempts to show 'how the press and broadcast media make use of information from various sources and how they organize their library and information departments to this end' " (Eagle, 1991).

News librarians will be able to unearth useful information; journalists will, most likely, be put off by its organization and language as well as the curious and formal examination of media research. This resource is a mixed bag.

391.   Bass, Frank. **The Associated Press Guide to Internet Research and Reporting.** Cambridge, MA: Perseus, 2001. 168p. index. illus. LC 20-01098300. ISBN 0-7382-0533-8.

Bass, director of computer-assisted reporting at the Associated Press, has compiled a nifty and inexpensive handbook for student and professional journalists. "Journalism hasn't changed; only the tools have," he states. "And while some journalists have maintained a certain sense of denial about the need to master new technology, few journalists long for a return to the old days and the old tools." Separate chapters address listservs and newsgroups, computer-assisted reporting, spreadsheets, databases, mapping, statistics, and tips for importing data. Chapter 11 focuses on "The Paper Chase," reminding both novice and experienced reporters that "while the Internet can be helpful in gaining access to paper documents and printing them out for safekeeping, not everything on a reporter's beat is computerized, and even less is available on the Internet." A useful essay on "Copyright on the Internet" by George Galt also is featured. Researchers might also wish to consult *The Investigative Reporter's Handbook* (entry 407) or Christopher Callahan's *A Journalist's Guide to the Internet* (Allyn & Bacon, 1999).

392.   **Black Press Handbook: Sesquicentennial, 1827–1977.** Washington, D.C.: National Newspaper Publishers Association, 1977. 116p.

Although haphazardly organized, this handbook does serve to mark the 150th anniversary of the black press and the birth of *Freedom's Journal.* Several pages of advertisements precede the table of contents. Included are articles on "The Black Press Assessed," "Challenges Still Confront Black Press," the Black Press Archives, and a brief history of the black press. The directory, now out of date, lists National Newspaper Publishers Association member newspapers by state, and includes address, telephone number, and circulation. Managers and editors are listed with biographical information. There is no index.

393.   Chater, Kathy. **The Television Researcher's Guide.** 2d ed. Hertfordshire, England: BBC Television Training, 1995. 156p. ISBN 0-948694-80-7.

"A lot of people are going to disagree with my methods and conclusions," Chater writes in the foreword. "All I can say is they've worked all right for me so far." This basic guide is written from a British perspective, and will appeal to those who are beginning to acquaint themselves with the broad field of television. The first half of the guide offers chapters on finding facts, finding people, finding visual material, and keeping records. The second half lists organizations and addresses, which, oddly, are not television-specific. Instead, they deal with a variety of issues ranging from the environment to religion, rather like a mini *Encyclopedia of Associations.* Users might also be interested in Chater's *Research for Media Production* (Focal Press, 2002) and Jacobson's *Television Research* (entry 408).

394. Cohen, Elliot D., and Deni Elliott, eds. **Journalism Ethics: A Reference Handbook.** Santa Barbara, CA: ABC-CLIO, 1997. 196p. (Contemporary Ethical Issues Series). index. LC 97-26874. ISBN 0-87436-873-1.

Most useful in this primer are the well-written introduction by Elliott and the chapter on Issues in Journalism Ethics, written by practitioners and focusing on basic themes such as "Anonymous Sources," "Deceiving Sources," "Forms of News Bias," "Journalism Ethics and the Coverage of Elections," and "Conflicts of Interest." There also are important chapters on landmark court cases and codes of ethics. A chapter on biographical sketches profiles selected figures in media ethics, mostly contemporary teachers and scholars, but it is nonetheless a highly selective collection of 36 names ranging from Ida Tarbell to Steve Weinberg. That glitch aside, this is appropriate for use in the newsroom as well as the classroom.

395. **Coverage in a Time of Terror: Tips You Can Use When the Pressure's On.** Special Edition Poynter Report. St. Petersburg, FL: The Poynter Institute, 2001. 52p.

"The argument is over," writes Jim Naughton. "News is what breaks, not soothes." With that, the user is drawn into a collection of brief, frequently poignant essays on covering crisis and terrorism, many written within hours of the September 11, 2001, events. More than 30 articles are arranged in sections on "Finding the Story," "Journalists and the Story," "Visualizing the Story," Exploring the Ethics of the Story," "Leading the Story," "Covering the War Story," "Language and the Story," and "The Story Online." For anyone covering disaster, this will serve as a sobering tip sheet. Researchers might also wish to consult *Crisis Journalism: A Handbook for Media Response* (entry 396), published by the American Press Institute.

396. **Crisis Journalism: A Handbook for Media Response.** American Press Institute, 2001.

Similar in scope to the Poynter Institute's *Coverage in a Time of Terror* (entry 395), this guide by the American Press Institute is available online at americanpressinstitute.org. Brief articles are organized in sections on "Planning, Reporting and Writing," "Design and Visuals," "Guiding the Creative Process," "Roles of Other Newsroom Areas," "Ethics, Values and Diversity," "The Business of News," "The Multimedia Story," and "Leadership/Reflections." An Afterword section includes an essay by Lloyd Dobyns. He writes, "Jumping to your death to escape burning to death may or may not be a rational act, but it clearly illustrates for all of us that sometimes there is no good choice. At that point, the ethical admonition, 'Do what's right,' makes no sense; nothing is right, not for the jumper, not for the media. In whole, we did more right than wrong."

397. Croteau, Maureen, and Wayne Worcester. **The Essential Researcher.** New York: HarperCollins, 1993. 624p. LC 91-58264. ISBN 0-06-271514-3; 0-06-273040-1 (pbk).

Subtitled "A Complete, Up-to-Date, One-Volume Sourcebook for Journalists, Writers, Students and Everyone Who Needs Facts Fast." from identification of toxic chemicals to discussion of libel law, this breathless guide is a handy source for reporters seeking instant gratification, fast facts, and little background. Journalists will be interested in the chapter on "Access to Information," with sections on databases and state freedom of information laws, and "The Journalist's Notebook," which includes information on press associations and organizations. Although not "essential," it has its uses.

398.   Dill, Barbara. **The Journalist's Handbook on Libel and Privacy.** New York: Free Press, 1986. 262p. index. LC 86-551. ISBN 0-02-908070-3.

Dill designed this to be a "comprehensive newsroom handbook on libel and privacy," and offers discussion and examples of court cases on libel law, actual malice, due care, opinion privilege, privacy law and embarrassment, and false light. (Remember the Cherry sisters' libel case? "The reviewer had depicted the youngest of the sisters, Addie, as 'the flower of the family, a capering monstrosity of 35,' and he wrote that when Addie and her sisters Effie and Jessie sang a eulogy to themselves, 'The mouths of their rancid features opened like caverns, and sounds like the wailing of damned souls issued therefrom.' " The judge agreed with the reviewer.)

A 60-page question-and-answer chapter lists more than 150 questions grouped in sections such as "A Suit is Filed," "Before the Trial," "At the Trial," "Reporting and Editing Process," "Official Proceedings," "Privacy," and "Photography." Those most likely to consult this chapter are journalists seeking quick answers to one or two questions such as: "Does personal information about a reporter come out in a libel trial?" "What about name-calling? Is that opinion?" "Is there any forgiveness for mistakes in 'hot news,' when a story is produced on deadline?" and "How protective is 'allegedly'?" A table of cases and subject index will guide the user through the libel and privacy maze.

Bruce W. Sanford's *Libel and Privacy* (Aspen, 1999, with supplements) also provides useful information. Michael G. Crawford's *The Journalist's Legal Guide* (Carswell, 1996) focuses on press law in Canada. See also *Media Law: A Legal Handbook for the Working Journalist* (entry 402), *The First Amendment Handbook* (entry 401), and *News Media and the Law* (entry 624).

399.   Ellis, Barbara G. **The Copy-Editing and Headline Handbook.** Cambridge, MA: Perseus, 2001. 337p. ISBN 0-7382-0459-5. index.

Ellis calls copy editors the "unsung 'brain trusts,' the mainstays behind any newspaper's success" and dedicates this practical and frequently humorous handbook to these "guardians of language and facts." Part 1 is an exhaustive primer on headlines—writing, counting, and punctuating them, as well a section on the art of writing feature heads and a master list of "forbidden words." Part 2 focuses on copyediting, with chapters on organization, leads, quotes, numbers, attribution, grammar and usage, more forbidden words, and captions. Accuracy and libel are discussed in part 3. In addition to citing rules of usage and issuing cautions about using clichés ("cutting edge," "push the envelope," and "not playing with a full deck" are on the hit list), Ellis provides hundreds of samples of sharp headlines and captions, and some that completely missed the mark. "Many perceive that head writing must be fun when they see this famous 'winner' crafted by a master for an otherwise ho-hum story about two famous New York detectives named Jack who raided what then was called a 'sporting palace': Pair of Jacks take full house." She also offers a wealth of good advice and reminders for both novice and experienced copy editors: "Aside from being sensitive to words that may result in a lawsuit, don't forget good taste or get so hardened about all the bad news you process that you get cynical about people and the world around you. A heartless headline could mislead or be inappropriate or inaccurate."

400.   Finnegan, John R., Sr., and Patricia A. Hirl. **Law & the Media in the Midwest.** St. Paul, MN: Butterworth Legal Publishers, 1984. 352p. ISBN 0-86678-119-6.

Dedicated "to all the hardy and irrepressible souls who gather the news for the doorsteps and airwaves of the Midwest," this handbook answers questions about media law in Illinois, Iowa, Minnesota, Nebraska, North Dakota, South Dakota, and Wisconsin. It aims at working journalists, editors, publishers, and broadcasters. Separate chapters on access to places, meetings, records, and courts, and protecting sources offer an overview of the issue, introduce some hypothetical questions on that aspect of media law, and then give a state-by-state account of answers to those questions. The chapter on libel addresses confidential sources and defenses for libel. There also is a valuable explanation of how to use the law books and references cited throughout the book. Although there is an index of statutory materials, use is hindered by the lack of a subject index. At times, one must resort to flipping through chapters to find information on reporters' privilege or the Freedom of Information Act, for example. Regardless, Finnegan, then vice president and editor of the St. Paul Pioneer Press and Dispatch, and Hirl, a media lawyer, have produced a useful, although now dated, sourcebook on media law for the nonspecialist.

401.   **The First Amendment Handbook.** 5th ed. Arlington, VA: The Reporter's Committee for Freedom of the Press, 1999.

The prolific RCFP continues to serve journalists by providing timely, well-organized, and readable reference materials and handbooks for working journalists who "need to be aware of the many potential pitfalls that await them, and of how they might avoid them. They need to know their rights, and how to fight back when they are threatened. The First Amendment Handbook is an important weapon in that fight." It also is available online at rcfp.org/handbook.

Those who seek a "just the facts" approach to the First Amendment will find this a suitable and solid source. Journalists seeking timely information quickly and students looking for a general overview can brief themselves on libel, privacy, surreptitious recording, confidential sources and information, prior restraints, gag orders, access to courts, access to places, Freedom of Information Acts, and copyright. In the section on invasion of privacy, there are discussions on intrusion, publication of private facts, false light, misappropriation, right of publicity, defenses, and a "Reporter's Privacy Checklist," consisting of a dozen questions on consent, obtaining information, and content.

Each chapter also offers practical "what to do if..." and "how to avoid..." advice. What to do when you are subpoenaed? "Receiving a subpoena does not mean that the marshal will be coming to the door to arrest you. It is simply notice that you have been called to appear at a deposition or other court proceeding to answer questions or to supply certain documents. You may not ignore a subpoena, however."

402.   Galvin, Katherine M. **Media Law: A Legal Handbook for the Working Journalist.** Berkeley, CA: Nolo, 1984. 228p. LC 84-060496. ISBN 0-917316-75-4.

Galvin says that the purpose of this guide is to "distill the overabundance of information on how law and the media interact into one convenient reference manual which deals with the primary issues you are sure to face from one day to the next." She also cautions that "this book is not and does not pretend to be a substitute for the advice of a competent media lawyer." Chapters cover freedom of expression, censorship, libel, privacy and the First Amendment, free press and fair trial, privilege, newsroom searches, access to news sources and records (including detailed information on the Freedom of Information Act), and government regulation of electronic media. A subject and name index is provided. See also Dill's *The Journalist's Handbook on Libel and Privacy* (entry 398), *The First Amendment Handbook* (entry 401), the *National Association of Broadcasters Legal Guide to Broadcast Law and Regulation* (1994), and the massive *Newsgathering and the Law* (Michie, 1997).

403.   Gora, Joel M. **The Rights of Reporters: The Basic ACLU Guide to a Reporter's Rights.** New York: Avon, 1974. 254p. LC 74-21647. ISBN 0-380-00188-8.

The author pulls no punches on the subject of reporters' rights: "This guide sets forth your rights under present law and offers suggestions on how you can protect your rights... [but] offers no assurances that your rights will be respected." Directed at the non-specialist, the guide is arranged in question-and-answer format by subject, and is part of a series of American Civil Liberties Union handbooks on rights. Sections discuss First Amendment principles, protecting sources, gathering news, publishing news, covering courts, libel and invasion of privacy, and the underground press. Appendixes include summaries of state shield laws.

Although this is not a new book, the questions are still valid, even if some answers have changed. (The author recommends that "if you encounter a specific legal problem in an area discussed in one of these guidebooks, show the book to your attorney.") Questions raised include "Who owns a reporter's notes or materials?"; "Can the police arbitrarily deny a press pass to a reporter?"; "Apart from national security, are there any other grounds for imposing a prior restraint on what reporters may publish?"; "Is radio or television broadcasting of court proceedings allowed?"; "Can the press urge a court to decide a case one way or the other?"; "Who comes within the description of a 'public figure'?"; and "What kinds of reporting deficiencies will result in a finding of actual malice?" For more timely information, consult *The First Amendment Handbook* (entry 401).

404.   Haws, Dick. **Touring the Newsroom: An Inside Look at Newspapers.** Ames, IA: Iowa State University Press, 1993. 96p. LC 93-12934. ISBN 0-8138-2292-0.

This is a strange amalgamation of stylebook, handbook, career guide, encyclopedia, and tourbook. According to the author, its focus is on newsroom people—"Who they are, what they do, why they do it." There is no index, so users must scan the table of contents to pinpoint areas of interest. Topics are arranged alphabetically and include a wide range of subjects: anonymous sources; budget meetings; clichéd leads; demotions, promotions, firings, and lateral pirouettes; flacks; innuendo, journalism by; plagiarism; and rumor stories. Under the entry for "ethics codes," the author writes: "In the best of worlds, the newsroom would be something like the ideal kindergarten. Whenever the happy new employee would enter, all the veteran editors and reporters would drop whatever they were doing, gather 'round the new recruit and carefully explain all of the newsroom's practices and traditions and answer all of the newcomer's questions." Haws then goes on to explain that "life in the newsroom isn't like this." This casual, conversational, humorous, and frequently glib overview of some key issues in newspaper reporting, editing, publishing, and marketing will appeal to some students of journalism.

405.   Horowitz, Lois. **A Writer's Guide to Research.** Cincinnati, OH: Writer's Digest Books, 1986. 135p. index. LC 86-4052. ISBN 0-89879-222-3.

The beginning researcher is targeted in this dated "travel guide" to the research process. Unfortunately, there is little discussion of online searching, a research skill now essential to the journalist. Instead, there is sometimes simplistic, sometimes cursory treatment of "quick-and-dirty research," original research, and using books, magazines, and newspapers in research. ("Are newspapers really research tools? Indeed they are. Newspapers are time capsules, freeze-frames of life as it existed in a certain time and place.") Other chapters discuss research tips, general reference sources ("the old regulars"), indexes, government documents, statistics, pictures, and experts. Horowitz, author of *Knowing Where to Look: The Ultimate Guide to Research* (Writer's Digest, 1988) knows her sources and has some excellent advice for novice library users. The serious researcher will want to make a brief stop here, then forge on. Writers will find additional useful research tips in Mona McCormick's *The New York Times Guide to Reference Materials* (Times Books, 1985), Bruce L. Felknor's *How to Look Things Up and Find Things Out* (Morrow, 1988), and *Search Strategies in Mass Communication* (entry 430).

406.   Horton, Brian. **Associated Press Guide to Photojournalism.** 2d ed. New York: McGraw-Hill, 2001. 223p. LC 00-048672. ISBN 0-07-136387-4.

Although not a traditional handbook, this revised edition of the Associated Press Photojournalism Stylebook is a unique handbook of news photography tips and techniques written in an effective narrative style. Its use as a ready reference source by photographers on-the-go is diminished, however, by lack of an index. Users must rely on the table of contents, which is divided into chapters on "The Look: Composition, Style, Cropping," "News: Sensitivity, Thinking, Instinct—and Curiosity," and features, sports, portraits, lighting, and electronic photography. According to Hal Buell's foreword, this book is "about the essence of photography, about the editor's and photographer's minds at work seeking that most elusive of all journalistic ends, a fine picture that tells those who see it something about their world." It also is very practical, giving the photographer covering a basketball game, for example, this advice: "Using a 180mm lens, work the midcourt area. The lighting will be better because you aren't shooting up into a black backdrop. And, the pictures can be better because you'll get more eye level contact and fewer armpits and elbows in your photos."

407.   Houston, Brant, Len Bruzzese, and Steve Weinberg. **The Investigative Reporter's Handbook: A Guide to Documents, Databases and Techniques.** 4th ed. Boston, MA: Bedford/St. Martin's, 2002. 589p. index. LC 2001095266. ISBN 0-312248237.

This is the most important book reporters will find while hacking away at mountainous piles of records and documents. As was true of the first and second editions edited by John Ullman and Steve Honeyman (St. Martin's Press, 1983 and 1991) and the third edition by Steve Weinberg (St. Martin's, 1995), this book continues to be relevant and groundbreaking. It has its uses as a journalism textbook as well, and instructors are encouraged to put this title at the top of their reading lists. The authors write: "Every journalist can be an investigative journalist. There is nothing magical about becoming one. It requires an intense curiosity about how the world works—or fails to work. Such curiosity must be accompanied by skepticism stopping short of cynicism or nihilism, abetted by undying outrage that expresses itself through comforting the afflicted and afflicting the comfortable.

Such traits lead to exposes, not because of luck but because chance favors the prepared mind. If these vital traits are present, the rest is teachable."

This new edition offers even more to "prepare the mind," with new case studies and special emphasis on new information technologies, Internet resources, and lists of the most important Web sites. It is organized in sections on "The Basics: How to Investigate Anyone or Anything," "Investigating Individuals, Institutions and Issues," and "Putting It All Together." Individual chapters deal with secondary sources, primary documents, computer-assisted reporting, international investigations, people trails, investigating government (five chapters on legislative branch, executive branch, education, law enforcement, and the judicial system), licensed professionals, for-profit businesses, nonprofits, health care, insurance, financial institutions, utilities, transportation, real estate, environmental issues, and an insightful new chapter on "Investigating the World of the Disadvantaged." Here, the authors allude to their previous comments about the "cliché of investigative journalism" as "comforting the afflicted and afflicting the comfortable." They write, "Many of the afflicted are poor. Many of the afflicted poor are racial and ethnic minorities. Many are also women, juveniles, the aged and the physically disabled." Included are important tips on "documenting the world of poverty," children and families, and confidentiality. Chapters on organizing and writing, and ethics and accuracy round out the volume.

This book is organized and written by individuals who know what they are talking about. Houston is executive director of Investigative Reporters and Editors (IRE), associate professor at the University of Missouri School of Journalism and an experienced reporter; Bruzzese is deputy director of IRE, assistant professor of journalism at the University of Missouri School of Journalism, editor of *The IRE Journal,* with 20 years daily reporting and editing experience; Weinberg, now a freelance writer, is the former executive director of IRE. This resource serves experienced journalists well, and teaches journalism students a thing or two about the reporting process.

There are a number of practical guides aimed at writers, such as *Writer's Guide to Internet Resources* (Macmillan, 1998), and Misti Jackson's *On the Net: Resource Guide for Writers* (Virtualbookworm.com Publishing, 2002), but none is aimed so precisely at the needs of working and student journalists as *The Investigative Reporter's Handbook.* Users also will be interested in Houston's *Computer-Assisted Reporting: A Practical Guide* (IRE, 1998) and publications such as *Access to Electronic Records* (entry 389), *Access to Juvenile Courts, Access to Places, How to Use the Federal FOI Act,* and the *Photographer's Guide to Privacy* (entry 419), all produced by the Reporters Committee for Freedom of the Press and available online.

408. Jacobson, Ronald L. **Television Research: A Directory of Conceptual Categories, Topic Selections, and Selected Sources.** McFarland, 1995. 138p. index. LC 94-44118. ISBN 0-7864-0033-1.

This multifaceted source is part handbook, part bibliography, part directory, and part research guide. Jacobson informs the user that "this directory consists of an alphabetical ordering of television-related categories." His 29 "conceptual categories" range from advertising to public television. Each category offers a brief overview of the field or subject, a listing of topics for research or lectures, and an unannotated bibliography of sources. For example, topic suggestions for "News, Documentary and Public Affairs" include "biographical study of a current television journalist" and "history of public service announcements on television"; the sources section lists approximately 70 current book titles relating to news and public affairs. In a separate section, Jacobson lists reference sources of particular interest to the television researcher. Journalism graduate students and new mass communications instructors will identify many uses for this guide.

For a beginning television research guide written from a British perspective, consult Chater's *The Television Researcher's Guide* (entry 393).

409. Jeter, James Phillip, Kuldip R. Rampal, Vibert C. Cambridge, and Cornelius B. Pratt. **International Afro Mass Media: A Reference Guide.** Westport, CT: Greenwood, 1996. 297p. index. LC 95-9304. ISBN 0-313-28400-8.

The authors explain that the word "Afro" in this book "is intended to be a global term used to refer to people who trace their ancestors to Africa and people who live in certain countries on the continent." Media systems in Africa south of the Sahara, North Africa, the Caribbean region, and Afro-America are examined in thoughtful and detailed chapters on setting and philosophical contexts; mass media development and government relations; media education, training, and development; and new technologies. Chapters are then broken down into discussions of media in individual countries. In a discussion of Libya, for example, it is noted that "Even though the press had been censored heavily since the coup, Qadhafi and the RCC [Revolutionary Command Council] recognized early in 1972 that censorship was insufficient to bring all thought into conformity with the goals of the Revolution. The RCC moved to eliminate all newspapers with the exception of its official organ. It suspended the publication of the 10 daily newspapers early in 1972 and later, the same year, their licenses were revoked. Little remained of the Libyan press as a result of these actions. Even the ASU's official organ, Al-Thawra, was shut down for a variety of reasons: it was badly written; its editorials were unsound; the intellectuals did not write for it." This is useful both as a scholarly introduction to and history of the media in Africa; it also may serve as a ready reference source.

410. Kamalipour, Yahya R., and Hamid Mowlana, eds. **Mass Media in the Middle East: A Comprehensive Handbook.** Westport, CT: Greenwood Press, 1994. 333p. index. LC 93-50536. ISBN 0-313-28535-7.

Aimed at a wide audience of students, scholars, professionals, and "globally inclined writers, readers, and researchers," this examination of the mass media in 21 Middle Eastern countries "arose from a recognition of the woeful lack of detailed information on the region's media systems." The Middle East is defined as all Arab countries, as well as Afghanistan, Cyprus, Iran, Israel, Pakistan, and Turkey. Much of the information is encyclopedic in nature, with lessons in geography, history, economics, and politics. Alphabetically arranged entries contain background information, and descriptions of print media, electronic media, new technologies, motion pictures, media ownership, regulation, services and agencies, and references. A politically correct, frequently vague, and sometimes opaque introduction does not diminish the vitality and candor of many of the individual essays. The introduction, for example, speaks of "the rise of Islamic resurgence as a major revolutionary social and political force, the use of channels of communication as an important vehicle for mobilization, and the integration of modern means of communication into the old social networks" as well as the difficulty of determining "with any great certainty the political and cultural changes including the processes of communication and those of the mass media in the contemporary Middle East." The essay on Syria (written by Arvind Singhal and Vijay Krishna) says that "The print media in Syria is strongly influenced by the ruling Ba'ath Party. In a sense, most Syrian journalists are 'employees' of the Ba'ath Party, with an explicit or implicit mission to propagate the party's ideology." It also states that "the government strongly believes that the mass media and their messages have an important role to play in the development of the Syrian society and hence regulates it closely." In light of recent world events, an updated volume would be an important addition to the reference literature.

411.   Keever, Beverly Ann Deepe, Carolyn Martindale, and Mary Ann Weston, eds. **U.S. News Coverage of Racial Minorities: A Sourcebook, 1934–1996.** Westport, CT: Greenwood Press, 1997. 387p. index. LC 96-53850. ISBN 0-313-29671-5.

The authors write that "No other volume approaches this Sourcebook in the breadth and depth of its scrutiny of the intersection of U.S. news and race." This appears to be true. This scholarly reference work examines the portrayal of Native Americans, African Americans, Hispanic Americans, Asian Americans, and Pacific Islanders primarily in the U.S. news media. The preface indicates that "these five groups are occasionally referred to as racial minorities in this book. The authors confronted a daunting problem when challenged to come up with a collective term for these groups. They settled on *minorities* reluctantly, knowing that in many times and places in the United States each of these groups has been—and is—a numerical majority and sometimes a political and economic one as well. The authors also recognize that the term *minority* assumes a white Euro-American point of view." Each chapter offers a historical overview and a critical evaluation of newspaper, magazine, and some broadcast coverage of minorities from 1934 on, with emphasis on coverage during and after several extraordinary historical moments such as the 1934 passage if the Federal Communications Act, the 1941 bombing of Pearl Harbor, the1945 atomic bombing of Hiroshima, the 1957 integration of Little Rock, and the 1974 resignation of Richard Nixon. This unique resource also offers a comprehensive subject, name, and title index.

412.   Kessler, Lauren, and Duncan McDonald. **The Search: Information Gathering for the Mass Media.** 2d ed. Belmont, CA: Wadsworth Publishing Co., 1992. 241p. index. LC 91-13843. ISBN 0-534-16278-9.

This revised edition of *Uncovering the News: A Journalist's Search for Information* (Wadsworth, 1987), is described by the authors as an "outgrowth" of their "first information-gathering book." Written for the student, this accessible handbook describes techniques for gathering information, research strategies, and reference sources useful to the journalist. New to this edition are a unique glossary of sources, chapters on interviewing and writing, and "master searches." These searches, according to the preface, use "contemporary public policy topics" and provide "an in-depth look at how we really acquire and evaluate information." There also are chapters on "Developing and Using Search Strategies," "Discovering the Library," "Specialty Libraries," "Electronic Libraries," "Government: The Information Colossus," "The Culture of Commerce," and "Experts and Where to Find Them." The authors, who teach in the School of Journalism at the University of Oregon, recognize that any discussion of this sort also should include issues of ethics in information gathering. A chapter on "Trust, Truth and Thoughtful Assumptions" and Appendix, "Access and Integrity," lay a foundation for discussions of credibility and ethics.

413.   Mandell, Judy, comp. and ed. **Magazine Writers Nonfiction Guidelines.** Jefferson, NC: McFarland, 1987. 392p. index. LC 86-43088. ISBN 0-89950-239-3.

Aimed at the novice and freelance writer this is a collection of official writers' guidelines for more than 200 newsstand and airline magazines and selected periodicals. Mandell says that "this book should help the writer who is uncertain about where to send the piece he or she has written as well as the writer who already has a periodical in mind but doesn't quite know his or her angle." Titles included range from *Fishing World* to *Hustler.* A title and subject index is provided. See also *Writer's Market* (entry 374), which is updated annually.

414. Morse, Grant W. **Guide to the Incomparable New York Times Index.** New York: Fleet Academic Editions, Inc.: 1980. 72p. LC 79-87815. ISBN 0-8303-0159-3; 0-8303-0160-7 (pbk).

It takes 72 pages of text and illustrations to explain how to use the index to the "newspaper of record" effectively. Morse says, "Herein one will find what you always wanted to know about *The New York Times Index*, but never dared ask." If one does not close the book after that statement, one will find a brief history of the versatile index, then explanations and illustrations of headings, subdivisions, cross-references, entries, and miscellaneous information (biographical, reviews, deaths, etc.). The appendix includes an illustrated step-by-step guide on using *The New York Times* microfilm: Copy down full citation, find microfilm reel (illustration: hand closes in on microfilm box), remove reel from box, place on microfilm reader, and turn to correct date, page, and column. (It does not, however, show the user how to thread the film on the machine, which is what really foils most nonusers of microfilm.) Researchers interested in the history and development of *The New York Times Index* might wish to consult Cates's 'The New York Times Index" in *Distinguished Classics of Reference Publishing* (Oryx, 1992).

415. **Newsroom Management Handbook.** Washington, D.C.: American Society of Newspaper Editors Foundation, 1985. LC 85-70343. ISBN 0-943086-04-3.

The American Society of Newspaper Editors has produced a loose-leaf notebook on newsroom management that is accessible and easily used by even the most harried city editor. According to the introduction: "Our idea is that if you are well-organized, and have half an hour to solve your crisis, you can read the general discussion before turning to the list of do's and don'ts. If you are both well-organized and prescient, you can order the books on the future reading list. If you're the typical editor, and have ten minutes, you can scan the do's and don'ts—and maybe squeeze in a call to The Newspaper Center."
Divided into sections on "The Editor as Manager," "The Editor as Real Person," and "The Editor as Money Manager," these 25 essays (some of which originally appeared in *ASNE Bulletin* or *Presstime*) are written by experts such as Robert Giles, C. K. McClatchy, and Judy Clabes. Subjects include hiring and firing, turnover, labor relations, burnout and stress, management style, and setting salaries. In "The Total Newspaper," Susan Miller tells us that "Real editors yell. They yell at reporters. They yell at copy editors. They yell at everyone in every other department. Real editors are a dying breed." This collection of pithy and well-written articles serves as a realistic overview of potential problems in the newsroom and, fortunately, balances itself with some down-to-earth answers and responses. For more and detailed discussion, see Giles's *Newsroom Management* (entry 539).

416. Newton, David E. **Violence and the Media: A Reference Handbook.** Santa Barbara, CA: ABC-CLIO, 1996. 254p. (Contemporary World Issues). index. LC 96-22269. ISBN 0-87436-843-X.

Similar in format to other Contemporary World Issues series publications, this is part handbook, part bibliography, and part directory, and is best used as a general overview of the subject. Included are brief biographies of individuals who have contributed to research on violence and the mass media, a chronology of events, and chapters on Documents and Opinions, resources, and organizations. Serious researchers might also wish to consult *Violence and Terrorism in the Mass Media: An Annotated Bibliography* (entry 111).

417.   On Assignment: Covering Conflicts Safely. New York: Committee to Protect Journalists.

The introduction states that "In the early months of 2002, Wall Street Journal reporter Daniel Pearl was abducted and executed by his captors while pursuing a story about Islamic militants in Pakistan. The kidnapping, which came only weeks after eight reporters were killed covering the conflict in Afghanistan, was a terrible reminder for journalists around the world of their vulnerability."

This brief but sobering handbook, available online at cpj.org/briefings/2003/safety/safety.html, offers advice on protective gear, health insurance, and health precautions as well as minimizing risk in conflict zones, rules of war, captive situations, and stress reactions. "From its years of research, CPJ recognizes that the journalists who are most at risk are often local reporters. They, and their news companies, often cannot afford body armor or expensive training courses. Some of them live with daily risks, different from the risks addressed in this handbook."

On body armor: "The most important thing to remember about body armor is this: Bulletproof vests are not bullet proof. Body armor may stop some projectiles, but one can still suffer serious injury or die as a result of the blunt trauma inflicted by high-caliber or high-velocity bullets."

On helmets: "Journalists working in conflict zones should also consider wearing combat helmets, which provide effective protection from flying shrapnel. A helmet, however, will not stop a round fired by a military assault rifle."

On clothing and culture: "Bright and light colors that reflect a lot of sunlight may make a journalist too conspicuous. But wearing camouflage or military green could make journalists targets. Depending on the terrain, dark blue or brown may be preferable. In particular, some photojournalists prefer black because it doesn't reflect light, but some combatants, especially rebel forces, often wear black."

Journalists might also wish to consult *Danger: Journalists at Work,* a "safety manual" published online by the International Federation of Journalists.

418.   Paul, Nora M. Computer-Assisted Research: A Guide to Tapping Online Information for Journalists. 4th ed. Chicago, IL: Bonus Books, 1999. Index. 205p. ISBN 1-566251370.

According to the back cover of this guide, it is "the authoritative source on Internet use for journalists." That may well be true. Journalists in a hurry will appreciate this practical, thorough, and accessible guide to online sources. Paul gets right to the point when defining computer-assisted journalism or CAJ: "CAJ can be broken down into four Rs: Reporting, Research, Reference, and Rendezvous. Each of these four functions is critical to newsgathering." Her guide, focusing on the latter three Rs, is arranged in chapters on the Internet Toolbox, the World Wide Web, Types of Material Online: Comparisons of Commercial Services and Web Sites, and Issues with Online Research. The chapter on

Directories, Bibliography and Index is filled with tips, insights, and Web sites useful for locating experts, getting background information, and finding facts and statistics. Paul, an experienced news and journalism librarian, and now the director of the Institute for New Media Studies at the University of Minnesota, knows the value of a decent index, and she provides the user with not only a subject index, but links to Web sites, an index by Web site name, and an index to people. Users will also find relevant information in *The Online Journ@list* (entry 420), Christopher Callahan's *A Journalist's Guide to the Internet: The Net as a Reporting Tool* (Allyn & Bacon, 2002), and Brant Houston's *Computer-Assisted Reporting: A Practical Guide* (IRE).

419.   Photographers' Guide to Privacy. Arlington, VA: The Reporters Committee for Freedom of the Press, 1999.

Published by the RCPF and now available online at rcpf.org/photoguide/index.html/, this brief guide is a useful primer on privacy issues affecting news photographers, camerapersons, videographers, and editors. An introduction offers definitions of intrusion, private facts, false light, and misappropriation, but the bulk of the publication is a state-by-state summary of privacy cases from federal and state courts.

420   Reddick, Randy, and Elliot King. The Online Journ@list: Using the Internet and Other Electronic Resources. 3d ed. Fort Worth, TX: Harcourt College Publishers, 2001. 277p. index. LC 00-26101. ISBN 0-15-506752-4.

Reporters and students in search of a one-volume, jargon-free guide to the Internet and other online sources will want personal copies of this thoughtful and well-organized resource aimed at working journalists. It describes search strategies and points out sources that a reporter on deadline will use time and again. The first two chapters provide introductory material, an overview of "The World Online," and information on bulletin board services and commercial databases. Chapter 3 introduces the World Wide Web, with sections on "Working the Web" and "When the Web Goes Wrong." Separate chapters cover e-mail, online communities search strategies, Internet beyond the Web, network news-Web publishing, law and ethics (with an interesting section on "Erased Files—Not"), and "Getting More Out of Your Browser." Especially useful is chapter 8, "Evaluating Net Information," with sections on protocol weight and domain checks. Three appendixes are packed with names and addresses of services, sites, resources, and providers. This is one of the most useful and approachable tools available for journalists seeking quick and intelligent access to online sources. Other impressive sources are Nora Paul's *Computer-Assisted Research: A Guide to Tapping Online Information* (entry 418) and Christopher Callan's *A Journalist's Guide to the Internet: The Net as a Reporting Tool* (Allyn & Bacon, 2002). *The Internet Handbook for Writers, Researchers, and Journalists* (Guilford, 1997) also has its uses but is fast becoming dated.

421.   Rivers, William L., Wallace Thompson, and Michael J. Nyhan. Aspen Handbook on the Mass Media 1977–79 Edition. New York: Aspen Institute for Humanistic Studies, 1977. 438p. index. LC 77-14556. ISBN 0-03-023141-8; 0-915436-67-1 (pbk).

Although it is clearly outdated, this handbook and directory represents a monumental effort to harness the literature of communications. Subtitled "a selective guide to research, organizations and publications in communications," it is much more than that. First published in 1973, and updated in 1975, this volume is the last edition published. One has only to scan the table of contents to grasp the depth and breadth of information here: communications research in universities, nonacademic institutions, and within organizations; communications organizations (in advertising and public relations, broadcasting, educational and instructional media, film and photography, journalism, new communications technologies, print media); communications law courses; special libraries; communications periodicals (subdivided by subject); books and films on communications; communications bibliographies. All entries are generously annotated. There is a subject and title index.

422.   Robertson, Stuart M. **Robertson's Newsroom Legal Crisis Management: What to Do When a Crisis Hits.** Dunedin, Ontario: Hallion Press, 1991. 80p. ISBN 0-9695155-0-2.

"This book will help you resolve legal crises in the newsroom by anticipating the steps you have to take and the decision you will have to make under fire," according to the introduction. Robertson, a Toronto lawyer, focuses on Canadian law and examines 10 situations in which editors, news directors, and reporters face tough calls: "When the search warrant arrives," "When the police ask you to help," "When a public event closes up," "When a gag order is made," "When an accused confesses to a crime," "When a competitor beats you to a story," "When a source requests anonymity or indemnity," "When a secret arrives in the newsroom," "To name or not to name," and "When a libel complaint arrives." Robertson also writes in the introduction that "there are few legalisms in here. There are very few cases and statute citations—just enough so that your lawyer can be steered quickly to the key authorities." If your lawyer needs to be "steered," however, perhaps you need a more experienced media law expert. Robertson also is the author of the *Media Law Handbook: A Guide for Canadian Journalists, Broadcasters, Photographers, and Writers* (International Self-Counsel Press, 1983).

423.   Rosen, Philip T. **International Handbook of Broadcasting Systems.** New York: Greenwood Press, 1988. 309p. index. LC 87-29986. ISBN 0-313-24348-4.

Twenty-eight experts examine broadcasting in 24 countries in this essay handbook. John Lent takes on Cuba and India; Benno Signitzer and Kurt Luger look at Austria; and Marvin Alisky reports on Chile, Mexico, and Peru. Other countries included are Australia, Belgium, Brazil, Canada, China, the Federal Republic of Germany, Great Britain, Hungary, Israel, Italy, Japan, Kenya, Korea, Nigeria, Saudi Arabia, the Soviet Union, Sweden, and the United States. According to the introduction, "At present no reference work exists where one can readily ascertain what the broadcast structure is in a given nation and how it came to be. By filling this void, we hope that our work will make a substantial contribution to the field of international broadcasting." This they have done.

Most essays include a bibliography; information on history, regulation, economic structure, programming, new technologies, broadcast reform; and a conclusion and/or forecast. What type of information can be found under broadcast reform? In Israel, for example: "The reaction against the 'leftist mafia,' a nickname coined for broadcasters, has been strongly felt in programming and personnel appointment policies. A popular TV satirical program was taken off the air in the late 1970s in response to harsh political criticism. The television prime-time weekly news magazine, broadcast on Friday nights, was cancelled in the mid-1980s on the grounds that the Israeli people should not be exposed to 'demoralizing' news on the Sabbath eve."

424. Somers, Paul. **Editorial Cartooning and Caricature: A Reference Guide.** Westport, CT: Greenwood, 1998. 205p. index. (American Popular Culture). LC 97-26181. ISBN 0-313-22150-2.

While exceedingly difficult to use as a reference guide, this collection of bibliographic essays is nonetheless a well-written examination of the history of editorial cartoons in the United States from 1747 on. As both the table of contents and index are spare, researchers should be prepared to skim the text. The first four chapters offer Historical Background, History and Criticism, Anthologies and Reprints, and Reference Works and Periodicals. Chapter 5 lists more than 150 research collections. All chapters contain extensive notes and references. In addition, five appendixes offer a chronology and lists of historical periodicals, theses and dissertations, and single-artist anthologies.

Somers writes "From Ben Franklin to Mike Ramiriz, America has produced a long line of artists—left, right, and center—idealists and cynics whose work has tried to keep politics honest." Surprisingly (and sadly), this source is not illustrated except for a lone reproduction of Franklin's "join or die" snake.

425. Steinle, Paul. **Professional Field Guide for Television News.** Radio-Television News Directors Association. 54p.

According to the 15-line preface, "This field guide is intended to maximize the effectiveness of reporters and camera-persons." Despite its size, this is a basic but surprisingly comprehensive news reporting primer. Chapters cover "Key Aspects of TV Reporting" (service, ratings, accuracy, clarity, reporting in context, teamwork and communication, responsibility, and credos); "Operating in the Field: Reporting Team"; "Breaking News Coverage"; "Live Shots"; "Enterprise Reports"; "Interviews"; "Interviewing Technique"; "Video Technique: Shooting and Composing, Some Fine Points"; and "Tell It Like It Is." Both novice and experienced journalists will benefit from advice such as "Help the interviewee look normal" and observations such as "A camera does not necessarily tell the truth, even in live shots."

426. Stempel, Guido H. III. **Media and Politics in America: A Reference Handbook.** ABC-CLIO, 2003. 237p. (Contemporary World Issues). index. LC 20-2154378. ISBN 1-57607-845-0.

Part handbook, part directory, part biographical source, and part bibliography, this is described as a "gateway to knowledge about political communication." Stempel, professor emeritus at the Scripps School of Journalism at Ohio University and director of the Scripps Survey Research Center, offers chapters on "History and Evolution of Political Communication," "Problems in Political Communication," and "The Process of News Communication," as well as a simple chronology of events, a selection of biographical sketches of major political communicators, an explanation of important legal documents and court cases (ranging from the Declaration of Independence to *Hustler Magazine v. Falwell*), listings of associations and organizations, and an annotated bibliography of book citations, journal articles, and Web sites. This is a handy resource for reference librarians and a useful primer for undergraduate students. Stempel also is the author *Mass Communication Research and Theory* (entry 556).

427. Swartz, Jon. D., and Robert C. Reinehr. **Handbook of Old-Time Radio: A Comprehensive Guide to Golden Age Radio Listening and Collecting.** Metuchen, NJ: Scarecrow, 1993. 806p. index. LC 92-42120. ISBN 0-8108-2590-2.

Old-time radio or OTR covers a surprisingly lengthy time span "from 1926, when NBC was incorporated, to 1962, by which time the character of radio had shifted dramatically," according to the introduction. Part 1 contains history and background information on radio networks and broadcasting. Part 2 is "Program Category Logs," more than 4,500 programs listed by program type: music and variety; comedy; children's programs; adventure, crime, and mystery; drama anthology; soap operas; quiz and audience participation; news; talk and information; sports and religious; and armed forces and foreign. This section is not annotated. Part 3 makes up the bulk of the guide, with a 400-page descriptive program log. More than 2,000 programs are listed alphabetically by title, and include information such as network, years broadcast, featured performers, and brief descriptions of programs or story lines. Annotations in this section vary in depth and quality of writing, but contain dates, numbers, and names found nowhere else. "It is important to remember that more episodes are being found every day," according to the introduction, "and that the numbers of available episodes that we have listed are very conservative." This specialized source, with separate name and program indexes, will appeal to journalism historians and radio news fans. Users might also be interested in *Radio's Golden Years* (entry 151).

428.   Tapping Officials' Secrets: A State Open Government Compendium. 4th ed. Arlington, VA: The Reporters Committee for Freedom of the Press, 2001.

Described as a "comprehensive guide to open government law and practice in each of the 50 states and the District of Columbia," 51 outlines "detail the rights of reporters and other citizens to see information and attend meetings of state and local governments." The fourth edition has been updated to include the latest on disclosure of drivers', voter registration, and autopsy records, and is available as a one-volume print source, on CD-ROM, or online at www.rcfp.org/tapping/. Also included is this appeal: "The Reporters Committee for Freedom of the Press is pleased to make this comprehensive guide to open records and meeting laws available to you at no cost. We hope you will find it useful and consider buying a copy (or just contributing directly) to help underwrite our efforts and enable us to keep producing publications that help journalists overcome the daily legal hurdles they encounter."

Most of these guides are divided into separate sections on access to records and access to meetings, and answer questions on requesting records (including what and whose records are covered), fees, exemptions and other limitations, open and closed record categories (bank, hospital, personnel, police records), obtaining records, and court actions. The section on meetings focuses on statutes, exemptions and other limitations, open and closed meeting categories (e.g., budget sessions, parole board meetings, real estate negotiations), and right of access. The Reporters Committee for Freedom of the Press (entry 776) produces numerous how-to-do-it guides for reporters, and this is the most ambitious and comprehensive to date.

429.   Thomas, Erwin K., and Brown H. Carpenter, eds. Handbook on Mass Media in the United States: The Industry and Its Audiences. Westport, CT: Greenwood Press, 1994. 325p. illus. index. LC 93-30984. ISBN 0-313-27811-3.

"The Industry" consists of advertising, books, cable, films, magazines, newspapers, public relations, radio, recordings, and television; "Its Audiences" are comprised of minorities, women, children and youth, the disabled, religious audiences, and sports fans. Contributors are authorities, and include the likes of Maurine Beasley and Bruce Garrison. Succinct industry and audience profiles average 20 pages in length and include selective bibliographies. Tables and figures (e.g., "Rankings of Newspapers on Coverage of Women," "Daily Newspaper Reading Audience," "The Structure of the Record Industry") further enhance the readability and accessibility of this well-organized source aimed primarily at college students and general readers seeking definitions and general overviews.

430.　Ward, Jean, and Kathleen A. Hansen. **Search Strategies in Mass Communication.** 3d ed. New York: Longman, 1997. 371p. index. LC 96-33780. ISBN 0-8013-1755-X.

　　　This textbook presents a model for mass communication research that can easily be adapted for use as a handbook. Searching the literature of mass communications can be a strenuous experience, but Ward and Hansen, of the University of Minnesota School of Journalism and Mass Communication, demystify and simplify the process. Chapters on "Digging into Institutions," "Approaching Libraries: Tactics and Tools," and a revised chapter on "Using Electronic Information and Data Tools" identify specific reference sources and other library tools and discuss public and private institutions. Additional chapters cover interviewing, polls and surveys, selecting and synthesizing information, and social responsibility and the search strategy. New to this edition is a case study that illustrates each step of the search strategy model. General and topical tool indexes ease the user into the valuable contents.

431.　West, Bernadette, Peter M. Sandman, and Michael R. Greenberg, eds. **The Reporter's Environmental Handbook.** 2d ed. New Brunswick, NJ: Rutgers Univ. Press, 1995. 346p. index.

　　　Brief articles on 27 health and environmental issues, covering subjects from asbestos to leaking underground storage tanks, make up the bulk of this well-designed and well-written handbook aimed at reporters seeking background on this broad topic. Carefully vetted by experts in the field, this book also is an excellent ready reference source for librarians and a primer for students. Briefings include sections on "Identifying the Problem," "Correcting the Problem," "Pitfalls," and "Sources for Journalists." Some articles include "Important Points for Researching a Story"; for example, in the briefing on incinerators, reporters are reminded to "Find out how much it will cost to burn a load of trash. Because of the technology, incinerators can cost more than landfills in the short-run." Also included are essays on "The Language of Risk," "Handling an Environmental Emergency: A Case Study in Finding Sources," and "Tracking Down a Company's Environmental Record," as well as an invaluable glossary, defining terms such as baghouse, aggregate risk, bottom ash, cluster, daughter products, hazardous identification, surface water, and threshold limit value.

SELECTED CAREER GUIDES AND HANDBOOKS

432.　Adams, Jeff, and Jim Blau. **Job Surfing: Media and Entertainment: Using the Internet to Find a Job and Get Hired.** New York: Princeton Review Publishing, 2002. ISBN 0-375-76236-1. 339p. index.

　　　More entertainment than media-focused, this is nonetheless a current career guide for both college students and working professionals seeking to begin or change careers. The tone is glib, the language is the jargon of the industries, and the authors write with unbridled enthusiasm—"So read on with your computer fired up and at the ready so you can point and click your way along as you separate the wheat from the chaff." The "Entertainment and the Media: The Present" chapter is divided into sections on television, film, and stage; music; media; graphic design; and "desk jobs"; the section on media is further subdivided into Journalists and Broadcast Media Technicians. Listed are job sites on the Web as well as news organizations that offer internships. A useful section on "Online Tips, Tools, and Tricks" offers advice on honing computer skills, learning basic Internet information, creating online résumés, and locating online job resources. In addition, more than 100 job-related Web sites are critically reviewed. Journalismjobs.com is cited for being "the very model for what an industry-specific job site should be: It's professionally designed and maintained, is easy to navigate, has a large number of current job postings, and is entirely free." On the author's five-microphone scale, with "zero microphones being 'completely useless' and five microphones being 'visit it, bookmark it, use it,'" it receives a stellar five microphone rating. (101hollywood.com, on the other hand, receives one microphone and is "most useful for: finding out how many clueless people there are out there who would really like to be working in the film industry.")

433.   Ferguson, Donald L., and Jim Patten. **Opportunities in Journalism Careers.** rev. ed. Lincolnwood, IL: VGM Career Books, 2001. 149p. LC 00-53372. ISBN 0-658-01050-6.

In the foreword to this compact, yet invaluable overview guide, Morley Safer writes, "If you are too lazy or too sure of yourself to 'go look it up,' don't even think of becoming a reporter." He also says, "I do not know of a single soul who fell into this line of work. It is not the kind of job that you might want to do, it is work that you must do. There are, for some, enormous financial rewards, but generally the reward is in the work itself." The authors then go on to describe that work in chapters on the nature of newspaper work, electronic media, magazines and newsletters, public relations, and supporting careers. Especially valuable are the appendixes, with recommended reading lists, societies and associations, and colleges and universities with journalism programs. There is no index, but students who are considering a journalism degree and anyone seeking basic journalism career information will want to read this cover to cover.

434.   **The Journalist's Road to Success: A Career and Scholarship Guide.** Princeton, NJ: Dow Jones Newspaper Fund, 1962– . Annual.

This directory is consistently the most timely, accurate, and comprehensive guide for budding journalists in search of career guidance and financial aid. Endorsed by the Association for Education in Journalism and Mass Communication and the Association of Schools of Journalism and Mass Communication, this is an essential source for anyone seeking a journalism scholarship, and is now available online at djnewspaperfund.dowjones.com/fund/. There are sections on news careers, choosing the right college, online opportunities, and internships. Other sections focus on "Applying for a Newspaper Job," "Before the Interview," "What to Do When the Phone Rings," "Skills Test," and "Your Resume." The bulk of the guide is the chapter on "Jobs, Scholarships, Internships and Groups," which is further subdivided into state-by-state lists of colleges offering journalism and mass communications majors. In addition, it contains comprehensive information on minority scholarships and fellowships, minority internships, minority training programs, job fairs, general grants, scholarships and internships, and continuing education grants. This should be the first stop for any student considering a newspaper career.

435.   Mogel, Leonard. **The Magazine: Everything You Need to Know to Make It in the Magazine Business.** Sewikley, PA: GATFPress, 2001. 4th ed. 224p. ISBN 0-88362-223-8.

436. Mogel, Leonard. **The Newspaper: Everything You Need to Know to Make It in the Newspaper Business.** Sewikley, PA: GATFPress, 2000. 248p. LC 99-64460. ISBN 0-88362-235-1.

437. Mogel, Leonard. **Creating Your Career in Communications and Entertainment.** Sewikley, PA: GATFPress, 2001. ISBN 0-88362-208-4.

Mogel has produced a series of informal media career guides, similar in scope and format, with many offering his "tips and sage advice."

Whether planning a career as an animatronics specialist or foreign correspondent, those interested in book publishing, magazine publishing, newspaper publishing, television, radio, movies, special effects, advertising, public relations, or new media will discover a load of practical advice for getting a foot in the door in the *Creating Your Career in Communications and Entertainment* volume. Those seeking more specific guidance to careers in journalism, however, will be better served by Mogel's *The Newspaper* or *The Magazine*. In *The Newspaper,* for example, he writes, "For quick, analytic reporting of news events, newspapers clearly win the media war. This book discusses the medium as it exists today and how it is meeting competition from the other deliverers of news." Chapters include overviews of *USA Today, The Wall Street Journal,* and *The New York Times*; small newspapers; newspaper companies; writing departments, Sunday papers, news-gathering services, newspaper design, operation, circulation, advertising, marketing, new media, newspaper organizations, and publications. "The Case for Journalism School" is a brief but detailed examination of the largest and top-rated schools. Searching for information on newspapers, magazines, Web sites, and other resources, however, can be tedious and time-intensive; indexes in all volumes would make them far more accessible. Mogel also is the author of *Making It in Broadcasting* (Collier, 1994).

438. Morgan, Bradley J., ed. **Magazines Career Directory: A Practical, One-Stop Guide to Getting a Job in Magazine Publishing.** 5th ed. Detroit, MI: Visible Ink Press, a division of Gale Research, 1993. 318p. (Career Advisor Series). ISBN 0-8103-9440-5.

439. Morgan, Bradley J., ed. **Newspapers Career Directory: A Practical One-Stop Guide to Getting a Job in Newspaper Publishing.** 4th ed. Detroit, MI: Visible Ink Press, a division of Gale Research, 1993. 344p. (Career Advisor Series). ISBN 0-8103-9438-3.

440. Morgan, Bradley J., ed. **Radio and Television Career Directory: A Practical One-Stop Guide to Getting a Job in Radio and Television.** 2d ed. Detroit, MI: Gale Research, 1993. 334p. (Career Advisor Series). ISBN 0-8103-5612-0.

These somewhat dated titles from the Career Advisor Series (formerly part of the Career Directory Series published by Career Press) are vastly improved and far more readable products than their predecessors. Gone are the encouraging and annoying gung-ho platitudes. The user is left with "Advice from the Pro's" (background articles written by experts in the field), a section on "The Job Search Process" (from résumés to networking), and a job opportunities databank (an alphabetical listing of publishers or stations with hiring information and job opportunities). Volumes are similar in format and each contains a master index. Articles in the radio and television volume range from "The TV Weatherperson: Where Illusion and Science Meet" to "Becoming a Producer Isn't Hard Unless You Want to Be a Good One." The newspaper and magazine volumes are just as diverse and focus on both business and editorial careers.

441. Seguin, James A. **Media Career Guide: Preparing for Jobs in the 21st Century.** 3d ed. Boston, MA: Bedford/St. Martin's, 2002. 92p. index. LC 20-01091362. ISBN 0-312-39556-6.

This concise, down-to-earth guide offers sound career advice and, according to the author, "attitude checks" for college students majoring in media and communications. Users will home in on two specific sections on "Where the Jobs Are" and the "Job Directory," which are further subdivided by subjects such as advertising, institutional communications, magazine publishing, new media, radio, television, video games/interactive, and video production. The bulk of the handbook is 33 "tips," ranging from "Promote yourself without being obnoxious" to "Don't burn your bridges." Sample résumés also are included.

442. Swann, Phil, and Ed Achorn. **How to Land a Job in Journalism.** Betterway Books, 1988. 180p. LC 88-019401. ISBN 1-55870-101-X.

Even though this is not a recently published title, it offers some practical advice and provides a reality check for those considering a career in journalism. Chapters focus on competition in a tight job market, getting started, job interview tips, and an effective "Loading Your Weapon" chapter on cover letters and résumés. Actual letters (names and dates are blacked out) are used to illustrate what *not* to do. For example, one editor's response to a sloppy résumé is as follows: "The resume is a mess. If you can't do better than cross out the name of the motel you lived in and hand write a new address, you're not going to get far." It even has an index.

Other titles of potential interest include: *The Mulligan Guide to Sports Journalism Careers* (VGM Career Horizons, 1998); *Vault Reports Career Guide to Media and Entertainment* (Vault Reports, 2003); *The News Media* (Lucent Books, 2002); *Getting Started in Journalism* (NTC, 1997); *Career Opportunities in Television, Video and Multimedia* (Facts on File, 1999); *Career Opportunities for Writers* (Facts on File, 2000); *Breaking Into Broadcasting* (KasterZ, 1996); *How to Launch Your Career in TV News* (VGM, 1993); *Job Surfing: Media and Entertainment* (Princeton Review Publishing, 2002); and *Opportunities in Television and Video Careers* (McGraw-Hill, 2003). In addition, some professional organizations publish career handbooks and guides or make them available on their Web sites; see chapter 14 for URLs.

10
Stylebooks

Many newspapers adhere to Associated Press style, but determine their own rules and guidelines for local issues and names. As a result, these newspapers produce electronic or print stylebooks primarily for in-house use. For the most part, this chapter includes the best-known, most widely used, and most widely available newspaper, magazine, and broadcast stylebooks. Also included in this chapter are selected books on English-language usage aimed primarily at the journalist.

443. Bagnall, Nicholas. **Newspaper Language**. Oxford, England: Focal Press, 1993. 221p. ISBN 0-7506-0399-2.

Bagnall sets the tone of this handbook on the first page of chapter 1, "What Is Newspaper English?" He writes that "you would have to be a very pompous journalist before you could write that someone was 'making every endeavour to locate a document.' You leave that kind of thing to your bank manager. You write, as you would say, 'He is doing his best to find it'. Bank managers write in that way because they are unwilling to admit that they have lost something and they want to keep their dignity."

Banker bashing aside, this is a survey of and commentary on British newspaper writing. It is not a standard stylebook or usage guide, but does include chapters on "Journalism and Journalese," "Bad Habits," "The Personal Touch: Questions of Style," "Punctuation," and "Grammar." The index is detailed, which is helpful, as chapter subheadings are sometimes opaque. The "Sequence and Structure" chapter, for example, is subdivided as follows: "Storytelling props: 'As'—'After'—'Following'—'Before'—Ways of avoiding Clutter—Clauses within clauses—Chinese puzzles—Double conditionals—Art of short sentences—Uncoiling a serpent—A good example." It is interesting to note that Bagnall frequently ignores his own advice by using passive voice instead of active, using "pedantic and oratorical" speech when there are "perfectly good equivalents in ordinary speech," and wasting words. Most users seeking style and language guidance will be better served by sources such as Berner's *Language Skills for Journalists* (entry 444) and Bernstein's *The Careful Writer* (entry 445).

444. Berner, R. Thomas. **Language Skills for Journalists.** 2d ed. Boston, MA: Houghton-Mifflin, 1984. 249p. index. LC 83-82323. ISBN 0-395-34098-5.

Designed as a journalism textbook, "a number of changes have been implemented [in this second edition] to make the book easier to use as a reference." These changes include the use of subheadings, a glossary, and a list of frequently misspelled words. Berner admits that "grammar is not a sexy topic. 'Investigative journalism' sounds exciting; 'grammar' doesn't. But grammar describes the writing and speaking characteristics of a people. And journalism students should realize that if they want their stories read or listened to, they must adhere to their readers' and listeners' conventions of grammar." Berner meets journalists on their own turf, using examples of correct and incorrect grammar in newspapers, magazines, and newscasts. Chapters on writing, sentences and paragraphs, functional grammar, conventional grammar, modification, punctuation, and meaning are further subdivided. For example, the chapter on writing includes subsections on "Needless Detail," "Stating the Obvious," "Weak Phrasing," and "Prepositional Pile-Up." So well organized is the table of contents that the user probably will have no need to consult the index, which also is a model of organization and detail.

Especially useful to the journalist is the discussion of meaning. A single misused word can change the whole tone and meaning of an article or newscast. Here the author explores "high-sounding words and phrases," tampering with meaning, and double meanings, using examples such as "mandatory flotation device," "locational preference," and "combat emplacement evacuator" (a shovel). Berner says, "Ignorance may be an excuse for talking and writing like this, but it is not an excuse for journalists reporting such nonsense."

445. Bernstein, Theodore M. **The Careful Writer: A Modern Guide to English Usage.** New York: Atheneum Press, 1965. 487p. LC 65-12404. ISBN 0-689-70555-7.

Even those who are not prone to reading dictionaries and encyclopedias will delight in *The Careful Writer.* Bernstein, an assistant managing editor of *The New York Times* who died in 1979, was a wordsmith who tempered his criticisms with witticisms. He writes: "A monologophobe (you won't find it in the dictionary) is a writer who would rather walk naked in front of Sak's Fifth Avenue than be caught using the same word more than once in three lines. What he suffers from is synonymomania (you won't find that one, either) which is a compulsion to call a spade successively a 'garden implement' and an 'earth turning tool.' The affliction besets journalists in general and sports writers in particular...The simple verb 'say' never seems to be good for more than one inning; then writers or editors feel they must rush in all kinds of bush league relief pitchers."

He also writes, "Thus, unless one belongs to that tiny minority who can speak directly and beautifully, one should not write as he talks. To do so is to indulge in a kind of stenography, not writing." He goes a step further and tells us where these guidelines to good usage have come from: "practices of reputable scholars and writers, past and present...observations and discoveries of linguistic scholars...predilections of teachers of English...observation of what makes for clarity, precision, and logical presentation...personal preferences of the author—and why not (After all, it's my book)...experience in critical examination of the written word as an editor of *The New York Times.*"

Arranged in dictionary format, most examples of use and abuse were taken from newspapers. Bernstein also is the author of *Do's, Don'ts, and Maybes of English Usage* (Times Books, 1977); *Miss Thistlebottom's Hobgoblins* (Simon & Schuster, [c1971], 1984); and *Watch Your Language* (Macmillan, 1965).

446. Block, Mervin. **Rewriting Network News: Wordwatching Tips from 345 TV and Radio Scripts.** Chicago: Bonus Books, 1990. 221p. index. LC 90-80011. ISBN 0-929387-15-5.

Block writes: "Though mistakes are often our best teachers, no one has awarded prizes for the most memorable mistakes of the year. The Museum of Broadcasting hasn't showcased mistakes. And no one has published a collection of faulty news scripts. Writers have had no opportunity to learn from a broad range of other newswriters' mistakes—until now. To help meet the need, this book provides examples from several hundred flawed scripts, plus correction, comments and suggestions for improvement."

Although not a traditional style guide, this is an effective approach to identifying and correcting problems in grammar, style, and broadcast writing. Block was hired by CBS News in 1977 to be the style and mistake watchdog. He reviewed all radio and television scripts and produced a weekly newsletter ("The project's intention was to spotlight sins, not sinners").

Included in this book are those faulty scripts, his memos, and suggestions. Each is printed in a different typeface, so using this source is a bit confusing at first.

Entries are arranged alphabetically and include discussions ranging from "Farther/Further" to "Host," for which Block uses the following example: "Today Mr. Carter is hosting a meeting in Plains, Georgia, dealing with economic matters." Block writes that "host" is a noun, not a verb, and goes on to list other nouns that "careful writers don't use as verbs: author (authored), ax (axed), gift (gifted), guest, (guested), impact (impacted), mentor (mentored), message (messaged), parent (parented). Block will have even the most careful writer blushing in embarrassment and scurrying to retrieve and correct copy. Under "Superfluous Words," Block cites that "People were handing beer out to anyone and everyone, kissing total strangers and shouting again and again." " 'Total' is unneeded," according to the author. "Also avoid 'perfect strangers.' No one is perfect. And no bystanders are innocent." Block also is the author of *Writing Broadcast News—Shorter, Sharper, Stronger: A Professional Handbook* (Bonus Books, 1997), *Writing News for TV and Radio* (Bonus Books, 1999), and *Broadcast Newswriting: The RTNDA Reference Guide* (Bonus Books, 1994). For a similar, but crankier, critique of newspaper writing, consult Roscoe C. Born's *The Suspended Sentence* (Scribner, 1986; Iowa State University Press, 1993).

447. Botts, Jack. **The Language of News: A Journalist's Pocket Reference.** Ames, IA: Iowa State University Press, 1994. 216p. index. LC 93-29910. ISBN 0-8138-2494-X.

"Journalists need grammar," says Botts, "despite some educational theories to the contrary." He continues, "This effort will have been worthwhile if the volume survives the test of all such work: daily use by journalists who care."

He also writes that the English language "rewards the serious and the patient, those students of language who always try to improve and who place the audience and the audience's understanding first." This well-organized manual aimed at the journalist writing on deadline is arranged in sections on grammar, common language blunders, usage (with very effective chapters on "Close Doesn't Count" and "Sham, Scam, Puff and Fluff"), and the news story. Botts uses many practical examples to illustrate, for example, wrong case of pronouns or the difference between "after" and "following." "Years of service on Associated Press Managing Editors Writing and Editing Committees gave me hundreds of examples for raw material," he says. "Editors throughout the nation may recognize some of their examples taken from wire stories." True to its title, the book itself can actually fit in a large pocket, and is more portable and less threatening than larger tomes. What's more, the table of contents and index provide quick and easy access.

448. Bremner, John B. **Words on Words: A Dictionary for Writers and Others Who Care About Words.** New York: Columbia University Press, 1980. 406p. LC 80-256. ISBN 0-231-04492-5; 0-231-04493-3 (pbk).

Bremner has the journalist in mind as he writes in the introduction, "I have witnessed the steady growth of literary ignorance during a career of more than a third of a century as a professional journalist, a professor of journalism and a newspaper consultant." But he doesn't scold the students of journalism. He blames the teachers, "many of whom either blame their students' previous teachers or pass the buck to later ones. Worse, many young teachers are being taught not to teach grammar. What used to be the first art of the trivium has become trivial." With his position on that issue firmly established, Bremner goes on to define and discuss words and their correct and incorrect usage, and includes "some verbal gamesmanship and excursions into mythology and literary allusion." A "gatekeeper," for example, is " 'communicologese' for editor, a gatekeeper is one who mans a gate to control what copy will get through him and how it will be played. Rarely in the history of the press has an editor ever identified himself as a gatekeeper." The book is arranged in dictionary format. And speaking of words, researchers might also wish to consult the Banished Words Web site maintained at Lake Superior State University (www.lssu.edu/banished/), where one may submit a word or phrase for "banishment."

449.   Brooks, Brian S., James L. Pinson, and Jean Gaddy Wilson. **Working With Words: A Handbook for Media Writers and Editors.** 5th ed. Boston: Bedford/St. Martin's, 2003. 369p. LC 20-02103649. ISBN 0-312-39790-9.

"With employers complaining that too many recent college graduates are deficient in language skills, it's falling more and more on journalism educators to fill the gap that secondary education has too often left," according to the authors. They continue, "The challenge is to lift even some of the brightest students from what employers consider a remedial level of grammar and usage understanding to that demanded of working professionals. That's what we're trying to do in this book, and that's part of what we think sets it apart from others." In this they succeed. This thoroughly revised and updated edition is both handy and hefty, packed with detailed explanations of and solutions to grammar and usage problems that working journalists encounter daily. It will be especially helpful to harried copy editors on deadline, as both the table of contents and index are well organized. Part 1, "Grammar and Usage," is arranged in chapters on phrases, clauses and sentences; subjects and objects, subject-verb agreement; verbs; modifiers; connecting words; and usage. Part 2 is "Mechanics," focusing on punctuation and spelling. Part 3 is "Style," with chapters on "Writing as a Journalist," "Sexism, Racism, and Other 'isms'," and conciseness. A new section on "Writing Methods for Different Media" addresses varying issues in writing for news, broadcast, and the online media. Also included in each chapter are resources available on the Web.

This is a unique guide in that it illuminates grammatical errors and flawed writing, but offers effective and matter-of-fact first aid without making the writer or editor feel moronic.

450.   Campbell, Richard M. **Stylebook.** Toronto: The Toronto Star, 1983. 148p.

A one-page introduction set in 14-point type and an understated title are the only introductory materials to 148 pages of *Toronto Star* style. Managing editor Ray Timson writes, "Campbell used every reference book he could find and assessed changes in style recommended by a host of *Star* editors over the years. And then he began writing, and I think you will find passages here that are absolutely delightful and unique among contemporary stylebooks." If stylebooks can be delightful, surely this one qualifies. It would be nice to know, however, which style and usage books and dictionaries Campbell used most frequently. On "Xanthippic," Campbell says, "Xanthippe was the name of Socrates' shrewish wife, and by extension, it applies to any peevish and ill-tempered woman. But you'd be xanthippic too if you had to put up with the Socratic method all day long." There is no index. "No index is necessary," counters Timson. "Everything we have to say about spelling, punctuation, abbreviation, libel, contempt of court, is listed alphabetically." This is true. Campbell has produced a most engaging, frequently humorous, and occasionally brilliant book of Canadian newspaper usage and style. Would that other stylebooks were written with such flair.

451. **The Canadian Press Stylebook: A Guide for Writers and Editors.** Toronto, Canada: The Canadian Press, 1993. index. ISBN 0-920009-10-7. (The following description is based on the 1993 edition. A 12th edition was published in 2002.)

The official stylebook of The Canadian Press has undergone numerous revisions since its first edition in 1940, and, according to the introduction, it has now "been redone from intro to index" with every chapter "freshened or revised to reflect the priorities and sensitivities of the '90s." Previous editions were arranged alphabetically by subject; the new edition groups material in the following categories: policies, general, legal, the working journalist, useful tools, and illustrating the news. The index is particularly well designed and allows easy access to the contents. This is fortunate, as material in the general section ranges from obituaries to foreign news, and grammar and style are dealt with in the "useful tools" section. This spiral-bound guide is a formidable publication, nearly 500 pages long, and covers in impressive detail both the major issues and minutiae of newspaper writing and editing. Other Canadian Press publications include the *BN Stylebook* (broadcast news) and the *Guide du Journaliste for French-language writing.* The Canadian Press also publishes *BN NewsTalk,* focusing on broadcast news, and *The Canadian Press Caps and Spelling.*

452. Cappon, Rene J. **The Associated Press Guide to Good Writing.** Reading, MA: Addison-Wesley, 1982. 140p. LC 82-73305. ISBN 0-201-10320-6.

The AP Guide to Good Writing is best described by Jack Cappon himself. This is "extended shoptalk—a continuation of the discussions, formal and informal, with newswriters intent on improving themselves in their craft." Here are Cappon's rules on and gripes about the use and abuse of language. According to the introductory material, however, the book cannot adequately describe "the gurgles and sighs and the groans that rise from behind his desk when he comes upon sentences that are particularly well turned or upon writing that is lazy or pompous or dull." Cappon, AP newsfeatures editor, offers a loosely organized volume with no index, so the user will have to browse, skim, and scan. The table of contents can lead you to general areas of interest such a news writing, leads, tone, pitfalls, quotes, color ("small, specific detail"), pseudo-color (clichés, etc.), features, and usage.

He concludes with a "Bestiary" section, a "compendium for the careful and the crotchety" or "a collection of usages which I regard as bestial." Of "literally," Cappon writes, "Disastrous as a casual intensifier because it means that something is factually and precisely true. The Mets literally slaughtered the Cardinals last night would have left at least nine corpses. I would never use literally in a million years. I mean that figuratively." And on one of his favorite phrases, "pre-dawn darkness": "Hackneyed journalese. Write pre-dawn darkness if you're also prepared to write pre-dusk brightness. It is a poetic phrase that has been worked to death, that's all. A substitute is needed. How about 'ere Aurora rose'? No? Then let us return, simply, to before dawn." Cappon's admonishments are enough to strike fear in the hearts of all. He says, "If you write disinterested when you mean uninterested you are wrong, period. Other entries, I admit, may be open to discussion—but not if I'm handling the copy." Enough said. This is a lively companion volume to the *Associated Press Stylebook and Briefing on Media Law* (entry 461). Cappon also wrote *The Associated Press Guide to News Writing* (IDG Books, 2000) and *The Associated Press Guide to Punctuation* (entry 453).

453.   Cappon, Rene J. **The Associated Press Guide to Punctuation.** Perseus, 2002. 96p. LC 20-2112483. ISBN 0-7382-0785-3.

Described as a companion volume to *The Associated Press Stylebook* and *Briefing on Media Law* (entry 461), this is a witty and wise rulebook on punctuation. "For many millenniums, language meant speech and speech only," writes Cappon. "Not until some Mesopotamian spoilsports devised a workable alphabet did writing make the scene, albeit in cuneiform and solely for commercial use or to lavish fulsome praise on kings and kinglets." He continues, "It was to make up for the loss of speech accouterments that punctuation gradually developed." Arranged alphabetically from ampersand to slash, brief chapters explore the use and misuse of 16 punctuation marks. On the semicolon: "The semicolon is a compromise. It drifts, somewhat nebulously, between the period and the comma. To be pedantic, the semicolon means a shorter pause than the period and a longer pause than the comma. Long or short pause, good stylists try to avoid it as too formal; decked out, as it were, in a starched shirt and a black suit. You would do well to keep semicolons at a minimum. There usually are options." Cappon also is the author of *The Associated Press Guide to News Writing* (IDG Books, 2000) and *The Associated Press Guide to Good Writing* (entry 452).

454.   **The Chicago Manual of Style.** 15th ed. Chicago, IL: The University of Chicago Press, 2003. 956p. index. LC 20-03001860. ISBN 0-226-10403-6.

Although not a newspaper or broadcast style manual, the formidable *Chicago Manual of Style* is used most frequently in book and magazine publishing. First published in 1906, this fifteenth edition now contains extensive discussions on electronic and online publishing. The first four sections are concerned with aspects of bookmaking, such as manuscript preparation, copyediting, proofs, and rights and permissions. The bulk of the book is the detailed style section with chapters on punctuation, spelling, names and terms, numbers, foreign languages, quotations, illustrations and captions, tables, mathematics in type, abbreviations, documentation, indexes, and so on. Other useful references are Joseph M. Williams's *Style,* also published by the University of Chicago Press; *United States Government Printing Office Style Manual* (2000) for printers, writers, and editors; and *Electronic Style: A Guide to Citing Electronic Information* (Mecklermedia, 1996).

455.   Copperud, Roy H. **American Usage and Style: The Consensus.** New York: Van Nostrand Reinhold, 1980. 433p. LC 79-11055. ISBN 0-442-21630-0; 0-442-24906-3 (pbk).

"Disputed points" of usage are compared in this consolidation and revision of Copperud's *A Dictionary of Usage and Style* (Hawthorn, 1964) and *American Usage: The*

Consensus (Van Nostrand Reinhold, 1970). Consulted for this consensus were: Bernstein's *The Careful Writer* (entry 445); Margaret M. Bryant's *Current American Usage* (Crowell, 1965); Copperud's own *A Dictionary of Usage and Style* (Hawthorne, 1964); Bergen and Cornelia Evans's *A Dictionary of Contemporary American Usage* (Random House, 1957), Rudolf Flesch's *The ABC of Style* (Harper & Row, 1964); Wilson Follett's *Modern American Usage* (Hill & Wang, 1966); H. W. Fowler's *A Dictionary of Modern English Usage* (Oxford University Press, 1965); and several dictionaries including Webster's *New International Dictionary, Third Edition; Random House Dictionary of the English Language;* and the first edition of the *Oxford English Dictionary.* "I decided that a more useful purpose would be served by comparing the views of these books, and indicating where the weight of opinion lay," writes Copperud.

Entries are arranged in dictionary format and range in length from a few lines to several pages. If an entry contains only one opinion, then it is the consensus of the authorities. Copperud writes, "Dictionaries of usage often disagree, but they have one quality in common: prescription. It could not be otherwise, for the authors are saying to the reader, 'I know best.' Yet correct usage, whatever that may be, is not a matter of revealed truth, but oftener than not reflects taste or opinion."

The entry for "critique" reads as follows: "Criticized by Evans, Flesch, and Fowler as pretentious for criticism, review, notice. This view seems dated and pedantic. Dictionaries give it as standard as a noun, but only Webster lists it as a verb (critique the performance). The use is widespread, however, and will probably gain recognition." Even though this is a consensus, Copperud gives himself the last word.

456. Crump, Spencer. **The Stylebook for Newswriting: A Manual for Newspapers, Magazines, and Radio/TV.** Corona del Mar, CA: Trans-Anglo, 1979. 112p. LC 79-2440. ISBN 0-87046-052-8; 0-87046-051-X (pbk).

According to Crump, "this guide, unlike the wire services' stylebooks, is intended primarily for the writer associated with a local newspaper, radio/TV news outlet or magazine." Entries are arranged alphabetically and focus more on style than basic English usage because "the journalist should be a person who knows how to use our language because of schooling and aptitude." He also says this book is compatible with the *Associated Press Stylebook and Briefing on Media Law* (entry 461) and the *UPI Stylebook* (entry 484), although its emphasis is on local news. For example, he allows a "more avant garde position" on courtesy titles and provides guides for writing about local sports.

457. **Disability Style Guide.** San Francisco, CA: National Center on Disability and Journalism.

Available online at ncdj.org/styleguide, this brief, no-frills stylebook is described as a "work in progress, a living document," and can be downloaded as a pdf document. Users are encouraged to "copy and reproduce part or the entire style guide provided any part reproduced is distributed free or at cost of your reproduction and not for profit." Arranged alphabetically, terms such as "able-bodied," "suffers from," and "invalid" are included. "Mute," for example is described as a "derogatory term referring to a person who physically cannot speak. It also implies that people who do not use speech are unable to express themselves, which is not true." This guide offers reporters quick access and answers to disability reporting issues.

458.   The Economist Style Guide: The Bestselling Guide to English Usage. 8th ed. London: Profile Books, 2003. 169p. index. LC . ISBN 1-86197-535-X.

Formerly subtitled "The Essentials of Elegant Writing," *The Economist* takes great pride, as it should, in its writing. The introduction states that "on only two scores can *The Economist* hope to outdo its rivals consistently. One is the quality of its analysis; the other is the quality of its writing." If you want readers, according to the introduction, "do not be hectoring or arrogant. Those who disagree with you are not necessarily stupid or insane. Nobody needs to be described as silly: let your analysis prove that he is."

This new and improved edition has addressed some biased language as well. The introduction still states that we should "Avoid, where possible, euphemisms and circumlocutions promoted by interest-groups. The hearing-impaired are simply deaf." (*The Associated Press Stylebook and Briefing on Media Law* might quibble with this. "Deaf describes a person with total hearing loss. For others use *partial hearing loss* or *partially deaf.*") But the following guideline, which appeared in an earlier edition of the *Economist Style Guide* has now been removed: "It is no disrespect to the disabled sometimes to describe them as crippled."

Part 1 is "The Essence of Style," with sections on capitals, currencies, figures, hyphens, metaphors, proofreading, spelling, and titles. Part 2 offers illuminating illustrations of the differences between "American and British English," and part 3 is a "Fact Checker and Glossary," dealing with a variety of subjects ranging from currencies to stock market indexes.

This is a guide for a selected audience.

459.   Evans, Harold. Newsman's English: A Guide to Writing Lively, Lucid and Effective Prose. New York: Holt, Rinehart and Winston, 1972. (Editing and Design: A Five Volume Manual of English, Typography and Layout). 224p. index. LC 77-160163. ISBN 0-03-091349-1.

Harry Evans on "Good English": "English is a battlefield. Purists fight off invading yes-men, dropouts, hobos, killjoys, stooges, highbrows and coeds. Vulgarians beseech them to trust the people because the people speak real good. Grammarians, shocked by sentences concluding with prepositions, construct syntactical defences up with which we will not put. Officials observe that in connection with recent disturbances there does not appear to have been a resolution of the issue. And journalists race to the colourful scene to report the dramatic new moves."

In other chapters he discusses words, language, the structure of news story leads, accuracy, and editing. Other books in this five-volume collection are *Handling Newspaper Text, News Headlines, Picture Editing,* and *Newspaper Design.*

460.   Fiske, Robert Hartwell. The Dictionary of Concise Writing: 10,000 Alternatives to Wordy Phrases. Oak Park, IL: Marion Street Press, 2002. 412p. LC 20-02008142. 0-9665176-6-0.

Fiske writes that "wordiness is a flaw of style—in how we express our language. Today, the style is prevailingly shoddy. In almost everything we read and hear, there is complexity instead of simplicity and obscurity instead of clarity. This is particularly inexcusable in written material, where words can be reworked." In a talkative paragraph on the subject of wordiness, he states that "In replacing a wordy phrase by one less wordy or by a single word or in deleting the phrase altogether, I have tried to show how wordiness can encumber clarity and that it can be corrected. The sentence examples have been edited only to remedy the wordiness diagnosed; rarely are they syntactically and stylistically indefectible." The first part of the guide is divided into sections on "The Perfectibility of Words," "Of Polish and Panache," "Clues to Concision," "The Imperfectibility of People," "Wordiness Everywhere," and "The Age of Shoddiness." Part 2, the bulk of the book, is the "Dictionary of Concise Writing," where the author offers alternative wording to phrases such as "for all intents and purposes," "despite the fact that," and "close scrutiny." On the subject of "journalese," he writes, "Moreover, despite the confines of their columns, few newspaper and magazine writers have yet to learn much about using the shorter phrase or the single word." Have yet to learn much about? Fiske is the author of *The Dimwit's Dictionary: 5,000 Overused Words and Phrases and Alternatives to Them* (Marion Street Press, 2002) and editor and publisher of the online journal *The Vocabula Review* (www.vocabula.com).

461.   Goldstein, Norm, ed. **The Associated Press Stylebook and Briefing on Media Law.** rev. ed. Cambridge, MA: Perseus, 2002. 383p. LC 20-02105974. ISBN 0-7382-0740-3.

Most newspapers today either use *The Associated Press Stylebook and Briefing on Media Law* (formerly *The Associated Press Stylebook and Libel Manual*) or have designed their own stylebooks, based on AP style, to incorporate local rules and guidelines. In the style section, entries are arranged in dictionary format, and include usage information, correct and incorrect usage, abbreviations, and related topics. Some entries merely offer correct spelling and/or capitalization. A "stylebook key" illustrates how entries are organized and explains the significance of entries printed in boldface type, italics, and so on. Sports and business style issues are covered in separate sections.

The media law portion of the book explores defenses and privileges; public officials, figures, and issues; privacy; and copyright. It offers a framework for discussion of libel but is not meant to serve as a textbook on libel.

This is not a flamboyant book of wordplay and display, but it is *the* book of newspaper style. All working journalists, journalism students, and newspaper freelancers should own and consult the most current edition of this stylebook. But do not ignore other books of style and usage such as the incomparable *The Elements of Style* (entry 481). For a lengthy discussion of bias in writing—an issue many stylebooks fail to address in any detail—see Marilyn Schwartz's *Guidelines for Bias-Free Writing* (entry 478).

462.   Grover, Robert O., ed. **U.S. News & World Report Stylebook: A Usage Guide for Writers and Editors.** 9th ed. Washington, D.C.: U.S. News & World Report LP, 2001. 246p. LC 20-01001693. ISBN 1-931469-10-5.

According to the spare introduction, "Most of the entries provide cold, dry, practical answers to such value-free questions as whether certain numbers should be rendered in words or in figures. Other entries go to the heart and soul of a publication, encompassing everything from how to deal with quotations that include vulgarity and obscenity to how to handle language that reflects gender, racial, ethnic, or religious bias." Entries, ranging from "guerrillas/gorillas" to "sentence rhythm," are alphabetically arranged in this comprehensive and clear style guide. Users are reminded that "for questions not explicitly addressed in this book, use analogy and, should that fail, use common sense in consultation with the style editor." An interesting side note: *U.S. News & World Report* supports adult literacy programs with a percentage of profits from stylebook sales.

463. Hale, Constance, and Jessie Scanlon. **Wired Style: Principles of English Usage in the Digital Age.** New York: Broadway Books, 1999. 198p. index. LC 99-087038. ISBN 0-7679-0372-2.

"You might call *Wired Style* an experiment in nonlinear, networked editing," according to the authors. "When a new technical term, a bullshit buzzword, or an especially gnarly acronym hits our screens, we send emails to various editors and style divas. *Wired Style* is the result of those online discussions, which are guided by actual usage rather than rigid rules. When it comes to a choice between what's on the Web and what's in Webster's, we tend to go with the Web. Like new media, *Wired Style* is dynamic and rule-averse." With that context provided in the lively and irreverent introduction (and with a nod of apology to Strunk), journalists and new media writers will find good uses for this unique, specialized, digital age stylebook. Arranged alphabetically, entries include attention economy, backward compatibility, disintermediation, Hacker Ethic, YOYOW (that's "you own your own words"), skunkworks, and meatspace. A separate Style FAQ answers questions such as: "If someone sends me an email—or posts something to the Net—can I cite it in a published article?" and "Do email quotes differ from spoken quotes?" The authors advise online journalists to "Write the way people talk. Don't insist on 'standard' English. Use the vernacular, especially that of the world you're writing about. And avoid lowest-common-denominator editing: don't sanitize and don't homogenize."

464. Hicks, Wynford. **English for Journalists.** 2d ed. London: Routledge, 1998. 144p. index. ISBN 0-415-17008-7.

This spare but frequently eloquent British guide addresses fundamental style and grammar problems with clarity and politeness. It is divided into sections on the use of English, grammar (rules, mistakes, and confusions), spelling, punctuation, reporting speech, house style, style, and words. On jargon, Hicks writes, "The computer industry has spawned its own ugly terminology—answer-back, boot up, end-user, formatted, throughput, input, hardware, software. It is apt for that industry since it conveys particular, precise meanings to those who work with computers." He continues, "But journalists (except those on computer magazines) should avoid such terms as 'throughput'. We already have words to describe those ideas. They may be less trendy, but they are at least as clear as computer jargon and certainly more elegant." Hicks also is the author of *Writing for Journalists* (Routledge, 1999).

465. Holley, Frederick S. **Los Angeles Times Stylebook.** New York: New American Library, 1979, 1981. 239p. LC 80-28897. ISBN 0-452-00552-3.

Each page of this style and usage book illuminates the blunders and gaffes we make as communicators. Although it emphasizes newspaper style for the *Los Angeles Times* and uses numerous examples from Southern California, "this present volume is intended to be of help to anyone engaged in writing or editing—not just *Times* staff members, not just newspaper people, not just journalism students." A two-page bibliography lists other style and usage books, many of which are mentioned in this chapter. There is no index, but arrangement is alphabetical and entries are cross-referenced. There is even an entry for "zzyzx," which says: "you may not believe it, but it's a good one to end an alphabetical listing with. This community near Baker was founded as a religious and health spa and is now being used as a base for desert studies by a consortium of seven California colleges. It was named with the intention of its being 'the last word in the language,' and it surely is."

466. Kalbfeld, Brad. **Associated Press Broadcast News Handbook: A Manual of Techniques & Practices.** New York: McGraw-Hill, 2001. 476p. ISBN 0-07-136388-2.

"No book is created in a vacuum, but few grow as directly from another as this one." Based on the *Associated Press Stylebook and Briefing on Media Law* (entry 461), this volume aims at radio and television journalists. Included are essays reflecting on getting, telling, and producing the story, with numerous examples, and more than 300 pages of broadcast style. Arranged alphabetically, this handbook addresses the many concerns that only broadcast journalists face. For example, the entry for "quotations in the news" reads, "Quotations are hard to handle on the air: The anchor or reporter must change inflection to telegraph that the words were said by someone else. Whenever possible, use tape. A quotation is a poor substitute for the sounds of the person saying the words. If tape isn't available, paraphrase the quote if at all possible."

467. Kessler, Lauren, and Duncan McDonald. **When Words Collide: A Media Writer's Guide to Grammar and Style.** 5th ed. Belmont, CA: Wadsworth, 2000. 240p. index. LC 99-35245. ISBN 0-534-56133-0.

"Note that the first paragraph in this chapter contains two fragments, incomplete constructions considered grammatical errors," the authors write. "We did that on purpose, not because we don't know how to write a complete sentence. We broke the full-sentence rule to create a punchy, emphatic introduction that we hoped would grab your attention. Some rules can be broken to create especial effects. But they must be known first before they can be flouted."

Aimed at students, teachers, and professionals, this guide is divided into two sections. Part 1 tackles grammar and style, with chapters on parts of speech; the sentence; agreement; case; passive voice; punctuation; spelling; the three Cs—clarity, conciseness, and coherence; style; and sense and sensitivity (covering sexism, heterosexism, racism, ageism, and able-bodyism). Part 2 is an alphabetical guide to usage and grammar. This spiral-bound book does not replace *The Associated Press Stylebook and Briefing on Media Law* (entry 461) or *The Elements of Style* (entry 481), but is appropriate for any writer needing a refresher course in grammar, or English and journalism instructors seeking an up-to-date and well-organized supplemental textbook. A useful companion volume for students is *Exercises for Kessler and McDonald's When Words Collide.* The authors, journalism faculty members at the University of Oregon, also wrote *The Search: Information Gathering for the Mass Media* (entry 412) and *Mastering the Message: Media Writing with Substance and Style* (Wadsworth, 1989).

468. Lippman, Thomas W., comp. and ed. **The Washington Post Deskbook on Style and Usage.** 2d ed. New York: McGraw-Hill, 1989. 243p. index. LC 88-26729. ISBN 0-07-068414-6.

"At a newspaper, the word 'style' has two meanings: the rules of grammar, punctuation, capitalization and usage that we apply to our written output, and the overall tone or approach," Lippman writes in the introduction. He continues, "Obviously no single tone or style of writing is appropriate for every article in a publication that reports about every subject, from the cosmic to the trivial, from the tragic to the humorous. Our writing style will change with the material. But our technical style should not."

Such is the premise of the revised edition of this well-respected stylebook. Brief chapters discuss standards and ethics, legal issues, role of the ombudsman, and writing obituaries. Then the book begins to take on the appearance of a traditional stylebook with an alphabetically arranged "Using the Language" section, which constitutes the bulk of the guide.

With Watergate, *The Washington Post* assumed a unique role in journalism. As Ben Bradlee wrote in the first edition, "Although it has become increasingly difficult for this newspaper and for the press generally to do so since Watergate, reporters should make every effort to remain in the audience, to stay off the stage, to report history, not to make history." He also writes "we fully recognize that the power we have inherited as the monop-oly morning newspaper in the capital of the free world carries with it special responsibili-ties: to listen to the voiceless, to avoid any and all acts of arrogance, to face the public with politeness and candor." These are words for all journalists, in or out of Washington, to heed.

469.   MacDonald, Ron. **A Broadcast News Manual of Style.** 2d ed. White Plains, NY: Longman, 1994. 384p. index. LC 93-6072. ISBN 0-8013-1110-1.

A lengthy introduction sets the tone of this manual of radio and television style and usage. "In broadcast writing we try to use conventional words—words our listeners are accustomed to hearing and using in their daily lives. This means broadcast news writing tends to the casual rather than the formal," MacDonald writes. He continues, "There is no attempt to make this a scholarly document." MacDonald mentions the Associated Press and United Press International guides (entries 461, 484) and says they are "excellent in most cases" but they were "adapted partly from style and usage guides that were developed for the newspaper wires where a quite different approach to newswriting is recommended." In this manual, style also includes "such things as page formats, how to cue tapes and the like, for both radio and television."

The usage guide constitutes the bulk of the volume. It is arranged in dictionary format and includes cross-references. The eight appendixes range in subject from area codes to codes of ethics. There are sections on style and formats; the law; and "Getting Words on Paper," with discussions of paragraphs, number usage, pronunciation, and lis-tener problems. There is a brief index.

In the introduction, the author writes: "There are some great writers working in broadcast newsrooms—but not many. For most, the hourly deadlines and demands for even briefer stories make graceful and precise writing impossible. But those very pressures make precision necessary. When you have only a fraction of a minute to tell a complex story, precision of language is essential—using the exact word to convey the precise thought."

On "hopefully," he advises, "Do not use HOPEFULLY as an adverb in the sense of 'it is to be hoped' at the beginning of a sentence: 'Hopefully, the car will arrive on time.' That means the car is full of hope. There's a deep urge in all of us, I think, to use hopefully and thankfully that way. Don't." And on "comparable": "Often mispronounced. It is KAHM-pur-uh-buhl."

The following guides to pronunciation in broadcasting also might be useful: *The Spoken Word: A BBC Guide* (British Broadcasting Corporation, 1982) and Eugene Ehrlich's *NBC Handbook of Pronunciation* (HarperPerennial, 1991).

470.   Macdowall, Ian, comp. **Reuters Handbook for Journalists.** Oxford, England: Butterworth-Heinemann Ltd., 1992. 183p. LC 92-5673. ISBN 0-7506-0551-0.

"The reputation of Reuters rests on its accuracy, speed and reliability." So says the dedication, which also states that this handbook is a "memorial to Ian Macdowall's passionate, life-long commitment to the highest standards of news writing." Macdowall, equipped with an Oxford English degree, worked with Reuters for 33 years as a sub-editor, foreign correspondent, and Chief News Editor, and died in 1991. Macdowall's preface states that the "cardinal principle which should underlie the work of any news agency is honesty." It is unfortunate that his preface is marred by lax copyediting (i.e., a phrase praising editors and correspondents is repeated). There is no table of contents or index; there is merely an alphabetical assembling of all that is uniquely Reuters.

According to the introduction by F. W. Hodgson, editor of Butterworth-Heinemann Media List, "Reuters, the international news organisation, has developed a keen sense of the problems of style and word accuracy in the course of collecting news and distributing it to subscriber newspapers around the world. As a result its house style guide has grown in response to the varied demands of its service until it has become a leading work of reference in its own right, with perhaps the greatest penetration and widest coverage of all new writing style books."

Users are urged to consult *The Associated Press Stylebook and Briefing on Media Law* (entry 461) and reach their own conclusions.

471.   Martin, Paul R., ed. **The Wall Street Journal Guide to Business Style and Usage.** rev. ed. New York: Simon & Schuster, 2002. 261p. LC 20-01040376. ISBN 0-7432-1295-9.

According to the introduction, "Some quirky *Journal* customs were passed along orally (as distinct from verbally) for years from copy editor to copy editor, and few even remembered their origins. A 16-page booklet for the news staff in 1970 provided a list of banned words, for example, that included buck, shift, shut and shot. Why? 'The reasons should be obvious,' the guide said, cryptically. In fact, the ban reflected editors' fears that inept or capricious typesetters would turn these innocent words into embarrassing ones." No banned wordlists are included in this revised edition of the *Wall Street Journal Stylebook,* arranged in dictionary format, and including nearly 4,000 entries. Many entries are based on *The Associated Press Stylebook and Briefing on Media Law* (entry 461).

472.   **News Watch Diversity Style Guide.** San Francisco, CA: San Francisco State University.

Available online at newswatch.sfsu.edu/guide, this is a comprehensive, current, and indispensable resource for reporters and editors. It was designed with the assistance of the Asian American Journalists Association, National Association of Black Journalists, National Association of Hispanic Journalists, National Lesbian and Gay Journalists Association, the Native American Journalists Association, the National Center of Disability and Journalism, and the South Asian Journalists Association. In addition, the Detroit Free Press's "100 Questions and Answers About Arabs: A Journalist's Guide" was consulted. Nearly 400 entries are arranged alphabetically and offer concise explanations of labels considered derogatory as well as usage of preferred terms. Entries range from "circle the wagons" ("Avoid. Offensive phrase when used to describe people who are protecting

Should I use "black-hearted" or "blind to the truth"? Is it "firefighter" or "fireman"? Is it a "developing country" or "newly industrialized country"? One of the issues journalists grapple with daily is political correctness and the language of bias. This concise and enlightening guide focuses on scholarly writing but is applicable to media writing; it is an important reference for editors, copy editors, and reporters. The author admits in the preface that "there is no such thing as truly bias-free language and that our advice is inevitably shaped by our own point of view—that of white, North American (specifically U.S.), feminist publishing professionals." She also states that "our aim is simply to encourage sensitivity to usages that may be imprecise, misleading, and needlessly offensive." Chapters cover gender; race, ethnicity, citizenship and nationality, and religion; disabilities, sexual orientation, and age. The entry for "Eskimo," for example, reads: "Of or pertaining to a group of peoples of northern Canada, Greenland, Alaska, and eastern Siberia. Although Eskimo is still widely used, it is a pejorative term that was adopted by Europeans (it means, roughly, 'eaters of raw meat'). The term Inuk (plural, Inuit) is preferred by Arctic and Canadian peoples and is the recommended alternative; also spelled with two n's: Innuk, Innuit."

The comprehensive index provides editors and reporters on deadline quick and easy access to the contents. This is an important source that should probably be an annual or biannual publication.

479. Sellers, Leslie. **Doing It In Style: A Manual for Journalists, PR Men and Copy-Writers.** London: Pergamon Press, 1968. 321p. LC 68-21107. ISBN 0-8203791-4; 0-8103791-0 (pbk).

Sellers, then production editor of the *Daily Mail,* states that this is "more than a style book—much more. It is the practical newspaperman's Fowler and should have a place at every journalist's bedside as well as in his office." Entries are arranged in dictionary format, with detailed descriptions, definitions, examples, and, of course, a British slant. For example, " 'The Queen' always takes the article, even if she makes the headline difficult by doing so. 'Queen' alone means any old queen, and that upsets people." Entries range from a few sentences to essay-length discussions of newspaper design, misused words, headlines, and picture cropping.

480. Siegal, Allan M., and William G. Connolly. **The New York Times Manual of Style and Usage.** rev. and expanded ed. New York: Times Books, 1999. 364p. LC 99-10630. ISBN 0-8129-6388-1.

"At its best, edited with restraint," according to the foreword, "style is the ingredient that enables any single issue of *The New York Times* to supply the minimum daily requirement of crisis and struggle and triumph without homogenizing the insights and wit of scores of individual writers." Further, "if that first kind of style is a form of painting, the second kind—the stylebook style—is framing and canvas. Its structure of spelling, grammar and punctuation supports and protects the writer's craft." Both "styles" are exhibited in this artfully revised edition of a standard reference tool. The foreword spells out *The New York Times's* goals and objectives in publishing this volume. Although designed for *The New York Times* writers and editors, any journalist will benefit from this close, thorough, and lively examination of newspaper style and usage. Entries are arranged alphabetically in dictionary format and range in subject from A.M.E. (African Methodist Episcopal Church) to zeitgeist ("When it appears in an English phrase, lowercase the German noun").

481.   Strunk, William Jr., and E. B. White. **The Elements of Style.** 4th ed. Boston: Allyn & Bacon, 2000. 105p. index. LC 78-18444. ISBN 0-205-31342-6; 0-205-30902-X (pbk).

These fundamentals of style and usage should be absorbed if only because E. B. White says so. In the introduction, White writes, "Amplification has reared its head in a few places in the text where I felt an assault could successfully be made in the bastions of its brevity." He continues, "The reader will soon discover that these rules and principles are in the form of sharp commands. Sergeant Strunk snapping orders to his platoon." There are 11 rules of usage, 11 principles of composition, and 21 style "suggestions." "A Few Matters of Form" discusses the use of exclamations, numerals, and hyphens ("The hyphen can play tricks on the unwary, as it did in Chattanooga when two newspapers merged—the *News* and the *Free Press.* Someone introduced a hyphen into the merger, and the paper became *The Chattanooga News-Free Press,* which sounds as though the paper were news-free or devoid of news"). A 27-page chapter contains listings of commonly misused words and expressions, arranged alphabetically. New to this edition is a foreword by Roger Angell, White's stepson. He says, "This edition has been modestly updated, with word processors and air conditioners making their first appearance among White's references, and with a light redistribution of genders to permit a feminine pronoun or female farmer to take their places among the males who once innocently served him." There is an index, but do not use it: Read it all. White concludes, "I still find the Strunkian wisdom a comfort, the Strunkian humor a delight, and the Strunkian attitude toward right and wrong a blessing undisguised." If a journalist consults but one book of rules in his or her career (besides the *Associated Press Stylebook and Briefing on Media Law,* entry 461), pray it is *The Elements of Style.*

482.   Swan, Jennifer, ed. **Sports Style Guide & Reference Manual: The Complete Reference for Sports Editors, Writers and Broadcasters.** Chicago: Triumph, 1996. 375p. ISBN 1-57243-101-6.

From high-sticking ("carrying a hockey stick above shoulder level") to oarsman ("do not change oarsman to oarswoman to reflect gender when referring to a member of a rowing crew"), this specialized stylebook is useful on both reference and sports desks. Entries in the style guide are arranged alphabetically and include correct spelling and usage guidelines. Part II contains an entry for "every major sport covered by American newspapers," and includes information on terms, governing bodies, leagues and teams, and scoring. While aimed at sports editors and writers, this resource will also be invaluable to less sports-minded individuals who don't know the difference between a triple bogey and a triple double.

483.   **21st Century Manual of Style.** Edited by the Princeton Language Institute. New York: Dell Publishing Co., 1993. 350p. LC 92-13645. ISBN 0-440-50489-9.

The self-congratulatory introduction reads like advertising copy for a new product: "breathes new relevance and flexibility into the classic style guide," "efficient and comprehensive," and "all-new, authoritative lexicographical compilation of cutting-edge information and insight." In conclusion, the introduction states that "Traditional style manuals must give way to the *21st Century Manual of Style*—a new reference standard compiled with the contemporary writer's style needs and concerns in mind." Designed by a lexicographer from the Princeton Language Institute, this guide offers easy access and answers to many style questions. Part 1, "Form: From A to Z," is alphabetically arranged and "gives concise, immediate gratification on all matters of style." Part 2 is "Description," with sections ranging from aircraft names to nobility titles. Part 3, "Rules of Punctuation," offers "grammar-at-a-glance." It is described (redundantly?) on the cover as being "completely comprehensive," but it does not, for example, offer a listing for Smokey the Bear. *The Associated Press Stylebook and Briefing on Media Law* (entry 461), however, tells us that it is "not Smokey the Bear." Use "Smokey" or "Smokey Bear." This source is useful as a supplemental style guide.

484.   UPI Stylebook. 3d ed. Lincolnwood, IL: National Textbook Company, 1992. 436p. LC 91-68422. ISBN 0-8442-5336-7.

United Press International now publishes one stylebook for both print and broadcast journalists in this revised guide subtitled "The Authoritative Handbook for Writers, Editors & News Directors." A usage guide in dictionary format makes up the bulk of this publication, but there also are sections on financial news, sports, writing for print, writing for broadcast (including phonetics and emergency coverage guidelines), libel, wire style for print and broadcast news, news pictures, and audio.

Users may wish to compare entries in *The Associated Press Stylebook and Briefing on Media Law* (entry 461) with the *UPI Stylebook*. For example, UPI defines a "rad" as follows: "Used to describe the actual exposure received by an individual. Stands for roentgen absorbed dose. Technically defined as the amount of radiation required to deliver 100 ergs of energy to 1 gram of substance. Often used interchangeably with rem by nuclear officials, but not really the same in that rad refers to the exact exposure an individual has received and rem refers to the level of radiation in a place whether or not people are there. One rad equals 1,000 millirads."

The *AP Stylebook* simply states that rad is "the standard unit of measurement for absorbed radiation. A millirad is a thousandth of a rad. There is considerable debate among scientists whether there is any safe level of absorption."

485.   Walsh, Bill. Lapsing Into a Comma: A Curmudgeon's Guide to the Many Things That Can Go Wrong in Print—and How to Avoid Them. Lincolnwood, IL: Contemporary Books, 2000. 246p. index. LC 99-53468. ISBN 0-8092-2535-2.

Walsh, the *Washington Post's* business copy desk chief, writes in his lively and literate introduction, "I've been a journalist 19 years now, and about 10 years ago I decided to make a point of jotting down every interesting style issue that came up. Often the issue was something not covered in the AP stylebook, the traditional newsroom bible. In other cases it was something covered in that stylebook but widely ignored by writers and copy editors—or something that exposed flaws in the stylebook's advice or in the conventional wisdom. These nuggets form the core of this book." He continues, "I doubt you'll find my advice predictable. I mix traditionalism (never, ever, use *which* when you mean *that*) with a streak of liberalism (don't believe what you've heard about hopefully). I make a case for *media* as a singular noun, and I argue that using the active voice isn't always preferable." With that context, users should be prepared to use the index to access these "nuggets," as his table of contents is a bit on the whimsical side. There are chapters on "Holding the (Virtual) Fort," "Giving 110 Percent," "Matters of Sensitivity," "He Said, She Said," "The Big Type," and "Dash It All, Period." The style guide itself is arranged alphabetically and includes entries such as "Doctors Such as Laura" ("Physicians are doctors. People with doctorates are people with doctorates"). and "Reese's Monkeys" ("Unless they're chocolate on the outside and peanut butter on the inside, you probably mean Rhesus monkeys"). Even if you are not in the market for an alternative stylebook, this curmudgeon's guide is an entertaining read from cover to cover. Users also will want to check out The Slot, his Web site at www.theslot.com/ (entry 283). His forthcoming book is titled, yes, *The Elephants of Style*.

11
Catalogs

486.   Akeroyd, Joanne V. **Alternatives: A Guide to the Newspapers, Magazines, and Newsletters in the Alternative Press Collection in the Special Collections Department of the University of Connecticut Library.** 2d ed. Storrs, CT: The Library, 1976. 128p. (Bibliographic Series, no. 5). LC 77-620500.

Although quite dated, this library catalog of approximately 1,500 titles (250 of which were on subscription in 1976) is an excellent general guide to alternative or underground publication titles. In part 1, titles are arranged alphabetically and list publisher and issuing group. Those included in the *Alternative Press Index* (entry 183) are marked. Part 2 is a subject listing. Akeroyd warns here that "right wing materials have not all been cataloged, so the list under 'Right Wing' is only partially representative of what is in the collection." Titles are arranged geographically (46 states and 21 foreign countries) in part 3. Entries range from *Attitude Check* (Vista, CA: Movement for a Democratic Military, 1970) to *No More Teachers Dirty Looks* (San Francisco, CA: Bay Area Radical Teachers Organizing Collective, 1970–73). For further information on Connecticut's Alternative Press Collection, see entry 724. Those seeking other alternative publications and collections should consult *Danky's Undergrounds: A Union List of Alternative Periodicals in Libraries of the United States and Canada* (entry 498). Another useful source is Joseph R. Conlin's *The American Radical Press, 1880–1960* (Greenwood, 1974).

487.   Ballantyne, James, ed. **The Researcher's Guide: Film, Television, Radio and Related Documentation Collections in the UK.** 6th ed. London: British Universities Film & Video Council, 2001. 310p. ISBN 0-901299-71-5.

Formerly the *Researcher's Guide to British Film and Television Collections,* this expanded guide, directory, and catalog to nearly 250 major film and television archives and collections in the United Kingdom is a well-organized and time-saving information and location source for researchers. Ballantyne, incidentally, does the user a great service by defining both archives and collections, and explaining what can and cannot be found in each. The directory section is subdivided into chapters on national archives; regional archives; other national, regional, and local collections; television companies; newsreel and production libraries; specialized collections; and associated information and documentation sources. Alphabetically arranged entries include name of collection, address, telephone and fax numbers, contact person, historical background, holdings information, storage facilities, cataloging and arrangement of collection, "junking" policies (weeding and disposal), and access to the collection. Some of the information is quite detailed: One film collection is stored in "wooden cupboards in Northamptonshire Studies Collection room. No control of temperature or humidity." Signed articles constitute the first 60 pages, and range in subject from research to copyright. The six appendixes are loaded with data, including bibliographies of books and periodicals, lists of research organizations, and sources available in Ireland.

488. Brigham, Clarence S. **History and Bibliography of American Newspapers, 1690–1820.** Westport, CT: Greenwood Press, 1975. (2 vols. Reprint of 1947 edition with additions and corrections from 1961, published by the American Antiquarian Society.) 1,508p. 2 vols. LC 75-40215. ISBN 0-8371-8677-3.

Brigham, the late head of the American Antiquarian Society, traveled 29 states and the District of Columbia, consulted more than 500 libraries, and studied more than 2,000 newspapers to compile this bibliography of early American newspapers. The first installment was published in the Society Proceedings in 1913. Once the final installment was printed in 1927, revision began almost immediately. In all, he spent more than 30 years meticulously compiling these geographical lists that give a short history of each newspaper, as well as dates of publication and locations. Half of the second volume includes lists and indexes. Brigham states, with justifiable pride, that the editors of the Union List of Newspapers began their list with the year 1821, apparently believing that Brigham's coverage of newspapers through 1820 was so comprehensive that there was no need to retrace his steps. Edward C. Lathem's *Chronological Tables of American Newspapers, 1690–1820: Being a Tabular Guide to Holdings of Newspapers Published in America Through the Year 1820* was published by the Society in 1972. For data on newspapers published after 1820, see Gregory's *American Newspapers, 1821–1936* (entry 503).

489. British Film Institute. **Catalogue of the Book Library of the British Film Institute.** 3 vols. Boston, MA: G. K. Hall, 1975. 3 vols. 2,540p. index. LC 75-332053. ISBN 0-8161-0004-7. **First Supplement, 1983.** 2 vols. ISBN 0-8161-0388-7.

Although the emphasis is placed on film studies in the British Film Institute Library, a large collection of books on television from the early 1960s to the 1980s is available. For a listing of periodicals in the BFI, see *British Film Institute: Film and Television Periodical Holdings* (entry 506). Useful author, title, subject, and script indexes are provided. Coverage is worldwide.

490. Brown, Warren, comp. **Check List of Negro Newspapers in the United States, 1827–1946.** Jefferson City, MO: Lincoln University, 1946. 37p.

Brown's modest list consists of 467 "Negro newspapers published in the United States since the founding of 'Freedom's Journal' in 1827," only a fraction of the publications which have been unearthed in the past five decades. Interestingly, Potter's *A Reference Guide to Afro-American Publications and Editors, 1827–1946* (entry 516), which supplements this list with indexes, offers some telling background on Brown; he ignored and omitted some important editors such as Marcus Garvey. Brown's catalog is austere, with a 10-line prefatory note, minimal holdings information, and no indexes. Entries are arranged simply by title. "The list gives the location of all known copies of these papers, the names of their editors, as well as the dates of founding and expiration, wherever these could be ascertained." Many expiration dates are marked simply with question marks. This is a flawed but important historical source. For comparison consult Pride's *A Register and History of Negro Newspapers in the United States, 1827–1950* (entry 517). For comprehensive listings of current and historical African American newspapers and periodicals, consult

Henritze's *Bibliographic Checklist of African American Newspapers* (entry 505) and *African-American Newspapers and Periodicals* (entry 500).

491.   Buechele, Lisa F. **Newsfilm Index: A Guide to the Newsfilm Collection 1954–1971.** Jackson, MS: Mississippi Department of Archives and History, 1985. 539p. index. LC 85-620005. ISBN 0-938896-45-8.

Although the catalog indicates that this newsfilm is "a collection of unedited newsfilm from a television station in Jackson, Miss.," most is footage from WBLT-TV, the NBC affiliate in Jackson. The newsfilm entries, which constitute the bulk of the index, are arranged chronologically. Each includes a record number, descriptive title, physical location of the film record, technical access information (e.g., silent or sound film), date, length in feet, reel position, and description of event. There also is an index arranged chronologically by year. Film records range from "Linda Joy Lackey, the 1961 Maid of Cotton, arrives in Jackson" to "James Meredith is interviewed upon his arrival in Canton, Miss., ending his 'Walk Against Fear.'" Civil rights materials are marked with an asterisk. Those researching media coverage of the civil rights years will find a wealth of material through this index.

492.   Burger, Barbara Lewis, comp. **Guide to the Holdings of the Still Picture Branch of the National Archives and Records Administration.** Washington, D.C.: Published for the National Archives and Records Administration by the National Archives Trust Fund Board, 1990. 166p. index. LC 90-5834. ISBN 0-911333-83-5.

The Still Picture Branch contains 6 million photographs and graphics dating from 1774, and provides a rich documentary history of the United States. This guide describes in detail these materials, organized by record group and series. Part 1 includes Federal Records in the Still Picture Branch as of October 1989; part 2 is Donated Material, which is arranged in chronological order. The guide is immensely accessible to researchers. The index lists materials by broad subject, making this guide less daunting to use for those who are unfamiliar with record groups and such. There is even information on ordering reproductions. According to introductory material, "To the best of our knowledge, all of the illustrations in this guide are in the public domain and there are no restrictions on their use."

A sample entry reads, "RG 75, Records of the Bureau of Indian Affairs, 1868–1979, ca. 130,000 items. 75.1 Photographic prints taken by William S. Soule, Ben Wittick, and John K. Hillers showing Arapaho, Cheyenne, Kiowa, Commanche, Navajo, and Apache Indians, 1868–75 (BAE). Portraits of members of Indian tribal delegations during their visits to Washington, D.C., photographed by Alexander Gardner, 1872 (ID). Portraits of American Indian chiefs and warriors, including Geronimo and Sitting Bull, 1880–1910. Studio portraits of unidentified American Indians from southeastern Idaho reservations, 1897. (SEI)."

This is an exhaustive and powerful guide to American documentary photography.

493.   Burrows, Sandra, and Franceen Gaudet. **Checklist of Indexes to Canadian Newspapers.** Ottawa, Canada: National Library of Canada, 1987. 148p. index. ISBN 0-660-53735-4.

The authors indicate this is the first comprehensive listing of Canadian newspaper indexes and that it resulted from a survey sent to approximately 4,000 libraries, newspapers, archives, and historical societies in Canada. The introduction details scope and methodology, and the book contains a copy of the original survey and letter. Entries are not arranged by newspaper title, but geographically by province, then alphabetically by city and institution. Fortunately, there is an alphabetical list of newspaper titles at the end of the checklist, as well as a geographic index by province and city. Entries in French and English contain address, telephone number, name of index, title of newspaper indexed, institution, frequency and place of publication, dates indexed, format of index, number of entries, and, if available to researchers, restrictions and charges. The National Library also produces a *Checklist of Indexed Canadian Newspapers: A Checklist Based on the Holdings of the Newspaper Division.* Useful guides to indexed newspapers in the United States include the *Lathrop Report on Newspaper Indexes: An Illustrated Guide to Published and Unpublished Newspaper Indexes in the United States and Canada* (Wooster, OH: Norman Lathrop Enterprises, 1979–80) and Milner's *Newspaper Indexes: A Location and Subject Guide for Researchers* (entry 511).

494. Campbell, Georgetta Merritt. **Extant Collections of Early Black Newspapers: A Research Guide to the Black Press, 1880–1915, With an Index to the Boston Guardian, 1902–1904.** Troy, NY: Whitson Publishing Company, 1981. 401p. LC 80-51418. ISBN 0-87875-197-1.

Some sources defy categorization. Campbell's guide could easily be placed with bibliographies and bibliographic guides or indexes, as it has a little bit of everything. She carries on where Armistead Pride's *The Black Press: A Bibliography* (entry 99) left off. This is a bibliographical guide to black newspapers published between 1880–1915 and available in special collections. More than 1,800 newspapers are known to have existed during that time span, and she locates and documents 180 of them. Entries include location of collections, holdings and dates, and availability on microform. In addition, a prototype index of the *Boston Guardian* is included. Campbell notes that "only one extant black newspaper has been indexed for publication. Fittingly, it is an index to the first black newspaper, *Freedom's Journal.*" There is no index to other features, but this source is well worth wading through. The foreword, preface, and first chapter contain valuable information regarding the *Pride* research, and puts the subject matter in historical perspective. Researchers also will want to consult *Bibliographic Checklist of African American Newspapers* (entry 505) and *African-American Newspapers and Periodicals: A National Bibliography* (entry 500).

495. Communications Library, University of Illinois, Urbana. **Catalog of the Communications Library.** 3 vols. Boston: G. K. Hall, 1975. ISBN 0-8161-1174-X.

Eleanor Blum, then communications librarian, and author of *Basic Books in the Mass Media* (entry 12) and *Mass Media Bibliography* (entry 13), says in her introduction that this catalog is the "largest collection of English-language books on the subject assembled as a single unit." That subject is communications and includes mass communications, communication theory, advertising, press freedom, popular culture, newspapers, radio, television, cable, magazines, and book publishing. When the catalog was published, the library held more than 12,500 monographs and 400 continuations and journals. Communications researchers would do well to tap this important catalog and collection. *A Selected Bibliography of Publications, 1949–1972,* published by the Institute of Communications Research, University of Illinois (1973), might also be useful.

496. Cox, Susan M., and Janice L. Budeit, comps. **Early English Newspapers: Bibliography and Guide to the Microfilm Collection.** Woodbridge, CT: Research Publications, 1983. 106p. LC 83-6787. ISBN 0-89235-076-8.

English newspapers from 1603 to the mid-1800s at the British Museum and Bodleian Library were microfilmed by the publisher and listed here. Entries, arranged alphabetically by title, contain little else except dates of publication and reel information. This has been updated periodically, most recently in 1993. Other publications that might be more useful include the *Census of British Newspapers and Periodicals, 1620–1800* (University of North Carolina Press, 1927) and *Guide to Early British Periodicals Collections on Microfilm with the Subject, Editor, and Reel Number Indexes* (University Microfilms International, 1980).

497. Danky, James P., ed. **Native American Periodicals and Newspapers, 1828–1982: Bibliography, Publishing Record, and Holdings.** Maureen E. Hady, comp., in association with the State Historical Society of Wisconsin. Westport, CT: Greenwood Press, 1984. 532p. index. LC 83-22579. ISBN 0-313-23773-5.

Danky and Hady prepared this guide to periodicals and newspapers by and about Native Americans "in order to assist faculty and students doing research as well as Native Americans seeking their past." They list 1,164 titles, of which the State Historical Society, with the largest collection of Native American publications, houses more than 800. Titles no longer published are included as well as literary, political, and historical journals. Users would do well to read the lengthy introduction, which provides a historical overview and describes scope and methodology. Detailed entries are numbered, arranged alphabetically by title, and list publication dates, frequency of publication, address, telephone number, number of pages in the last issue examined, availability in microform, title variations, and holdings. Cover pages of more than 40 Native American publications, ranging from *The Medicine Bundle* to *Native Women's News,* are included as well. This source wins the prize for accessibility—included are separate subject, editor, publisher, geographical, catchword and subtitle, and chronological indexes. In the introduction, Danky writes, "Daniel F. Littlefield and James W. Parins provided assistance in identifying and locating titles while doing research for their historical guide to the Native American press (*American Indian and Alaska Native Newspapers and Periodicals,* Greenwood Press, 1984 [entry 508]). Many materials were exchanged during the course of the project, but, beyond that, we reaped the benefits of both their scholarship and professionalism."

498. Danky, James P., ed. **Undergrounds: A Union List of Alternative Periodicals in Libraries of the United States and Canada, 1974.** Madison, WI: State Historical Society of Wisconsin, 1974. index. LC 74-8272. ISBN 0-87020-142-5.

According to Danky, "My own definition of an alternative periodical, and this is purposely left very broad, is one that is politically and culturally to the left of center; i.e., a publication that expresses views not normally presented in the daily press." Complete with psychedelic cover art and matching typography, this guide to more than 3,000 titles is more than a checklist—it is the statement of an era. Compiled from lists prepared by nearly 200 librarians, *Undergrounds* is a comprehensive listing of alternative publications in the United States and Canada. Entries are arranged alphabetically by title and include place of publication, publisher, where indexed, format, holdings, and holding institution. There is a geographic index but no subject index, because "the problems inherent in stereotyping alternative publications persuaded me not to attempt this. I also felt that this would have been potentially unfair to the publications and misleading to researchers." Nonetheless, a subject index to this important source, no matter how misleading, would be most helpful.

The following sources might also provide useful information: Gail Skidmore and Theodore J. Spahn's *From Radical Left to Extreme Right* (Scarecrow, 1987) and the *Utne Reader,* a bimonthly periodical devoted to reprinting the "best of the alternative press." For historical information on the underground press in Great Britain, consult *The Underground and Alternative Press in Britain* (Harvester Microform), published annually in the 1970s and 1980s.

499. Danky, James P., and Maureen E. Hady. **Newspapers in the State Historical Society of Wisconsin: A Bibliography with Holdings.** 2 vols. New York: Norman Ross, 1994. LC 92-60505. ISBN 0-88354-700-7 (vol. 1); ISBN 0-88354-701-5 (vol. 2).

Those unfamiliar with the holdings of the State Historical Society of Wisconsin might be inclined to bypass this two-volume source, thinking it is a local listing of titles. Be advised that the Society boasts the second-largest collection of newspapers in the United States, and is the Wisconsin project center for the United States Newspaper Program. According to the introduction, the Society possesses a national collection from the seventeenth century to the present, and has 11,000 bound volumes, 100,000 reels of positive and negative microfilm and more than 17,000 sheets of microprint covering the 50 states, United States possessions, and 13 Canadian provinces. Compiled by experts, this unparalleled guide to an amazingly accessible collection is a researcher's dream. It does have limitations, however, as spelled out by none other than publisher Norman Ross: "This guide informs us of every newspaper held in the State Historical Society of Wisconsin. However, what it doesn't do is tell us all of the newspapers ever published in Wisconsin and held anywhere, which would have been very useful to researchers, especially those located outside Wisconsin. That could have been accomplished if OCLC had agreed to provide us with the complete database we wanted to purchase. But they did not."

Volume 1 is an alphabetical listing, by city, of Wisconsin newspapers. Entries include title, county, publisher and publication dates, frequency of publication, and holdings. Volume 2 is primarily a geographic listing to newspapers in the United States (sans Wisconsin) and Canada. Separate alphabetical, audience, and chronological indexes are included with each volume. Thanks to Danky and Hady, who, despite technical, organizational, and political glitches, have crafted yet another seminal source in newspaper and periodical bibliography.

500. Danky, James P., and Maureen E. Hady, eds. **African-American Newspapers and Periodicals: A National Bibliography.** Cambridge: Harvard University Press, 1998. 740p. LC 98-26099. ISBN 0-674-00788-3.

More than 6,500 publications by and about African Americans are detailed in this exhaustive and meticulous source in which information "was gained through direct examination of each issue of every title." The editors continue: "The bibliography covers literary, political, and historical journals as well as general newspapers and feature magazines. It includes titles that have long ceased publication as well as those that still appear. This work is the most extensive yet compiled, and its titles represent many phases of African-American thought and action, from the religious, abolitionist, and educational press of the antebellum era to the publications of nationalists, Hip Hop musicians, and business and professional groups that appear today." Introductory material sets the volume in historical context, and describes the breadth of the African-American Newspapers and Periodicals Bibliography Project at the State Historical Society of Wisconsin. Entries are arranged alphabetically by title and include publication years frequency; current editor and address; previous editors; subscription rates; publisher; information on photographs, advertising, drawings, and illustrations; indexing; variation in title; subject focus; and library holdings. With separate geographic, subjects/features, editors, and publishers indexes, this resource also is highly accessible. Danky indicates that this catalog will be updated and made available in electronic format in the future. "There is still a tremendous amount of material that has not been recovered," he writes. The project "has identified thousands of titles that were reported as published but which cannot be located today." Users might also wish to consult Henritze's *Bibliographic Checklist of African American Newspapers* (entry 505).

501.   Dick, Ernest J. **Guide to CBC Sources at the Public Archives.** Ottawa, Canada: Public Archives Canada, 1987. 125p. index. LC 87-174326. ISBN 0-662-54911-2.

Described as a "centralized index" to a decentralized organization, this catalog attempts to list the Canadian Broadcasting Corporation collections in seven divisions of the Archives. The 782 entries are listed in English and French by administrative division (Head Office, English Services Division, etc.). Categories and series are arranged alphabetically within chapters. Entries contain a brief description, program title, administrative unit, PAC division holdings, accession number, extent of holdings, and dates. Included are name, book title, program title, and subject indexes. The author cautions that "this guide is not intended to lead a researcher to a particular document or broadcast, but rather to indicate whether the PAC holds potential sources for a particular research project." He also says that "the researcher should be aware that there exist collections in virtually all archives in Canada, not to mention archives outside the country." For further information on the CBC and Public Archives, see entry 764. Also available is the *Inventory of the National Film, Television, and Sound Archives* (Public Archives, 1983), which lists primarily Canadian Film Institute media.

502.   Dooley, Patricia L., David Klaassen, and Richard Chapman. **A Guide to the Archives of the National News Council.** Minneapolis, MN: Silha Center for the Study of Media Ethics and Law, University of Minnesota, 1986. 25p. (No. 86031).

The National News Council "officially terminated operations" in 1984, but its archives are rich with records and reports on press freedom, press accountability, and relations between press and public. This is not an official catalog of the collection, but a general description of what can be found at the archives, such as National News Council Records, administrative and financial records, working files (including complaints papers), and audiotapes and videotapes. A detailed inventory, however, is planned. The NNC was organized as an "independent and private National News Council . . . to receive, to examine, and to report on complaints concerning the accuracy and fairness of news reporting in the United States, as well as to initiate studies and report on issues involving the freedom of the press."

503.   Gregory, Winifred, ed. **American Newspapers, 1821–1936.** New York: Kraus Reprint Corp., 1967. (Reprint of 1937 edition, published by the Bibliographical Society of America). 791p.

Picking up where Brigham left off in 1820 (*History and Bibliography of American Newspapers, 1690–1820,* entry 488), Gregory lists newspapers published in the United States and Canada through 1936. Entries are arranged alphabetically by state or province, and subdivided by city and newspaper. Dates of publication, symbol and holdings, and variations of titles are included. Gregory notes that "we have attempted to eliminate all titles already appearing in the previous union lists in this series." Also excluded are fraternal, religious, and labor union publications.

504. Hamilton, Dave. **A Guide to the Negro Newspapers on Microfilm: A Selected List.** DeKalb, IL: Northern Illinois University, 1972. 56p. ERIC Report ED 062240.

Designed to fill gaps in the 1953 guide to *Negro Newspapers on Microfilm: A Selected List* (entry 573), this 1972 guide is divided into three sections. More than 200 titles arranged alphabetically by title make up part 1. Entries include dates of publication and reel and title number. Part 2 lists newspapers geographically by state, then city. Part 3 is a listing of microfilm reels and titles. Hamilton writes that "when an investigation by this author revealed that several newspapers appearing on the film had not been included in the (1953) guide, a thorough canvassing was undertaken to discover other possible discrepancies."

505. Henritze, Barbara K. **Bibliographic Checklist of African American Newspapers.** Baltimore, MD: Genealogical Pub. Co., 1995. 206p. bibliog. index. LC 94-79984. ISBN 0-8063-1457-5.

In this exhaustive source, Henritze lists 5,539 African American newspapers and periodicals published in the United States. As the foreword explains, "Little did anyone know in 1946 that Brown [*Check List of Negro Newspapers in the United States,* entry 490] only identified one-tenth of the actual number of African American newspapers." Henritze consulted more than 100 sources (listed in an appendix) to compile this checklist. She warns the user that "this book is not a union list of newspapers, which lists available issues (long runs or individual issues) of specific papers and the repositories that house them. Although the source codes may give clues to repositories, the search for specific individual issues is left to the researcher." Entries are spare but provide a valuable starting point for researchers; included are title, city, state, frequency of publication, dates published, and possible sources. Arrangement is geographic by state and city, then alphabetically by title. Fortunately, there is a title index. This is not the first source to document African American newspapers; but it is essential when researching any aspect of journalism history and African American journalism. Researchers also should be aware of *African-American Newspapers and Periodicals: A National Bibliography* (entry 500), a comprehensive resource covering more than 6,500 newspapers and periodicals.

506. Ingram, Joan, ed. **British Film Institute. Film and Television Periodical Holdings.** London: British Film Institute, 1983. 40p. index. ISBN 0-85170-143-4.

More than 1,600 film and television periodicals from 50 countries are available at the British Film Institute. Entries in this guide are arranged alphabetically by title and list variations in title, country of origin, language, and holdings. Cross-references and a geographic index are included. For information on other BFI holdings, see the *Catalogue of the Book Library of the British Film Institute* (entry 489).

507. Langman, Larry. **The Media in the Movies: A Catalog of American Journalism Films.** Jefferson, NC: McFarland, 1998. 333p. index. LC 97-46949. ISBN 0-7864-0433-7.

From "Torchy Gets Her Man" to "Citizen Kane," 1,025 films released from 1900 to 1996 with magazine, newspaper, television, and radio journalism themes are chronicled. Alphabetically arranged entries include date, distributor, director, screenwriter, synopsis, and cast, but, unfortunately, no character names. Researchers might also wish to consult Ness's *From Headline Hunter to Superman: A Journalism Filmography* (entry 514) and compare, for example, descriptions of movies such as "A Certain Rich Man": "A small-town newspaper provides part of the background for this sprawling silent drama based on the 1909 novel by William Allen White. Jean Hersholt arrives in town to start a newspaper and unknowingly places his money in a bank whose owner is short of funds. Hersholt falls in love with Claire Adams, but when she rejects him, he decides to leave town. Robert McKim, a wheat dealer in financial trouble, threatens Adams, who loves Carl Gantvoort, the banker's son. He tells her that many in town will suffer if she does not marry Hersholt, who will take his funds with him when he leaves. She then reluctantly agrees to the marriage. Twenty years later, Hersholt becomes an alcoholic, leaving his wife to run the paper, now owned by her former boyfriend. The angry Hersholt shoots Gantvoort and bolts from the town. When they learn about her husband's eventual death, Adams and Gantvoort rekindle their love and marry." The classic films on the lives of broadcast and print reporters, editors, publishers, and photojournalists are all here, but there are some surprises as well. Who would guess that "The Ghost and Mr. Chicken" ("inept newspaper typesetter Don Knotts, always aspiring to be a great reporter") or "Then Came Bronson" ("disillusioned young reporter") contained journalistic themes?

508.   Littlefield, Daniel F., and James W. Parins. **American Indian and Alaska Native Newspapers and Periodicals, 1826–1924.** Westport, CT: Greenwood Press, 1984. 482p. index. (Historical Guides to the World's Periodicals and Newspapers). ISBN 0-313-23426-4. **American Indian and Alaska Native Newspapers and Periodicals, 1925–1970.** Westport, CT: Greenwood Press, 1986. 553p. index (Historical Guides to the World's Periodicals and Newspapers). ISBN 0-313-23427-2. **American Indian and Alaska Native Newspapers and Periodicals, 1971–1985.** Westport, CT: Greenwood Press, 1986. 609p. 3 vols. index. (Historical Guides to the World's Periodicals and Newspapers). LC 83-1483. ISBN 0-313-24834-6.

These three volumes represent as comprehensive a historical and reference guide as there probably ever will be to newspapers and periodicals edited or published by American Indians or Alaska natives. The series also includes those publications "whose primary purpose was to publish information about contemporary Indians or Alaska natives," according to the authors. Canada and Mexico are not included. The native press consists of tribal newspapers, nontribal newspapers, intertribal newspapers and periodicals, and literary periodicals; the nonsectarian reform press and independent press concerns itself with reform periodicals and independent newspapers and periodicals; the sectarian press of native-language periodicals and English-language periodicals; and the government-supported press focuses on the Indian school press and Indian agency periodicals. Magazine titles and essays are arranged alphabetically, and contain history (including affiliations with parties, organizations, or tribes), information sources (bibliography, indexing, location), and publication history. The introduction in all three volumes provides a historical overview and briefs the reader on the time period covered. Volume 1 describes more than 200 publications. Volumes 2 and 3 were compiled with the aid of more than 30 contributors. As a result, volume 2 contains more than 500 listings, and volume 3, which takes the user through 1985, lists more than 1,000 titles. Students of Native American journalism are assured of a comprehensive listing of titles when these volumes are used with Danky's impressive *Native American Periodicals and Newspapers, 1828–1982* (entry 497).

Littlefield and Parins caution that this last volume is the "beginning of research...and not the end." Notes in the *Native Press Research Journal* (edited by Littlefield and Parins) update these volumes. In a 1988 issue, the editors say, "Despite our efforts to be exhaustive in coverage, many titles were not included because they were unknown at the time or, for some reason, copies were not available for examination. Thus as a regular feature of the *Journal,* we include publication histories for titles that are now available from the pre-1985 period. Also as need arises, we include 'Publication Histories: Recent Titles.'"

James E. Murphy and Sharon M. Murphy's history *Let My People Know: American Indian Journalism, 1828–1978* (University of Oklahoma Press, 1981) contains useful information as well. Researchers might also wish to consult *The Newspaper Indian: Native American Identity in the Press 1820–90* (University of Illinois, 1999).

509.   Mass Communications History Center. **Sources for Mass Communications, Film, and Theater Research: A Guide.** Madison, WI: State Historical Society of Wisconsin, 1982. 176p. index. LC 81-13569. ISBN 0-87020-211-1.

This resource and its update, *Sources for Mass Communications, Film, and Theater Research: 1986 Guide Update* (State Historical Society of Wisconsin, 1986), describe more than 500 manuscript collections at both the Mass Communications History Center of the State Historical Society of Wisconsin and the Wisconsin Center for Film and Theater Research of the University of Wisconsin at Madison. Included are materials on mass communications, journalism, broadcasting, and the press acquired through mid-1979; items collected prior to World War I are not listed. Entries contain contents description, subject, format, donor, and pertinent holdings information.

510.   Mehr, Linda Harris, ed. **Motion Pictures, Television, and Radio: A Union Catalog of Manuscript and Special Collections in the Western United States.** Boston, MA: G. K. Hall, 1977. index. 210p. LC 77-13117. ISBN 0-8161-8089-X.

Researchers on the West Coast will find they do not have to travel far to uncover more than 40 special collections in mass media. Entries in this catalog, a project of the Film and Television Study Center, are arranged by institution. It is important to note that this is a guide only to printed material such as papers, scripts, and photograph collections. No films or television programs are included. Name and subject indexes are provided.

511.   Milner, Anita Cheek. **Newspaper Indexes: A Location and Subject Guide for Researchers.** 3 vols. Metuchen, NJ: Scarecrow Press, 1977, 1979, 1982. index. LC 77-7130. ISBN 0-8108-1066-2 (vol. 1); 0-8108-1244-4 (vol. 2); 0-8108-1493-5 (vol. 3).

Although Milner warns the user that "these three volumes are not comprehensive," they are certainly the most comprehensive available. She received approximately 800 responses from the more than 2,800 questionnaires mailed to libraries, newspapers, historical societies, publishers, booksellers, and "selected individuals." Entries in each volume are arranged geographically by state, then country, and include the name of the newspaper, date indexed, and a repository symbol. Each volume also contains listings of repositories arranged alphabetically by symbol. Included here, when available, are subjects covered, reference and photocopy charges (no doubt now dated), catalogs available, interlibrary loan policies, and so on. There also are brief sections on American foreign-language newspapers, church publications, specialized subjects, and miscellaneous newspapers. Users should consult all volumes. Information is updated in later volumes but is not duplicated or cumulated. An updated volume reflecting current holdings from the 1990s to the present would be invaluable.

512.   Museum of Broadcasting. **The Catalog of the Museum of Broadcasting: The Radio and Television Collections.** Douglas F. Gibbons, ed. New York: Arno Press, 1980. LC 80-23579. ISBN 0-405-13969-1.

513.   Museum of Broadcasting. **Subject Guide to the Radio and Television Collection of the Museum of Broadcasting.** New York: Arno Press, 1979. 186p. LC 79-106857.

From "See It Now" to D-Day network coverage, thousands of radio and television programs and scripts are described in these two guides. Included is programming from ABC, CBS, NBC, NPR, and PBS. In the subject guide, entries are arranged by broad subject headings and list accession numbers, title, and date. For easiest access, remember to use both catalogs, as the lack of a keyword index in the subject guide renders it an unwieldy source. When searching, for example, for a program on the Truman Tour of the White House, one would find it indexed under "Architecture, American." The guide does indicate that "more complete program details may be found by consulting the Museum's card catalog."

514.   Ness, Richard R. **From Headline Hunter to Superman: A Journalism Filmography.** Lanham, MD: Scarecrow, 1997. 787p. index. LC 97-5526. ISBN 0-8108-3291-7.

More than 2,000 films focusing on journalism and the journalist are described in this exhaustive catalog of classics as well as little-known films. American films released from 1909–1996 make up the bulk of this work, but significant international films also are included. According to Ness, "the definition of 'journalist' has been for the most part confined to those who work in a news or editorial capacity. Consideration has been given to off-shoot areas such as columnists, photographers, sportswriters and critics, although listings have been somewhat more selective in these areas." Arranged chronologically by year, then alphabetically by film title, entries include source information, cast of characters and players, director, and story line. Some of the film descriptions, while detailed, also are choppy and uneven, and similar in format and tone to weekly soap opera roundups. For example, in *A Certain Rich Man,* produced in 1921, "Hersholt comes to the town of Sycamore Ridge to start a newspaper. When Adams refuses to marry him he decides to leave, but McKim wants to keep him, or at least keep his money in the town bank to cover shortages. Adams is in love with Gantwoort [sic], whose father runs the bank, and McKim threatens the family with financial ruin unless she marries Hersholt. She does, and twenty years later he is a drunk and she is working for the paper. Hersholt shoots Gantvoort, who now runs the paper, and then is killed in a railroad accident. The title refers to McKim, who reforms when his wife dies and gives his money to the townspeople whose businesses he helped ruin in his rise to the top. The film became the source of a feud between author White and producer Hampton. The conflict is briefly addressed in the television film "Mary White" (q.v.), based on the author's reminiscences of his teenaged daughter." Researchers will want to compare this resource with *The Media in the Movies: A Catalog of American Journalism Films, 1900–1996* (entry 507).

515. Pactor, Howard S., comp. **Colonial British Caribbean Newspapers: A Bibliography and Directory.** Westport, CT: Greenwood Press, 1990. 144p. index. (Bibliographies and Indexes in World History, no. 19). LC 90-35630. ISBN 0-313-27232-8.

From Antigua to Trinidad, this specialized catalog focuses on nearly 700 colonial British Caribbean newspapers published from the 1700s to the present time, and will appeal to scholars and students of Caribbean journalism and newspaper history. Entries are organized by colony or country, then chronologically by date of first issue. A typical entry is spare: Pactor lists, when available, publishing dates, editors, circulation, historical notes, and holdings. This is an unattractive source, with unevenly spaced type, and occasional grammatical and typographical errors. The main drawback, however, is Pactor's breadth of research; he notes that "the findings reported here are the result of a Research Summer Grant provided by the College of Journalism and Communications at the University of Florida." That, in itself is not a problem; it is an important collection. Had he examined, for example, other sources such as *Newspapers in Microform* (entry 528), he would have been able to include more comprehensive information.

516. Potter, Vilma Raskin. **A Reference Guide to Afro-American Publications and Editors, 1827–1946.** Ames, IA: Iowa State University Press, 1993. 104p. index. LC 91-17167. ISBN 0-8138-0677-1.

This guide supplements Brown's *Check List of Negro Newspapers in the United States, 1827–1946* (entry 490), and provides some revealing information on Brown's research. His original list of 467 titles does not include names of important editors such as Marcus Garvey, T. Thomas Fortune, and Adam Clayton Powell. Further, Potter cites some spelling errors and inconsistencies in form. "I have not altered his inconsistencies," Potter states. "Brown's contribution is archival. Where can one find these primary sources? He identifies the institutions and the particular issues they hold. It is a heroic piece of work, but the alphabetical format limits its usefulness as a research tool; however, the four supplemental indexes should facilitate its use." Potter offers information on African American women journalists prior to 1890, and provides useful geographic, editor, and year-of-publication indexes, along with an updated publications index. Beyond this, it is still, basically, Brown's *Check List,* inconsistencies and all. Researchers would be better served by Pride's *A Register and History of Negro Newspapers in the United States, 1827–1950* (entry 517), Henritze's *Bibliographic Checklist of African American Newspapers* (entry 505), and *African-American Newspapers and Periodicals: A National Bibliography* (entry 500).

517. Pride, Armistead Scott. **A Register and History of Negro Newspapers in the United States, 1827–1950.** Evanston, IL: Northwestern University, 1985, 1950. 426p.

This guide is Pride's doctoral dissertation and is the result of a 1946 microfilming project of black newspapers published before 1900 in the United States (see entry 529). Of the more than 2,700 newspapers listed here, more than 2,000 then had no known holdings in the United States. (The largest collection of black newspapers is located, according to Pride, at the Kansas State Historical Society, but the State Historical Society of Wisconsin also has a sizable collection). Pride cites other useful lists and studies of black newspapers such as Detweiler's *The Negro Press* in the United States (McGrath [c1922], 1968) and Warren Brown's *Check List of Negro Papers in the United States 1827–1946* (entry 490). The first section of the guide offers a regional overview of the black press in essay format. In the second section, entries are numbered and arranged alphabetically by state, then town or city, with information on title and variations, publication dates, and holdings and depositories. Pride also published *The Black Press: A Bibliography* (entry 99). See also Hamilton's *A Guide to the Negro Newspapers on Microfilm: A Selected List* (entry 504) and *African-American Newspapers and Periodicals: A National Bibliography* (entry 500).

**518.	Public Affairs Video Archives Catalog.** West Lafayette, IN: Public Affairs Video Archives. School of Humanities, Social Science, and Education. West Lafayette, IN: Purdue University, The Archives, 1988– . Semiannual. unpaged.

According to the introduction in the initial catalog published in 1988, "the staff of the Archives put in many hours watching tapes, entering descriptions, and correcting errors to produce this catalog. It will, no doubt, contain errors. We attribute them to the growing pains of a new organization monitoring the programming of a network telecasting 17,520 hours per year with no fixed schedule." This loose-leaf catalog of C-SPAN (Cable-Satellite Public Affairs Network) programming does not duplicate materials included in Vanderbilt's *Television News Index and Abstracts* (entry 212).

Entries are arranged by subject and include title and identification number, location and dates, length of program, and names and titles of participants. Of particular interest to journalism researchers will be the Journalists' Roundtable and the National Press Club newsmaker luncheons. House and Senate committee and subcommittee hearings, State Department and Pentagon briefings, White House special events, and, infrequently, Canadian Parliament sessions are all included.

**519.	Riley, Sam G. Index to Southern Periodicals.** Westport, CT: Greenwood Press, 1986. 459p. LC 85-27232. ISBN 0-313-24515-0.

This index is really a union list of more than 7,000 consumer, medical, literary, legal, religious, business, and general interest magazines published in the South from 1764–1985. The South includes Alabama, Arkansas, Florida, Georgia, Kentucky, Louisiana, Mississippi, North Carolina, South Carolina, Tennessee, Texas, Virginia, and, until the Civil War, Maryland. Entries are arranged chronologically and include title, place published, dates, and, when available, repository information. Alphabetical and geographic lists of periodical titles are included. According to Riley, this list "should help dispel the image held by others, notably Northeasterners, of the literary South as a 'Sahara of the Bozart,' a place of genteel lassitude where men and women do not like to write, or think." A companion volume is Riley's *Magazines of the American South* (entry 586).

**520.	Rouse, Sarah, and Katharine Loughney, comps. 3 Decades of Television: A Catalog of Television Programs Acquired by the Library of Congress 1949–1979.** Washington, D.C.: Motion Picture, Broadcasting, and Recorded Sound Division, Library of Congress, 1989. 688p. illus. index. LC 86-20093. ISBN 0-8444-0544-2.

From "60 Minutes" segments to *The Readers' Digest's* ever-popular film adaptations of body organ articles ("I Am Joe's . . ."), this catalog is a 30-year time capsule of American television programming reflecting a selective picture of broadcast journalism. Titles of series, serials, documentaries, speeches, and primetime programs are arranged alphabetically within 41 subject and genre sections such as biography, social documentary, public affairs, and talk show. Minimal descriptive information such as title, date, production company, shelf number, and format is given, and, occasionally, a one-sentence summary or listing of "contents" of show is attached. Excluded are television commercials and daily network news broadcasts. Introductory material focuses on the Library of Congress's Television Archive and the development of the collection and catalog, with an enlightening account of acquisition practices and other issues such as technology and copyright, which have shaped this large and quirky collection. The catalog is entertaining to read and easy to use (there is a 53-page content descriptor index). Researchers are reminded that "Like all other audio and moving image materials in the collections of the Motion Picture, Broadcasting, and Recorded Sound Division of the Library of Congress, the TV shows in the archive can be seen in the Library's viewing facilities, without charge, by those doing research of a specific nature leading toward a publicly available work. All viewing is by advance appointment." The Library currently receives about 4,000 titles per year, and, according to the catalog, there are plans for an updated guide. For those interested in radio programming, see *Radio Broadcasts in the Library of Congress, 1924–1941* (entry 524).

521. Rowan, Bonnie G., and Cynthia J. Wood. **Scholars' Guide to Washington, D.C. Media Collections.** Baltimore, MD: Johns Hopkins University Press, 1994. 189p. index. (Scholars' Guide to Washington, D.C., vol. 14). LC 94-2028. ISBN 0-943875-54-4; 0-943875-55-2 (pbk).

In an introductory essay entitled "Through the Media Maze," University of Maryland Professor Douglas Gomery, College of Journalism, proclaims that "The greatest collection of accessible information in the world lies in Washington, D.C. This may seem boastful, but it is altogether true." Others might argue that Washington, D.C. holds the greatest collection of inaccessible information. Regardless, one does not have to be a scholar or Washington journalist to find uses for this accessible source, sponsored by the Woodrow Wilson International Center for Scholars. This series "seeks to facilitate connections between the astonishing and often unexpected scholarly resources of the nation's capital and those who have scholarly or practical needs for them—or even simply a desire to satisfy their intellectual curiosity." Media collections include, according to the foreword, photographs, film, television, sound recordings, newspapers, news magazines, and news clippings. Most of the 131 main entries focus on major collections of unique media materials located in the District of Columbia. A typical entry contains address and telephone number, contact person or head of reference, a useful "Advice to Researchers" section, and descriptions of available material. The broad name and subject index does not include individual items in large collections but is invaluable, for example, when trying to quickly sort through Smithsonian and Library of Congress listings.

522. Schreibman, Fay C., comp. **Television News Resources: A Guide to Collections.** Washington, D.C.: Television News Study Center, George Washington University, 1981. 27p. LC 82-146621.

In this guide to American television news sources in 20 collections in the United States, Schreibman lists useful sources for the novice television researcher and includes information on news documentaries, and network and local station news archives. It is not a "how-to" guide, but a very brief listing of what is out there. There is no index.

523. Scott, Randall W. **The Comic Art Collection Catalog: An Author, Artist, Title, and Subject Catalog of the Comic Art Collection, Special Collections Division, Michigan State University Libraries.** Westport, CT: Greenwood Press, 1993. 1,435p. index. (Bibliographies and Indexes in Popular Culture, no. 2). LC 93-7599. ISBN 0-313-28325-7.

The introduction states that "If you are reading this in the twenty-first century, it is possible that you would be better served by consulting the Michigan State University Libraries' on-line catalog. Until then this will serve you well for titles published before Fall 1990." It also says, "To date, the Michigan State University collection is regrettably alone in its broad scope, extensive holdings, and detailed cataloging. This catalog in book form will likely stand for many years as the outline of the first century of comics collecting in research libraries." This tome represents the unique holdings of a massive research collection, and is listed here because of its emphasis on U.S. newspaper comic strips and criticism of comics. From "Shoe" to "Brenda Starr," the lives and times of fictionalized journalists are chronicled along with bibliographical antics of superheroes and studies on masochism in the comics. The straight alphabetical listing includes author, title, and subject entries. Information on using this accessible special collection also is included in the introduction.

524.   Smart, James R., ed. **Radio Broadcasts in the Library of Congress 1924–1941.** Washington, D.C.: Motion Picture, Broadcasting, and Recorded Sound Division, Library of Congress, 1982. 149p. LC 81-607136. ISBN 0-8444-0385-7.

This guide describes audio recordings of live radio broadcasts aired through 1941 and available in the Library of Congress. Records are arranged in chronological order and list title of broadcast, station call letters, and length of program. Undated records are listed alphabetically in a separate section. There is a title and performer index. Users might also be interested in *3 Decades of Television: A Catalog of Television Programs Acquired by the Library of Congress, 1949–1979* (entry 520).

525.   Thompson, Julius E. **The Black Press in Mississippi 1865–1985: A Directory.** West Cornwall, CT: Locust Hill Press, 1988. 144p. index. LC 88-561. ISBN 0-933951-16-7.

"Here is the mind of the Negro. Here is a weekly chronicle of the black experience, for the press freezes what is happening in a community and preserves it for posterity," according to Henry Lewis Suggs in the foreword. He does not overstate; this is indeed a remarkable and unique history of Southern black journalism. This directory lists more than 400 newspapers, magazines, pamphlets, newsletters, even college catalogs, and, according to Thompson, "every known publication by blacks in Mississippi from 1865 to 1985." Entries are arranged by county, then alphabetically by title, and include, when available, location, publishing dates, frequency, size, subscription rate, circulation, publisher and editor, a brief description, and holdings information. Too, there are five indexes (title, publisher/editor, organization, city, chronological), which provide complete access to contents. In an important statement, Suggs writes that "Oftentimes in black periodicals the dates are incorrect, narratives exaggerated and editorial opinions injected into feature articles. And in the case of Mississippi, the black press was both a hazardous and, to a limited degree, haphazard operation. Nevertheless a black press existed, and the editors and publishers were motivated by the same factors that stimulated newspaper publishing as a whole. And in general, Thompson's directory is a statement that blacks in Mississippi did not enjoy freedom of the press until the advent of the civil rights movement." A companion volume is Thompson's *The Black Press in Mississippi 1865–1985* (University Press of Florida, 1993).

526.   Thorpe, Frances, ed. British Film Institute. **TV Documentation: A Guide to BFI Library Services Resources.** London: Library Services, The Institute, 1985. 67p. LC 86-169903. ISBN 0-85170-181-7.

The British Film Institute has produced numerous useful guides to film and television. This one describes television research resources in the Library Services and Stills, Posters and Designs Collection of the BFI. Short chapters outline library book collections, periodicals, television scripts, special collections, press clippings, television publicity, the Television Stills Archive, and the British National Film and Video Catalogue, which ceased publication in 1991. Also of interest might be SilverPlatter's *International Directory of Film and TV Documentation Collections,* made available online in 2002 and covering nearly 150 international archives and collections.

527.   United States Library of Congress. Catalog Management and Publication Division. **Newspapers in Microform: Foreign Countries, 1948–1983.** Washington, D.C.: Library of Congress, 1984. 504p. index. LC 75-644000. ISSN 0097-9627.

According to the introduction, "this catalog necessarily reflects efforts made in the United States to film foreign newspapers." It also advises the user that "the number of newspapers included here varies widely from country to country. In many developing nations there is no obvious urgency about reducing newspapers to microform, and there is no particular reason why the state library of a central European nation should report its holdings of microfilmed newspapers to the Library of Congress." Foreign newspapers are separated from newspapers published in the United States (entry 528) in this *Newspapers in Microform* publication "because the availability of foreign newspapers in microform is so different from that of U.S. newspapers and because the information in each instance generally serves different interests." Domestic and foreign holdings of newspapers are listed, and even those newspapers that cannot be obtained in the United States are included. Entries are arranged alphabetically by country, then by province or city. When available, publication dates are listed. There also is a title index.

528.   United States Library of Congress. Catalog Management and Publication Division. **Newspapers in Microform: United States, 1948–1983.** 2 vols. Washington, D.C.: Library of Congress, 1984. index. LC 75-644000. ISSN 0097-9627.

The introduction offers an explanation of *Newspapers in Microform's* sometimes confusing publishing record. For example, it is important to note that the dates 1948–1983 refer to the years material was cataloged or received at the Library of Congress, not the actual time period the material covers. There also is a brief history of the publishing record of *Newspapers on Microfilm.* The Library's definition of "newspaper" is broad: "When a particular question does arise, the Library's editors will accept a publication as a newspaper if it is listed by Brigham or Gregory, appears in the newspaper directories of Rowell or Ayer to 1929, or is described in Ayer's *Directory of Newspapers and Periodicals* [now *Gale Directory*] since 1930 as having a depth of more than 10 inches (140 agate lines) and a format of at least four columns. This bibliography thus includes religious, collegiate, labor, and other special-interest papers that were excluded in *Newspapers on Microfilm.*"

Entries are arranged alphabetically by state, then city and title. Volume 1 lists newspapers published from Alabama to Oregon; volume 2, Pennsylvania to Wyoming, plus a title index. Publication dates, frequency of publication, variations in titles, and holdings are included. For a listing of foreign newspapers, including those published in Canada, see *Newspapers in Microform: Foreign Countries* (entry 527). The Serials Division of the Library of Congress also publishes a biennial listing of *Newspapers Currently Received in the Library of Congress.*

529.   United States Library of Congress. Photoduplication Service. **Negro Newspapers on Microfilm: A Selected List.** Washington, D.C.: Library of Congress, 1953.

Armistead Pride's *A Register and History of Negro Newspapers in the United States, 1827–1950* (entry 517) was one of the forces behind the microfilming project of the Library of Congress and its later publication of *Negro Newspapers on Microfilm*. In 1946, the Committee on Negro Studies of the American Council of Learned Societies began the project of microfilming the Negro newspapers published in the United States in the last century.

530.   **United States Newspaper Program National Union List.** 5th ed. Dublin, OH: OCLC, 1999. ISBN 1-55653-150-8. United States Newspaper Program National Union List. 102 microfiches, 1 book (various pagings).

The United States Newspaper Program (USNP) is a national microfilming project supported by the federal government to identify, locate, catalog, maintain, and preserve newspapers published in the United States from the eighteenth century to the present. Funded by the National Endowment for the Humanities and supported by the Library of Congress, it has been a catalyst for libraries to add information about newspaper holdings to their local online catalogs. This union list documents location and holdings information through 1998 of newspaper repositories participating in the USNP. Entries are arranged alphabetically by title, and include publication dates, place and frequency of publication, numerical and chronological designation, variations of title, and bibliographic notes. Local records list repository, format of newspaper, and a chronological summary of issues held in all collections. Geographic, chronological, and subject indexes are included.

12
Miscellaneous Sources

MISCELLANEOUS REFERENCE SOURCES

Some resources are not easily categorized; others are simply one-of-a-kind. Instead of forcing them into the designated chapters, they are singled out here. They merit inclusion because of their importance, relevance, and unique qualities. I admit I have taken some liberties and included a few works that are not necessarily referential in nature.

531. Beasley, Maurine H., and Sheila J. Gibbons. **Taking Their Place: A Documentary History of Women and Journalism.** Washington, D.C.: The American University Press, 1993. index. 374p. LC 92-041011. ISBN 1-879383-09-1; 1-879383-10-1 (pbk).

This revised edition of Donna Allen's *Women in Media: A Documentary Source Book* (Women's Institute for Freedom of the Press, 1977) is a reflective and powerful documentary history of women in print and broadcast journalism from colonial times to the present. Useful as a reference source, sourcebook, and history text, the 24 chapters focus on subjects such as suffrage periodicals, women's pages, war correspondents, ladies' periodicals, and "stunt reporter and sob sisters." Each chapter includes historical background and primary material. It is painstakingly documented, providing hundreds of citations, resources, and endnotes. The 49-page overview alone lists 234 notes.

Users might also be interested in Judith G. Clabes' *New Guardians of the Press: Selected Profiles of America's Women Newspaper Editors* (R. J. Berg, 1983), Barbara Belford's *Brilliant Bylines: A Biographical Anthology of Notable Newspaperwomen in America* (Columbia University Press, 1986), or Madelon Golden Schilpp and Sharon M. Murphy's *Great Women of the Press* (Southern Illinois University Press, 1983). Although not biographical anthologies, the following history sources are not to be overlooked: Ishbel Ross's *Ladies of the Press: The Story of Women in Journalism by an Insider* (Harper & Brothers, 1936), Kay Mills's *A Place in the News: From the Women's Pages to the Front Pages* (Dodd, Mead, 1988, Columbia University Press, reprint with new preface, 1990), and Marion Marzolf's *Up From the Footnote: A History of Women Journalists* (Hastings House, 1977).

532. Compaine, Benjamin, and Douglas Gomery. **Who Owns the Media? Competition and Concentration in the Mass Media Industry.** 3d ed. Mahwah, NJ: L. Erlbaum, 2000. (LEA's Communication Series). 604p. bibliog. index. LC 99-089794. ISBN 0-8058-2935-0; 0-8058-2936-9 (pbk).

Economic and political aspects of the media are examined in this important update of *Anatomy of the Communications Industry: Who Owns the Media,* published in the early 1980s. The authors write that "the real answers to most of the everyday expressions of concern about or praise for the media lie with the owners and managers of American print, film, and electronic media companies." With chapters on newspapers, television, radio, magazines, theatrical films, book publishing, the Hollywood film industry, and the online information industry, this book also provides numerous graphs and tables, providing a timely snapshot of the burgeoning communications industry.

533. Cray, Ed, Jonathon Kotler, and Miles Beller, eds. **American Datelines: Major News Stories from Colonial Times to the Present.** rev. ed. Urbana: University of Illinois Press, 2003. 412p. index. LC 20-02027190. ISBN 0-25207-116-6.

This is an odd collection of newspaper articles and editorials covering some of the most important events and people in American history.

534. Densmore, Dana, ed. **Syllabus Sourcebook on Media and Women.** Washington, D.C.: Women's Institute for Freedom of the Press, 1980. 47p. LC 80-52917. ISBN 0-930470-06-0.

According to the introduction, the purpose of this sourcebook is to provide a collection of syllabi for departments and teachers looking to institute courses on women and the media, and to offer new ideas for existing courses. It may be too dated to fulfill its initial purpose, but historians and instructors may still find some uses for the 60 syllabi listed (some developed by well-known scholars such as Maurine Beasley and Sheila Gibbons). The table of contents is arranged by subject (e.g., general, film, minorities and women, image, art) and the book contains a name index as well. Entries typically contain a course description and outline.

535. **Editorials on File. New York: Facts on File News Service, 1970–** . Semimonthly. ISSN 0013-0966.

Of great interest to writers of commentary, columns, and editorials this publication reprints about 200 editorials and editorial cartoons published in more than 150 newspapers in the United States and Canada. Indexes are published monthly and cumulate on a quarterly, six-month, nine-month, and annual basis.

536. **Facts on File Weekly World News Digest. New York: Facts on File News Service, 1940–** . Weekly. ISSN 0014-6641.

This is a unique, weekly summary of national and world news events gleaned from more than 70 newspapers and magazines. It includes charts and graphs, maps, and statistics and offers a cumulated subject index. It also is available online.

537. Fensch, Thomas, ed. **Television News Anchors: An Anthology of Profiles of the Major Figures and Issues in United States Network Reporting.** Jefferson, NC: McFarland, 1993. bibliog. index. 308p. LC 92-50940. ISBN 0-89950-769-7.

Selected articles on news anchors and network television news published from 1957 to 1991 make up this collection. Articles range from a 1968 *New Yorker* article on Chet Huntley and David Brinkley (in which author William Whitworth states that the newsmen took "their place in American popular culture beside such immortal duos as Blanchard and Davis, Abbott and Costello, Roy Rogers and Trigger, and Fibber McGee and Molly") to "Women in Journalism Anchored by Lack of Substantial Change," by Kenneth Clark. This title could be useful as a secondary textbook or biographical source. Indexing is adequate, but bibliographic annotations are spare.

538. Ghiglione, Loren, ed. **Gentlemen of the Press: Profiles of American Newspaper Editors; Selections from the Bulletin of the American Society of Newspaper Editors.** Indianapolis, IN: R .J. Berg, 1984. 435p. ISBN 0-89730-110-2.

More than 100 newspaper editors are profiled in this collection of *ASNE Bulletin* (now *American Editor*) articles published from the 1950s through the 1980s. Included are the likes of Vermont Royster, Ralph McGill, Turner Catledge, William Henry Grimes, Norman E. Isaacs, and J. Donald Ferguson. Users might also be interested in Judith G. Clabes's *New Guardians of the Press: Selected Profiles of America's Women Newspaper Editors* (R. J. Berg, 1983).

539. Giles, Robert H. **Newsroom Management: A Guide to Theory and Practice.** Detroit, MI: Media Management Books, Inc., 1991. (Previously published by R. J. Berg, 1987). 742p. bibliog. index. LC 87-71124. ISBN 0-9621094-0-1.

Giles explains that his book "is based on many of the behavioral-science theories about management," "is both theoretical and practical," and should be "useful as a textbook for students and a reference for publishers, editors and other practitioners." That it is. In addition to discussions of management theories, styles of management, leadership, newsroom management, conflict, and stress, there are a glossary of terms, a detailed index, and an extensive, unannotated bibliography. Giles, former executive editor of *The Detroit News,* was at the helm during Detroit's newspaper strike in the 1990s, so users might be especially interested in his chapters on "Stress and Survival," "Managing Conflict in the Newsroom," and "Pay, MBO, and Other Rewards."

540. Hansen, Kathleen A., Nora Paul, and Bruce Whatley. **Behind the Message: Information Strategies for Communicators.** Boston: Allyn & Bacon, 2004. ISBN 0-205-38680-6.

This title was announced as *Journalism: A Guide to the Reference Literature* was going to press.

541. Hilliard, Robert L., and Michael C. Keith. **The Broadcast Century and Beyond: A Biography of American Broadcasting.** 3d ed. Boston: Focal, 2001. index. 341p. LC 00-52113. ISBN 0-240-80430-9.

"We make no pretense of possessing the erudition of Erik Barnouw, certainly America's foremost broadcast historian with his trilogy *A Tower in Babel, The Golden Web,* and *The Image Empire,*" according to the authors. "Nor do we pretend to compete with the collection of information and data in Christopher H. Sterling and John Michael Kittross's *Stay Tuned.* We have tried to provide an easily readable work, for the student and public alike, that deals with the key events, issues, and people in this first century of broadcasting that have altered forever the way we perceive the world."

Keeping this in mind, the user will find, in time line and retro box format, an entertaining, general, sometimes simplistic, but frequently useful source of ready reference material on the history of broadcasting and broadcasters, complete with index.

542. Hohenberg, John, ed. **The Pulitzer Prize Story.** New York: Columbia University Press, 1959. 375p. LC 59-7702. ISBN 0-231-08663-6.

543. Hohenberg, John, ed. **The Pulitzer Prize Story II: Award-Winning News Stories, Columns, Editorials, Cartoons, and News Pictures, 1959–1980.** 472p. bibliog. index. LC 80-16880. ISBN 0-231-04978-1.

These collections of Pulitzer Prize–winning journalism prove to be useful references as well as inspiring reading. Other Pulitzer collections include *The Pulitzer Prize Archive* (entry 551) and *The Pulitzer Prizes in Journalism, 1917–1985* (entry 577) on microfilm. See also *The Pulitzer Prizes* at www.pulitzer.org (entry 279).

544. Hollis, Daniel Webster III. **The ABC-CLIO Companion to the Media in America.** Santa Barbara, CA: ABC-CLIO, 1995. 352p. illus. index. (ABC-CLIO Companions to Key Issues in American History and Life). LC 95-013097. ISBN 0-87436-776-X.

This entertaining "companion" of approximately 200 articles is a current handbook, encyclopedia, and reference guide to the mass media in the United States. Articles on events and leading figures in journalism are arranged alphabetically, and include suggestions for further reading. There are some startling omissions—Ben Bradlee does not rate an entry and neither does "60 Minutes." Still, a substantial index and numerous cross-references make this a useful supplemental ready reference source.

545. Kahn, Frank J. **Documents of American Broadcasting.** 4th ed. Englewood Cliff, NJ: Prentice-Hall, 1984. 501p. index. LC 83-11025. ISBN 0-13-217133-3.

This fourth edition is completely revised, and contains both a general and legal decision index. According to Kahn (who earned a law degree since the third edition was published in 1978), this book "remains a collection of primary source materials in the field of public policy formulation in broadcasting and related media. The laws, commission materials, court decisions, and other documents span electronic media development from their prehistory to the 1980s in chronological fashion." Ranging from "The Radio Act of 1912" to "TV in the Courtroom," each document entry includes background information and a brief bibliography.

546. **Law and the Media.** Stuart M. Robertson, series ed. Ottawa, Canada: Canadian Bar Foundation.

This five-book series was written with the Canadian journalist in mind. Included are the following titles: *Journalists and the Law* by Robert S. Bruser and Brian MacLeod Rogers (1985); *The Charter and the Media* by John D. Richard and Stuart M. Robertson (1985); *Defamation Law in Canada* by Gerald A. Flaherty (1984); *A Reporter's Guide to Canada's Criminal Justice System* by Harold J. Levy (1986); and *Privacy Law and the Media in Canada* by Gordon F. Proudfoot (1984). See also Robert Martin and G. Stuart Adam's *A Sourcebook of Canadian Media Law* (Carleton University Press, 1994).

547. Mayer, Ira, ed. **The Knowledge Industry 200.** White Plains, NY: Knowledge Industry Publications, 1987. 421p. ISBN 0-86729-262-8; 0-8103-4254-5 (Gale Research Company edition); ISSN 0736-6795.

Profiles of the 200 leading media companies in the United States (circa 1987), both public and private, are arranged alphabetically. Some changes are evident since the previous edition was published in 1983. Outdoor advertising is no longer counted as media, and new categories include syndicated services and computer software. CBS, however, was still number one. Profiles include information such as revenue rank, total number of employees, number of media employees, total assets, media assets, media revenue breakdown, corporate officers, directors, company description, and recent acquisitions/divestitures. The editor comments on the large number of mergers and acquisitions in the industry and says that this book reflects "such major changes through the end of November 1987 in the appropriate profiles." For a timely statistical analysis of concentration of mass media ownership, see Compaine and Gomery's *Who Owns the Media?: Competition and Concentration in the Mass Media Industry* (entry 532).

548. Merrill, John C., and Harold A. Fisher. **The World's Great Dailies: Profiles of Fifty Newspapers.** New York: Hastings House, 1980. 416p. bibliog. index.

This book profiles the "great dailies," which, according to Merrill and Fisher, "represent the very best in the world's journalism." See also the Media Research Institute's *America's Leading Daily Newspapers* (R. J. Berg, 1983).

549. Miller, Sally M., ed. **The Ethnic Press in the United States: A Historical Analysis and Handbook.** Westport, CT: Greenwood Press, 1987. 437p. index. LC 85-31699. ISBN 0-313-23879-0.

Twenty-seven chapters describe twenty-eight ethnic presses (Latvian and Lithuanian presses are covered in one chapter). The definition of "press" varies from essay to essay. Some discuss only newspapers; others are broader and include broadcasting. Arranged alphabetically by ethnic group and written by specialists, each essay provides an analysis and historical overview. The Italian press "regrettably could not be covered because no specialist was sufficiently free of constraints to undertake the assignment." Black and Native American presses also are omitted, because they "would not reflect the immigration and adaptation processes." Miller goes on to explain that "these chapters focus on groups which typically chose to immigrate to the United States and underwent the subsequent adjustment process."

550. Mott, Frank Luther. **American Journalism; A History 1690–1960.** 3d ed. New York: Macmillan, 1962. 901p.

A classic general survey journalism text, *American Journalism* also serves as a fine historical reference. The third edition includes a section on the electronic media, albeit the electronic media of the 1950s. (The first and second editions were published in 1941 and 1950.) There are numerous bibliographical notes. The prolific Mott also authored the five-volume *A History of American Magazines* (Harvard University Press, 1930–1968) covering the years 1741–1930, and edited *Interpretations of Journalism: A Book of Readings* (F. S. Crofts, 1937) with Ralph D. Carey.

Although not generally considered reference works, the following titles are mentioned here simply as further examples of noted general history texts: John Tebbel, *The Media in America* (Thomas Y. Crowell, 1974); Erik Barnouw's three-volume *A History of*

Broadcasting in the United States, published by Oxford University Press: *Tower of Babel: To 1933* (1966), *The Golden Web: 1933–1953* (1968), and *Image Empire: From 1950* (1970); Sidney W. Head, Christopher H. Sterling, and Lemuel B. Schofield, *Broadcasting in America: A Survey of Electronic Media* (Houghton Mifflin, 1994); Theodore Peterson, *Magazines in the Twentieth Century* (University of Illinois Press, 1964); Michael Emery and Edwin Emery, *The Press and America* (Prentice-Hall, 1992); Willard G. Bleyer, *Main Currents in the History of American Journalism* (Houghton Mifflin 1927); Frederic Hudson, *Journalism in the United States from 1690–1872* (Haskell, 1969, reprint of 1873 ed.); Isaiah Thomas's, two-volume *The History of Printing in America* (B. Franklin, 1972, reprint of 1874 ed.); Robert Rutland, *The Newsmongers* (Dial, 1973); and Anthony Smith, *The Newspaper: An International History* (Thames and Hudson, 1979), to name a few.

551.   The Pulitzer Prize Archive: A History and Anthology of Award-Winning Materials in Journalism, Letters, and Arts. Heinz-Dietrich Fischer and Erika J. Fischer, eds. Munich, Germany: K. G. Saur, 1987– .

This series includes the following titles: Volume 1: *International Reporting 1928–1985: From the Activities of the League of Nations to Present-Day Global Problems* (1987); Volume 2: *National Reporting 1941–1986: From Labor Conflicts to the Challenger Disaster* (1989); Volume 3: *Local Reporting 1947–1987: From a County Vote Fraud to a Corrupt City Council* (1989); Volume 4: *Political Editorial 1916–1988: From War-Related Conflicts to Metropolitan Disputes* (1990); Volume 5: *Social Commentary 1969–1989: From University Troubles to a California Earthquake* (1992); Volume 6: *Cultural Criticism 1969–1990: From Architectural Damages to Press Imperfections* (1993); and Volume 13: *Editorial Cartoon Awards 1922–1997* (1999). Other volumes focus on nonfiction literature and belles lettres. Each volume offers lists of winners and selected reprints of Pulitzer Prize–winning articles. Researchers might also wish to consult *The Pulitzer Prizes* at www.pulitzer.org/ (entry 279).

552.   Riblet, Carl Jr. The Solid Gold Copy Editor. Washington, D.C.: Falcon Press, 1972. LC 72-95673. ISBN 0-202-38000-9; 0-202-38001-7 (pbk).

Aimed at newspaper copy editors, this classic textbook outlines what Riblet considers his "method" for writing headlines, editing ("When to Improve It, When to Leave It Alone"), and speed. Numerous examples and lessons are provided. Other copyediting guides, such as Judith Butcher's *Copy-Editing: The Cambridge Handbook for Editors, Authors and Publishers* (Cambridge University Press, 1992) and Karen Judd's *Copyediting: A Practical Guide* (Crisp Learning, 2001), focus on book or magazine publishing but may provide some relevant lessons. Users might also be interested in *Washington Post* copy desk chief Bill Walsh's Web site The Slot (entry 283).

553.   Rose, Brian G., ed. TV Genres: A Handbook and Reference Guide. Westport, CT: Greenwood Press, 1985. 453p. bibliog. index. LC 84-22460. ISBN 0-313-23724-7.

Although *TV Genres* focuses mostly on entertainment television programming (the western or situation comedy), there also are essays on television news, docudrama, television documentary, sports television, and talk shows. Each genre essay is written by an expert in the field, and includes an overview, historical development, themes and issues, bibliography, and videography.

554. Slide, Anthony, ed. **Selected Radio and Television Criticism.** Metuchen, NJ: Scarecrow Press, 1987. 203p. index. LC 86-27891. ISBN 0-8108-1942-2.

Slide says that this mixed bag of 100 short articles on television and radio published from the 1920s to the 1950s is for "students and scholars of popular entertainment needing an immediate insight into contemporary commentary on radio and television." Immediate, perhaps, but for insight, this is not the source. Suffice it to say that 30 years' worth of radio and television criticism is crammed into fewer than 200 pages. Slide also edited *International Film, Radio, and Television Journals* (entry 589).

555. **Standard Rate and Data Service (SRDS) Publications.** Wilmette, IL: Standard Rate and Data Service.

SRDS sources, used primarily as guides for placing advertising, offer unique statistical snapshots of the mass media. They include *Radio Advertising Source; Direct Marketing List Source; Newspaper Advertising Source; Business Publication Advertising Source; Interactive Advertising Source; Circulation; Community Publication Advertising Source; Hispanic Media and Market Source;* and *Technology Media Source.*

556. Stempel, Guido H., III, David H. Weaver, and G. Cleveland Wilhoit, eds. **Mass Communication Research and Theory.** 3d ed. Boston: Allyn & Bacon, 2003. 440p. LC 20-2066662. ISBN 0-20-535923-X.

Stempel, Weaver, and Wilhoit, masters of research methods, have crafted a well-written and organized guide to mass communication research. Formerly *Research Methods in Mass Communication,* the editors state that there are two "major differences" in this edition. "One is the emphasis put on industry applications of mass communication research. We felt a need to do this in part so that students would be aware of such applications. We also felt it was necessary to assess what media researchers were doing against the context provided by academic researchers." Students will be relieved to open this book and find a virtual step-by-step guide to broadcast, newspaper, public relations, and advertising research. Nearly 30 scholars contributed chapters on statistics, data analysis, survey research, content analysis, ethics, measurement, and secondary analysis. Prior to publication of the first and second editions of this source in 1981 and 1989, commonly used research texts included Nafziger and White's *Introduction to Mass Communications Research* (Louisiana State University Press, 1963) and Nafziger and Wilkerson's *Introduction to Journalism Research* (c1949, Greenwood, 1968). See also Roger D. Wimmer and Joseph R. Dominick's *Mass Media Research: An Introduction* (Wadsworth, 1987) and Anders Hansen's *Mass Communication Research Methods* (New York University Press, 1998).

557. Sterling, Christopher H., and Timothy R. Haight. **The Mass Media: Aspen Institute Guide to Communications Industry Trends.** New York: Praeger; Palo Alto, CA: Aspen Institute Publications. 1978. 457p. bibliog. index. LC 76-24370. ISBN 0-275-24020-7.

Described by the authors as a "statistical abstract of the communications industries," this dated but classic guide offers more than 300 tables of data, organized in seven subject categories, on growth of media industries, ownership, economics, employment and training, content trends, media audiences, and United States media industries abroad.

These are further broken down into specific media categories (books, newspapers, magazines, radio, television, etc.). A detailed table of contents and subject index allow easy access to a wealth of information. This is a remarkable gathering of data, and even though the book is more than 25 years old, it is still useful in carrying out Sterling and Haight's objective: "to provide a single reference source for the most significant statistics describing communication industry trends in the United States since 1900." Too, "there is a strong historical tone" to this guide. Would that it were updated to include the 1980s and 1990s. Sterling is also editor of the *Electronic Media: A Guide to Trends in Broadcasting and Newer Technologies* (Praeger, 1984) and coeditor (with James K. Bracken) of *Mass Communication Research Resources: An Annotated Guide* (Lawrence Erlbaum, 1997).

558.   Summers, Harrison B., ed. **A Thirty-Year History of Programs Carried on National Radio Networks in the United States, 1926–1956.** New York: Ayer, 1971. (Reprint of 1958 edition). (History of Broadcasting: Radio to Television series). LC 78-161155. ISBN 0-405-03572-1.

This typed and single-spaced source, compiled in 1958, is hard on the eyes, but is an excellent overview of what the editor calls the "rise and the beginning of the fall of network radio." This is a year-by-year account of national radio network programs, but only those officially scheduled during the month of January of each season. Consequently, this means that special programs and summer replacement shows are excluded. In addition to variety and music programs, the following are included: magazine-type variety, human-interest programs, informative drama, sports broadcasts, news commentary, public affairs and forums, and daytime news. This volume is part of the *History of Broadcasting: Radio to Television* series, which also includes *History of Radio to 1926* (1938) and *Bibliography on Educational Broadcasting* (1942).

559.   Wachsberger, Ken, ed. **Voices from the Underground.** 2 vols. Tempe, AZ: Mica Press, 1993. LC 92-082780. ISBN 1-8794610-3-X.

This two-volume curiosity is an ambitious attempt to synthesize the disparate voices of the 1960s and early 1970s. It provides a look, with examples of primary material and with the perspective of hindsight, into the angst, innocence, and ignorance of the underground press. Volume 1 consists of *Insider Histories of the Vietnam Era Underground Press,* with 26 essays on underground papers. Volume 2, *A Directory of Sources and Resources on the Vietnam Era Underground* is an impressive reference source offering lengthy chapters on "The Underground Press of the Vietnam Era: An Annotated Bibliography," "Directories of Special Collections on Social Movements Evolving from the Vietnam Era," and "Preserving the U.S. Underground and Alternative Press of the 1960s and '70s: History, Prospects, and Microform Sources."

560.   Weaver, David H., and G. Cleveland Wilhoit. **The American Journalist in the 1990s: U.S. News People at the End of an Era.** 3d ed. Mahwah, NJ: L. Erlbaum, 1996. 299p. bibliog. index. (LEA's Communication Series). LC 96-17622. ISBN 0-8058-2135-X; 0-8058-2136-8 (pbk).

While the second edition depicted "A Portrait of United States News People and Their Work," the third edition, according to the authors, addresses "(a) the role perceptions of journalists working in America's news media over the last quarter of the century; (b) the changes in the backgrounds and education of those choosing journalistic life; (c) professional attitudes, beliefs, and values of journalists; and (d) the problem of retaining the best and brightest people in journalism." Chapters focus on characteristics of journalists, education and training, job conditions and satisfaction, professionalism, minority journalists, and women in journalism. An interesting chapter on "Journalists' Best Work" reveals that "stories about personalities and celebrities, social problems and protests, and general human interest were more likely to be chosen by journalists in 1992 as examples of their best work than in 1982, when crime news and state or local government news were the most common topics." Although not classified as a traditional reference source, journalism librarians will admire the detailed bibliography and meticulous index, and plant a copy at the reference desk.

561. Wilhoit, G. Cleveland, and David H. Weaver. **Newsroom Guide to Polls and Surveys.** Washington, D.C.: American Newspaper Publishers Association, 1980. 82p. index.

The authors write, "With the help of this guide and other persons knowledgeable in survey research, we hope that many journalists will better understand, critically evaluate and accurately report surveys and polls." The guide is arranged in sections on evaluating survey questionnaires, interviewing, sampling, and results, and includes a section on reporting those results. This is aimed at the working journalist. A subject and name index is provided. Wilhoit and Weaver also wrote *The American Journalist in the 1990s: U.S. News People at the End of an Era* (entry 560).

562. Wilson, John. **Understanding Journalism: A Guide to Issues.** London: Routledge, 1996. 304p. index. ISBN 0-415-11598-1; 0-415-11599-X (pbk).

Written from a British perspective, this is a fascinating foray into both the mechanics and ethics of journalism. Neither stylebook nor traditional handbook, this is nonetheless a useful reference for journalism students as well as working journalists. There are chapters on Regulators, Editorial Values, Trouble Spots, Violent Events, Special Treatment, Disputed Practices, Politics, State Interests, The Public, Social Values, Regional Values, and The Law. Each are further broken down into dozens of mini-essays focusing on, for example, impartiality, balance, objectivity, straight dealing, and independence, to name a few. Each is artfully written, to the point, and frequently quite humorous. On accuracy, Wilson writes: "Because of this propensity for news to travel badly, some American journals use 'fact checker.' They check essential facts in copy by going back to primary sources or as near as they can get to them. Their remit runs from the momentous to the trivial. They are not confined to bald facts. They question judgements because they have to be justified by the facts. American media-study circles have referred to a 'fetishism of facts' and that fact checkers are 'obsessed with facticity,' like accusing a doctor of being obsessed with cure. By comparison, British and other European journalism seems careless of fact and scandalously lax in judgement. It is an exaggerated impression." He continues, "But the way it works on weekly news magazines with time to consider each line would not fit readily into hurried daily news in newspapers or on radio and television. And when fact checkers were mooted for the BBC, staff derided the idea, saying they would accept only fat checques."

NEWSPAPER AND SPECIAL COLLECTIONS ON MICROFORM

Although not necessarily standard reference sources, these selected microforms provide access to important and unique subject collections on the press and journalism, and are thus included. Many of these collections may now be found online.

563.   ABC News Transcripts and Index. Woodbridge, CT: Research Publications. Available on microfiche.

Complete transcripts of ABC news programs such as "Nightline," "20/20," "This Week with David Brinkley," and "ABC News Special" are available from 1969 on. The *ABC News Index* (entry 182) allows access by subject, name, and program. It also is available online at ABCnews.com.

564.   The African American Press Collection. Ann Arbor, MI: UMI. Available on microfilm.

More than 80 publications, published from 1837 to the present, and ranging in title from *Colored American* to the *Journal of Religious Education of the African Methodist Episcopal Church* are included in this collection.

565.   Alternative Press. Ann Arbor, MI: UMI. Available on microfilm.

Examples of alternative newspapers and periodicals, from *Mother Jones* to *The Black Scholar,* are documented in this collection covering 1986 to the present.

566.   BBC Summary of World Broadcasts. Ann Arbor, MI: UMI. Available on microfilm (1939–1972) and microfiche (1972–1997).

Selected, transcribed news broadcasts from the former USSR, Central Europe, Asia-Pacific, the Middle East, and Africa, Latin American and the Caribbean and monitored by the British Broadcasting Company (BBC) are included in this collection. See also BBC Monitoring Online (entry 222).

567.   Black Newspaper Collection. Ann Arbor, MI: UMI. Available on 2,038 reels of microfilm.

The 19 black newspapers in this collection were published from 1896 to the present and represent, according to UMI, "the voices of the Black Experience in America." Included are such newspapers as the *Amsterdam News* (New York), *Call and Post* (Cleveland), *Muslim Journal* (Chicago), *Michigan Chronicle* (Detroit), *Post Tribune* (Dallas), and the *Los Angeles Sentinel.* The *Black Newspapers Index* (entry 186) indexes key black newspapers and is arranged by name and subject. See also *Negro Newspapers on Microfilm* (entry 573).

568.   CBS News. Ann Arbor, MI: UMI. Available on microfilm and microfiche.

Complete CBS news and public affairs transcripts from 1975 to the present are available in this collection. In addition, some news broadcasts transcripts from 1963 to 1975 are available on microform. Transcripts range from "The CBS Evening News with

Walter Cronkite," to "60 Minutes." The *CBS News Index* (entry 192), prepared by CBS News, is arranged by name and subject. This material is now available online at cbsnews.com (entry 258).

569.   Civil War Newspapers. Ann Arbor, MI: UMI. Available on microfilm.

More than 300 newspapers from 29 states and published from 1861 to 1865 are included in this collection. "Of special interest are the editions of Frank Leslie's *Illustrated Newspaper,* which published nearly 3,000 pictures of battles, sieges, and other war scenes."

570.   Dougherty Collection of Military Newspapers. Ann Arbor, MI: UMI. Available on 58 reels of microfilm.

More than 2,000 Army, Navy, Air Force, Marine, National Guard, Coast Guard, and Merchant Marine publications, mostly from World War II, the Korean War, and Vietnam, are included in this unique collection. There also are issues from the Mexican War, Spanish-American War, and World War I.

571.   Early American Newspapers. Ann Arbor, MI: University Microfilms International Research Collections. Available on 1,845 reels of microfilm.

Almost 2,000 reels of microfilm make up this collection of selected newspapers published as early as 1789. Included are the following: *The Albany Evening Journal,* 1830–1873; *The Baltimore American and Commercial Advertiser,* 1799–1902 and 1903–1920; *The Boston Herald,* 1848–1879; *The Boston Transcript,* 1848–1915; *The Philadelphia Public Ledger,* 1836–1934; *The Pennsylvania Freeman,* 1836–1841 and 1844–1854; *The York Recorder,* 1800–1830; and "Iowa Frontier Newspapers," 1838–1859, a selection of newspapers published from Dubuque to Muscatine. Readex Microprint Corp. also produced a collection entitled *Early American Newspapers (1704–1820),* which includes all existing newspapers listed in Brigham's *History and Bibliography of American Newspapers, 1690–1820* (entry 488).

572.   Meet the Press, 1957–1986. Ann Arbor, MI: UMI. Available on microfiche.

This collection contains full text transcripts of "Meet the Press," the longest-running television public affairs program. Each fiche holds one transcript. An annual chronology lists programs and provides names and titles.

573.   Negro Newspapers on Microfilm: A Selected List. Library of Congress.

Approximately 200 black American newspapers from the mid-1800s to the mid-1900s constitute this collection. See also the *Black Newspaper Collection* (entry 567).

574.   Newspapers Along America's Great Trails. Ann Arbor, MI: UMI. Available on microfilm.

Newspapers published along the famous wagon trails are chronicled in this unusual collection. It contains thousands of newspapers from hundreds of communities along, for example, the Wilderness Road, Santa Fe Trail, Oregon Trail, Chisholm Trail, Cumberland Road, and the Lewis and Clark Expedition. The collection can be accessed by state or specific trail.

575.   Newspapers from the Depression Years, 1929–1938. Ann Arbor, MI: UMI. Available on 868 reels of microfilm.

Full runs of nine newspapers published during the stock market crash and the Depression years were compiled to make up this massive collection. Included are *The Wall Street Journal, San Francisco Chronicle, Charleston News and Courier,* and *Tulsa World.* According to explanatory notes, "Students and researchers can explore the economic machine of Wall Street as it faltered and then faded. The human despair of ruined lives and fortunes is also chronicled." Of course, most newspapers published during this time would reflect that.

576.   Public Television Transcripts. Woodbridge, CT: Research Publications. Available on microfiche.

Transcripts of programs such as "The MacNeil/Lehrer Newshour," "Adam Smith's Money World," "Bill Moyers' Journal," and "Healthline" from WNET in New York and other public television stations are available in this collection. Backfiles date to original air dates.

577.   Pulitzer Prizes in Journalism, 1917–1985. Ann Arbor, MI: UMI, 1986. Available on 56 reels of microfilm.

Available in this collection are full text versions of every copyright-cleared Pulitzer Prize awarded in journalism from 1917–1985. Included are winners in editorial writing, local reporting, public service reporting, cartoons, and foreign correspondence, as well as commentary, criticism, feature writing, and special awards. *The Pulitzer Prizes in Journalism, 1917–1985: A Guide to the Microfilm Edition* includes reel number, chronology, news organization, author, prize category, and subject index.

578.   Underground Press Collections, 1963–1985. Ann Arbor, MI: UMI. Available on microfilm.

Nearly 1,000 alternative and underground newspapers published during the 1960s through 1985 are available in yearly segments. Newspapers such as *The Village Voice* and *The Berkeley Barb* are included. Also included in this collection are the *Hoover Supplement,* with more than 250 titles from the newspaper archives at the Hoover Institution on War, Revolution and Peace, and the University of Missouri–Columbia Underground Press Collection, with 123 titles published in the early 1960s through the late 1970s. This large collection offers a cumulative table of contents.

HISTORICAL GUIDES TO THE WORLD'S PERIODICALS AND NEWSPAPERS

Greenwood Press has published a number of important guides to various specialized aspects of journalism history in a series on Historical Guides to the World's Periodicals and Newspapers. Following are citations and brief descriptions of some of the books in the series. Many are amalgamations of bibliography, encyclopedia, handbook, guidebook, catalog, and directory. Most follow the same format and contain alphabetically arranged profiles of newspapers or journals written by scholars and other experts, as well as location information. A few titles, such as American Indian and Alaska Native Newspapers and Periodicals (entry 508) are listed in other chapters. In addition, Greenwood publishes a

Contributions to the Study of Mass Media and Communication series. While these titles are not necessarily reference works, they range in subject from Native Americans in the News: Images of Indians in the Twentieth Century Press to The Best of the Rest: Non-Syndicated Newspaper Columnists Select Their Best Work, and should be noted.

579. Chielens, Edward E., ed. **American Literary Magazines: The Eighteenth and Nineteenth Centuries.** Westport, CT: Greenwood Press, 1986. 503p. index. LC 85-24793. ISBN 0-313-23985-1.

More than 50 contributors profile 92 "quality" literary magazines founded before 1900.

580. Daniel, Walter C. **Black Journals in the United States.** Westport, CT: Greenwood Press, 1982. 432p. bibliog. index. LC 81-13440. ISBN 0-313-20704-6.

Descriptive profiles of about 100 black-oriented magazines and journals are included.

581. Endres, Kathleen L., and Therese L. Lueck, eds. **Women's Periodicals in the United States: Social and Political Issues.** Westport, CT: Greenwood Press, 1996. 529p. bibliog. index. LC 96-7144. ISBN 0-313-28632-9.

From *The Birth Control Review* to *The Celibate Woman Journal,* this resource profiles about 75 publications, and, according to the editors, "attempts to cover a wide range of social, economic, and political issues—from abolitionism to temperance, from moral reform to birth control, from suffragism to antisuffragism, from pacifism to feminism." Endres and Lueck also edited *Women's Periodicals in the United States: Consumer Magazines.* Users might also wish to consult Mary Ellen Zuckerman's *A History of Popular Women's Magazines in the United States, 1792–1995* (Greenwood Press, 1998).

582. Fisher, William, ed. **Business Journals of the United States.** Westport, CT: Greenwood Press, 1991. 328p. ISBN 0-313-25292-C.

More than 100 business serials, ranging from the *Wall Street Journal* to the *Journal of Portfolio Management,* are described. Users might also be interested in Kathleen Endres's *Trade, Industrial, and Professional Periodicals of the United States* (1994), a title in this series.

583. Lora, Ronald, and William Henry Longton, eds. **The Conservative Press in Eighteenth- and Nineteenth-Century America.** Westport, CT: Greenwood Press, 1999. 401p. bibliog. index. LC 98-51934. ISBN 0-313-31043-2.

584. Lora, Ronald, and William Henry Longton, eds. **The Conservative Press in Twentieth-Century America.** Westport, CT, Greenwood Press, 1999. 744p. bibliog.. index. LC 98-51891. ISBN 0-313-21390-9.

Nearly 40 journals published between 1787 and 1879, and 65 published mostly in the 1900s are profiled in these volumes. Titles such as the *Baptist Quarterly Review, Southern Magazine, Porcupine's Political Censor, Christian Anti-Communism Crusade Newsletter,* and *Sword of the Law* depict the range of conservative points of view.

585.   Nourie, Alan, and Barbara Nourie, eds. **American Mass Market Magazines.** Westport, CT: Greenwood Press, 1990. 611p. LC 89-17084. ISBN 0-313-25254-8.

General interest magazines published in the United States from the eighteenth century to the present are examined in 106 profiles. Titles range from the *American Whig Review* to *Crawdaddy.*

586.   Riley, Sam G. **Magazines of the American South.** Westport, CT: Greenwood Press, 1986. 346p. index. LC 85-8012. ISBN 0-313-24337-9.

About 90 literary and popular magazines published in the South (Confederate states and pre–Civil War Maryland) and dating as far back as 1764 are profiled. The companion volume is Riley's *Index to Southern Periodicals* (entry 519).

587.   Riley, Sam G., ed. **Corporate Magazines of the United States.** Westport, CT: Greenwood Press, 1992. 277p. index. LC 91-33481. ISBN 0-313-27569-6.

Twenty-nine contributors describe more than 50 corporate or company magazines, from *The Gerber News* (founded in 1935) to *Macworld: The Macintosh Magazine* (1984).

588.   Riley, Sam G., and Gary W. Selnow, eds. **Regional Interest Magazines of the United States.** Westport, CT; Greenwood Press, 1990. 432p. ISBN 0-313-26840-1.

Eighty-six general-interest magazines focusing on particular geographical regions are profiled. A companion volume is Riley and Selnow's *Index to City and Regional Magazines of the United States* (Greenwood Press, 1989).

589.   Slide, Anthony, ed. **International Film, Radio, and Television Journals.** Westport, CT: Greenwood Press, 1985. 428p. bibliog. index. LC 84-8929. ISBN 0-313-23759-X.

Fifty contributors offer essays on more than 150 journals, with emphasis on film publications.

590.   Sloane, David E. E., ed. **American Humor Magazines and Comic Periodicals.** Westport, CT: Greenwood Press, 1987. 648p. index. LC 86-27155. ISBN 0-313-23956-8.

More than 100 humor magazines published in the last 200 years are examined. Brief annotations of more than 400 additional titles also are included.

591.   Sullivan, Alvin, ed. **British Literary Magazines: The Augustan Age and the Age of Johnson, 1698–1788.** Westport, CT: Greenwood Press, 1983. 427p. index. ISBN 0-313-22871-X. **British Literary Magazines: The Romantic Age, 1789–1836.** Westport, CT: Greenwood Press, 1983. 491p. index. ISBN 0-313-22872-8. **British Literary Magazines: The Victorian and Edwardian Age, 1837–1913.** Westport, CT: Greenwood Press, 1984. 560p. index. ISBN 0-313-24336-0. **British Literary Magazines: The Modern Age, 1914–1984.** Westport, CT: Greenwood Press, 1986. index. LC 82-21136. ISBN 0-313-24336-0.

These four volumes cover British literary journals published from 1698 to the present. In all, essays for 369 magazines are included, with more than 400 discussed in appendixes.

13
Core Periodicals

592.   American Editor. 1925– . American Society of Newspaper Editors, 11690B Sunrise Valley Dr., No. B, Reston, VA 20191-1409. www.asne.org. six issues/year. ISSN 1083-5210.

Formerly *The Bulletin of the American Society of Newspaper Editors* (ASNE Bulletin), this periodical continues to offer relevant material and some of the best writing in journalism literature. For those who find that literature dull, over-researched, preachy, or simplistic, this trade journal grasps both the ongoing and cutting-edge issues in newspaper journalism and presents a tight, well-written, original, and attractively packaged collection of articles and columns nearly every month. Each issue is usually 30–40 pages long. Topics of great concern to most editors, such as minorities in the newsroom, journalism education, and journalistic ethics receive a great deal of attention. Unfortunately, the journal is not widely indexed, but researchers may visit the Web site for quick links to past issues of *American Editor* available online. Recent articles include "Explaining Why We Do the Things We Do," "How Do You Prevent Risk-Taking From Going Too Far?," "Reporters Must Learn to Use the Internet Wisely," "Multicultural Staffs Are a Matter of Good Business," and "Meanwhile, On the Unemployment Front." Regular departments include book reviews, freedom of information, "Pages Across the Nation," "Diversity—What Are You Going to Do?," and "Credibility Conversation." This illustrated magazine's cover art usually deserves a second look. The memorable "In Search of Credibility" cover, for example, featured an Indiana Jones–like newsman, clutching a vine, and wielding both a bullwhip and carrier's sack of newspapers.

593.   American Journalism. 1982– . American Journalism Historians Association, Department of Communication Studies, California State University at Sacramento, 6000 J St., Sacramento, CA 95819-6070. Quarterly. ISSN 0882-1127.

With its small circulation and understated appearance, this scholarly and readable publication is not considered the premier journalism history periodical. It does, however, offer some creative articles, a large book review section, and an alternative to *Journalism History* (entry 618). *American Journalism* embraces all aspects of American journalism history, including broadcasting and general communication; advertising and public relations are covered as well. Each issue examines a cross section of Americana, and includes three or four main articles such as "Hemingway as Negligent Reporter: New Masses and the 1935 Florida Hurricane" and "Science Journalism and the Construction of News: How Print Media Framed the 1918 Influenza Pandemic." There are usually 5–10 book reviews, which vary in quality and timeliness. The first issue of each volume contains an index to the previous volume. It is currently indexed in *America: History and Life, His-*

torical Abstracts, ComIndex (entry 194), *Peace Research Abstracts Journal,* and *Communication Abstracts* (entry 195).

594.   American Journalism Review. 1977– . 1117 Journalism Building, University of Maryland, College Park, MD 20742-7111. www. ajr.org; www.newslink.org. Monthly. ISSN 1067-8654.

Formerly *Washington Journalism Review,* the *American Journalism Review,* published by the University of Maryland's College of Journalism, broadened its title in the early 1990s, finally reflecting what the contents had offered for years: a national review source. AJR might not currently have the national prestige that *Columbia Journalism Review* (entry 600) enjoys, but it has carved quite a niche for itself in the last two decades.

Its four or five main articles are generally thought-provoking, well researched, and well written, and cover a wide spectrum of issues. A 2003 issue, for example, offered the following articles: "Higher Examination" (the education beat); "Air of Uncertainty" (covering health issues at Ground Zero); "Blinded by History" (the 2002 midterm election); "Poll Crazy"; and "Endangered Journalists" (covering Colombia). Print and broadcast journalism receive fairly equal coverage. Regular features include "Free Press," "First Amendment Watch," "Broadcast Views," "The Newspaper Business" by John Morton, and book reviews.

Gone is "Take 2," which featured newspaper blunders, similar to Columbia Journalism Review's "lower case." (It is, however, available on the online version of AJR.) The November 1995 issue displayed the following unforgettable "Caption From Hell" published in the *Journal-Star,* Lincoln, Nebraska: "Wava Staub (left) and Rosie Dauner, both of Omaha, board a Fun Tours bus, while Rosie Dauner stands behind. Both are from Omaha. (The other lady in blue on the right) is Ruth Nelson, but she's dead now. It might be better to crop her out of the picture.) (I need this picture back)." There is now a "Cliché Corner" feature, which focuses on media overuse and abuse of phrases such as "under the radar," "shock and awe," and "Adlai Stevenson moment."

AJR also publishes an annual "Directory of Selected News Sources." It is currently indexed in *Access, Readers' Guide to Periodical Literature* (entry 209), and *PAIS International in Print* (entry 208), to name a few. (According to the 2003 Ulrich's, AJR also is conveniently indexed in *Dental Abstracts.*)

595.   Australian Journalism Review. 1979– . Journalism Education Association, c/o School of Communication, Information & New Media, University of South Australia, St. Bernards Road, Magill SA 5072. Semiannual. ISSN 0810-2686.

North American journalists will discover some thought-provoking and highly readable material in this journal which has, during the last decade, proved itself to be a formidable international media watchdog. As would be expected, many items are scholarly in nature, but there also are contributions from journalists and government officials. A 1992 issue, emphasizing international issues and journalism ethics, offered the following articles: "Television Journalism and Image Ethics," "How Queensland Political Parties Promoted Crime: The 1992 Election," "Agendas in Indonesian Responses to Australian Journalism: Some Journalists' Perspectives," "A Sense of Deja Vu: Canadian Journalism Education Ponders Its Future," and "Reporting French Politics." A 1994 issue published articles ranging from "Sources of News—Who Feeds the Watchdogs?" to "A Suggested Core Curriculum in Journalism Education." A 2002 issue included the following: "Overlooked and Underused: How

Australia's First Public Journalism Project Treated Women and Indigenous People." It is, unfortunately, published only twice a year, and the two issues are frequently published as one volume. Researchers might also wish to consult *Australian Studies in Journalism* (School of Journalism and Communication, University of Queensland) and the *Pacific Journalism Review* (School of Communication Studies, Auckland University of Technology), covering the South Pacific, Asia-Pacific, Australia, and New Zealand.

596.   British Journalism Review. 1990– . University of Luton Press, University of Luton, 75 Castle St., Lutons, Beds LU1 3AG, United Kingdom. www.bjr.org.uk. Quarterly. ISSN 0956-4748.

Despite its relative newcomer status, the *British Journalism Review* has made its mark, consistently providing a lively, engaging, and thought-provoking examination of British media, and frequently, in comparison, American media, while serving up its share of snide observations and overwritten prose. Cal McCrystal's "Should We Stop the Muck-spreading?," published in a 1995 issue, is but one example of the magazine's provocative writing: "One question invariably comes up whenever I dine or drink with Americans in London: Why is it, someone politely asks, that British newspapers are more prurient than American newspapers? To the diplomat's wife or the visiting businessman I usually offer the same answer: we are prurient because our readers require it. And why should this be so? Because, I reply, prurience has become an emanation so central to our culture that weightier subjects tend to sink from sight beneath it (Out of sight, out of mind!). This situation suits government very nicely, I suggest, despite parliament's occasional lamentations about it. An electorate guided by its copulatory organs is 'safer' than one motivated by its power to reason." In 2003 Phillip Knightley writes in "History or Bunkum": "The Pentagon made it clear from the beginning of the war against Iraq that there would be no censorship. What it failed to say was that war correspondents might well find themselves in a situation similar to that in Korea in 1950. This was described by one American correspondent as the military saying: 'You can write what you like—but if we don't like it we'll shoot you.' The figures in Iraq tell a terrible story."

Each issue features 8 to 10 articles, an editorial, and lengthy book reviews. Researchers and others with any interest in the British media will appreciate the journal's accessibility and range of topics. Selected articles and index (1989–1999) are available on the Web site.

597.   Broadcasting & Cable. 1931– . Reed Business Information, 245 W. 17th Street, New York, NY 10011. www.broadcastingcable.com. subscriptions to Box 6399, Torrence, CA, 90504. Weekly. ISSN 1068-6827.

Formerly entitled *Broadcasting,* this is one of the must-read, most-read trade sources for current information on the broadcast industry. Television, radio, cable, satellite, and home video are covered, as well as updates on programming, legislation, business news, technology, advertising, and FCC actions. Business and advertising are emphasized. *Broadcasting & Cable* is widely indexed. The business news of broadcasting also is covered in *Mediaweek* (entry 623) and *TelevisionWeek,* formerly *Electronic Media* (entry 638). For those who seek a Canadian broadcasting magazine, Broadcaster is available from Business Information Group. For information and ideas on news programming see *The Rundown* (Standish Publishing Company), a weekly newsletter on trends in local television news aimed at broadcast executives.

598.   C:JET (Communication: Journalism Education Today). 1967– . Journalism Education Association, Inc., Kansas State University, 103 Kedzie Hall, Manhattan, KS 66506. www.jea.org. Quarterly. ISSN 0010-3535.

This professional journal is on the must-read list of most secondary school journalism teachers and advisers. Its mission is to "provide educational materials to JEA members on a wide variety of topics related to all aspects of scholastic media with lesson plans, teaching tips, current research, and other resources." Five to 10 articles plus regular features usually constitute the whole of *C:JET,* but occasionally proceedings of national meetings or special reports are printed. The book review section highlights important publications, but is occasionally marred by careless copyediting (for example, four errors are spotted in a review of *The Associated Press Stylebook*). This journal addresses universal themes such as "Truth, Responsibility, and the Myth of Objectivity" and "Journalistic Responsibility" as well as subjects only an adviser or teacher could love ("Yearbook Journalism Teaching Aids"). It is indexed in *Current Index to Journals in Education* (entry 197).

599.   College Media Review. 1956– . College Media Advisers, Department of Journalism, University of Memphis, Memphis, TN 38152. www.collegemedia.org. Quarterly. ISSN 0739-1056.

College Media Review is designed for college media advisers and managers, focusing on issues in publishing print and electronic college newspapers, magazines, and yearbooks. This thin journal, published twice a year, covers topics from press freedom to newspaper style. A 1994 issue, for example, sported the following articles: "A World of Difference" (on multicultural staffing), "Editorial Choice and the Maserati Level" (selecting poetry for campus literary magazines), and "Dressing Up That Dull Editorial Page." Regular features and departments include technology, legal issues and ethics, advising, and book reviews. It is indexed in *Higher Education Abstracts.*

600.   Columbia Journalism Review. 1962– . Columbia University, Graduate School of Journalism, Journalism Building, 2950 Broadway, New York, NY 10027. www.cjr.org. Bimonthly. ISSN 0010-194X.

Few journalism reviews have been applauded and booed, praised and spanked as much as *Columbia Journalism Review.* Some reviews (*Montana Journalism Review, Access, Cryano's Journal*) have just faded away. Others (*MORE, feed/back, Chicago Journalism Review*) have gone out kicking and screaming. Some continue to move steadily along (*SJR: St. Louis Journalism Review* [entry 635] and *Australian Journalism Review* [entry 595]), serving their regions and readers. *CJR,* however, has been accused of being petty, petulant, pedantic, and picky. It also has been lauded for single-handedly raising the standards of journalism. In truth, it lies somewhere in between. The contents page spells out, in an excerpt from the magazine's founding editorial, what *CJR* stands for: "To assess the performance of journalism…to help stimulate continuing improvement in the profession, and to speak out for what is right, fair, and decent." Those are difficult words to live up to, but *CJR* has done a satisfactory job. There have been times when the writing was not so lively, and when *CJR* itself should have been listed in the "Darts" section of its own "Darts and Laurels."

Regardless, this is the basic journalism review, with *American Journalism Review* (entry 594) following close behind. The six or seven main articles in each issue are usually investigative or analytical. Articles in a 2003 issue include a special report on *The New York Times* in the wake of the Jayson Blair incident; "Toward a New Deal: Rethinking

Objectivity in a World of Spin"; "The Avenger" (on Seymour Hersh); " 'A Thousand Flowers'" (the media in Iraq); and "Recovery Plan" (report on Reuters). The "lower case" feature on the inside back cover still publicizes press bloopers such as "County Wants Eyes Out for Child Abuse" from *The Davis (CA) Enterprise* (1/31/03) and "Reader Requests Tanning Procedure for Hunter's Wife," from *The Express-News* (San Antonio, 8/1/87). Cumulative indexes are available. *CJR* is indexed in sources such as *Humanities Index,* (entry 199), *Readers' Guide to Periodical Literature* (entry 209), and *Political Science Abstracts,* and is available full text online via numerous services such as LexisNexis.

601.   Communicator. 1946– . Radio-Television News Directors Association, 1000 Connecticut Avenue, N.W., Suite 615, Washington, D.C. 20036. www.rtnda.org. Monthly. ISSN 0033-7153.

Formerly the *RTNDA Communicator,* the *Communicator* is aimed at news directors, reporters, and producers and addresses all aspects of radio and television news. It is an important source for the broadcast journalist. Its mission is to "give the reader the latest information on issues of importance: news judgment, ethics and decision-making, newsroom management and staffing, professional development, industry trends and practices, and more." Journalistic ethics are examined closely here, as well as technology and newsroom management issues. Each issue is packed with a variety of relevant and, on the whole, well-written material. In addition, the *Communicator* offers current articles on its Web site.

Examples of stories in a 1995 issue are: "Ten Years After" (on the people who managed television newsrooms a decade ago); "Addicted to News" (on physical addiction to your job and its deadlines); "Raising Ethical Issues"; and "Trend-Setting Stand-Ups." Departments and columns include "Tough Calls" (news directors' responses to ethical questions), legal issues, and newswriting. In 2003, the publication addressed issues such as "Focus on ENG/SNG" and "Back in Business." Users might also wish to consult TVnewz.com, a webzine for television news professionals.

602.   Copy Editor: The National Newsletter for Professional Copy Editors. 1990– . McMurry Newsletters, 1010 E. Missouri Avenue, Phoenix, AZ 85014. www.copy-editor.com. Bimonthly. ISSN 1049-3190.

Most trade journals in journalism aim at the reporter, editor, or publisher. Although working editors at the copy desk will find items of interest in journalism reviews and membership newsletters, few publications are designed specifically for them. (*Righting Words, The Journal of Language and Editing,* published in the late 1980s, was one of those magazines.) Copy editors, or the "Rodney Dangerfields of journalism," according to a 1987 *Editor & Publisher* article, will find here brief articles, information, arguments, and decisions on issues they must deal with daily (or nightly) at the desk. Journalism instructors who teach editing will also identify some useful teaching aids here; selected articles are available on the Web site. An eight-page 1995/96 issue contains articles ranging from "The Elements of Cyberstyle," to "Remembrance of Things Past Perfect" in addition to a question-and-answer feature, dictionary update, resources listings, technology updates, and a "Hot Button" feature. A 2003 issue offers fewer feature articles but is still packed with examples and advice. The impressive editorial advisory board boasts names such as Carl Sessions Stepp of *American Journalism Review* and the University of Maryland; Allan Siegal from *The New York Times*; and other names from newspapers and magazines, Columbia University Press, and *Encyclopaedia Britannica.*

603.   Critical Studies in Media Communication. 1984– . National Communication Association, 1765 N Street, N.W. Washington, D.C. 20036. www.arches.uga.edu. Quarterly. ISSN 1529-5036.

Formerly *Critical Studies in Mass Communication,* this is now a "forum for cross-disciplinary scholarship treating issues related to mediated communication." The three or four research and theoretical articles in each issue of this scholarly journal for specialists focus on "interpretive approaches" to any and all aspects of media communication including television, radio, newspaper, video, new media, and film. Its policy states that it encourages a "broad range of methodological and theoretical approaches to the analysis of mass media institutions, histories, technologies, and messages, including the intersections of mass media and culture." Article titles in a 2002 issue range from "It's Still a White World Out There: The Interplay of Culture and Economics in International Television Trade" to "Mediating Terrorism: Text and Protest in Interpretations of The Siege." Critical book reviews are lengthy, but shorter notes on some books are also included.

This journal is indexed in numerous sources including *Current Index to Journals in Education* (entry 197), *Communication Abstracts* (entry 195), and Matlon's *Index to Journals in Communication Studies* (entry 206), and is available full text online via services such as Gale Group and ISI. Researchers might also wish to consult the *Web Journal of Mass Communication Research* (www.scripps.ohiou.edu/wjmcr), an online, refereed publication launched in 1997.

604.   Design. Journal of the Society for News Design. 1979– . Society for News Design, 1130 Ten Rod Road, F-104, North Kingstown, RI 02852. www.snd.org. Quarterly. ISSN 1520-4243.

Formerly the *Journal of the Society of Newspaper Design, Design's* format has changed from magazine to tabloid back to magazine in the last two decades, and it has been reduced to a quarterly, but each issue since the first in 1979 has been well-designed and packed with the kind of stories and graphics found in few magazines. This is the only periodical devoted exclusively to newspaper design. The contents pages continue to reflect the most respected names in publication design in addition to providing a forum for talented newcomers. Articles are well-written and timely, with emphasis on color, technology, typography, redesign, and graphics. As one might expect, graphic art is innovative and the color is superb. A wide array of slick, beautiful, and innovative magazines such as *Graphis* (Graphis Inc.), *Step Inside Design* (formerly *Step by Step Graphics,* Dynamic Graphics, Inc.), *How* (F & W Publications), *Communication Arts* (Coyne & Blanchard), and *Print* (RC Publications, Inc.) should be examined when studying publication design and graphics, but *Design* is the only one that consistently answers the professional prayers of newspaper artists and designers. Journalism students and instructors, and especially school and college newspaper advisers, would also do well to consult *Design*.

605.   Editor & Publisher, The Newsmagazine of the Fourth Estate. 1884– . Editor & Publisher Company, Inc., 770 Broadway, New York, NY 10003-9595. www.editorand publisher.com. Weekly. ISSN 0013-094X.

Some jobhunters pick up *E&P* to scour the classified advertising section, but savvy print journalists will at least scan the contents each week. Doing so is much easier than in years past; the old, cluttered "Index to Issue" page was replaced with a detailed contents page subdivided by news, sections, and departments. This was an important redesign element for one of the most important trade magazines and "the oldest publishers and advertisers newspaper in America."

News stories and features cover all aspects of newspaper journalism. Regular features include information on technology, syndicates, and "Newspeople." In a "-30-" column, formerly "Shop Talk at Thirty," a journalist (e.g., editor, publisher, professor) will air a grievance, offer an opinion, or "talk shop." Annual special features include a directory of journalism awards and fellowships and syndicate directory. For news on the Web, a photo of the week, and an *E&P* online weekly poll, visit the Web site at editorandpublisher.com.

The *Editor & Publisher 100th Anniversary 1884–1984* issue was published in 1984 and offers a decade-by-decade account of American journalism history. Editor & Publisher, Inc. also publishes the *Editor & Publisher International Yearbook* (entry 354) and *Editor & Publisher Market Guide Directory.* Editor & Publisher is indexed in *Business Periodicals Index* (entry 189) and *Graphic Arts Literature Abstracts.* Available full text online through sources such as Gale Group, H. W. Wilson, and ProQuest.

606.   Folio: The New Dynamics of Magazine Publishing. 1972– . Media Central, 470 Park Avenue S., 8th floor, New York, NY 10016. www.foliomag.com. 16 issues/year. ISSN 0046-4333.

Formerly *Folio: The Magazine for Magazine Management,* this publication was redesigned and renamed in late 2002. A wide range of journalistic, design, ethical, publishing, and management issues punctuate articles entitled "The New Rage of Science," "Online Reloaded," and "The Worst-Case Survival Guide for B-to-B Magazines." Three or four feature stories and regular columns and departments such as "Magz," "Magazine Marketplace," and "Enterprise Zone" combine to make this an upscale, timely, and important management publication. More changes appear to be in its future, however, with the recent departure of the editor in chief and a gradually, but noticeably thinner publication. It is indexed in several sources including *Business Periodicals Index* (entry 189) and is available full text online via services such as Gale Group and Dialog.

607.   Gazette: The International Journal for Communication Studies. 1955– . Sage Publications, Inc., 2455 Teller Road, Thousand Oaks, CA 91320. Bimonthly. ISSN 0016-5492.

Formerly *Gazette: The International Journal for Mass Communication Studies,* this scholarly international journal now covers "the international community of communication scholars, with a particular focus on communication and international relations; communication and development; and new information and communication technologies." Each issue contains three or four lengthy (15–30 pages) articles focusing on a theme. For example, the February 2003 issue dissects "Determinants of International News Production" with articles such as "Homogeneity Around the World? Comparing the Systemic Determinants of International News Flow Between Developed and Developing Countries"; "Organizational Determinants of International News Coverage in Korean Newspapers"; and "Individual Perceptions of International Correspondents in the Middle East: An Obstacle to Fair News?" This important title in international journalism is indexed in sources such as *Communication Abstracts* (entry 195), *International Political Science Abstracts,* and *PAIS International in Print* (entry 208), and is available full text online from services such as EBSCO and Gale Group.

For another international perspective and current international press news, see *Global Journalist Online* (www.journalism.missouri.edu/globalj/index.html), the monthly bulletin of the International Press Institute.

608. **Grassroots Editor. 1960– .** International Society of Weekly Newspaper Editors, Institute of International Studies, Missouri Southern State College, 3950 E. Newman Road, Joplin, MO 64801-1595. www.mssc.edu/iswne/groots.htm. Quarterly. ISSN 0017-3541.

Issues in community and weekly journalism are raised in this plain and outspoken magazine, "a journal for newspeople." Five or six feature articles comprise the bulk of the 20 or so pages allotted for each black-and-white issue. (Users also may review some recent issues on the Web site.) There are few ads and illustrations, so all attention is focused on the generally well-written and succinct articles on publishing, managing, and editing the community and weekly newspaper. Recent articles include "Newspaper Front-Page Ads— The Good, the Bad and the Ugly," "Building a Community by Building a School Newspaper," "A Case Study of One Daily's Cooperative Project," and "One Toke Over the Line? When the Watch Dog Becomes the Guard Dog." *Publishers' Auxiliary* (entry 632) also addresses the needs of the weekly and should be examined in addition to this source.

609. **The Harvard International Journal of Press Politics. 1996– .** Sage Publications, Inc., 2455 Teller Road, Thousand Oaks, CA 91320. Quarterly. ISSN 1081-180X.

The *Journal's* focus is on journalism and public policy, international news, and communications. Indexed in numerous indexes including *Communication Abstracts* (entry 195) and *PAIS International in Print* (entry 208), it is available full text online via services such as EBSCO and ISI.

610. **The Internet Newsroom. 1995– .** Bergman Publishing LLC, P.O. Box 2625, Glen Allen, VA 23058-2625. Monthly.

Labeled "Your Guide to the World of Electronic Factgathering," this no-frills, advertising-free newsletter contains vast amounts of background material on Web sites potentially useful to journalists and news researchers, and grassroots how-to-do-it advice on using the Internet. According to its mission statement, this publication "focuses its energies on those organizations and individuals using the Internet for research and information. TIN searches for, then summarizes, those Web sites that make excellent sources for information." A recent issue included the following articles: "Women's Health Concerns," "Lewis & Clark Reach 200," "Pet Adoption," "Commerce on the High Seas," "The World of Video Games," and "The Boy from Hogwarts." A regular feature is "Notable Netsites," a compendium of a dozen or so Web sites of particular interest to journalists and information professionals. Published monthly, this is a timely, well-conceived package bursting with information, addresses, briefs, and advice. Further, a recent publisher's note revealed that "The Internet Newsroom is finally going electronic. We may be saying goodbye to the hard copy version as early as the September [2003] issue." Users might also consult the *IRE Journal* (entry 611.)

611. **The IRE Journal. 1978– .** Investigative Reporters & Editors, Inc., 138 Neff Annex, School of Journalism, University of Missouri, Columbia, MO 65211. www.ire.org. six issues/year. ISSN 0164-7016.

There is no better acronym than *IRE* for the muckraking crew of investigative journalists who crank out this tabloid six times a year. The *Journal* reminds us, however, that "When we refer to investigative reporting, it is meant in the broadest sense. All good reporters, whether full-time investigative reporters or those assigned to government, science, education, finance or other traditional beats, do investigative work." This journal provides us with consistently accurate, occasionally humorous, engaging, and in-depth articles on reporting and writing the tough stories. One recent cover story focuses on "Following the Faithful: Investigative Reporting and Religion" while another looks into "Assisted Living." Each issue usually contains a cover story, three or four feature articles, a FOI Report, tip sheets, and background on court cases. In addition, former editor Steve Weinberg (currently a Senior Contributing Editor and coauthor of *The Investigative Reporter's Handbook,* entry 407) contributes a first-rate book review column. Students, reporters, editors, and information specialists all will profit from this unique tabloid, which is available full text online via services such as Factiva, Gale Group, and ProQuest.

For additional and up-to-the-minute reports, check out the Web site (entry 682), which offers, for example, an "Extra! Extra!" feature listing examples of investigative reporting on Web sites of newspapers and broadcast stations. Other Investigative Reporters & Editors publications include *The Investigative Journalist's Morgue* (entry 185) and *The IRE Books,* summaries of investigations.

612.   **Journal of Broadcasting and Electronic Media. 1956– .** Broadcast Education Association, 1771 N Street N.W., Washington, D.C. 20036. www.beaweb.org. Quarterly. ISSN 0883-8151.

Read *Broadcasting & Cable* (entry 597) for the most current news and information in this broad field, and then sit back with this periodical, formerly *Journal of Broadcasting,* for scholarly treatment of radio, television, and satellite broadcasting and their effect on the world at large. Given its far-reaching subject matter, it is indexed in numerous sources such as *Communication Abstracts* (entry 195), *Current Index to Journals in Education* (entry 197), *PAIS International in Print* (entry 208), and Matlon's *Index to Journals in Communication Studies* (entry 206). Recent research articles include "Does Audience Skepticism of the Media Matter in Agenda Setting?," "Television Exposure and the Public's Perceptions of Physicians," and "Making News Memorable: Applying Theory to the Production of Local Television News." The many book reviews tend to be well written and range in length from notes to essays.

613.   **Journal of Communication. 1951– .** International Communication Association, Oxford University Press, 2001 Evans Road, Cary, NC 27513. Quarterly. ISSN 0021-9916.

This journal "seeks to be a general forum for communication scholarship and that publishes articles and book reviews examining a broad range of issues." Articles also tend to be less technical than those in other scholarly publications. It is indexed in numerous sources including *America: History and Life, Current Index to Journals in Education* (entry 197), *Communication Abstracts* (entry 195), *Matlon's Index to Journals in Communication Studies* (entry 206), and *Social Sciences Index* (entry 211) and is available online via services such as Factiva and Gale Group.

Articles on "Television News and the Cultivation of Fear of Crime," "The World's Nicest Grown-Up: A Fantasy Theme Analysis of News Media Coverage of Fred Rogers," and "The Impact of Background Radio and Television on High School Students' Homework Performance" appeared in one recent issue. The large critical book review section is one of the best features of this journal. See also the *Canadian Journal of Communication* (Simon Fraser University), *Communication Research* (Sage), *The Howard Journal of Communications* (Taylor & Francis), and the *Journal of Communication Inquiry* (Sage).

614.   Journal of Mass Media Ethics. 1985– . Lawrence Erlbaum Associates, Inc., 10 Industrial Drive, Mahwah, NJ 07430-2262. jmme.byu.edu. Quarterly. ISSN 0890-0523.

Journalistic ethics is a frequent focus in most trade journals, almost to the point of overkill. This periodical, however, became one of the most important in the field early on, and devotes itself exclusively to the topic. (In 1989, Barry Bingham launched Fineline, a newsletter on journalistic ethics, but it lasted only two and a half years.) The journal has grown from an upstart, semiannual publication to a well-respected, quarterly refereed journal with an all-star staff and editorial advisory board. The journal's original stated purpose was "bridging real and imagined gaps between media professionals and academics who have practical and philosophical concerns over the ethical performance of the media." In this endeavor it still succeeds, with a balanced mix of theoretical, philosophical, and practical articles written by those whose names we associate with media ethics: Clifford Christians, Lou Hodges, Bob Steele, Bob Logan, editors Jay Black and Ralph D. Barney, and book review editor Deni Elliott, to name a few. The first issue focused on mass media codes of ethics, and other issues have centered on newsroom ethics, professional ethics, ethics in photojournalism, credibility, privacy, and objectivity. A 2003 issue offered the following: "The Academy and Cyberspace Ethics," "The Rhetoric of Hate on the Internet: Hateporn's Challenge to Modern Media Ethics," "Continuities and Discontinuities in Ethical Reflections on Digital Virtual Reality," and "Reformatting Ethics." Book reviews continue to employ spirited and thought-provoking writing. It is indexed in numerous sources including *Communication Abstracts* (entry 195), *Humanities Index* (entry 199), and *PAIS International in Print* (entry 208). Abstracts also are available on the Web site.

Black and Barney, along with Bob Steele, are authors of *Doing Ethics in Journalism: A Handbook with Case Studies* (Allyn & Bacon, 1999), useful as a reference source and practical supplementary textbook. Users will also be interested in the twice yearly *Media Ethics* magazine (Emerson College), and the annual *Social Responsibility: Business, Journalism, Law, Medicine* (Washington and Lee University).

615.   Journalism and Communication Monographs. 1966– . Association for Education in Journalism and Mass Communication, 234 Outlet Pointe Blvd, Suite A, Columbia, SC 29210-5667. Quarterly. ISSN 1522-6379.

As the title indicates, each thin monograph (formerly *Journalism and Mass Communication Monographs*) is a thoroughly documented piece of research on some narrow aspect of journalism. Its mission statement includes the following: "One of the goals of the monograph series from the beginning has been to publish scholarly work from the entire field, whether the methodology was historical, legal, behavioral, or whatever." Many of these monographs fall into the "historical" and "whatever" categories, and include "Getting the Story Out of Nazi Germany," "The Press Corp and the Kennedy Assassination," "From the Back of the Foxhole: Black Correspondents in World War II," "Egyptian Radio: Tool of Political and National Development," "Literary Newswriting: The Death of an Oxymoron," "Journalism Professionalism as an Organizational-Level Concept," "Setting the Record Straight: A Proposal for Expanding the Role of Retraction in Libel Litigation," "Packaging

Reality: The Influence of Fictional Forms on the Early Development of Television Documentary," "Crafting the National Pastime's Image: The History of Major League Baseball Public Relations," and "Communication and Journalism from 'Daddy' Bleyer to Wilbur Schramm." Although this refereed publication appeals to a special audience, it belongs in most journalism collections. It is indexed in *America: History and Life, Communication Abstracts* (entry 195), *Resources in Education* (entry 210), and *Historical Abstracts,* and is available full text online via services such as ProQuest and Gale Group.

616.   Journalism and Mass Communication Educator. 1945– . Association for Education in Journalism and Mass Communication, 234 Outlet Pointe Blvd, Suite A, Columbia, SC. 29210-5667. excellent.com/utk.edu/jmce. Quarterly. ISSN 1077-6958.

Formerly *Journalism Educator,* this nontechnical, refereed publication for professors and administrators considers all aspects of college journalism education. This unadorned little journal, with few illustrations or photographs, sometimes contains articles that are less than bombastic. Still, it approaches the real issues in undergraduate journalism education such as plagiarism, censorship, grading, computers and training, and internships. Article titles in a 1996 issue, for example, range from "Broadcast Newsroom Hiring and Career Preparation" to "The European Debate in 1894 on Journalism Education." Each issue carries six or more articles, and regular features include book reviews and faculty news. It is indexed in *Current Index to Journals in Education* (entry 197) and *Communication Abstracts* (entry 195), to name a few, and is available full text online via services such as Factiva, ProQuest, and Gale Group. A separate *Journalism and Mass Communication Directory* (entry 362) also is published by the AEJMC.

617.   Journalism and Mass Communication Quarterly. 1924– . Association for Education in Journalism and Mass Communication, 234 Outlet Pointe Blvd, Suite A, Columbia, SC 29210-5667. Quarterly. ISSN 1077-6990.

This is the best-read or most-skimmed scholarly research journal in the field for a number of reasons: It is indexed in more than 40 indexes and abstracts, including *Communication Abstracts* (entry 195), *Humanities Index* (entry 199), *Psychological Abstracts,* and *PAIS International in Print* (entry 208), and is available full text online via services such as Factiva and Gale Group. It considers practically every aspect of journalism and communications in the world; each issue contains book and textbook reviews by scholars in the field and listings of new publications. Unfortunately, it no longer offers "Articles on Mass Communication in U.S. and Foreign Journals," a feature consisting of one-sentence summaries of several hundred articles subdivided by subject (thus devising a semblance of a journalism index). Quantitative research is emphasized, and the "Information for Contributors" section states that this journal "strives to be the flagship journal of the Association for Education in Journalism and Mass Communication and to be a premier journal in the field." Each issue usually features a dozen or so articles, ranging from "Going Negative: Candidate Usage of Internet Web Sites During the 2000 Presidential Campaign" to "Prior Restraints on Photojournalists." One issue on "Media Behavior" offered a wide selection of articles on media in the public arena, media and government, theory and methodology, and media management and organization. Cumulative indexes are published, and annual subject and author indexes are available in each winter issue.

618.   Journalism History. 1974– . E. W. Scripps School of Journalism, Ohio University, Athens, OH 45701-2979. Quarterly. ISSN 0094-7679.

A spare, but important scholarly research journal, *Journalism History* concentrates on historical aspects of journalism and mass communication in the United States. Special issues have centered on the Constitution, and, in a bold move, the black-and-white cover was changed to yellow for the special issue on sensationalism. Each issue includes six or more lengthy articles as well as book and electronic media reviews and reports on current research. A 1994 issue offered the following articles: "Race, Money, Politics and the Antebellum Black Press," "The Press and Tails of Darwin: Victorian Satire of Evolution," "Journalistic Impartiality on the Eve of Revolution: *The Boston Evening Post, 1770–1775*," and "The Black Press in the 'Nadir' of African Americans." A recent issue detailed "The Myth Becomes the Mythmaker: Bat Masterson as New York Sports Writer" and "When a Newspaper Was Accused of Killing a President: How Five New York City Newspapers Reacted." Cumulative indexes are available. *Journalism History* is indexed in publications such as *America: History and Life, Historical Abstracts, and Humanities Index* (entry 199), and is available full text online via services such as ProQuest and H. W. Wilson. See also *American Journalism* (entry 593). In addition, Carfax Publishing Ltd.'s *Newspaper and Periodical History, Media History,* and *Historical Journal of Film, Radio and Television* offer a British slant on selected issues in journalism history.

619.　Mass Communication and Society. 1973– . Lawrence Erlbaum Associates, Inc. 10 Industrial Avenue, Mahwah, NJ 07430-2262. Quarterly. ISSN 1520-5436.

Formerly *Mass Communications Review,* this plain, scholarly journal published by the Mass Communication and Society Division of the AEJMC focuses on "original research and scholarship on mass communication processes and effects with the goal of contributing to a theoretical base of knowledge." Writing levels vary, but most articles are aimed at an academic audience. The editorial board and editorial staff consist of an impressive collection of well-known scholars, but the journal reads and looks as if it could use a surge of adrenalin. Articles in a 2003 issue include "Television Reporters' Perceptions of How Television and Newspaper Competition Affects City Hall Coverage," "Pacing in Children's Television Programming," and "Parasocial Breakups: Measuring Individual Differences in Responses to the Dissolution of Parasocial Relationships." Cumulative indexes are available. It is indexed in *Sociological Abstracts* and available full text online via services such as Gale Group and EBSCO.

620.　The Masthead. 1948– . National Conference of Editorial Writers, 6223 Executive Boulevard, Rockville, MD 20852. Quarterly. ISSN 0025-5122.

Some of the best writing on journalism is featured in this straightforward, well-packaged publication. Editorial and commentary writers in both print and broadcast face unique problems and situations, and *The Masthead* addresses these issues. One issue, for example, takes on the state of broadcast editorials; another challenges opinion page readership. In addition to these topical "Masthead Symposium" pieces, this 30–40 page quarterly offers reports, features, editorial cartoons, and book reviews useful to any editorial journalist. Journalism instructors will use this in the classroom as well. *The Masthead* is currently indexed in *America: History and Life and Historical Abstracts.* Magazines addressing editorial cartoons include, among others, *Target: The Political Cartoon Quarterly,* which ceased publication in 1987, *Cartoonist Profiles* (Cartoonist Profiles) and *Witty World* (Witty World Pubs.). Available full text online via EBSCO.

621.   Media. 1994– . Canadian Association of Journalists, St. Patrick's Building 316B, Carleton University, 1125 Colonel By Drive, Ottawa, Ontario K1S 5B6, Canada. Quarterly. ISSN 1198-2209.

In 1994, the 24-year-old *Content* merged with the *Canadian Association of Journalist's Bulletin.* The quarterly *Media* is the result. Its goal is to "reflect and promote high professional standards for journalistic research and writing, which is topical, practical and current in relation to the issues it covers, as well as keeping tabs on developing and evolving techniques and technologies of our trade." In this it succeeds. Columns on writing and the Internet ("Journalismnet" by Julian Sher) are reflective of current issues in the profession. "A Writer's Toolbox" and "Tools of the Trade' offer practical advice, and the numerous book reviews are timely .

The Ryerson Review of Journalism (Ryerson School of Journalism) also is a timely and useful barometer of issues in Canadian journalism.

622.   Media Law Reporter. 1977– . Bureau of National Affairs, Inc., 1231 25th Street N.W., Washington, D.C. 20037. Weekly. ISSN 0148-1045.

This weekly journal presents U.S. Supreme Court and important federal and state court decisions pertaining to media law and communications. A topical index, classification guide, tables of cases, and an index digest allow full access to the text of cases on antitrust, broadcast media, disclosure, fair trial and free press, libel, privacy, and prior restraint. There are annual cumulations. *Media Law Reporter* is indexed in *Legal Resource Index.* For further information, background material, and so on, consult publications such as *Communications and the Law* (William S. Hein & Co.) and *News Media and the Law* (entry 624). For a British perspective, try Tolley's *Communications Law* (Tolley).

623.   Mediaweek. 1966– . VNU Business Publications, 770 Broadway, New York, NY 10003. Weekly (47 issues/year). www.mediaweek.com. ISSN 0155-176X.

Labeled "The News Magazine of the Media," this weekly looks suspiciously similar to the magazine *Adweek.* Indeed, they share the same publisher and follow much the same format. For the news executive on the go, there are snippets of breaking news on all aspects of the media including cable, network television, radio, and magazines. The publication sports a "Market Indicators" section containing a one- or two-sentence wrap-up of the state of national television, net cable, spot television, radio, and magazines for that week. For example, in the 16 June 2003 issue, we learn that the spot television market is "tightening," that magazines are "strong," and "men's and women's health and fitness titles are shaping up." Users in need of up-to-the-minute information may consult an online version of current headlines for no charge at mediaweek.com. It is indexed in several indexes including *Business Periodicals Index* (entry 189) and *Management Contents* and available full text online via services such as Gale Group and Dialog. Users also will be interested in *NewsInc.* (entry 626), which covers the business of newspaper, *TelevisionWeek,* formerly *Electronic Media* (entry 638), and *I Want Media* (www.iwantmedia.com), a weblog on the media industry.

624.   News Media and the Law. 1973– . Reporters' Committee for Freedom of the Press, 1815 N. Fort Myer Drive, Suite 900, Arlington, VA 22209. four issues/year. ISSN 0149-0737.

From "Cameras in the Courtroom" to "Rap Sheet Access," this journal covers all aspects of broadcast and print media law. Numerous brief articles cover court cases and news events. Be forewarned, however, that this news-flash publication does not contain any in-depth material. Regular and occasional departments include "Broadcasting and Copyright," "Libel & Privacy," "Confidentiality," "Freedom of Information," and "Newsgathering." Many issues feature nifty pullout sections such as "Access to Electronic Records" (entry 389), "Secret Justice: Alternative Dispute Resolution," and "Media Privacy vs. the Public Interest." It is indexed in several sources including *Legal Resource Index* and is available full text on line via services such as Factiva and ProQuest. For texts of cases, consult *Media Law Reporter* (entry 622). *Communications and the Law* (William S. Hein & Co.) might also be a useful resource. Those seeking a British perspective might consult Tolley's *Communications Law* (Tolley).

625.   News Photographer. 1946– . National Press Photographers Association, Inc., 3200 Croasdaile Drive, Suite 306, Durham, NC 27705. www.nppa.org. Monthly. ISSN 0199-2422.

This is not merely a picture magazine, although it is full of black-and-white and color photographs. *News Photographer,* one of a handful of publications designed specifically for the professional photojournalist, also could be an educational tool for publishers, editors, news directors, graphic artists, and journalism students. Photos appearing in *News Photographer* can become topics of discussion in journalistic ethics sessions and hands-on photojournalism classes. Each issue contains several features and departments such as "NewsViews," "Pictures of the Month," "Common Cents," and "Ethics Matters." It is indexed in *Graphic Arts Literature Abstracts* and available full text online via sources such as Gale Group. Users also will be interested in *Reportage: The International Magazine of Photojournalism* (Reportage Publishing), launched in London in 1993, and *The Digital Journalist,* a monthly Web magazine (digitaljournalist.org).

626.   NewsInc. 1989– . The Cole Group, P.O. Box 3426, Daly City, CA 94015-0426. www.colegroup.com/newsinc/. Weekly. ISSN 1043-7452.

NewsInc., "the weekly newsletter on the business of the newspaper business," was acquired in 1997 by The Cole Group, which also publishes *The Cole Papers,* a monthly newsletter on technology and journalism. According to the Web site, "It brings readers a thorough and complete look at issues that effect newspapers: performance of publicly traded companies, mergers and acquisitions, circulation issues, advertising issues, marketing issues and a strong look at new media issues."

Short articles and news briefs are included in its 10 or 12 pages. Articles are timely, and busy editors and publishers will appreciate the brevity and clarity of articles such as "McPaperless: USA Today to Open Drive-In Window on the World Wide Web" and "Handy Guide to 1Q Stock Performance for Newspapers." *NewsInc.* is available full text online with a subscription to the print edition and also via services such as Factiva and Gale Group. Readers of *NewsInc.* will also want to scan *Presstime* (entry 631) and perhaps *MediaWeek* (entry 623).

627.   Newspaper Research Journal. 1979– . Association for Education in Journalism and Mass Communication, 234 Outlet Pointe Blvd, Suite A, Columbia, SC 29210-5667. Quarterly. ISSN 0739-5329.

The Newspaper Division of the AEJMC produces this scholarly journal devoted entirely to the study of newspapers. Various articles consider all aspects of the newspaper industry, including management, circulation, editorial, readership, libel, ethics, and technology. *NRJ* strives to provide a "bridge between journalism scholars and newspaper professionals and a forum for practical research on and discussion of issues of interest to both." Each issue contains about a dozen articles, 12–15 pages in length; the quality of writing varies. An "Editors' Comments" section usually contributes a brief but reflective warts-and-all commentary on research, its uses and failures, readership, and the frequently tenuous relationship between practitioners and scholars. Articles range from the nontechnical or practical ("Pagination and the Newsroom: A Question of Time") to the highly theoretical and/or quantitative ("A Parsimonious Regression Model to Predict Metropolitan Circulation in Outlying Counties"). The book review section is small but satisfying. *NRJ's* mammoth editorial board is a "who's who" of journalists, ranging from Bob Giles, Nieman Foundation, to Bruce Garrison, University of Miami. This is a basic title for print journalism collections, but it has been ignored by many major indexing services. Fortunately, it is indexed in *Communication Abstracts* (entry 195), *Sage Urban Studies Abstracts,* and, strangely enough, *Peace Research Abstracts Journal,* and is available full text online via services such as ProQuest.

628.   Nieman Reports. 1947– . Nieman Foundation for Journalism at Harvard University, One Francis Avenue. Cambridge, MA 02138. www.nieman.harvard.edu/reports/contents.html. Quarterly. ISSN 0028-9817.

Lucius Nieman, founding editor and president of the *Milwaukee Journal,* died in 1935. His wife, Agnes Nieman, on her death in 1936, willed most of her estate to Harvard University to promote excellence in journalism. In 1930 the Nieman Foundation awarded its first fellowships. Fellows spend a year at Harvard, and this publication highlights their work there. The work of past fellows is published also.

Any subject in journalism is fair game. A 1994 issue contains seven articles on "Reviving the Labor Beat," "Annals of a Libel Suit: Excerpts of Janet Malcolm Trial," "Spain's Private TV Invigorates News Coverage," and "Speaking in Tongues." An issue published in 2003 covers Medical Reporting, including more than 20 brief articles ranging from "Portraits of Living with the Dead" to "Documenting Native Approaches to Wellness." The Nieman Foundation sponsors a Watchdog Journalism Project and publishes a special section in the report on "Watchdog Reporting." Each issue also typically contains "Nieman Notes," a "Curator's Corner" by publisher Bob Giles, and, consistently, the most thought-provoking and well-written book reviews available on journalism and related topics. It is indexed in some unlikely sources, namely *Annual Bibliography of English Language and Literature* and *Middle East: Abstracts and Index.* It is available full text online via services such as Factiva and Gale Group.

629.   Online Journalism Review. 1998– . Annenberg School for Communication, University of Southern California, University Park Campus, Los Angeles, CA 90089. www.ojr.org. Weekly. ISSN 1522-6883.

"Because the Annenberg School gives us an academic base a step removed from the travails of commercial Web sites, we believe we can explore issues with depth, vigor and impartiality—and even irreverence. We don't want to be bores or scolds." There is little chance of this. This is a timely, unique and well-written (if occasionally overstated)

Web-based review source, focusing on all aspects of new media and online journalism. "Our role, then, is to apply standards. We want to identify who is best serving the public on the Web and who, hiding in the cloak of journalism, belongs in different garb. We want to support the truth tellers, label the entertainers and expose those who would let excess commercial interests sway their judgment. We analyze new technology and assess how it affects journalism—who is using it best, who is perverting its intent. We survey the Internet on a daily basis and look for strengths and flaws." There are sections on the workplace, technology, business, law, and ethics, as well as a "Future of News" page that offers, for example, essays on dashboard computing and newspapers in the digital age. A "Site Reviews" page posts articles ranging from "East Coast Sites Uneven" to "How Useful is WSJ's Redesign?" Executive Editor Joshua Fouts, director of USC's Online Journalism and Communication Center, and a staff of Web producers and print and broadcast journalists, as well as Annenberg faculty, staff, and students, contribute to this important resource. Users might also want to check out OJR's sister publications, *OnlineJournalism.com* and *Japan Media Review* as well as *Contentious* (www.contentious.com), which examines issues affecting "writers, editors, and others who create content for online media."

630.   Press Gazette. 1965– . Quantum Publishing Ltd., Quantum House, 19 Scarbrook Road, Croydon, Surrey CR9 1LX, United Kingdom. www.pressgazette.co.uk. Weekly. ISSN 0041-5170.

Formerly the *UK Press Gazette,* this "journalists' weekly" publishes "vital news and developments from the world of newspapers, magazines, TV, radio and the Internet" in the United Kingdom. Several pages of news and opinion, classified ads, regular columns ranging from "Cyberview" to "Dear Dr. Deadline," and a glut of information on media technology are part of this untidy but timely package. An online version is available on the Web site, but only by subscription. A similar publication focusing on media in the United States is *Mediaweek* (entry 623).

631.   Presstime. 1979– . Newspaper Association of America, 1921 Gallows Road, Suite 600, Vienna, VA 22182-3900. www.naa.org/presstime/index.html. Monthly. ISSN 0194-3243.

An indispensable source of practical information on newspapers, this official publication of the NAA (formerly the official voice of the American Newspaper Publishers Association) focuses on every aspect of the newspaper industry, from home delivery to employee relations. It is most useful to the editors, managers, and publishers who assemble budgets, deal with postal regulations, purchase equipment, or handle advertising. The journal, however, also includes general interest articles on writing and editing, management, and design for classroom and newsroom reading. Each issue usually contains eight or more well-written articles by staffers, and reports from regular departments such as the Digital Edge, Line Item, profile, advertising and marketing, and distribution. All copy is tidy, well-organized, and easy to locate. *Presstime* also features a "special report" on hot topics in the newspaper industry such as "Content Management: The Next Generation." Cover art and special reports usually emphasize current issues or trends in the business such as minorities in the newsroom, women in news management, first-time managers, readers, free circulation, and digital technology. Indexed in sources such as *Graphic Arts Literature Abstracts* and *Statistical Reference Index,* it also is available full text online via LexisNexis. In addition, the Web site offers an online archive. Readers of *Presstime* also will be interested in the monthly tabloid *Newspapers & Technology* (Conley Magazines) and *NewsInc.* (entry 626).

632.   Publishers' Auxiliary. 1865– . National Newspaper Association, 1010 N. Glebe Road, Arlington, VA 22201-4749. Monthly. ISSN 0048-5942.

"The newspaper industry's oldest newspaper" aims at publishers and editors of weekly, community, semiweekly, and small daily newspapers. It is now published as a weekly e-mail digest "ePubAux," with the redesigned print edition converting from a weekly to a monthly. Most aspects of newspaper publishing are covered, as well as the specific legal, business, and editorial issues confronting weeklies and small dailies. In spite of its large circulation, its only major indexing sources are *Graphic Arts Literature Abstracts* and *ABI Inform.* See also *Grassroots Editor* (entry 603), which focuses specifically on the weekly paper.

633.   Quill. 1912– . Society of Professional Journalists, Eugene S. Pullman National Journalism Center, 3909 N. Meridian Street, Indianapolis, IN 46208. www.spj.org. Monthly. ISSN 0033-6475.

These days, *Quill* is far more than a tool of the Society of Professional Journalists. It has become a mix of house organ, journalism review, and journalism news report. Articles are written by those from the academic and professional communities. In one issue, the following articles appeared: "The Many Shades of Journalism Ethics," "Truth Isn't Only Valuable in Stories," "Avoiding Public Panic," "Deciding Which Pieces to Leave Out," "Why Don't We Name Juveniles?" and "Getting Past Biases Is a Tough Act." The emphasis is on print journalism, although articles on broadcasting are included. Regular columns and departments include letters, freedom of information, ethics, diversity, and international journalism. In addition, *Dallas Morning News* writing consultant Paula Larocque contributes a "Mastering the Art" column. It is indexed in *Humanities Index* (entry 199) and *ABI Inform.* Available full text online via services such as Gale Group and H. W. Wilson. *Quill* continues to be an attractive, readable, and nicely packaged journalism magazine that examines the ethics of journalism as ably as any journalism review.

634.   Quill & Scroll. 1926– . Quill & Scroll Society, School of Journalism and Mass Communication, University of Iowa, Iowa City, IA 52242. www.uiowa.edu/~quill-sc/. four issues/year. ISSN 0033-6505.

The official magazine of the International Honorary Society for High School Journalists covers all aspects of the high school press, and does it very well. Recent *Quill & Scroll* articles have centered on technology, graphics, writing and revising, censorship, and libel. Articles are written primarily by journalism instructors and media professionals. This is an excellent source for current information on scholarships and careers in journalism, and it is indexed in *Current Index to Journals in Education* (entry 197).

635.   SJR: The St. Louis Journalism Review. 1970– . 8380 Olive Boulevard, St. Louis, MO 63132. www.webster.edu/~review. 10 issues/year. ISSN 0036-2972.

It accurately labels itself "a critique of metropolitan media and events," and a self-promotion reads, "It is a newspaper's duty to print the news and raise hell: when it doesn't, people turn to the *St. Louis Journalism Review.*" The *Review* is not a particularly pretty tabloid, but it is a lofty-thinking, intelligently written, and occasionally muckraking example of a regional journalism watchdog. Each issue contains short features, news sections and columns, and some longer national pieces. Both print and broadcasting are examined. It is indexed in *Alternative Press Index* (entry 183) and *PAIS International in Print* (entry 208), and available full text online via services such as Factiva, Northern Light, and Gale Group.

636.   SPR: Student Press Review. 1925– . Columbia Scholastic Press Association, Columbia University, Box 11, Central Mail Room 5711, New York, NY 10027-6902. www.studentpressreview.com. Quarterly. ISSN 1523-729X.

By far the most attractive of the scholastic press publications, *Student Press Review* (formerly *The School Press Review*), emphasizes writing and editing in the high school press and frequently offers future-oriented articles such as "In the College Press: What High School Journalists Can Expect." An "Ethical Matters" section examines issues confronting the high school press, with special emphasis on plagiarism. This review, indexed in *Current Index to Journals in Education* (entry 197), is a useful supplement to *Quill & Scroll* (entry 634). Back issues are available on the Web site.

637.   Television Quarterly. 1962– . National Academy of Television Arts and Sciences, 111 West 57th Street, Suite 1020, New York, NY 10019. Quarterly. ISSN 0040-2796.

All aspects of television broadcasting are covered in this attractive and readable quarterly. A substantial number of articles address television news. Articles in a 2003 issue include: "The Downward Spiral of Television News," "Scarce, Scarcer, Gone! What's With the Fairness Doctrine?," "Television's Troubling Indian Images," and "Diversity in Prime Time: Not a Priority in Television." Each issue also includes timely book reviews. It is indexed in publications such as *Communication Abstracts* (entry 195) and *PAIS International in Print* (entry 208) and is available full text online via services such as H. W. Wilson, Gale Group, Factiva, and ISI.

638.   TelevisionWeek. 1982– . Crain Communications, Inc., 360 N. Michigan Avenue, Chicago, IL 60601. www.tvweek.com. Weekly. ISSN 0745-0311.

Formerly *Electronic Media, TelevisionWeek* now covers "tv and only tv. We will be your one-stop must-read that connects the dots between programming, advertising, regulation and finance." In its previous incarnation, *Electronic Media* was a timely and substantial tabloid covering national television, radio, and cable news; its exhaustive coverage of the information superhighway and other electronic issues positioned it as an important source for the print media industry as well, especially those newspapers and magazines involved in marketing electronic products. It remains to be seen if *TelevisionWeek* will carve a similar role, but the inaugural issue in March 2003 was promising. For example, it includes a special report called "NewsPro: The State of TV News," an annual survey of "Washington's newsmakers." Senator John Edwards is described as "Looks Most Like Patient in Dentist's Chair"; the winner of the "Most in Love with the Sound of His or Her Own Voice" title is Terry McAuliffe, chairman of the Democratic National Committee. Regular features include newsmakers, ratings, converging media, roving eye, and a column by Tom Shales. TVweek.com is updated daily with important, up-to-the-minute news; it is indexed in *Business Periodicals Index* (entry 189) and *Business and Industry* and available full text online via services such as LexisNexis and Gale Group. Users might also wish to peruse *Mediaweek* (entry 623) and *Broadcasting & Cable* (entry 597). In addition, researchers might be interested in *Television and New Media* (Sage), a scholarly periodical launched in 2000 that "explores the field of television studies, focusing on audience ethnography, public policy, political economy, cultural history, and textual analysis."

639.   World Press Review. 1961– . The Stanley Foundation, 700 Broadway, 3d floor, New York, NY 10003-9536. Monthly. ISSN 0195-8895.

News and feature stories from foreign newspapers and magazines are reprinted in this monthly digest. Articles are culled from publications such as *The Economist, London Review of Books, Der Spiegel, Proceso, Hindustan Times, Toronto Star, Le Monde, Jerusalem Post,* and *Nikkei Weekly.* Each issue offers a cover story ("South Africa's Muddle," "Chemical Warfare, "Democracy By Design: Is the Middle East Buying the U.S. Hard Sell?") with five or six representative articles, and regular features on the nation, arts, books, Eye on the United States, science and technology, society, and commentary. "The World in Cartoons" is an international sampling of editorial and feature cartooning. When researching the international press, this digest of primary materials is unequaled. It is indexed in numerous sources, including *Academic Index, PAIS International in Print* (entry 208), and *Political Science Abstracts.* Users might also be interested in the *UTNE Magazine,* a bimonthly showcase of "the best of the alternative media."

640.   Writer's Digest. 1920– . F & W Publications, 1507 Dana Avenue, Cincinnati, OH 45207; Monthly. ISSN 0043-9525.

The Digest touches a lot of journalistic bases, and is a popular general-writing periodical with the same appeal and audience as most *Writer's Market* publications. Each 60- to 80-page issue speaks to both the fiction and nonfiction writer involved in print, television, and radio, as well as cartoonists and photographers. It is a cut above *The Writer* (Kalmbach) in terms of scope and number of "how-to-do-it" or ' how-I-did-it" stories. The mechanics of writing receive as much attention as the art of writing. It is indexed in *Access* and *Magazine Index,* and available full text online via services such as Factiva, Gale Group, and ProQuest.

A Features section showcases four to six full-length articles ranging from "You and Your Copy Editor" to "5 Ways to Write Fast." Columns and departments are arranged in sections on contests, inspiration, business, and technique, which includes columns on fiction, nonfiction, and scripts. Journalists and writing teachers can skim the contents page of *Writer's Digest*—"your monthly guide to getting published"—each month and find one or two articles useful for the newsroom or classroom. For example, in a 1995 article entitled "How Not to Write a Sentence," author David Fryxell admonishes writers for using "wimpy verbs" and provides examples of powerful writing from the King James Bible: "'Moses lifted up his hand, and with his rod he smote the rock twice.' Now, smote isn't a verb we use much nowadays, but it's a darned good one and maybe worth resurrecting." He continues, "But see how that Biblical sentence reads with its verbs anesthetized: 'Moses made an upward motion of his hand, and used his rod to impact the rock twice.'" Users should also consult the free Web site at www.writersdigest.com.

Other new or current periodicals worth noting include *Journalism Studies* (Routledge), a British publication launched in 2000 and *Journalism: Theory, Practice & Criticism* (Sage), an international scholarly journal.

14
Societies and Associations

Hundreds of organizations, some of them quite specialized, focus on journalism and the mass media. Listed here are the ones most germane to the field of journalism.

641. **Accuracy in Media,** 4455 Connecticut Avenue, N.W., Suite 330, Washington, D.C. 20008. 202-364-4401; 202-364-4098 (fax). ar1@aim.org. www.aim.org.

Described as a "non-profit, grassroots citizens watchdog of the news media that critiques botched and bungled news stories and sets the record straight on important issues that have received slanted coverage," the right-wing AIM researches and publicizes the public's complaints of media errors. It also broadcasts Reed Irvine and Cliff Kincaid's daily radio program called "Media Monitor" and publishes a weekly column. Accuracy in Media is affiliated with the Accuracy in Academia organization. The *AIM Report* is published twice a month.

642. **American Association of Sunday and Feature Editors,** c/o Penny Bender Fuchs, AASFE Executive Director, College of Journalism, 1117 Journalism Bldg. University of Maryland, College Park, MD 20742-7111. 301-314-2631. www.aasfe.org.

The AASFE is "dedicated to the quality of features in newspapers and the craft of feature writing." It maintains job listings on the Web site, sponsors an annual Excellence-in-Writing competition, and confers feature, specialty, and commentary writing awards.

643. **American Copy Editors Society,** 3 Healy Street, Huntington, NY 11743. www.copydesk.org.

ACES is a professional organization founded in 1997 primarily for newspaper copy editors. Its goal is to "provide solutions to copy desk problems, through training, discussion and an awareness of common issues." ACES sponsors a headline contest, lists job postings on its Web site, and confers the Merv Aubespin Scholarship.

644. **American Journalism Historians Association.** www.elon.edu/dcopeland/ajha/ajha1.htm.

This small organization was founded in 1981 and consists of journalism educators, researchers, and professional journalists interested in American and international mass media history. It publishes the quarterly *American Journalism* (entry 593).

645. **American Society of Journalists and Authors,** 1501 Broadway, Suite 302, New York, NY 10036. 212-997-0947; 212-768-7414 (fax). www.asja.org/index.php.

An organization of freelance nonfiction writers, the ASJA maintains a Writer Referral Service and publishes a monthly newsletter and the *ASJA Membership Directory.*

646. **American Society of Magazine Editors,** 919 Third Avenue, 22nd Floor, New York, NY 10022. 212-872-3700; fax: 212-906-0128; asme@magazine.org. www.asme. magazine.org.

Senior editors of print and online business and consumer publications are members of this professional organization founded in 1963. Its Web site offers access to a Job Bank for ASME and Magazine Publishers of America (entry 684) members.

647. **American Society of Media Photographers,** 150 North Second Street, Philadelphia, PA 19106. 215-451-2767; 215-451-0880 (fax). www.asmp.org.

Formerly the American Society of Magazine Photographers, membership consists of freelance magazine photographers. Founded in 1944, the ASMP conducts seminars and publishes the ASMP Professional Business Practices in Photography and the *ASMP Bulletin,* published 10 times a year.

648. **American Society of Newspaper Editors,** 11690B Sunrise Valley Drive, Reston, VA 20191-1409. 703-453-1122; 703-453-1133 (fax). www.asne.org/index.cfm.

Newspaper editors who set news and editorial policy for daily newspapers are members of ASNE. Founded in 1922, this organization publishes *The American Editor* (entry 592), formerly the *ASNE Bulletin,* and the annual *ASNE Proceedings* (entry 377). For further background on ASNE, researchers might wish to consult Paul Alfred Pratte's *Gods Within the Machine: A History of the American Society of Newspaper Editors, 1923–1993* (Praeger, 1995).

649. **American Sportscasters Association,** 225 Broadway, New York, NY 10007. 212-227-8080; 212-571-0556 (fax). www.americansportscasters.com.

Television and radio sportscasters make up this group, which sponsors seminars and workshops for student and other budding sportscasters. Its Hall of Fame was located in the MCI National Sports Gallery from 1998–2000; the Gallery has been closed, and the ASA continues to look for appropriate space for the Hall of Fame. The Association also publishes the quarterly *Insiders Sportsletter.* Researchers might also wish to contact the Association for Women in Sports Media at www.awsmonline.org.

650. **American Women in Radio and Television,** 8405 Greensboro Drive, Suite 800, McLean, VA 22102. 703-506-3290; 703-506-3266 (fax). info@awrt.org. www.awrt.org.

Radio and television professionals involved in administrative and creative aspects of the broadcasting industry are members. Founded in 1951, the association offers a CareerLine Online, maintains an educational foundation (The Foundation of American Women in Radio and Television, Inc.), and publishes the monthly *News & Views.*

651. **Asian American Journalists Association,** 1182 Market Street, Suite 320, San Francisco, CA 94102. 415-346-2051; 415-346-6343 (fax). national@aaja.org. www.aaja.org.

This organization, founded in 1981, focuses on educational and professional achievements of Asian American print and broadcast journalists as well as press coverage of Asian American issues. Members are journalists, students, and educators. The AAJA publishes with the South Asian Journalists Association a stylebook (*All American: How to Cover Asian America*) and *Dateline,* a quarterly newsletter. Job listings are posted on AAJAOnLine for members.

652.   **Associated Collegiate Press,** 2221 University Avenue SE, Suite 121, University of Minnesota, Minneapolis, MN 55414. 612-625-8335; 612-626-0720 (fax). www.student press.org/acp.

A division of the National Scholastic Press Association and publisher of *Trends in College Media,* now an online publication, the ACP critiques college newspapers, magazines, yearbooks, and broadcast stations, and provides rating services and critical analyses. It also offers ACPjobs online. Researchers might also wish to contact the Community College Journalism Association at www.ccjaonline.org.

653.   **Associated Press,** 50 Rockefeller Plaza, New York, NY 10020. 212-621-1500; 212-621-1723 (fax). info@ap.org. www.ap.org.

More than 10,000 newspapers and broadcast organizations and stations subscribe to the AP, a news agency that gathers and transmits news reports and photographs by satellite and cable. AP journalists work out of more than 240 news bureaus around the world. It was founded in 1848 when six New York papers (the *Sun, Herald, Tribune, Express, Courier* and *Enquirer,* and *Journal of Commerce*) set up the New York Associated Press or NYAP. The AP publishers numerous handbooks, books, and guides, notably *The Associated Press Stylebook and Briefing on Media Law* (entry 461).

654.   **Associated Press Managing Editors,** 50 Rockefeller Plaza, New York, NY 10020. 212-621-1552; 212-621-1567 (fax). apme@ap.org. www.apme.com/index.shtml.

Members include managing editors and news and editorial executives of Associated Press newspapers. It sponsors the Public Service Award, International Perspective Award, APMEOnline Convergence Award, and the Freedom of Information Award. Publications include the weekly online APME Update online, APME News, and special reports. The APME was founded in 1933.

655.   **Associated Press Photo Managers.** appm@ap.org. www.apphotomanagers.org.

Founded in 2002, APPM members "hold management or leadership-level responsibilities and are charged with overseeing photojournalism of any newspaper or any nationally circulated general news magazine published in the United States or Canada, including online editions of those publications."

656.   **Associated Press Sports Editors.** apse.dallasnews.com.

The stated purpose of APSE is to "improve professional standards of newspaper sports departments, to discuss and attempt to resolve problems of newspaper sports departments, to improve communication between sports departments and other newspaper departments and newspaper management and to recognize professional excellence among the membership." The APSE sponsors the annual Red Smith Award and publishes the bimonthly APSE newsletter.

657.   Association for Education in Journalism and Mass Communication, 234 Outlet Pointe Blvd., Columbia, SC 29210-5667. 803-798-0271; 803-772-3509 (fax). www.aejmc.org.

This important professional organization of more than 3,000 college and university educators was founded in 1912, and publishes the following: *Journalism and Mass Communication Educator* (entry 616), *Journalism and Communication Monographs* (entry 615), *Journalism and Mass Communication Quarterly* (entry 617), *Journalism and Mass Communication Abstracts* (entry 205), and the *Journalism and Mass Communication Directory* (entry 362). The AEJMC conducts research and compiles statistics on various aspects of journalism education. AEJMC Divisions include advertising, communication technology and policy, communication theory and methodology, cultural and critical studies, history, international communication, law, magazine, mass communication and society, media management and economics, media ethics, minorities and communication, newspaper, public relations, radio-television journalism, scholastic journalism, and visual communication. The Association of Schools of Journalism and Mass Communication (ASJMC), which includes administrators of journalism and mass communication programs, can also be reached at the AEJMC address. Both AEJMC and ASJMC are members of the Accrediting Council on Education in Journalism and Mass Communications (ACEJMC), which publishes a listing of accredited programs and accrediting standards.

658.   Association for Women in Communications, 780 Ritchie Highway, Suite 28-S, Severna Park, MD 21146. 410-544-7442; 410-544-4640 (fax). www.womcom.org.

Formerly Women in Communications, Inc., this national professional organization of women and men involved in all aspects of print and broadcast journalism, communications, public relations, advertising, publishing, and photojournalism, was founded in 1909. AWC publishes online *The Matrix,* a quarterly publication, and a monthly newsletter, and offers seminars and workshops, confers the Clarion Awards and the International Matrix Award, to name a few, and offers a national job bank. Researchers might also wish to contact the International Women's Media Foundation in Washington, D.C., and consult Elizabeth Burt's *Women's Press Organizations, 1881–1999* (Greenwood, 2000).

659.   Association of Alternative Newsweeklies, 1020 Sixteenth Street N.W., 4th Floor, Washington, D.C. 20036-5702. 202-822-1955; 202-822-0929 (fax). aan.org.

This trade association for more than 100 alternative newspapers was founded in 1978 and confers annual Alternative Weekly Awards that "recognize work that is well written, incisively reported and original, and that presents an effective challenge to established orthodoxies in a manner consistent with the mission of alternative newspaper journalism." It also offers job listings on its Web site.

660.   Association of American Editorial Cartoonists, 1221 Stoneferry Lane, Raleigh, NC 27606. 919-859-5516; 919-859-3172 (fax). pc99.detnews.com/aaec.

Dedicated to promoting editorial cartoon art in newspapers, magazines, and syndicates, members of this association founded in 1957 are professional editorial cartoonists for newspapers, magazines, and syndicates as well as student cartoonists. Publications include the annual *Best Editorial Cartoons of the Year* (entry 379). See also the Association for Canadian Editorial Cartoonists at www.canadiancartoonists.com.

661. **Association of Capitol Reporters and Editors.** capitolbeat.org.

Reporters who cover state and local government are members of this relatively new association founded in 1999. "This Association exists to advance public understanding of state government and the issues before state government, and to educate and share information with its members and the public on best practices, tools and techniques in state government reporting." ACRE maintains a listserv and offers on its Web site links to resources useful to statehouse reporters. It also lists job postings.

662. **Association of Health Care Journalists.** 204 Murphy Hall, University of Minnesota, 206 Church Street SE, Minneapolis, MN 55455-0418. 612-624-8877; 612-626-8251 (fax). ahcj@tc.umn.edu. www.ahcj.umn.edu.

The AHCJ is a nonprofit organization "dedicated to advancing public understanding of health care issues. Its mission is to improve the quality, accuracy and visibility of health care reporting, writing and editing." Established in 1997, it maintains a useful resource section on its Web site and publishes *Covering the Quality of Health Care: A Resource Guide for Journalists.*

663. **Broadcast Education Association,** 1771 N Street, N.W.,Washington, D.C. 20036-2891. 202-429-5354. www.beaweb.org.

The BEA, founded in 1955, is a professional association for educators, industry professionals, and students involved in teaching and research on radio, television, and electronic media. Publications include the quarterly *Journal of Broadcasting & Electronic Media* (entry 612), the *Journal of Radio Studies,* an annual membership directory, and its quarterly membership magazine *Feedback.* It also offers the BEA Job Bank online for institutional members.

664. **Canadian Association of Journalists,** St Patrick's Building, Carleton University, 1125 Colonel By Drive, Ottawa, Ontario K1S 5B6, Canada. 613-526-8061. www.eagle.ca/caj.

Formerly the Centre for Investigative Journalism, this professional organization of more than 1,500 print and broadcast journalists in Canada was founded in 1978. Its mission statement is clear: "The CAJ promotes excellence in journalism, encouraging investigative journalism. We serve as the national voice of Canadian journalists, and we uphold the public's right to know." The CAJ publishes the quarterly *Media* magazine (entry 621).

665. **Canadian Association of Newspaper Editors,** 890 Yonge Street, Suite 200, Toronto, Ontario M4W 3P4, Canada. 416-923-3567; 416-923-7206 (fax). www.cane.ca.

In 1999, the Canadian Managing Editors Conference broadened its perspective and reorganized as the CANE. Editors, executives, and newsroom managers at daily Canadian newspapers and news agencies are members.

666. **Canadian Newspaper Association,** 890 Yonge Street, Suite 200, Toronto, Ontario M4W 3P4, Canada. 416-923-3567; 416-923-7206 (fax). www.cna-acj.ca.

The CNA was founded in 1996 following the dissolution of the Canadian Daily Newspaper Association (founded in 1919) and the Newspaper Marketing Bureau. Its Web site is described as a "resource for both members of the CNA—the people who publish and work for newspapers in Canada—and for all those who love and read newspapers." It is packed with useful links and resources including "The Ultimate Online Guide to Canadian Newspapers" and "Careers in Daily Newspapers."

667.   Canadian Press, La Presse Canadienne, 36 King Street, E., Toronto, Ontario M5C 2L9. 416-364-0321; 416-364-0207 (fax). www.cp.org.

Described as "Canada's multimedia news agency," the Canadian Press and its broadcast division, Broadcast News, provide a "news-sharing co-operative of more than 600 Canadian newsrooms and news agencies from around the world." The CP was founded in 1917.

668.   College Media Advisers, c/o Ron Spielberger, Executive Director, Department of Journalism, University of Memphis, 3711 Veterans Avenue, Room 300, Memphis, TN 38152. 901-678-2403; 901-678-4798 (fax). www.collegemedia.org.

Founded in 1954, the CMA serves advisers and directors of college student newspapers, yearbooks, magazines, television and radio stations, and others interested in college media. It confers the annual Apple Awards, offers workshops, sponsors journalism competitions and contests, and maintains a job board. In addition, the CMA publishes a newsletter, the *College Media Review* (entry 599), the annual *Keeping Free Presses Free,* and the *Best of Collegiate Design.* It also maintains a listserv at https://lists.latech.edu/pipermail/cma-l/.

669.   Columbia Scholastic Press Advisers Association (CSPAA) and Columbia Scholastic Press Association (CSPA), Columbia University, Mail Code 5711, New York, NY 10027-6902. (CSPA telephone: 212-854-9400; fax: 212-854-9401; cspa@columbia.edu). www.columbia.edu/cu/cspa.

The CSPAA, founded in 1927, is a professional organization of teachers and advisers that focuses on the educational development of the student press. The CSPA is a national education association and clearinghouse for information on student magazines, newspapers, and yearbooks. The CSPA also evaluates member student publications and confers the Gold Circle and Crown Awards. Founded in 1924, it publishes *SPR: Student Press Review* (entry 636). It is sponsored by Columbia University.

670.   Committee of Concerned Journalists, 1850 K Street NW, Suite 850, Washington, DC 20006. 202-293-7394; 202-293-6946 (fax). mail@journalism.org. www.journalism.org/who/ccj/.

The CCJ, chaired by Bill Kovach, is described as a "consortium of reporters, editors, producers, publishers, owners and academics worried about the future of the profession." Hand-wringing aside, the committee, formed in 1997, generates numerous timely reports ranging from "Jessica Lynch—Media Myth-Making in the Iraq War" to "Why Has TV Stopped Covering Politics?" It organizes forums and conducts research, offers a "Traveling Curriculum for Mid-Career Journalists," and in 2001 published *The Elements of Journalism: What Newspeople Know and the Public Should Expect.* Its Web site, journalism.

org., is described as the "joint Internet presence" of The Project for Excellence in Journalism (entry 775) and the Committee of Concerned Journalists.

671. Committee to Protect Journalists, 330 7th Avenue, 12th Floor, New York, NY 10001. 212-465-1004; 212-465-9568 (fax). info@cpj.org. www.cpj.org.

Founded in 1981, this organization exists to "promote press freedom worldwide by defending the right of journalists to report the news without fear of reprisal." Members are journalists, media organizations, and human rights groups. The CPJ provides online coverage of attacks on the press, journalists killed in the line of duty, and journalists in prison, compiles statistics, and conducts research. It publishes an annual *Attacks on the Press* volume (entry 378), a biannual magazine, *Dangerous Assignments,* and an e-newsletter CPJ Update.

672. Criminal Justice Journalists, 720 7th Street NW, Third Floor, Washington, D.C. 20001. 202-448-1717; cjj@reporters.net. www.reporters.net/cjj.

Criminal Justice Journalists, which recently established an affiliation with the Jerry Lee Center of Criminology of the University of Pennsylvania, exists to "improve the quality and accuracy of news reporting on crime, law enforcement, and the judicial system" and offer resources and services for journalists covering crime, cop, court, and prison beats. It publishes *Crime and Justice News,* maintains a Cops & Courts Reporters Discussion List, and cowrote with IRE *Understanding Crime Statistics: A Reporter's Guide.* This nonprofit association was founded in 1997.

673. Education Writers Association. 2122 P Street NW, Suite 201, Washington, D.C. 20037. 202-452-9830; 202-452-9837; ewa@ewa.org. www.ewa.org.

More than 800 print and broadcast journalists as well as writers working for educational organizations are members of EWA, founded in 1947. It publishes a series of guides for reporters, maintains a listserv, and offers travel and study fellowships. EWA also publishes on its Web site a selection of "Reporter's Stories" on topics ranging from Graduation Rates to School Violence.

674. Ifra, Washingtonplatz 1, 64287 Darmstadt, Germany. 49.6151.733-6; 49.6151. 733-800 (fax). info@ifra.com. www.ifra.com.

Founded in 1961, IFRA (INCA-FIEJ Research Association—INCA stands for International Newspaper Colour Association and FIEJ is Fédération Internationale des Editeurs de Journaux) focuses on techniques and trends in newspaper publishing and printing, and "all issues related to the production of newspapers and to new media." It publishes the monthly *Newspaper Techniques* in English, French, German, Spanish, Russian, and Chinese. Researchers might also be interested in the IfraNewsplex (entry 746).

675. Inland Press Association, Inland Press Foundation. 2360 East Devon Avenue, Suite 3011, Des Plaines, IL 60018. 847-795-0380; 847-795-0385. www.inlandpress.org.

More than 850 newspapers are members of Inland, which describes itself as a "newspaper association specializing in high quality low cost training options for all newspaper departments." Member services range from training seminars to revenue studies. It also posts job listings on the Web site as well as an Idea Center and Best Practices.

676. **Inter American Press Association,** 1801 SW 3rd Avenue, 8th floor, Miami, FL 33129. 305-634-2465; 305-635-2272 (fax). info@sipiapa.org. www.sipiapa.com/ default.cfm.

Organized in 1942 to protect press freedom in the Americas, this association publishes individual country reports and resolutions on its Web site. It is affiliated with the IAPA Press Institute and the IAPA Scholarship Fund.

677. **International Association for Mass Communication Research,** School of International Services, The American University, 4400 Massachusetts Avenue, N.W., Washington, D.C. 20016-8071. 202-885-1621; 202-885-2494 (fax).

More than 2,500 individual and group members in 65 countries focus on journalism training and education and mass communication research. Subject divisions include communication technology policy, gender and communication, law, local radio and television, and media education research. It publishes the quarterly *IAMCR Newsletter.*

678. **International Federation of Journalists,** Residence Palace, 155 rue de la Loi (Bloc C), 1040 Brussels, Belgium. 32-2-235-22-00; 32-2-235-22-19 (fax). ifj@ifj.org. www.ifj.org.

Focusing on freedom of the press issues, the influential IFJ was founded in 1952 when it split from the International Organization of Journalists. It has more than 500,000 members in 100 countries in affiliated unions (The Newspaper Guild in the United States, The National Union of Journalists of UK and Ireland in the United Kingdom). In 2003, the IFJ and the IPI (entry 680) founded the International News Safety Institute, which, according to its new Web site (www.newssafety.com) will "promote practical actions and foster good practice in the provision of safety training, materials and assistance to journalists and media staff."

679. **International Food, Wine and Travel Writers Association,** P.O. Box 8249, Calabasas, CA 91372. 818-999-9959; 818-347-7545 (fax). ifwtwa@aol.com. www.ifwtwa.org.

According to the Web site, the IFWTWA "strives to be a gathering point and resource base for an active membership composed of professionals engaged in the food, wine and travel industries. The association's membership includes professionals in culinary arts and sciences, the wine-growing and production industry, and in the hotel and hospitality management industries."

In addition, members must publish a minimum of 10 articles per year. The IFWTWA publishes a monthly newsletter, *Press Pass,* but only for its membership of about 300.

680. **The International Press Institute (IPI),** Spiegelgasse 2, A-1010 Vienna, Austria. 43-1-512-90-11; 43-1-512-90-14 (fax). ipi@freemedia.at. www.freemedia.at.

Newspaper editors, editorial directors, and managers of broadcast organizations worldwide who influence news and editorial policy are members. The IPI, founded in 1951, works to safeguard press freedom and improve the flow of news and information. "Even though the size of the organization has changed, its philosophy remains the same: that freedom of expression is the right that protects all other rights and that this freedom needs to be promoted and defended." The IPI also conducts research and publishes the annual *World Press Freedom Review* and the quarterly *IPI Global Journalist* magazine.

681. **International Society of Weekly Newspaper Editors (ISWNE),** Missouri Southern State College, 3950 E. Newman Road, Joplin, MO 64801-1595. 417-625-9736; 417-659-4445 (fax). www.mssc.edu/iswne.

This organization's stated purpose is to "help those involved in the weekly press to improve standards of editorial writing and news reporting and to encourage strong, independent editorial voices." Membership consists of editors and editorial writers employed at weekly newspapers. The ISWNE, founded in 1954, sponsors the Golden Quill Award and the Eugene Cervi Award and publishes the quarterly *Grassroots Editor* (entry 608).

682. **Investigative Reporters and Editors,** University of Missouri, School of Journalism, 138 Neff Annex, Columbia, MO 65211. 573-882-2042; 573-882-5431 (fax); info@ire.org. www.ire.org.

Founded in 1975, this nonprofit educational organization is "dedicated to improving the quality of investigative reporting." It operates a database library, and sponsors workshops and seminars on investigative reporting techniques, public documents, and computer-assisted reporting through IRE's National Institute for Computer-Assisted Reporting (entry 766). IRE also maintains several listservs as well as a Campaign Finance Information Center and a Job Center. The IRE's Resource Center offers access to a massive story database as well as guides, tip sheets, and transcripts of television, newspaper, and magazine investigative reports. Publications include *The IRE Journal* (entry 611).

683. **Journalism Education Association,** Kansas State University, 103 Kedzie Hall, Manhattan, KS 66506-1505. 785-532-5532; 913-532-7309 (fax). www.jea.org.

This professional association of high school journalism teachers, publications advisers, and others interested in secondary school journalism aims to improve the quality and teaching of high school journalism. Founded in 1924, it sponsors journalism competitions, offers awards, publishes *C:JET* (*Communication: Journalism Education Today,* entry 598), and an annual membership directory.

684. **Magazine Publishers of America,** 919 Third Avenue, 22nd Floor, New York, NY 10022. 212-872-3700; 212-888-4217 (fax). www.magazine.org.

Formerly the Magazine Publishers Association, MPA members are publishers of consumer magazines. Affiliated with the American Society of Magazine Editors (entry 646), the MPA conducts seminars and workshops, maintains a Career Center, and oversees the Publishers Information Bureau.

685. **National Academy of Television Arts and Sciences,** 111 West 57th Street, Suite 600, New York, NY 10019. 212-586-8424; 212-246-8129 (fax); hq@natasonline.com. www.emmyonline.org/emmy/academy.html.

For television professionals actively involved in all aspects of the industry, this association seeks to advance the television arts and sciences through workshops, seminars, and publications, and recognizes innovation and creativity in the industry. It maintains a Job Bank, sponsors the annual Emmy Awards for News and Documentary, Sports, Daytime, Public and Community Service, and Technology, and publishes *Television Quarterly* (entry 637). Its archives at UCLA contain more than 20,000 television programs.

686.   National Association of Black Journalists, University of Maryland, 8701-A Adelphi Road, Adelphi, MD 20783-1716. 301-445-7100; 301-445-7101 (fax). www. nabj.org.

Print and broadcast journalists and student journalists working in all aspects of news are members of this association which "provides quality programs and services to and advocates on behalf of black journalists worldwide." The NABJ, founded in 1975, also maintains The NABJ Media Institute, which "seeks to provide professional development, technical training, historical documentation and entrepreneurial guidance for black journalists and students, relating to the media industry" and "seeks to teach, compile, disseminate and chronicle information about African Americans in the field of journalism, and acts as a clearinghouse for information to entities interested in the media and the connection with black journalists." In addition, the NABJ offers NABJobs Online and numerous fellowships and scholarships, and sponsors an annual careers fair as well as a speaker's bureau. Those interested in NABJ's history should consult Wayne Dawkins's *Black Journalists: The NABJ Story* (August Press, 1993). Researchers might also wish to contact the Capital Press Club at www.cpcomm.org.

687.   National Association of Broadcasters, 1771 N Street, N.W., Washington, D.C. 20036-2891. 202-429-5300; 202-429-4199 (fax); nab@nab.org. www.nab.org.

Founded in 1922, members include representatives from television and radio stations and the networks. The NAB acts as a watchdog for government censorship and represents the industry on issues in broadcasting legislation. It publishes *RadioWeek and Telejournal,* and other publications on radio and broadcast engineering, and maintains job postings on its Web site. The NAB also operates an Information Resource Center, with links to useful resources and sites at irc@nab.org.

688.   National Association of Hispanic Journalists, 1000 National Press Building, Washington, D.C. 20045-2001. 202-662-7145; 202-662-7144 (fax). nahj@nahj.org. www. nahj.org.

Formed in 1984 to provide a forum and support for Hispanic journalists, the association works toward fair and unbiased treatment of Hispanics in the media, and encourages the study and practice of journalism by Hispanics. Members are professional journalists, educators, and students. The NAHJ offers an online job bank, scholarships, seminars, and workshops, and confers a series of awards. Researchers might also wish to contact the National Federation of Hispanic Owned Newspapers.

689.   National Association of Minority Media Executives, 1921 Gallows Road, Suite 600, Vienna, VA 22182. 888-968-7658; 703-893-2410; 703-893-2414 (fax). namme executivedirector@worldnet.att.net.

Senior managers and executives are members of this "organization for media managers and executives of color working in newspapers, magazines, radio, television, cable and new media" Founded in 1990, "NAMME exists to encourage more diversity among the senior ranks of the media industry, as well as more informed discussion of how to better serve multi-cultural communities. NAMME also serves as a resource to the media industry on diversity issues." NAMME offers numerous fellowships and training programs, publishes the quarterly *NAMME News,* and offers job postings on the Web site.

690.   National Cartoonists Society, P.O. Box 713, Suffield, CT 06078. www.reuben. org.

Nearly 600 professional cartoonists are members of this organization, described as the "world's largest and most prestigious organization of professional cartoonists. As defined in the NCS by-laws, a professional is one who earns the majority of one's living by drawing cartoons. The by-laws define a cartoonist as 'a graphic story teller, whose drawings interpret rather than copy nature in order to heighten the effect of his or her message.' " The Society, founded in 1946, confers the Reuben Award for outstanding cartoonist of the year, and publishes a newsletter, *The Cartoonist.*

691.   National Conference of Editorial Writers, 3899 N. Front Street, Harrisburg, PA 17110. 717-703-3015; 717-703-3014 (fax); ncew@pa-news.org. www.ncew.org.

Aimed at newspaper, television, and radio editorial writers and journalism educators in the United States and Canada, this nonprofit professional organization is interested in raising the standards of editorial content and quality. It was established in 1946, and absorbed the National Broadcast Editorial Association in 1992. The NCEW also publishes *The Masthead* (entry 620) and *Beyond Argument: A Handbook for Editorial Writers.* A Job Bank is available on the Web site as well as an Online Forum.

692.   National Federation of Community Broadcasters, 1970 Broadway, Suite 1000, Oakland, CA 94612. 510-451-8200; 510-451-8208 (fax). www.nfcb.org.

The NFCB is described as a "national alliance of stations, producers, and others committed to community radio" and "advocates for national public policy, funding, recognition, and resources on behalf of its membership, while providing services to empower and strengthen community broadcasters through the core values of localism, diversity, and public service." It publishes a monthly newsletter, *Community Radio News,* maintains a listserv, and confers several awards including the Golden Reel and Silver Reel.

693.   National Federation of Press Women, P.O. Box 5556, Arlington, VA 22205. 800-780-2715. presswomen@aol.com. www.nfpw.org.

More than 3,500 professional women and men involved in all aspects of communications are members. The organization, founded in 1937, offers journalism scholarships and an annual Communicator of Achievement award. It also publishes the monthly *AGENDA.*

694.   National Lesbian and Gay Journalists Association, 1420 K Street N.W., Suite 910, Washington, D.C. 20005. 202-588-9888; 202-588-1818. info@nlgja.org. www.nlgja. org.

The NLGJA has more than 1,000 members and describes itself as an "organization of journalists, online media professionals, and students that works from within the journalism industry to foster fair and accurate coverage of lesbian, gay, bisexual and transgender issues." Founded in 1990, it offers a number of services including a mentorship program, student outreach and education program, and a job board. It publishes a quarterly *NLGJA News* and a *NLGJA Stylebook Supplement.*

695.   National Newspaper Association, P.O. Box 7540, Columbia, MO 65202-7540. 800-829-4662; 573-882-5800; 573-884-5490 (fax). www.nna.org.

Founded in 1885, this association's membership consists of more than 3,200 editors and publishers of community newspapers. It publishes the well-read *Publishers' Auxiliary* (entry 632) and sponsors contests and awards. The National Newspaper Association Foundation, which is composed of the board of directors and past presidents of the National Newspaper Association, offers educational training, seminars, conferences, journalism awards, and scholarships. Researchers might also wish to contact the Canadian Community Newspapers Association at www.ccna.ca.

696.   National Newspaper Publishers Association/Black Press of America, 3200 13th Street, N.W., Washington, D.C. 20010. 202-588-8764. www.nnpa.org.

Membership in this association, founded in 1940, consists of publishers of community newspapers dedicated to promoting the black press. In 2001, the NNPA and the NNPA Foundation launched the BlackPressUSA Network, described as the "nation's premier network of local Black community news and information portal." The Foundation also sponsors the Black Press Archives and Hall of Fame at Howard University, the A. Philip Randolph Messenger Awards for Excellence in publishing and reporting, Black Press Institute, and the NorthStar Center for Civic Journalism.

697.   National Press Club, National Press Building, 529 14th Street, N.W., Washington, D.C. 20045. 202-662-7500; 202-662-7512 (fax). npc.press.org.

The Press Club's membership of approximately 4,000 is comprised of print and broadcast journalists and others working in the news media. Nonvoting members include former journalists. Its constitution states: "The Club shall provide people who gather and disseminate news a center for the advancement of their professional standards and skills, the promotion of free expression, mutual support and social fellowship." It sponsors workshops on Washington reporting, seminars, social events, and journalism awards and contests, and publishes a weekly "Record" (back issues are available on the Web site). Members have access to the Eric Friedheim Library and News Information Center and an employment hotline. The NPC Luncheon Speakers series is broadcast on NPR and C-SPAN.

698.   National Press Photographers Association, 3200 Croasdaile Drive, Suite 306, Durham, NC 27705. 919-383-7246; 919-383-7261 (fax). info@nppa.org. www.nppa.org.

News photographers, editors, other professionals associated with photojournalism, and students are members of this association of more than 11,000 founded in 1946. The NPPA is "dedicated to the advancement of photojournalism, and acknowledges concern and respect for the public's natural-law right to freedom in searching for the truth and the right to be informed truthfully and completely about public events and the world in which we live." It conducts seminars, workshops, and newsphoto and newsfilm contests, such as Best of Photojournalism and Best of Television Photojournalism, and publishes *News Photographer* (entry 625). The NPPA also publishes an annual NPPA membership directory, sponsors a National Mentoring Program, and maintains a listserv. Its Job Information Bank for members is available on the Web site.

699.   National Scholastic Press Association, 2221 University Avenue SE, Suite 121, Minneapolis, MN 55414. 612-625-8335; 612-626-0720 (fax). www.studentpress.org/nspa.

Publisher of *Trends in College Media* and *Trends in High School Media*, now available online, the NSPA evaluates high school newspapers, magazines, and yearbooks, and sponsors numerous contests. It was founded in 1921.

700.   National Sportscasters and Sportswriters Association, Box 559, Salisbury, NC 28144. 704-633-4275.

Open to, obviously, sportscasters and sportswriters, this group of approximately 1,000 members maintains the National Sportscasters and Sportswriters Hall of Fame (www.nssahalloffame.com), confers awards for excellence in the field, and elects charter members to the U.S. Olympic Hall of Fame. It was founded in 1959.

701.   National Union of Journalists, Acorn House, 308 Gray's Inn Road, London WC1X 8DP, England. 020-7278-7916; 020-7837-8143 (fax). info@nuj.org.uk. www.nuj.org.uk.

This large trade union represents 34,000 members in England and Ireland. It publishes *Journalist* magazine 10 times per year. Its Web site indicates that the NUJ has launched the Scrooge Awards to "shame the worst-paying media employers in Britain."

702.   The Native American Journalists Association, University of South Dakota, 414 East Clark Street, Vermillion, SD 57069. 605-677-5282; 866-694-4264 (fax). info@naja.com. www.naja.com.

Native American print and broadcast journalists are members of NAJA, which was formed in 1984. Formerly the Native American Press Association, it publishes *NAJA News,* sponsors professional development fellowships and scholarships, and offers job listings on its Web site.

703.   Newspaper Association Managers, 70 Washington Street, Suite 214, Salem, MA 01970. 978-744-8940; 978-744-0333. www.nammanagers.com.

National, state, and regional newspaper association executives are members. This small group, founded in 1923, sponsors National Newspaper Week.

704.   Newspaper Association of America, 1921 Gallows Road, Suite 600, Vienna, VA 22181-3900. 703-902-1600; 703-917-0636 (fax). www.naa.org.

This influential organization was formed in 1992 when the following organizations merged: American Newspaper Publishers Association, Newspaper Advertising Bureau, International Circulation Managers Association, International Newspaper Marketing and Advertising Executives, International Newspaper Marketing Association, Association of Classified Advertising Managers, Newspaper Advertising Co-Op Network, and the National Research Council. Member organizations are newspapers in the United States and Canada, with some international members. The NAA, is especially concerned with press freedom issues, and according to the Web site, "focuses on six key strategic priorities that collectively affect the newspaper industry: marketing, public policy, diversity, industry development, newspaper operations and readership." The NAA also publishes *Presstime* (entry 631), and offers The Digital Edge Web site, which "publishes original analysis and advice for the development and management of digital-media businesses" and corresponding annual "Edgie" Awards.

705. **The Newspaper Guild,** 501 Third Street, N.W., Suite 250, Washington D.C. 20001. 202-434-7177; 202-434-1472 (fax). guild@cwa-union.org. www.newsguild.org.

Affiliated with the AFL-CIO, IFG, and the Canadian Labour Congress, the Newspaper Guild was founded in 1933 and is the largest union of journalists. It publishes *The Guild Reporter* (back issues are available on the Web site) and confers the Heywood Broun Award for outstanding journalistic achievement. See www.tngcanada.org for information on The Newspaper Guild Canada.

706. **Online News Association,** P.O. Box 741, Arlington, VA 22216-0741. 802-434-6176; 802-654-2560 (fax). helpdesk@journalists.org. www.journalists.org.

Online journalists, individuals who report, write, produce, edit, or design news for digital delivery, are members of ONA, founded in 1999. ONA conducts research such as the ONA Digital Journalism Credibility Study and sponsors, with Columbia University, the Online Journalism Awards.

707. **Organization of News Ombudsmen (ONO),** c/o Gina Lubrano, Executive Secretary, P.O. Box 120191, San Diego, CA 92112. 619-293-1525. ono@uniontrib.com. www.newsombudsmen.org.

News ombudsmen, often called reader advocates or public editors, are those who receive and investigate reader or viewer complaints and attempt to negotiate and settle disagreements. Founded in 1980, this international group of approximately 100 is comprised of both newspaper and television ombudsmen. More than half of them write weekly columns for their newspapers or contribute monthly columns to trade publications.

708. **Overseas Press Club of America,** 40 West 45th Street, New York, NY 10036. 212-626-9220; 212-626-9210 (fax). www.opcofamerica.org.

Foreign correspondents, editors, reporters, newscasters, photojournalists, and other professional journalists who are currently working or have worked overseas are eligible for membership. In addition, working newspeople with two consecutive years' foreign experience, freelance writers, and authors of foreign affairs books are members. Founded in 1939, this is the only organization devoted exclusively to overseas reporters. According to a 1988 issue of *Quill,* the Overseas Press Club has been designated a "Historic Site in Journalism" and the Algonquin Hotel in New York (where the group first met informally) is listed as the founding site. Researchers might also wish to contact the Foreign Press Association at www.foreignpressnewyork.com.

709. **Quill and Scroll,** School of Journalism, University of Iowa, Iowa City, IA 52242. 319-335-5795; 319-335-5210 (fax). quill-scroll@uiowa.edu. www.uiowa.edu/~quill-sc.

This international honor society for high school journalism students, founded in 1926, boasts 1 million members and more than 14,000 chapters in all 50 states and 44 foreign countries. Through the Quill and Scroll Foundation, it grants scholarships, conducts research and publishes surveys. In addition, it publishes *Quill & Scroll* (entry 634), handbooks, and a stylebook.

710. **Radio-Television News Directors Association and Foundation,** 1600 K Street, Suite 700, Washington, D.C. 20006-2838. 202-659-6510, 800-80-RTNDA; 202-223-4007 (fax). rtnda@rtnda.org; rtndf@rtndf.org. www.rtnda.org.

This professional society or the "association of electronic journalists" aims to improve the standards of electronic journalism through education, training, and research. The RTNDA includes heads of broadcast, cable, and network news departments as well as other broadcast journalists, teachers, and public relations practitioners. It sponsors workshops, the annual Edward R. Murrow Award, and a job bulletin online, maintains an Environmental Journalism Center of news resources and stories, and publishes the monthly *Communicator* (entry 601). It was founded in 1946 and lists more than 3,000 members. The RTNDF, according to its mission, "provides training programs, seminars, scholarship support and research in areas of critical concern to electronic news professionals and their audience." For information on The Radio and Television News Directors Association Canada see www.rtndacanada.com.

711.   Religion Newswriters Association, Religion Newswriters Foundation. P.O. Box 2037, Westerville, OH 43086-2037. 614-891-9001. www.religionwriters.com.

This trade association seeks to "advance the professional standards of religion reporting in the secular press as well as to create a support network for religion reporters." Founded in 1949, it maintains a message board and speakers bureau, holds writing and design contests, and offers training workshops.

712.   Society for News Design, 1130 Ten Rod Road, F-104, North Kingstown, RI 02852-4177. 401-294-5233; 401-294-5238 (fax). www.snd.org.

Formerly the Society of Newspaper Design, more than 2,600 newspaper designers, art directors, artists, editors, photographers, educators, and others involved in news design are members of this international organization founded in 1979. "Dedicated to improving news presentation and design in all media," SND publishes *Design* (entry 604) and the annual *Best of Newspaper Design* (entry 381). In addition, it offers an Online Designer's Toolbox on its Web site as well as a job bank. The SND Foundation offers research grants and internship programs. Researchers might also wish to contact The Society of Publication Designers at www.spd.org.

713.   Society of American Business Editors and Writers, University of Missouri, School of Journalism, 134 Neff Annex, Columbia, MO 65211-1200. 573-882-7862; 573-884-1372 (fax). sabew@missouri.edu. www.sabew.org.

Nearly 3,200 business, financial, and economic reporters, writers, and editors for newspapers and magazines, as well as educators and broadcast journalists, are members of this association founded in 1963. It maintains a Resume Bank and job postings for members, offers a listserv and electronic bulletin board, confers an annual Distinguished Achievement Award, and publishes the bimonthly newsletter *The Business Journalist* and an online membership directory. Researchers might also wish to consult the American Society of Business Press Editors at www.asbpe.org.

714.   Society of Environmental Journalists, P.O. Box 2492, Jenkintown, PA 19046. 215-884-8174; 215-884-8175 (fax). sej@sej.org. www.sej.org.

With more than 1,200 members in print and broadcast, the SEJ's stated mission is to "advance public understanding of environmental issues by improving the quality, accuracy, and visibility of environmental reporting." Founded in 1990, it produces the quarterly *SEJournal,* a daily *EJToday* news service, and biweekly *TipSheet.*

715.   Society of Professional Journalists, Eugene S. Pulliam National Journalism Center, 3909 North Meridian Street, Indianapolis, IN 46208. 317-927-8000; 317-920-4789 (fax). questions@apj.org. www.spj.org.

Formerly Sigma Delta Chi, The Society of Professional Journalists, this organization is now simply called The Society of Professional Journalists and is "dedicated to the perpetuation of a free press as the cornerstone of our nation and our liberty." It publishes the magazine *Quill* (entry 633), offers a job bank online, bulletin board, listserv, and daily PressNotes. SPJ sponsors many awards including the following: Sigma Delta Chi Awards, Eugene S. Pulliam First Amendment Award, Eugene C. Pulliam Fellowship for Editorial Writing, and the Mark of Excellence Awards for student journalism. Founded in 1909, this is the largest professional journalism organization in the United States.

716.   Special Libraries Association, News Division, 1700 Eighteenth Street, N.W., Washington, D.C. 20009-2514. SLA Headquarters: 202-234-4700; 202-265-9317 (fax). sla@sla.org. www.ibiblio.org/slanews.

Members of the Special Libraries Association News Division include librarians and others affiliated with news libraries in newspapers, magazines, and television. A primary objective of the Division is to "develop the usefulness and efficiency of news media libraries." It publishes *News Library News* and maintains a listserv; its Web site is packed with useful information and links for journalists.

717.   United Press International, 1510 H Street, N.W., Washington, D.C. 20005. 202-898-8000; 202-898-8057 (fax). www.upi.com.

This international wire service gathers news stories and photographs and disseminates them to member newspapers, radio, and television stations. UPI was formed in 1958 when United Press (founded in 1907) and International News Service (1909) merged. It has more than 6,500 subscribers worldwide, and more than 200 local news bureaus in the United States.

718.   Unity: Journalists of Color, Inc., 1601 North Kent Street, Suite 1003, Arlington, VA 22209. 703-469-2100; 703-469-2108 (fax). info@unityjournalists.org. www.unityjournalists.org.

UNITY is described as a "strategic alliance" of 7,000 journalists belonging to the Asian American Journalists Association, National Association of Black Journalists, National Association of Hispanic Journalists, and the Native American Journalists Association. It convenes an annual UNITY conference, with emphasis on networking and professional development for journalists of color.

719.   White House Correspondents Association, 1067 National Press Building, Washington, D.C. 20045. 202-737-2934. www.whca.net.

More than 600 print and broadcast journalists covering the White House are members of this association founded in 1914.

720.   White House News Photographers Association, 7119 Ben Franklin Station, Washington, D.C. 20044-7119. 202-785-5230; 301-428-4904 (fax). www.whnpa.org.

Newspaper, magazine, wire service, and television news photographers who cover the White House, Congress, and government agencies are members of this association founded in 1921. It publishes *The Eyes of History,* its annual contest book.

721. **World Press Freedom Committee,** 11690-C Sunrise Valley Drive, Reston, VA. 20191. 703-715-9811; 703-620-6790 (fax). freepress@wpfc.org. www.wpfc.org

Committee members include more than 40 journalism and communications organizations that defend press freedom and oppose state control of the media. It offers professional journalistic assistance, seminars, and workshops, and has developed hundreds of educational and training programs in Africa, Europe, Asia, and the Middle East.

15

Selected Research Centers, Archives, and Media Institutes

Only those collections available to researchers are included in this chapter. Excluded are private and in-house collections and archives and papers of individual journalists (for further information on archives, see Lucy Caswell's Gu.de to Sources in American Journalism History *[entry 19]). Those interested only in broadcasting, might also consult* Reruns on File: A Guide to Electronic Media Archives *(entry 357). Addresses of selected foundations are included, but for a comprehensive listing of funds and scholarships, see* The Journalist's Road to Success *(entry 434).*

722.   Alfred I. duPont Center for Broadcast Journalism, Columbia University, 2950 Broadway, New York, NY 10027. www.jrn.columbia.edu/events/dupont/dcbj.

The duPont/Columbia University Award winners in local news, national news, and public affairs from 1968 to the present are housed here. The purpose of the Center is to "enhance the Awards program with professional conferences and educational programs on issues of public policy and practice of broadcast journalism." It sponsors an annual duPont Forum with topics ranging from "Journalists, Lawyers & Public Officials: Overcoming Public Mistrust" (1997) to "Journalists in a Time of Crisis: Watchdogs or Lapdogs?" Some transcripts are available at www.dupont.org.

723.   Alicia Patterson Foundation, 1730 Pennsylvania Avenue, N.W., Suite 850, Washington, D.C. 20006. 202-393-5995; 301-951-8512 (fax). www.aliciapatterson.org.

Established in 1965, the Alicia Patterson Fellowship program is designed for professional journalists seeking to "pursue independent projects of significant interest." One-year grants are awarded, and fellows contribute to the *APF Reporter,* the foundation's quarterly magazine. Patterson, who died in 1963, was editor and publisher of *Newsday* for more than 20 years.

724.   Alternative Press Collections, Thomas J. Dodd Research Center, University of Connecticut, 405 Babbidge Road, Unit 1205, Storrs, CT 06269-1205. 860-486-2524. www.lib.uconn.edu/online/research/speclib/ASC.

Founded in the late 1960s, this special collection maintains more than 4,000 newspaper and magazine titles, books, pamphlet files, posters, buttons, and manuscripts. Publications focusing on the women's movement, civil rights, the peace movement and the Vietnam War, and the environment comprise the bulk of the collection, although publications of the conservative right (*Phyllis Schlafly Report*) and radical right (John Birch Society, Accuracy in Media publications) are well represented. Also located here is the Students for a Democratic Society Radical Education Project of handouts and tabloids that was the core of the original Alternative Press Collection. There is a printed catalog.

725. **American Antiquarian Society Library,** 185 Salisbury Street, Worcester, MA 01609-1634. 508-755-5221. library@mwa.org. www.americanantiquarian.org.

When studying the history of early American journalism, the Antiquarian Society Library is a key resource. It was the source of Readex Microprint Corporation's *Early American Imprints, 1639–1800,* a microform edition of every extant book, pamphlet, and broadside printed in the United States (see Brigham's *History and Bibliography of American Newspapers, 1690–1820,* entry 488). The Society also houses the most comprehensive collection of pre-1921 American newspapers in the United States, and Readex made this collection available on microfilm in a series entitled *Early American Newspapers, 1704–1821.* There also are extensive collections of amateur newspapers, and Bolivian, Chilean, and West Indian newspapers.

726. **American Press Institute,** 11690 Sunrise Valley Drive, Reston, VA 22091-1498. 703-620-3611; 703-620-5814 (fax). info@americanpressinstitute.org. www.american pressinstitute.org.

Founded in 1946, this nonprofit organization offers five-day seminars for mid-career, working newspaper journalists (United States and Canada) in advertising, general management, news/editorial, circulation, marketing, weeklies, and digital/new media. It also schedules online seminars, and offers fellowships to professional journalists and journalism educators. Its Media Center, founded in 1997, "focuses on the creative, technical and strategic challenges of conceiving, gathering, packaging and delivering online news and information." That same year, API and the Freedom Forum (entry 742) forged a "First Amendment" partnership; attendees at API classes in Washington also visit the Freedom Forum and its Newseum to participate in First Amendment discussions.

727. **Bettmann Archive,** Corbis Headquarters, Dexter-Horton Building, 710 Second Avenue, Suite 200, Seattle, WA 98104. 206-373-6000; 206-373-6100 (fax). www.corbis. com.

The Bettmann Archive was purchased by Corbis, a photo agency founded by Bill Gates, and in 1997, according to its Web site, "spent five years selecting images of maximum historical value and saleability for digitization. More than 1.3 million images (26 percent of the collection) have been edited and 225,000 have been digitized." Bettmann Newsphotos, which was part of the Bettmann Archive, offered the photographic collection of United Press International from 1907 to the present; International News Photos, 1912–1958; Acme Newspictures, 1923–1960; Pacific and Atlantic Photos, 1925–1930; and Reuters from 1985 to the present. In addition, the Bettmann Archive contained the Underwood and Underwood Collection of feature and news photography from 1880–1955 and the New York Daily Mirror collection from 1947–1961.

In 2002, the Archive was "moved to a state-of-the-art, sub-zero film preservation facility in western Pennsylvania" or as Dirck Halstead put it in an issue of the *Digital Journalist,* Corbis "was preparing to move the entire Bettmann Archive to a cave in western Pennsylvania." He continues, "The UPI files, alone, comprise millions of photographs taken by photographers working for the United Press, the International News Service, and Acme Newspictures. The collection is one of the most extensive in the world." Researchers interested in these images should contact Corbis to determine if they are still available. As of 2004, Corbis offered 70 million images.

728.   Black Press Archives and Gallery of Distinguished Newspaper Publishers, Moorland-Spingarn Research Center, Howard University, Washington, D.C. 20059. 202-806-7240, 202-806-6405 (fax).

The Black Press Archives, founded in 1973, is a repository for hundreds of black newspapers. In addition to the black newspapers received on subscription, the Archives also works in cooperation with publishers who send copies of their newspapers to be microfilmed.

729.   Broadcast Pioneers Library of American Broadcasting, Hornbake Library, University of Maryland, College Park, MD 20742. 301-405-9160; 301-314-2634 (fax). bp50@umail.umd.edu. www.lib.umd.edu/LAB.

Formerly the Broadcast Pioneers Library, this collection, along with the National Public Broadcasting Archives, is housed at the University of Maryland. The library offers numerous special collections on radio and television broadcasting history, ranging from the Communications Bar Association Archives to the National Association of Broadcasters Library and Historical Archive. There are oral histories, interviews with broadcasters and photographers, books, and pamphlets. According to the Web site, "LAB staff welcome all telephone and e-mail research requests."

730.   Canadian Broadcasting Corporation, Reference Library, P.O. Box 500, Station A, Toronto, Ontario M5W 1E6 Canada. 416-205-3311; archives @cbc.ca. archives.cbc.ca.

According to the Web site, "During the summer of 2001, the Department of Canadian Heritage approved a joint proposal from the CBC and its French counterpart, Radio-Canada, to create a Web site which would highlight selections from its radio and television archives. Using the latest technology, digital copies of selected programs would be made available online." Researchers should consult the CBC Archives Virtual Tour for detailed background on this massive project. Included on the site are topic and clip indexes as well as information accessing separate film, video, radio and photo archives.

731.   Casey Journalism Center on Children and Families, 4321 Hartwick Road, Suite 320, College Park, MD 20740. 301-699-5133; 301-699-9755 (fax). info@casey. umd.edu. casey.umd.edu.

The Center, affiliated with the Phillip Merrill College of Journalism at the University of Maryland, is described as a "national resource for journalists who cover children and families. Its mission is to enhance reporting about the issues and institutions affecting disadvantaged children and their families and to increase public awareness about the concerns facing at-risk children." It offers seminars, a CJC Weekly Summary, CJC Listserv, and The Children's Beat. It also awards Casey Medals for Meritorious Journalism.

732.   Center for Investigative Reporting, 131 Steuart Street, Suite 600, San Francisco, CA 94105-1238. 415-543-1200; 415-543-8311 (fax). center@cironline.org. www.muckraker.org.

Founded in 1977, this nonprofit organization describes itself as a "base for journalists in pursuit of hidden stories about the individuals and institutions that shape our lives. These are the hard stories, hard to assemble and hard to tell." The CIR conducts research and workshops on investigative reporting of public policy, health, crime and justice, international security, and environmental issues. Center publications include *Muckraker, Raising Hell: How the Center for Investigative Reporting Gets the Story,* and *Raising Hell, A Citizen's Guide to the Fine Art of Investigative Reporting.* Its Web site offers tips on "How to Become Your Own Muckraker."

733.   Center for War, Peace, and the News Media, 418 Lafayette Street, Suite 554, New York University, 10 Washington Place, New York, NY 10003. 212-998-7960; 212-995-4143 (fax). war.peace.news@nyu.edu. www.nyu.edu/cwpnm.

This organization was founded in 1985 to study media coverage of arms control and United States–Soviet Union relations. According to the Web site, "In 1993 the Center extended its original mission concerning the role of the media in the superpower conflict during the Cold War to explore the potential of media to contribute to international peace and security. The program's core mission is to examine and develop media-based strategies and approaches to prevent, lessen, manage, and help resolve international, national, ethnic and sub-state conflicts." In addition, the Center's Global Reporting Network focuses on analyzing and improving the reporting of international security stories. Programs affiliated with the Center are the Media Diversity Institute in London and the Center for War and Peace Journalism in Moscow.

734.   Communications Library, University of Illinois, 122 Gregory Hall, 810 South Wright Street, Urbana, IL 61801. 217-333-2216. gateway.library.uiuc.edu/cmx/About Lib/about.htm.

One of the finest communications collections in existence, this library collects books and periodicals on advertising and public relations as well as broadcasting, mass communications, magazines, newspapers, communication, photography, and typography. Emphasis is on television systems and programs, history, and communication theory and effect. Historical library holdings are listed in the *Catalog of the Communications Library* (entry 495) and online. A New Communications Newsroom is currently under construction in the library and users are invited to check it out via the new Web cam at gateway.library.uiuc.edu/cmx.

735.   Council for the Advancement of Science Writing, P.O. Box 910, Hedgesville, WV 25427. 304-754-5077. nasw.org.

This nonprofit educational organization focuses on the quality of science news writing as well as the relationship between the media and scientific community. The Council of scientists and journalists organizes training programs, seminars, fellowships, and other programs and publishes *A Guide to Careers in Science Writing.* It offers fellowships for journalists to attend the annual New Horizons in Science Briefing. Journalists seeking training in science writing may wish to contact the Council.

736.   C-SPAN Archives, Purdue Research Park, P.O. Box 2909, West Lafayette, IN 47996-2909. 877-ONCSPAN; 877-662-7726; 765-497-9699 (fax). info@c-spanarchives. org.

Purdue University began recording programs on Cable-Satellite Public Affairs Network (C-SPAN) in 1987 and in mid-1998 the Archives operations (formerly Public Affairs Video Archives) moved to C-SPAN. Every program aired since 1987—more than 80,000 hours—is indexed and archived. Researchers interested in all aspects of public affairs, Senate proceedings, congressional hearings, press conferences, and presidential debates that C-SPAN regularly covers will want to consult this archive. Copies of most available programs can be requested and used for education, research, or home viewing. Archives catalogs are available, but researchers should consult the Web site for further and more current information and access to indexes.

737. **The Dart Center of Journalism and Trauma,** Department of Communication, 102 Communications Building, Box 353740, University of Washington, Seattle, WA 98195-3740. 206-616-3223; 206-543-9285; info@dartcenter.org. www.dartcenter.org.

The Dart Center is described as a "global network of journalists, journalism educators and health professionals dedicated to improving media coverage of trauma, conflict and tragedy." It confers the Dart Award for excellent reporting on victims of violence; the Dart Foundation sponsors, with the International Society for Traumatic Stress Studies, the Dart Fellowship in Journalism & Trauma. The Web site is packed with useful resources, studies, and links.

738. **The Dow Jones Newspaper Fund,** P.O Box 300, Princeton, NJ 08543-0300. 609-452-2820, 609-520-5804 (fax); newsfund@wsj.dowjones.com. djnewspaperfund. dowjones.com.

The Dow Jones Newspaper Fund publishes *The Journalist's Road to Success* (formerly *Journalism Career and Scholarship Guide,* entry 434), and offers internships in online editing, news copy editing, and business reporting; scholarships; and training programs. It was founded in 1958 by editors of *The Wall Street Journal* to "improve the quality of journalism education and the pool of applicants for jobs in the newspaper business."

739. **European Journalism Centre,** Sonnevile-lunet 10, 6221KT Maastricht, The Netherlands. 31-43-325-40-30; 31-43-321-26-26 (fax). secr@ejc.nl. www.ejc.nl.

This nonprofit training institute for professional journalists, media executives, and journalism educators was founded in 1992 and launched its teaching programs in 1993. Its goals include promoting "high quality journalism through professional training, particularly in a European context" and to "create and support networks among media professionals within Europe and with other parts of the world." It offers training programs in reporting, media management, and technology. A unique feature on the Web site is the European Media Landscape, which provides an overview of the press in approximately 30 European countries. Researchers might also be interested in library services and publications from the European Institute for the Media in Düsseldorf (www.eim.org).

740. **FAIR (Fairness and Accuracy in Reporting),** 112 W 27th Street, New York, NY 10001. 212-633-6700; 212-727-7668 (fax). fair@fair.org. www.fair.org.

FAIR, founded in 1986, describes itself as a national media watch group. "We work to invigorate the First Amendment by advocating for greater diversity in the press and by scrutinizing media practices that marginalize public interest, minority and dissenting viewpoints. As an anti-censorship organization, we expose neglected news stories and defend working journalists when they are muzzled." It publishes the magazine *Extra!,* produces *CounterSpin,* a weekly radio program, and offers a Racism Watch Desk as well as FAIR Archives on its Web site.

741.   First Amendment Center, Vanderbilt University, 1207 18th Avenue S., Nashville, TN 37212. 615-727-1600; 615-727-1319 (fax). info@fac.org. First Amendment Center/Arlington, 1101 Wilson Blvd., Arlington, VA 22209. 703-528-0800; 703-284-3519 (fax). www.firstamendmentcenter.org.

"The First Amendment Center works to preserve and protect First Amendment freedoms through information and education. The center serves as a forum for the study and exploration of free-expression issues, including freedom of speech, of the press and of religion, the right to assemble and petition the government." It sponsors programs such as First Amendment Schools (with the Association for Supervision and Curriculum Development), which aims at changing the way schools educate children about the First Amendment. It also publishes numerous documents on free speech and freedom of information, which can be downloaded on the Web site.

742.   The Freedom Forum, 1101 Wilson Blvd., Arlington, VA 22209. 703-528-0800; 703-284-3770 (fax). news@freedomforum.org. www.freedomforum.org.

The Freedom Forum is primarily concerned with First Amendment issues, supports and sponsors programs focusing on freedom of the press and freedom of speech, and offers scholarships to journalism and mass communications students. It publishes numerous studies on world press freedom, newsroom diversity, and media ethics, and sponsors awards such as the Excellence in Urban Journalism Award and the Al Neuharth Free Spirit of the Year Award. The Freedom Forum also directs operations of the First Amendment Center (entry 741) and the Newseum, "the interactive museum of news," which was closed in 2002 to "permit Newseum staff to focus exclusively on planning and developing the new museum, which is scheduled to open in late 2006." A Cyber Newseum is available at www.newseum.org/cybernewseum.

743.   Freedom of Information Center, 133 Neff Annex, University of Missouri–Columbia, Columbia, MO 65211. 573-882-4856; 573-884-2604. foi@missouri.edu. www.missouri.edu/~foiwww.

According to the Web site, "We're here to serve the general public and the media on questions regarding access to government documents and information." The FOI Center studies on a daily basis "actions by government, media and society affecting movement and content of information." Established in 1958, the FOI Library acts as a First Amendment clearinghouse of more than a million articles and documents, and indexes and files information and documentation on access laws, press freedom, libel, student press, and censorship; many items are now available online. Journalists with research questions and problems may contact the Center. Researchers might also be interested in the Brechner Center for Freedom of Information at the University of Florida, Gainesville.

744.   Fund for Investigative Journalism, P.O. Box 60184, Washington, D.C. 20039-0185. 202-362-0260; 301-422-7449. fundfij@aol.com. www.fij.org.

The Fund for Investigative Journalism awards grants to journalists who are working on "investigative pieces involving corruption, malfeasance, incompetence and societal ills in general as well as for media criticism" and are without the "protection and backing of major news organizations."

745.   The Huck Boyd National Center for Community Media, 105 Kedzie Hall, Kansas State University, Manhattan, KS 66506-1501. 785-532-0721. huckboyd@ksu.edu. huckboyd.jmc.ksu.edu.

Founded in 1990, this research and teaching center should "serve and strengthen the local newspapers, radio stations, cable systems and other media that have a key role to play in the survival and revitalization of America's small towns" and is described in promotional material as "dedicated to the proposition that strengthening community media will help strengthen small communities." It is named for McDell "Huck" Boyd, a Kansas publisher and state leader who died in 1987. The Center publishes the *Community Newspaper Showcase of Excellence,* which features winners of the National Newspaper Association's Better Newspaper Contests. It also plans to provide a job bank on community journalism.

746.   Ifra Newsplex at the University of South Carolina, SCETV Telecommunications Center, 1040 George Rogers Blvd., Columbia, SC 29201. 803-737-8411; 208-728-9066. info@newsplex.org. www.newsplex.org.

Described as a "skunkworks for the news industry" and a "prototype multi-media micro-newsroom for demonstration, research and training in next-generation newshandling tools and techniques," *Ifra* (entry 674) has created Newsplex "to exercise the future of news." The facility will include a newsflow desk, news analysis area, and media docks for convergence journalists. Interestingly, USC's School of Library and Information Science also is involved in the project and was seeking funds for a news resourcer role, described as a "hybrid informatics journalist." Recent week-long seminar offerings include: Visual Journalism Summit, Adplexing, and a Media Scenarios Project. Newsplex also publishes *Ifra Newsplex Trends* on its Web site.

747.   Institute for New Media Studies, University of Minnesota, School of Journalism and Mass Communication, College of Liberal Arts 111 Murphy Hall, 206 Church Street, S.E., Minneapolis, MN 55455-0418. 612-625-0576. inms@umn.edu. www.inms.umn.edu.

The Institute's mission is clearly stated: It is a "center for creation, innovation, and examination of content and messages and the affects of new media technologies and techniques on their forms and functions. The goal is the imagining and testing of innovative forms, development of new knowledge about functions, and generation of greater understanding of the impacts of these changes in the media landscape." Toward this goal, director Nora Paul, named one of the Top 10 "wired women" in the world, writes, "It is through presentations, programs, research and writings that the 'knowing' of the Institute shall be formed. We are just at the beginning." The Institute, founded in 2000, sponsors conferences and workshops, conducts research, and has designed an innovative and accessible Web site.

748.   International Center for Journalists, 1616 H Street N.W., Washington, D.C. 20006. 202-737-3700; 202-737-0530. editor@icfj.org. www.icfj.org.

The ICFJ was founded in 1984 "to improve the quality of journalism in nations where there is little or no tradition of independent journalism." It conducts workshops and seminars and offers fellowships such as the Knight International Press Fellowship Program. The Center also maintains the International Journalists' Network at www.ijnet.org.

749.   International Women's Media Foundation, 1726 M Street, N.W., Suite 1002, Washington, D.C. 20036. 202-496-1992; 202-496-1977. info@iwmf.org. www.iwmf.org.

The IWMF's mission is "to strengthen the role of women in the news media around the world, based on the belief that no press is truly free unless women share an equal voice." Founded in 1990, it offers seminars and workshops, publishes the *IWMFWire* newsletter, and confers annual Courage in Journalism awards for international women journalists. Its Web site is packed with useful training resources and important links.

750.   J-Lab: The Institute for Interactive Journalism, University of Maryland, Philip Merrill College of Journalism, 7100 Baltimore Avenue, Suite 101, College Park, MD 20740-3637. 301-985-4020; 301-985-4021. news@j-lab.org. www.j-lab.org .

Described as a spin-off of the Pew Center for Civic Journalism, J-Lab's mission is to be an "incubator for innovative news experiments that use new technologies to help people actively engage in critical public issues." It confers the Batten Awards for Innovations in Journalism and offers on its Web site numerous examples of interactive journalism such as the BBC Iraq Navigator (an interactive map) and the Seattle Times "You Build It" Transportation Project Calculator.

751.   Journalism Library, Indiana University, School of Journalism, Ernie Pyle Hall, 940 E. 7th Street, Bloomington, IN 47405. 812-855-3517; 812-856-5391. libjourn@ indiana.edu. www.indiana.edu/~libjourn.

This journalism and mass communication library houses a comprehensive collection of books and serials, with exceptional holdings in media law, broadcasting, and print journalism. It also contains the Ernie Pyle collection of columns and memorabilia. It would behoove serious researchers to schedule some time in Indiana.

752.   Journalism Library and Library for Communication and Graphic Arts, The Ohio State University, 100 Journalism Building, 242 West 18th Avenue, Columbus, OH 43210. 614-292-8747; 614-247-6393 (fax). www.lib.ohio-state.edu/jouweb.

A large journalism collection, this library focuses on radio, television, newspapers, magazines, photography, motion pictures, and public relations. Ohio State University also houses the Cartoon Research Library in its special collections department.

753.   Journalism Library, University of Missouri, School of Journalism, 117 Walter Williams Hall, Columbia, MO 65211. 573-882-7502; 573-884-4963 (fax). www.missouri.edu/~jourss/.

Serious researchers should not bypass this substantial collection of books and periodicals on broadcasting, newspapers and magazines, media management, photography, and typography; it is among the most comprehensive journalism libraries.

754. **Knight Center for Environmental Journalism,** 382 Communication Arts Building, Michigan State University, East Lansing, MI 48824-1212. 517-355-7710; 517-432-1415. environmental.jrn.msu.edu.

Established in 1994, the Center focuses on environmental reporting and writing, conducts research, and organizes seminars. It also holds the Meeman Archives (entries for the Edward J. Meeman Award sponsored by the Scripps Howard Foundation National Journalism Awards), a collection of award-winning reporting on environmental journalism. Its Web site provides job postings and information on internships, scholarships, and fellowships.

755. **Knight Center for Science and Medical Journalism,** Boston University College of Communication, 640 Commonwealth Avenue, Boston, MA 02215. 800-992-6514; 617-353-4239; 617-358-2348 (fax). www.bu.edu/com/jo/science.

Described as a "global center for educating future generations of scientifically proficient and ethically grounded journalists," this Center is currently building a global reference service, a "library devoted to science and medical journalism, and a Web site in which journalists from around the world can exchange information, sources and perspectives on science, medical and public health issues." The University of Missouri also supports a Science Journalism Center (www.journalism.missouri.edu/research/resources.html).

756. **Knight Center for Specialized Journalism,** University of Maryland, 1117 Cole Field House, College Park, MD 20742-1024. 301-405-4817. knight@umail.umd.edu. www.knightcenter.umd.edu.

The Knight Center offers week-long seminars for print and broadcast journalists who cover specific beats or specialized topics. Recent courses include "Covering Business, After Enron" and "Civil Liberties in an Age of Terror: Seminar for Editorial Writers."

757. **Knight Foundation,** One Cascade Plaza, Eighth Floor, Akron, OH 44308. 216-253-9301.

The John S. and James L. Knight Foundation was founded in 1950 as a "private foundation independent of the Knight brothers' newspaper enterprises. It is dedicated to furthering their ideals of service to community, to the highest standards of journalistic excellence and to the defense of a free press." It funds the Knight Chairs in Journalism program, Knight Center for Specialized Journalism (entry 756), Knight Center for Science and Medical Journalism (entry 755), John S. Knight Fellowships for Professional Journalists, the Knight Bagehot Fellowships in Economics and Journalism, Knight International Press Fellowships, Knight Public Health Journalism Fellowships, and the Knight Science Journalism Fellowships. It also supports the Media Management Center at Northwestern University (entry 762) and the Knight Foundation Newsroom Training Initiative.

758. **Library of Congress, Motion Picture and Television Reading Room,** Broadcasting & Recorded Sound Division, Madison Building, Room 336, 101 Independence Avenue S.E., Washington, D.C. 20540-4690. 202-707-8572; 202-707-2371 (fax). www.loc.gov/rr/mopic.

Television collections include the NBC Television Collection (1948–1977), National Educational Television programs (1955–1969), PBS Collection, and the Television News Collection, including ABC Evening News from 1977–1992 and CBS from 1975–1993. It should be noted that "viewing facilities, which are available without charge, are provided for those doing research of a specific nature leading toward a publicly available work such as a dissertation, publication, or film/television production. We regret that the facilities may not be used for purely personal study or appreciation, nor in ways—such as preview—that conflict with commercial distribution." Researchers should consult the Web site for more specific information regarding access and hours.

759.   Library of Congress, Prints and Photographs Reading Room, Prints & Photographs Division, Madison Building, Room 337, 101 Independence Avenue, S.E., Washington, D.C. 20540-4690. 202-707-6394; 202-707-6647 (fax). www.loc.gov/rr/print.

U.S. News and World Report's files (1955–1985) are maintained here. In addition, there are thousands of negatives, transparencies, and prints from the Farm Security Administration documentation project and more than 100,000 negatives from Bain News Service, the first news photograph service. Researchers should consult the Web site for more specific information on collections, hours, and access. Users might also be interested in the Motion Picture Films and Sound and Video Recordings at the National Archives and Records Administration, www.archives.gov/research_room/media_formats/film_sound_video.html.

760.   The Media Institute, 1000 Potomac St., N.W., Suite 301, Washington, D.C. 20007. 202-298-7512; 202-337-7092 (fax). www.mediainst.org.

This nonprofit research facility and conservative think tank was founded in the late 1970s "to encourage and promote the development of knowledge and understanding of American media and communications." It focuses primarily on communications policy and First Amendment issues. It also offers a Copyright Colloquium, described as an "online forum for discussing and debating the many issues surrounding copyright and intellectual property in the digital age."

761.   The Media Laboratory, Wiesner Building, 20 Ames Street, Cambridge, MA 02139-4307. 617-253-5960; 617-258-6264 (fax). www.media.mit.edu.

This center for advanced study and research in new information technologies and communications media opened in 1985, and its charter was to "invent and creatively exploit new media for human well-being and individual satisfaction without regard to present-day constraint." Today, The Media Lab "continues to focus on the study, invention, and creative use of digital technologies to enhance the ways that people think, express, and communicate ideas, and explore new scientific frontiers." Research "comprises interconnected developments in an unusual range of disciplines, such as software agents; machine understanding; how children learn; human and machine vision; audition; speech interfaces; wearable computers; affective computing; advanced interface design; tangible media; object-oriented video; interactive cinema; digital expression—from text, to graphics, to sound; and new approaches to spatial imaging, nanomedia, and nanoscale sensing." The Web site is a colorful and well-designed introduction to all facets of its research interests and projects.

762.   Media Management Center, 301 Fisk Hall, Northwestern University, 1845 Sheridan Road, Evanston, IL 60208-2110. 847-491-4900; 847-491-5619. contact@media managementcenter.org. www.mediamanagementcenter.org.

Formerly the Newspaper Management Center, this teaching and research facility, founded in 1989, is supported by both the Knight Foundation and the Robert R. McCormick Tribune Foundation. It grew out of a Knight study by director John M. Lavine, then professor of media management and economics at the University of Minnesota and currently director of the Media Management Center, and is a joint project of Northwestern's Medill School of Journalism and J. L. Kellogg Graduate School of Management. The MMC offers seminars focusing on the development of senior leaders in the newspaper, broadcast, magazine, and new media industries, and sponsors the Women in Newspapers project.

763.   MediaResource, 99 Alexander Drive, P.O. Box 13975, Research Triangle Park, NC 27709. 800-223-1730; 919-549-0090 (fax) mediaresource@sigmaxi.org. www.mediaresource.org.

Founded in 1980 as part of the Scientists' Institute for Public Information (SIPI), Media Resource Service is a national, nonprofit organization that recognizes that reporting on issues in science, technology, and medicine can be challenging. It refers journalists to specialists who can translate technical information and jargon and who, most importantly, have agreed to answer questions from the media.

764.   National Archives of Canada, 395 Wellington Street, Ottawa, Ontario K1A ON3 Canada. 613-992-3884; 613-995-6274. www.archives.ca.

Formerly the Public Archives of Canada. the National Archives houses many of the Canadian Broadcasting Corporation's records. The CBC is Canada's principal broadcasting agency and its records are scattered. There is a printed guide, albeit dated, to the collections, *Guide to CBC Sources at the Public Archives* (entry 501), which leads the user through the Federal Archives Division, Manuscript Division, National Map Collection, National Photography Collection, and the National Film, Television and Sound Archives. Also available is ArchiviaNet, the Archives' online database, which provides access to numerous holdings. Special collections range from the Shugg Collection (Orvill Shugg was the first supervisor of the CBC Farm Broadcasts in 1939) to "Tuesday Night," a collection of kinescopes and videotapes of the weekly current affairs program. See also the Canadian Broadcasting Corporation Reference Library (entry 730).

765.   National Center on Disability and Journalism, 944 Market Street, Suite 829, San Francisco, CA 94102-4019. 415-291-0868; 415-291-0869 (fax). ncdj@ncdj.org.

The NCDJ's mission is to "educate journalists and educators about disability reporting issues in order to produce more accurate, fair and diverse news reporting." It produces teaching materials, such as a style guide and newsletter, for use in the classroom and sponsors mentorship programs and student internships. This nonprofit organization was founded in 1998 as the Disability Media Project.

766.   National Institute for Computer Assisted Reporting (NICAR), 138 Neff Annex, Missouri School of Journalism, Columbia, MO 65211. 573-884-7711; 573-882-5431 (fax). info@ire.org. www.nicar.org.

This important training organization created in 1989 is a joint effort of Investigative Reporters and Editors (entry 682) and the University of Missouri School of Journalism. It focuses on computer-assisted reporting and offers newsroom training in addition to seminars for journalists and journalism educators. NICAR also maintains an impressive Database Library at www.ire.org/datalibrary and publishes *Uplink.*

767.   National Press Foundation, 1211 Connecticut Avenue, N.W., Suite 310, Washington, D.C. 20045. 202-663-7280. www.nationalpress.org.

The mission of the National Press Foundation is to "provide professional development opportunities for editors, producers and reporters across the United States, helping them better understand and explain the impact of public policy on readers and viewers." It sponsors seminars for professional journalists and confers numerous awards including the Excellence in Online Journalism award and the Sol Taishoff Award for Excellence in Broadcast Journalism.

768.   National Women & Media Collection, Western Historical Manuscript Collection, 23 Ellis Library, University of Missouri, Columbia, MO 65201-5149. 573-882-6028. whmc@umsystem.edu. www.system.missouri.edu/whmc/nwm.html.

Founded in 1987, this collection focuses on women's roles in the media and the history of women in American journalism. Included are records of women's organizations and personal and professional papers of women journalists, educators, and press secretaries. A complete list of holdings is available on the Web site.

769.   New Directions for News. info@ndn.org. www.ndn.org.

NDN's vision is to be the "world's thought leader on the creation, application and consumption of news, information and media." Its mission: to provide "organizations worldwide with superior insights and guidance on the future role and use of news, information and media from a user point of view." Founded at the University of Missouri in 1987, this nonprofit organization moved to the University of Minnesota in 2000. NDN conducts research, organizes seminars and forums, and maintains a weblog at fastforward.ndn.org.

770.   News University.

The Poynter Institute (entry 774) and the John S. and James L. Knight Foundation are currently building News University, or NewsU, described as an "online training portal for journalists." Howard Finberg, former vice president for Internet Strategies and Technology and Central Newspapers, Inc., will direct the program.

771.   NewsLab, 1850 K Street N.W., Suite 850, Washington, D.C. 20006. 202-969-2536; 202-969-2543 (fax). mail@newslab.org. www.newslab.org.

NewsLab describes itself as a "non-profit resource for television newsrooms, focused on research and training. We serve local stations by helping them find better ways of telling important stories that are often difficult to convey on television." It develops workshops and produces handbooks and tip sheets, which are available on its Web site. Its newsletter, *NewsLab Report,* also is available online. It is affiliated with the Project for Excellence in Journalism (entry 775).

772.   Nieman Foundation for Journalism at Harvard University, One Francis Avenue, Cambridge, MA 02138. 617-495-2237; 617-495-8976 (fax). www.nieman.harvard.edu.

The original purpose of the Nieman Foundation was to "promote and elevate the standards of journalism in the United States and educate persons deemed especially qualified for journalism." Toward that end, the Nieman Foundation funds Harvard University's prestigious academic-year Lucius W. Nieman Fellowships for professional journalists, which now includes international journalists. It also publishes *Nieman Reports* (entry 628).

773. **Pacifica Radio Archive,** 3729 Cahuenga Boulevard West, North Hollywood, CA 91604. 818-506-1077; 800-735-0230; 818-506-1084. pacificaarchives.org.

More than 47,000 recordings made at Pacifica's five sister stations in Berkeley, Los Angeles, New York, Houston, and Washington, D.C., are housed here. Emphasis is on news, information talk, documentary, and political programs. A substantial portion of the collection focuses on alternative radio and the Vietnam War. It is searchable via the Web site.

774. **The Poynter Institute for Media Studies,** 801 Third Street South, St. Petersburg, FL 33701. 888-769-6837. www.poynter.org.

A nonprofit educational institution, the Institute (formerly Modern Media Institute) was founded in 1975 by Nelson Poynter, the late publisher of the *St. Petersburg Times* and chairman of the Times Publishing Company. Dozens of seminars focus on writing and editing, graphics and design, ethics, photojournalism, new media, and leadership. Most are aimed at professional print and broadcast journalists, but there also are programs for graduate students and teachers. Poynter's Eugene Patterson Library contains thousands of books and numerous periodicals, videotapes, and newspapers on all aspects of print and broadcast journalism, ethics, graphics and design, color, and newsroom management. The library is not open to the public, but is available to journalists and journalism researchers. Its Web site PoynterOnline (or "Everything You Need To Be a Better Journalist") is true to its description. This invaluable online resource offers news and analysis, links to organizations and relevant sites, and Jim Romenesko's "daily fix of media industry news, commentary, and memos." The Institute also publishes *Best Newspaper Writing* (entry 380) annually in cooperation with the American Society of Newspaper Editors.

775. **Project for Excellence in Journalism,** 1850 K Street, N.W., Suite 850, Washington, DC, 20006. 202-293-7394; 202-293-6946 (fax). mail@journalist.org. www.journalism.org/who/pej.

The PEJ, part of the Columbia University Graduate School of Journalism, "conducts research about journalism and provides journalists with tools to do better work. Additionally, the Project helps citizens gain a better understanding of what to expect from the press and how to demand it." It produces report and content studies, and reviews local television news. The PEJ sponsors the Committee of Concerned Journalists (entry 670) and its Web site, journalism.org, is described as the "joint Internet presence" of the Project and the CCJ. Also affiliated with the PEJ is NewsLab (entry 771).

776. **The Reporters Committee for Freedom of the Press,** 1815 N. Fort Myer Drive, Suite 900, Arlington, VA 22209. 800-336-4243 (Legal Defense Hotline); 703-807-2100. rcfp@rcfp.org.

Dedicated to preserving First Amendment rights for all journalists involved in news media, this voluntary association offers free legal advice, defense, and research assistance to all members of the working press, media scholars, and media lawyers. Publications include *The News Media and the Law* (entry 624), the biweekly *News Media Update,* and dozens of handbooks and special reports such as *How to Use the Federal FOI Act* and *The First Amendment Handbook* (entry 401).

777.   Robert C. Maynard Institute for Journalism Education, 409 Thirteenth Street, 9th Floor, Oakland, CA 94612. 510-891-9202; 510-891-9565. mije@may nardije.org. www.maynardije.org.

Cofounded in 1973 by Robert Maynard, editor of *The Oakland Tribune*, the Institute for Journalism Education was renamed following his death in 1993. The Institute offers several unique training and leadership programs for journalists, designed around a "Fault Lines" framework. According to the Web site, Maynard believed that the "five fault lines of race, class, gender, generation and geography are the most enduring forces shaping lives, experiences and social tensions in this country," and that "the Institute's Fault Lines framework helps journalists build a more diverse source list, have more voices in stories and determine which fault lines are at work in complex issues." Its Web site offers valuable links to articles, organizations, and resources focusing on journalism and diversity.

778.   Scripps Howard Foundation, P.O. Box 5380, 312 Walnut Street, Cincinnati, OH 45201. 513-977-3035; 513-977-3800 (fax).

The Foundation offers scholarships to undergraduate and graduate print and broadcast journalism students. It also bestows National Journalism Awards such as the Ernie Pyle Award for human interest writing and the Charles M. Schulz Award for college student cartoonists, and offers grants to nonprofit journalism organizations.

779.   Sigma Delta Chi Foundation, Eugene S. Pulliam National Journalism Center, 3909 N. Meridien Street, Indianapolis, IN 46208. 317-927-8000; 317-920-4789 (fax). questions@spj.org. www.spj.org/sdx.

The Sigma Delta Chi Foundation funds Sigma Delta Chi Awards, the annual Mark of Excellence Awards for journalism students, and the Eugene C. Pulliam Fellowship for Editorial Writers, and sponsors and supports activities of the Society of Professional Journalists (entry 715).

780.   Student Press Law Center, 1815 N. Fort Myer Drive, Arlington, VA 22209. 703-807-1904. www.splc.org.

Focusing on First Amendment rights of high school and college students, the Student Press Law Center, founded in 1974, is a clearinghouse of information on press freedom. It also offers legal aid to students and advisers dealing with censorship issues. Publications include the *SPLC Report,* available on its Web site.

781.   Vanderbilt Television News Archive, 110 21st Avenue South, Suite 704, Nashville, TN 37203. 615-322-2927. tvnews@library.vanderbilt.edu.

Researchers interested in broadcast history and the evolution of television news will want to review this Archive. All network television evening news programs (more than 30,000 broadcasts) and selected special news programs (9,000 hours) from August 5, 1968 to the present are stored on videotape in these archives. The evening news programs are indexed through 1995 in the *Television News Index and Abstracts* (entry 212); now available is TV-NewSearch, an online database of the entire archive. Special collections include Democratic and Republican National Conventions, press conferences, and Watergate hearings. "Face the Nation," "Meet the Press," and "Issues and Answers" from 1970 on also can be found here. Tapes are offered on a loan basis; examine the Archive Web site for further information on services and charges.

782.   **Wisconsin Historical Society Library,** Newspaper and Periodicals Section, 816 State Street, Madison, WI 53706-1482. 608-264-6535; 608-264-6520. www.wisconsinhistory.org/library.

This is the home of the second-largest collection of newspapers in the United States, with titles published in every state and Canadian province. Newspapers are available in bound volumes and micro-formats. It also houses the largest collections of Native American newspapers and U.S. and Canadian underground or alternative newspapers in North America and has one of the largest collections of African American, Asian American, Canadian, and Hispanic American newspapers. James Danky, newspapers and periodicals librarian, is one of the finest resources available, and is the author of numerous newspaper bibliographies. Researchers should consult the Web site for details about hours, catalogs, and holdings. (Note: The Pew Center for Civic Journalism indicates that its archive of 800 civic journalism projects will be housed at the Wisconsin Historical Society and will be available at some point to researchers.)

783.   **Women's Institute for Freedom of the Press,** 1940 Calvert Street, N.W., Washington, D.C. 20009-1502. 202-265-6707; 202-986-6355. www.wifp.org.

The nonprofit WIFP was founded in 1972, and focuses on women working in the media and women's issues in communications. It publishes the *Directory of Women's Media* now available on its Web site.

784.   **World Press Institute,** c/o Macalester College, 1600 Grand Avenue, St. Paul, MN 55105. 612-696-6360; 612-696-6306 (fax).

Founded in 1961, the World Press Institute's mission is to "promote and strengthen press freedom throughout the world." It sponsors a fellows program in the United States for foreign journalists. It is privately funded by media, corporate, and individual donations.

Author / Title Index

Subject Index

Diversity. *See* Bias-free word usage; Disabilities, reporting issues; Minorities; Stereotypes; *specific groups*
Documentaries, 28, 149
DotJournalism (Web site), 263
Dougherty Collection of Military Newspapers, 570
Dow Jones Newspaper Fund, The, 738

Editing, art and craft of, 118
Editorial cartoons/cartoonists, 64, 424, 535, 639, 660. *See also* Cartoons/cartoonists
Editorials, 364, 535, 620, 691
Editors: associations, 592, 642–43, 646, 654, 656, 661, 682, 684, 686, 713, 766; associations, newspaper, 377, 648, 665, 681, 744; biographies, 323, 331, 341; copy, 283, 299, 399, 552, 602, 643; guides for, 462, 482, 516; newspaper, 354, 415, 538, 605, 608, 642, 648
Education in journalism: associations, 668–69, 677, 682–83, 739, 777; college programs guides, 355, 437; directories, 327, 362; ERIC abstracts/database, 210, 229; financial aid (*see* Fellowships in journalism; Grants; Scholarships); journals, 197, 598, 616, 627; listservs, 301, 306; teacher resources, 277, 534, 765. *See also* Internship programs; Mentorship programs; Training seminars
Education Writers Association, 673
Electronic communications, 160, 710. *See also* Computer-assisted reporting
Electronic records access, 389
Email language usage guide, 463
Emmy Awards, 360, 685
Environment, 714, 724
Environmental Journalism Center, 710
ERIC (Educational Resources Information Center), 210, 229
Essays, 198
Ethics: foreign perspective, 117, 562; generally, 393–94, 412, 742; journals, 614, 633, 636; media, 22, 23
Ethnic groups, 47, 230–31, 375–76, 478, 549, 688, 718

Ethnic NewsWatch, 230
Europe, 126, 219, 236, 264, 721, 739. *See also* British journalism; France
European Institute for Media, 739
European Journalism Centre, 739
European Journalism Page (Web site), 264

FAIR (Fairness and Accuracy in Reporting), 740
Families as journalism focus, 731
Fellowships in journalism: environmental/science, 735, 754; generally, 689, 737, 748, 757; journalists, 673, 723, 726, 772, 784
Film: British, 487, 489, 506, 526; generally, 139, 510, 589; on journalism, 507, 514; research guides, 30, 487, 509; term definition, 163, 172–74
Financial aid, 434. *See also* Grants; Scholarships
First Amendment Center, 741–42
First Amendment rights: associations promoting, 740–43, 760, 776; generally, 140, 726, 780; handbooks on, 401–3; media and, 7, 36. *See also* Press freedoms
1stHeadlines (Web site), 265
Foreign correspondents, 82, 708
Foreign Press Association, 708
Foundation of American Women in Radio and Television, Inc., 650
Foundations: awards through, 658, 710, 712, 749, 767; fellowships through, 723, 737, 772; Knight, 757, 762, 770; scholarships through, 710, 778; women, 650, 658, 749
France, 126, 219
Freedom Forum, The, 726, 742
Freedom of Information Center, 743
Free expression, 75, 741–43
Free press. *See* Press freedoms
Fund for Investigative Journalism, 744

Gale Group resources, 202, 231–34
Gays, 29, 694
Gender stereotypes, 32, 85, 169, 478. *See also* Bias-free word usage

About the Author

JO A. CATES is currently Director of the library at Columbia College Chicago, a school for the arts and the media. She has been Regional Research Manager of Ernst and Young's Center for Business Knowledge in Chicago, former Head of the Transportation Library at Northwestern University in Evanston, Illinois, and former Chief Librarian of the Poynter Institute for Media Studies in St. Petersburg, Florida. She has an undergraduate degree in Journalism from Boston University and an M.S. in Library Science from Simmons College.

Dedication

For my beautiful grandchildren Katie, Mike, Brian, Conor, Cullen and Emeline. You are the perfect motivation for living a long healthy life.

Acknowledgements

This book is an outgrowth of the many encouraging words I have heard from clients, friends and colleagues that my approach to healthy eating and aging should reach a wider audience. A pivotal moment that moved me from thinking about writing to actually committing to it occurred when I realized there is a huge lack of information on how food can be a powerful tool for getting or staying healthy through later years. Anyone who is a part of the Baby Boomer generation knows that a healthy lifestyle will increase their chances of aging well. There's much about anti-aging creams, miracle supplements, medications and joint replacement but far too little about the way food plays a vital role in health and wellness in our later years. The food we eat literally becomes who we are - a powerful statement on food's importance.

I give special thanks to my children Joanna and Kenton and their spouses Timmy and Kate, for their encouragement and patience as I shared every bump on the road with them. Also Joe Saling, who gently but firmly insisted I clarify my message. Dolores Pucci held my hand during the last lap where I found that there's a whole lot more to publishing a book than simply writing it. From getting the message right to getting the cover right, I am deeply grateful to my many friends, clients and professional colleagues who encouraged me to stay with it and get it done. Thanks Diane Horn and Zoe Finch Totten for your favorable and encouraging comments.

Contents

1

You and Food

"Aging is not lost youth but a new stage of opportunity and strength." Betty Friedan

Simply stated, this book tells the story of vital aging and how real food changes everything about your health. It changes everything because the food you put in your body day after day, literally becomes you. It becomes your skin, your hair, your hearing and vision. It becomes your internal organs. It becomes your mind and your mood. That's why *real* food, not *pretend* food, is so important. I'm going to give you what you need to know to make positive change in a way that's designed to work into your busy lifestyle. This book will educate you in food and nutrition so well that you will feel confident that you are making the best choices for staying well and aging well.

My message is simple: if you are a Baby Boomer or someone who cares about having lifelong health, you need to eat **real food**.

Eating real food will increase your chances for a long healthy life exponentially. I am on the high end of the Boomer generation and I think it would be really cool to be a recipient of our President's Happy 100th Birthday greeting one day. If you want that too, listen up. Get yourself inspired by the notion that *food becomes you.* Nutritious food needs to be your best friend. When it is, amazing things will happen for you that no amount of anti-aging creams, facelifts, butt lifts or hair color will ever do for you. Imagine having more energy than you've had in years. Imagine that those aches and pains you thought were a part of normal aging are gone! For most of us, it is entirely possible.

Two things prompted me to write this book: one is the amazing ways in which my own health and the health of my clients improved when we changed our food. The other is I want to combat the widespread belief that aging is the primary cause of physical and mental decline. Aging is not the primary cause of decline; poor lifestyle habits are the reason many of us fall apart in old age. The changes I made in my food, moving from a chronic sugar habit to a balanced whole foods based diet, changed all my health markers for the better. I've seen the same results in the many clients I have worked with. Change your food and your body will change, inside and out.

The food choices you make affect your health more than almost anything else, even your genes. Scientists have found that genes only count for 30% of your health profile; the rest is lifestyle, and much of that relates to the food you eat. Food is my specialty. If you'd like to change your health for the better, follow me. I will take you step by step through the process of transforming your plate and your life into something really special.

The path to healthy eating I will take you on is not complicated. It does not separate food into a bunch of micronutrients where you have to think like a scientist to get it right. In fact, I think much of the confusion we experience today around food comes from overcomplicated food advice. Food should be simple. It should taste good. And most important, it should make you *feel* good. I can help you with that.

Today more than ever before we are called upon to be more responsible for our health. If you are noticing subtle shifts in your health, pay attention to them. They are signals that something is not right, either in your food, your lifestyle or maybe a combination of both. The good news is it is never too late to make changes for the better. I became aware of the way declining health started sneaking up on me in my late forties, even though I'd lived in a reasonably health-conscious way. It is in your late forties that the innate energy of youth will no longer overcome even the most subtly negligent lifestyle habits. Without the glow of youth, that bagel or muffin in the morning simply isn't enough to keep you energized or effectively regulate your blood sugar.

Employers and insurance companies are asking you to pay more of your health care costs because so many older adults are developing the diseases of a poor lifestyle. Cases of Type II diabetes, elevated cholesterol, high blood pressure, aching joints, gum disease, and even some forms of cancer are on the rise. These companies could lower premiums if they educated their subscribers on healthy eating instead of simply scheduling biometrics screenings. Because there has been so little clear-cut education about food, we must learn on our own how to be healthy through nutrition.

As part of the 78 million members of the baby boomer generation, you are nearing or are already enrolled in Medicare. As a part of that generation I am committed to helping myself and my fellow Boomers. The government is in a quandary about Medicare's sustainability but it has done little to educate Americans on the importance of eating healthy foods. Instead it continues to subsidize agri-business that mass produces poor quality packaged foods and foods laden with pesticides and chemical fertilizers. .

With few resources available to help you stay healthy through eating well, you must decide how much you want to be healthy in your older years and how to incorporate healthy eating into your plan. This book is here to help you.

You may be asking - what do I mean by *real food*? Real food is food in its original form. It is food that does not come in packages with additives and chemicals. It has not been treated with hormones or antibiotics, or pesticides or chemical fertilizers. An apple, brown rice, carrots, nuts, seeds, fish and chicken are all examples of real food. Some taste great in their perfectly plain state; others need a little dressing up with herbs and spices.

The truth is there are no shortcuts when it comes to real food and its preparation but it's also very easy when you plan it right. Like this morning, before I sat down to write, I had a balanced mix of protein and carbs. I sauteed kale with an organic egg and had one slice of whole grain toast. Nutritionally loaded. Satisfying and delicious. Easy - it took 10 minutes maximum to make and will keep me satisfied for at least 4 hours.

How does a breakfast like this happen? I keep a supply of kale in my freezer. I grow it for 3 seasons and freeze enough for the winter. I strip the kale from the stems, blanch it and put it in a freezer bag. I use this as my backup if I don't have any fresh kale in the refrigerator. Each time I want some, I take a handful, sauté it and add the egg and voila! One slice of toast and a cup of green tea complete it.

You could make a smoothie. Have fresh fruits on hand and bags of frozen fruit. Mix the fruit with more of the kale, and add a scoop of Greek yogurt. Add a scoop of whey protein. You can add nuts and seeds if you want. Done.

If you like oatmeal - mix water, whole oats, a teaspoon of cinnamon and a handful of walnuts or almonds in a slow cooker. Keep it in the fridge for the week and have it when you want it. Reheat, add half a sliced banana and enjoy. You can even swirl a poached egg into it for added protein.

All of these are real whole foods, filled with nutrients and energy. One may be ideal for you, and another not so much. That's the part that *you* need to determine, because every body has its own unique biology and it is only when you eat quality foods and see how your body responds to them that you really know what's best for you. I've been a health coach for some time and it continually fascinates me to see how unique we all are. The way you figure out what is best for you is to have real food as your baseline and take the time to pay attention to how the food makes you feel. Your body's reaction will tell you if the food is right for you. Just be sure you start the day with a good breakfast. It truly is the most important meal of the day.

Your life is busy. It doesn't get quieter a you get older, so to change your eating habits for the better you need simple manageable solutions. What I'll do for you is cut through all the confusion and give you tools you can work with. I include a detailed chapter called 'Back to the Kitchen', the place where it all needs to happen. You will find planning, stocking and cooking techniques. A simple description of each of the necessary food groups is included. The Back to the Kitchen chapter will give you the tools you need to make it easy for you to prepare simple real foods on a consistent basis. As you become proficient at preparing whole foods, you will see that it doesn't take much time. Real foods cook up quickly, and you will be eating chemical and preservative free foods. Doesn't that sound better? You will also find a multitude of resources in the Appendix, including a list for stocking your pantry and refrigerator, a 7 day menu plan and other relevant information for making the shift to healthy eating easy for you.

If you already have some health challenges, you will see how changing your food can improve your health. I include stories of many people who have changed their food, including former President Bill Clinton. You will see how each person's health improves from changing the food they eat.

Notice I haven't mentioned calories. Caloric focus is the domain of the diet industry and has led to less than 15% weight loss success overall. Even when a dieter loses weight by calorie restriction, it doesn't necessarily improve health in the way eating nutrient rich foods can. Picture the results of eating highly processed packaged foods filled with additives as compared with eating a plate filled with fresh vegetables, whole grains and lean meat. You will not see calorie counting and restrictive diets in this book. In my opinion they are a major cause of faulty metabolism, poor self-esteem and overweight. You will see how eating healthy instead of dieting will help you reach your ideal weight range and keep it there. When you eat healthy, food has a proper context in your life and you are not constantly thinking about it. You eat when you are hungry and if the food you eat is real and nutritious, your hunger signals turn off when they should.

Someone said old age is not for sissies As we age we lose the almost magical advantage of youth. With aging there are more challenges, but they are not insurmountable. If you read some of the literature on aging you might think there is no turning back - that your health and stamina are going right down the tube. *Remember this - it's simply not true for everyone - and food changes everything.*

Seek out your vibrant older friends and ask them what they do to be healthy. Most will tell you they eat real food, they move, and they don't stress a lot. When you lay a healthy foundation by eating well it will naturally cycle into other lifestyle improvements. Whatever you do, don't settle for what some regard as a new normal of aching joints, insomnia, poor vision, shortness of breath or Type II diabetes. With quality food, you can be vibrant for many many years.

I enrolled in a Gerontology studies program at the University of Massachusetts to get an idea of what may lie ahead for myself and the people I support. One book we were required to read was Merck's Manual on Health & Aging. I found it so distressing, describing aging as one loss after another, with the sense that all loss is inevitable. Had I not been steeped in the practice of self-care and helping clients focus on healthy lifestyles, I might have thought there was absolutely no hope in having much to look forward to in older years. Instead of books filled with dire predictions on aging we need inspirational stories of vital older folks who take their health seriously and take responsibility for their health. We have had only a few widely publicized heath gurus like Jack LaLanne and Richard Simmons as role models for healthy aging. Olga Kotelko of Vancouver made the news recently. She is 94 years old and is a world class athlete with more than 700 medals, all won after the age of 77. We need more role models like Jack, Richard and Olga, and one day you could be one of them.

Right now, I have a long bucket list. I don't know if I have one day or 30+ years ahead of me, but what I do know is that what I put in my mouth each day will directly affect how much or how little I will be able to do with my time left on this planet.

Do some thinking about what lies ahead for you. If you have not had the best diet for a long time, make one simple change today. If you are a 3 o'clock vending machine snacker as I once was, take an apple or some nuts to work and have those instead. Experiment with an herbal tea. Buy an organic vegetable. The possibilities are endless and it is never too late. Even those touched by unavoidable illness can optimize their health through quality foods. In the case of illness, quality foods are essential. In the next chapter we will look at the best foods to have in your kitchen and how to get them.

Now that you know my simple message, that food literally becomes you, I will be flipping the format in the next chapters. You will find the key points listed at the beginning of each chapter to give you an idea of the content. Feel free to hop around, skip a chapter that doesn't resonate with you, but always keep this simple message in mind: *food becomes you*. It will change everything for you.

Here's a quick recap of the key points in this first chapter
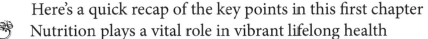 Nutrition plays a vital role in vibrant lifelong health
The food you eat becomes you
Health and stamina don't have to diminish with age

2

Nutrition Science Translated into Eating

*"Pay attention to your body. The point is everybody is different.
You have to figure out what works for you."*
Andrew Weil, M.D.

Key points in this chapter
- Malnutrition is the outcome of eating foods with few if any nutrients
- There is no single eating plan that is perfect for everyone
- Are you a Classic or a Junker?
- Five simple steps to get you started

You may ask yourself why the topic of food and nutrition has become so complex. Never before has healthy eating been so fraught with confusion. Scientists view nutrients as a collection of fats, carbohydrates and protein, with micro- and phyto - nutrients thrown into the mix. The diet industry and some old school dietitians view nutrition through the narrow lens of weight and calories. I ask you to leave that perspective to scientists and weight loss marketers and join me in looking at food in the simplest and most practical of ways. Real food keeps you satisfied and healthy. There is no need to look at it in any other way unless you really want to know about the scientific components of food molecules.

Then the question becomes what's the best eating plan for you? There is no single eating plan that is perfect for everyone. You are the outcome of your unique biology and life experience. What you need to be vital in your later years might be quite different from what you needed when you were 24. Life changes and nutritional needs can change too, whether we're talking age, or even seasons and geographic locations. However, no matter what your unique needs might be, at all times and in all places you need real food because real food is nutrient rich. That is what will give you the energy you need to ward off disease and maintain vitality up to the end of your life.

Could You Be Malnourished?

When you buy food in supermarkets and wholesale outlets you are inundated with labels that can be misleading. The result? Malnutrition *and* obesity. I used to think of malnutrition as a condition caused by having too little food, as in the faces of little starving children. But malnutrition can also come from eating a lot of food with few if any nutrients. When the food you eat has a shortage of nutrients, your brain, in its intelligence, will signal your appetite to look for more food. If you consistently eat low nutrient foods you will become malnourished and will overeat while trying to find the missing nutrients. That is why it is so important to make your first choices quality ones that will satisfy you. You'll get the nutrients you need from real food and won't need or want to overeat.

Ask Yourself: Are You a Classic or a Junker?

If you are someone who keeps your car for a long time, you value the importance of ongoing maintenance. My grandson owns a 1998 Honda Accord that was previously owned by a woman who never missed a scheduled maintenance. She sold it to Michael with the confidence that this new driver would be in good hands. (His encounter with a large turtle meandering across the road is another story, but suffice it to say, the turtle was spared thanks to Michael's compassionate decision to dodge the big fella.)

Much like cars, the classic/junker outcome is true for us humans. Let me explain.

The Junker Profile

As you go through the first few decades of life, you may be blessed with good health. You may get by on little sleep, eat junk food, smoke and use alcohol for several years and still look and feel good. The problem is you can't see what is happening on the inside. Illness doesn't happen overnight. It is the accumulation of many years of benign neglect or outright abuse. The lack of quality energy coming into your body and an unhealthy lifestyle will inevitably lead to decline. Overall sluggishness, body aches and dragging yourself out of bed in the morning are the first symptoms. If this is you, it's time to get your food right and give up the late nights and other lifestyle issues that harm you.

The good news is, even if you have neglected yourself for the first few decades of your life, you can recover and become healthier than you might have imagined. What I hope this book will do is convince you that aches, pains, sickness and decline are not a natural outcome of aging, but they are the signals that so far you haven't given your body the care and nurturing it needs to age well. *Food becomes YOU,* in every sense of the word. What you put in your body will forecast your health in your later years. Since food is my specialty, I will show you how to plan a way of eating that works for your lifestyle.

Becoming a Classic

To become a classic, you must make a clear decision about the kind of health you want in your later years and be willing to do the work to get there. We all know a sixty year old who looks forty five, and we also know a sixty year old who looks seventy five. There is no fooling nature by age 60. The life you are living shows up loud and clear, for better or worse.

If you are someone who continually nourishes yourself with quality food, in all likelihood you will become a classic. If you have a steady diet of highly refined and processed foods with few if any nutrients in them, I think you know where you might be headed.

Here's an appetizer of 5 simple steps to get you started:

1. Clear out the old and bring in the new

Do an inventory of your pantry and refrigerator. Replace foods that are highly processed with simple whole grains like whole oats, brown rice and quinoa, beans, lentils, nuts, extra virgin olive oil, peanut butter, hummus, plain yogurt, organic meats if you eat meat, wild fish and fresh fruits and vegetables. That way you can make good choices.

2. Improve the function of your digestive system

The digestive system is the entry point for nutrients and the exit point for waste. Eat slowly, chew thoroughly and relax while you eat to help your digestive system do its job. Think of your digestive system as one long road through your body. It holds many nerve endings that react to foods and stress. If you get butterflies in your stomach when you are nervous or upset you know what I'm talking about. Treat your system with care.

3. Educate yourself

Do not rely on advertising when you are looking for quality food. Grow your food or buy it organically when you can. As noted author Michael Pollan says "Eat real food, mostly plants, and not too much." Real food is fresh food, not a product made in a factory.

4. Know your biology

You've narrowed it down to quality food but you still don't feel great. You have gas some days or you get sinus infections. Do a little detective work by eliminating some of the foods you've been eating to see if you get some relief. Not all good foods are good for everyone. My friend Joe said "I get horrible gas when I eat hummus. It's home made by my grandmother with all fresh ingredients." The hummus isn't bad. It is just bad for Joe.

5. Keep your own health records and understand what they mean

I changed my food as I approached 50. I had elevated cholesterol and triglycerides and some achy joints. Refined sugar was my constant companion. I crowded out the sugar by eating organic fruits and sweet vegetables. My triglycerides plummeted and I raised my good cholesterol. I am healthier now than I was at age

50. It did not take medicine to change my numbers. It took changing my food.

If you've ever been to London, you might have stopped at Speaker's Corner in Hyde Park. When I'm feeling most passionate about getting my message out that food changes everything, I imagine a Speaker's Corner in downtown Boston where I leave all my inhibitions behind and shout at the top of my lungs **food becomes you!**

I think you know that is true too. Otherwise, you would not have opened this book.

Garden, Farm and Market to Kitchen

"When you're green inside, you're clean inside."
Dr. Bernard Jensen

Key points in this chapter
- Getting fresh foods should be your top priority
- Growing your own - Marie's Story
- Becoming a shareholder - Nurse Helen
- Visiting Farmers' Markets
- Smart grocery store tips

There are many ways to get good food, and fresh is always best. Getting fresh foods is my top priority. I do freeze some vegetables for winter as I live in a cold climate, but whenever possible I eat fresh. Food sources may include your own garden, a farm or the supermarket. In this chapter we will explore the various ways you can acquire your food. I'll share examples of the ways 3 different people maximized the quality of their food, each acquiring it from different sources.

The Gardener Type

You may be one of many novice gardeners, drawn to the allure of backyard or community gardening. Baby boomers like to stay current, and the trend toward growing your own has resulted in many a new boomer gardener, intrigued by the almost magical experience of planting and harvesting fresh vegetables. This is an ideal way to acquire fresh food, particularly if your garden is organic. Organic simply means that the soil and seeds, or seedlings planted in the soil, are nourished only by chemical free nutrients that come from food, leaf and paper compost and other organic sources. Vegetables grown this way give you vitamins and minerals. Growing organically is more earth-friendly than chemically fertilized plants and doesn't deplete the soil of important minerals.

Your climate will influence how much of a gardener you can be, but Barbara Damrosch, author of The Garden Primer, speaks of her husband's success in having fresh vegetables in Maine from May through much of the winter with the use of cold storage and careful planning. They grow root vegetables like carrots, parsnips, beets, and onions, along with potatoes and squash, which can be stored for many months without spoiling if they are in a dry cool place. Compare that with the average agri-business carrot, grown in a greenhouse and shipped 1800 miles on average before it reaches your plate. Knowing this inspires me to grow and buy local whenever possible.

A Gardener Is Born

Becoming a gardener requires patience and curiosity. Marie is a health-conscious boomer in her 60s and paid willingly for quality vegetables at her grocery store, but with a little time on her hands she decided to give gardening a try. She did some reading and joined a vegetable garden club to get some ideas. Living in New England, she had to wait until mid-May to get the soil ready. It was an experience in frustration. There were tree roots, abundant rocks and ugh! poison ivy in her yard. It wasn't looking good. But like most things in life, there is usually a solution. In Marie's case it was the installation of 2 raised beds. These simply are defined spaces that are above the ground and are bordered by cut wood, usually 12" to 36" high, depending on the gardener's access needs. You can even buy kits at a home supply store that are easily assembled. The beds are installed on level ground and filled with nutrient rich organic soil and compost, both of which you can buy at a garden shop or have delivered. With beds you don't have to turn over the ground, and you start with really good soil, an essential part of successful gardening.

Marie put in two beds, each 8' by 12' in a sunny section of her yard, giving her a great amount of space for growing. She decided to plant lettuce, beans, peas and dark greens in one bed, all planted by mid-May when the weather was still cool. She kept her attention on those, keeping the soil moist but not soaked. Over Memorial Day weekend she planted tomatoes, herbs and summer squash in the second bed, installing some wire towers to separate and control the direction of growth. To protect her garden from deer she had 6 foot wire fencing installed around the outside with an entry gate for access.

Marie still raves about the transformation that took place in less than 6 weeks. Little seedlings in the first bed became robust plants that landed on her dinner table. The tomato and squash plants were bushes and jungles, respectively. She was thrilled. Then Marie noticed that the vegetables she was growing tasted better than what she bought in the grocery store. She also had less waste because she only picked what she needed or blanched and froze the excess, or shared some with her neighbors. The only significant investment was the set up in the first year. After that, it was only seeds or seedlings and added compost to get a huge amount of fresh vegetables.

Think about your life and the time you have for gardening. Will it work for you? Is there something in Marie's story that sparked an interest in you? If so, start small and talk to gardeners you know. They love to share their knowledge.

Offerings from the Farm

If you are fortunate enough to have a local farm, you can visit and support your local farmer by buying direct from him or her. Small farms became nearly extinct with the onset of suburban sprawl from the fifties through the nineties, but we are fast recognizing the importance of having locally sourced food and farms. Foods that come directly from a local farm will be fresher and taste better, as Marie found from her own garden. Going all philosophical on you for a moment, this food has breathed the same air as you and had the same water as you, so it is likely to be most compatible with your body.

Farmers are also developing techniques for winter harvesting and cold storage of root vegetables so you can have them through the winter. To find a list of farms in your region and what they offer, visit www.localharvest.org and enter your zip code.

Since the late nineties many remaining small farms across the country have opened their fields to community supported agriculture projects (CSAs), where you can purchase a "share" of the land

and volunteer a specific number of work hours while the farmer plants and grows food for you. As a shareholder you are usually required to volunteer a set number of work hours, as you will see in the following story.

A Modern Sharecropper's Story

Helen, a Baby Boomer, was in her late forties, and married with 3 children, when I met her. She came to a soup making class I was giving, looking for healthy recipes that tasted good and were easy to make for her busy family. A former oncology nurse, Helen wanted to do the best she could to promote wellness in her family, and suspected that food played a major role. We wound up working together for the next 6 months, examining her lifestyle and making healthy eating a priority. Helen liked her sweets and snacks, but she was also very committed to staying healthy. Her experience in changing her food was similar to mine, in that once she started eating better quality food, her cravings for sweets lessened. This happens because your brain knows when your body has enough nutrients, and it will turn off the hunger signals when your nutrient need is satisfied. It's not so much about will power once you get your food right.

Helen didn't stop her focus on health when she got some healthy recipes and cooking techniques down. She edged even closer to her nutrient sources by dipping her toe into vegetable gardening. No, she didn't excavate her back yard. Her life was too busy for that. Instead, she asked me about the community garden I belonged to at the time, and how it worked. A community garden or community supported agriculture (CSA) is a garden planted by a farmer who sells shares to those who sign up and pre-pay for the expected yield from the garden. The farmer does all the heavy lifting and the shareholders agree to give a prede-termined number of labor hours to weed, harvest and distrib-ute the crops. Helen liked the idea, and here's what she said to me about the experience: "Peg introduced me to the concept of a CSA and encouraged me to join one in a nearby town in 2008. I joined and have been a member ever since. It has been an eye-opening experience for my whole family. I think they have more of an appreciation of where their food comes from and on several occasions my children helped with the harvesting, even though they complained the whole time. It is definitely hard work! After working in the fields I am always filthy and it takes several washes to get my clothes clean. It often takes several days to get the dirt fully out from under my fingernails despite all the scrubbing. My kids like to work at the distribution table much more than the harvesting. They greet the shareholders and replenish the bins of produce. It is always fun to see what is in the share each week. You never know what to expect and sometimes it is something really unusual or something that you have never tried before. The challenge is to get it all home, wash/scrub it, let it dry and then find room in the refrigerator. Our CSA also has a "pick your own" for various vegetables, fruit and flowers. It is always nice to come home with a small bunch of colorful blossoms and they usually last for most of the week until I go again."

I think you can see that despite the hard work of harvesting, Helen has a deep appreciation for her involvement in the process and the freshness of the food she puts on her table. And Helen is right about the dirt. Food that comes from the farm is dirty be-cause it's straight from the ground. It is not polished and perfectly shaped like the produce you see in the grocery store. Real food, organic food, is rough and rugged. It is very much alive the day you pick it up at the farm.

CSAs are by far the easiest way to get very fresh local vegetables. All you need to do is pick them up at a prearranged time and give just a few hours a season to helping out. Helen is a great example of someone who is committed to healthy living. In addition to her focus on food, she extended her health focus to her community and is passionately involved in a green living program that provides information and resources for recycling and clean living.

I would be remiss if I didn't mention Farmers' Markets. They are springing up like dandelions all over the country. It speaks to our desire to have fresh food. Farmers' Markets are made up of a group of local farmers who bring their food to sell directly to you in a central location like a town common or church parking lot. Check for their locations in your neighborhood at localharvest.org.

On to the Grocery Store

Grocery stores are loaded with choices, both good and bad. It is a place that should not be visited while hungry, because it is much harder to be discriminating when you are hungry. A personal trainer, steeped in knowledge about quality eating once said "Get me too hungry and I'll go right for the snack and pizza aisle". It's true for most of us.

Gloria is a busy professional who does not have time for her own garden or to participate in a CSA. She shops exclusively in grocery stores and has a set routine that works for her. She starts with a shopping list that reflects her menu plans for the upcoming week.

She goes when she's not hungry. She heads right to the produce section of the store and loads up on fruits and vegetables, looking for what's in season. She then goes to the healthy food section of the store (don't you wonder why they gave it that name - is it because the rest of the store has *un-healthy* foods?). You be the judge. It is in the healthy foods section that Gloria buys her packaged foods like grains, being careful to choose whole grains, and low sodium broths for soup, olive oil, vinegars, and other essential groceries. Even in the healthy food section Gloria is careful to check labels on items she buys infrequently to be sure the ingredients are acceptable. She buys some organic and some conventional foods, always with a focus on ingredients. Since Gloria and her family are not vegetarian, she moves to the meat and fish sections where she buys small amounts of meat and wild fish. She buys hormone-free and antibiotic-free meat, organic when it is available. She buys organic eggs and almond milk. She may also buy some snack foods in the healthy food section, checking to be sure they are free of trans fats and high fructose corn sugar. She opts for nuts, popcorn and dried fruits instead of energy bars. She does not buy soda, even though some brands now show up as "healthy foods". They are not.

Even the most successful gardener and CSA shareholder needs to go to the grocery store for some items. Whether the grocery store is a supplement or primary source of food, here are a few tips for getting quality food:

1. Make a shopping list before you go. Check your pantry and refrigerator to see what you need. Menu planning helps too.

2. Think unpackaged, whole foods first. These are foods that don't come in a box.

3. If you eat meat, buy antibiotic and hormone free meats. Look at the labels. "Natural, Choice, or Premium"" is not enough. Choose lean meats that are in the butcher's cabinet and packed fresh for you. The same is true for fish, which should be caught in the wild, not farm raised. Plan to make meat a condiment on your plate rather than the main event. This makes quality meat more affordable and leaves room in your belly for the other things on your plate. It might interest you to know that since US large beef processors in the US began injecting Bovine Growth Hormone in their cattle, the European markets will not purchase US beef.

4. Buy vegetables of many colors, flavors and textures. Each color gives you specific vitamins that support your health. Varying flavors give your taste buds experiences other than sweet and salty by adding bitter, sour and pungent to the mix. Texture gives you variety and chew appeal. Buying in season will give you the freshest and most economical choices and will lend itself to variety through the year. In the winter I eat a lot of root vegetables like carrots, beets, onions, squash and sweet potatoes. Spring is the time for greens including early lettuce, peas, spinach and green beans. Summer is a free for all of zucchini, summer squash, cucumbers, tomatoes, kale, chard, herbs, eggplant, peppers. Fall harvest brings butternut squash, beets, apples and pears. Just when I'm getting a little tired of one season's vegetables, the weather changes and there's a whole new list of choices.

5. While you are in the produce section, don't forget your fruits. Buying seasonally is the best way, choosing the luscious watery fruits of summer like melon, peaches, plums and berries

to keep you cool, and moving on to apples and pears in autumn, followed by dried fruits in the winter.

6.   Check out the bulk grains. If your market sells in bulk, buy your grains and legumes like beans and lentils there. They will be fresher than packaged products and you can choose as much or as little as you will eat in the next few weeks.

The foods I have listed are your essential foods. Beyond that, you might want to round out your shopping with some other foods like eggs, cheese, whole grain cereal and bread, beverages, oils and vinegars, snacks and treats. I distinguish between snacks and treats because you might need to have something in between meals to maintain your best energy, and that can be a healthy snack like cheese, hummus, nuts, or a whole grain cracker. Treats are always fun to have but only occasionally. In all cases, carefully read the label and know that the label defines the nutrients per serving. Check salt and sugar content per serving carefully. High blood pressure and Type II diabetes are epidemic and most salt and sugar comes from packaged foods or foods you have in restaurants, not from your salt shaker or sugar bowl. Ingredients should be real food with little or no additives or chemicals. If the label shows more than 5 ingredients or words that you do not recognize, choose something else.

Remember, whatever you bring home is what you are likely to eat. Bring home quality food and you will boost your odds for vital aging.

Another alternative is the independent distributor. Companies are beginning to develop online delivery services from distribution depots for added convenience. Time and experience will tell the quality and value of these offerings. Theoretically these foods should be fresher than those that have gone from distributor to supermarket, but careful evaluation of the quality and origin of the food should be a part of your decision of whether to use them or not.

I gave you some details about essential foods to buy in the grocery store. Now I will break it down even further. If it's been awhile since you brought much of anything home, you might need an actual shopping list. First you'll need to get your kitchen stocked with essentials like spices, herbs, oils, vinegars and other condiments. Take some time to purchase all these flavor essentials so you can mix up the flavors of your food from Asian to Tex-Mex and everything in between. Once you have that foundation in place, this list should stock you up with just about everything you need to feed yourself for a week.

Weekly Shopping List for a Single Boomer

1 lb. brown rice
1/2 lb. quinoa
1 lb. whole oats
1 can organic black beans
1 can kidney beans
2 onions
2 lemons
1 loaf Ezekial sprouted wheat bread
3 peaches (warm weather) apples (cold weather)
2 plums (warm weather) pears (cold weather)
1 pt. blueberries or other berries in season
1 bunch partially ripe bananas
1 avocado
1/2 lb raw nuts

1 package organic chicken or vegetable broth
1/2 doz. organic eggs
1 package hummus
1 bunch green vegetable (chard, kale, spinach)
1 bunch broccoli
1 yellow squash
1 eggplant
1 head of cauliflower
1 red pepper
1 package organic cherry tomatoes
2 cucumbers
1 head green lettuce or tub of pre-washed greens
1/2 pound wild seafood
1/2 pound skinless chicken breast
1 bar dark chocolate
1 box Rya whole grain crackers
tea or coffee optional

Shopping for Two?

Experiment with doubling or tripling the meat/fish, nuts, eggs, bread, fruits and vegetables until you find your sweet spot for two.

Next Steps

Now if you are saying, "Okay, now I have all this food, what the heck do I do with it?" here are a few ideas:

Cook a batch of brown rice and a batch of quinoa. Here's how to do it:

Rinse 1 cup of dry rice and place in a saucepan with 2 cups of water or half water and half broth. Bring to a boil and reduce the heat to low. Cover and simmer for about 40-60 minutes. It's best if you have a glass cover on your pan so you can see when the liquid is absorbed.

For the quinoa, rinse 1 cup of dry grain and place it in a saucepan with 2 cups of water. Bring to a boil, reduce the heat and simmer for 15-20 minutes. Remove from heat, let sit 10 minutes, then fluff with a fork.

These two bowls of grains can be the foundation for several dishes. Each one will give you 3 cups of cooked grains.

While the grains are simmering, you can chop some onion and/or garlic, along with cucumber and combine with the juice of a lemon and a little olive oil. Mix it into one of the grains, probably the quinoa.

I like to keep the rice unflavored until I prepare a meal and then season it accordingly. By adding unique flavors to each dish, the rice can be made to taste very different. You might want to use one scoop in a salad, another in a soup, and yet another in a stir fry. Each dish will make the rice taste different since you will be adding unique flavors to each of the three dishes. You might add oil and vinegar to the salad, cumin and coriander to the soup, and liquid aminos and ginger to the stir fry.

You can also prepare some oatmeal, mixing 1/4 cup whole oats with 1 cup of water. Make it in larger quantities and reheat it through the week. Oats can be cooked in a saucepan or a slow cooker.

I like to alternate my breakfasts, sometimes having oatmeal with banana, cinnamon and nuts, and other mornings having sauteed greens with an egg and piece of toast. Of course when warm weather comes I shift to cooler foods for all my meals.

Keep checking your foods and your preferences and cooking will start to get simple for you. And did I mention pleasurable? Trust me, it will.

What I've given you here is a very basic and balanced shopping list of all the basic food groups. You can change the specific grains, fruits and vegetables to your liking and create the meal combinations you like best. Changes in the weather will lead you to make changes in your shopping list. You won't be looking for hot soups and stews in July and you may not want cold salads in January. Eating in sync with your climate makes for a nice variety of menus so you won't get bored.

4

Cause and Effect: Good Food/Good Health Poor Food/Poor Health

"Take care of your body. It's the only place you have to live."
Jim Rohn

Key points in this chapter
- the real cause of death is not disease
- The Boomer generation: Fast Food and the Diet Industry
- Two pathways to aging
- Health predictors: Genetics 30% ; lifestyle 70%
- Naming your preventable health challenges

In 2011 I heard David Katz MD, MPH, FACPM, FACP, an authority on nutrition and weight management, speak at a health conference in New York. Dr. Katz is a leader in integrative medicine and patient-centered care. I was struck by something he said that I'd never heard framed quite this way, but it made perfect sense to me.

The Center for Disease Control lists the top causes of death in the US in this order: heart disease, cancer, chronic respiratory diseases and stroke. Dr. Katz said these diseases are NOT the major causes of death. Poor nutrition, lack of exercise and smoking are the real <u>causes</u> of death. The resulting diseases are the <u>effects </u>of these lifestyle habits. This distinction really struck me. It opened the door to the idea that these diseases are not inevitable; instead they may be the outcomes of poor lifestyle choices. All the major causes of death are potentially **preventable.** This is not to say that these diseases are **always** preventable because some people, despite their good lifestyle practices may still fall ill due to genetics or environmental factors over which they have no control. But for most of us, a pro-active lifestyle will help prevent these diseases that have so long been identified as a natural part of aging. Did you ever realize you had so much control over your health destiny before?

When you think cause and effect as Dr. Katz explained, you begin to see the reasons for illness. It doesn't happen simply because you are getting older. Unless you have an overwhelming genetic or environmental link to a disease, the quality of your health will be a reflection your lifestyle choices, especially your food. The good news is, your body will respond to positive change. You can get better. I got better when I replaced my daily sugar and white flour fixes with more fruits, vegetables whole grains and nuts. My elevated triglycerides, a factor associated with heart disease, dropped more than 200 points in just 6 months of healthy eating. Seeing how easily my body healed by simply changing my food encouraged me to want to help everyone feel better. In the years I have been health coaching, I have seen the same results in countless others. If your choices haven't been the best in the past, don't give up. Quit dieting and make your course correction to a healthy way of eating. It is quite amazing how quickly you can improve your health when you improve your food. Food becomes you.

The Birth of Fast Food Restaurants

Baby Boomers were the first to grow up with fast food and move away from real food. I don't think of fast food as real because most of it is highly processed, filled with preservatives and stored for months. Looking from that perspective, how real could it be? How many nutrients could still be in this kind of food? Not many. Fast food has also taken its toll on the waistline. In the 1950s, the decade in which most boomers were born, 33% of Americans were overweight; today more than 66% are overweight. As Americans have gained weight, weight loss programs have flourished. Instead of looking at modern lifestyle and the shifts in food choices that caused obesity, marketers steered consumers toward quick fix diets that would be the magic bullet for restoring svelte bodies.

Weight Watchers opened its doors in 1963; Jenny Craig in 1985. Both offer their own brand of highly processed foods for weight loss. Weight Watchers emphasizes points. Using a points system completely detaches you from the experience of nourishing yourself. You are much more than points. Jenny Craig provides expensive meals with the objective of weight loss. We all know people who have tried these plans, only to lose weight and gain it back again. Maybe you are one of them. There's a reason diet plans have lifetime membership options. Diet plans on average have a 15% success rate; the other 85% keep coming back, or switch from one diet to another.

In most cases, chronic illness doesn't happen by accident. Neither does health. Both are outcomes of family pre-dispositions and/or lifestyle. Genetics account for about 30% of your risk or benefit. Lifestyle accounts for a whopping 70% of your risk or benefit. Lifestyle is the segment you have most control over and with careful attention you can build your defenses against any familial tendencies toward illness. It is not the doctor or the medicine that will prevent these diseases. Doctors may have the means to manage disease, but the choices you make with nutrition and lifestyle are what can prevent or heal disease. Isn't that amazing? I think it's the best kept secret of all. Barring an unavoidable event in your life or an overwhelming genetic pre-disposition, it is your lifestyle that causes health or disease. You are steering the boat.

Midlife is the time we have to get honest with ourselves about what is a genetic pre-disposition and what is a sensitivity that has been caused by the lifestyle choices we make. If heart disease is in your family, be extra diligent about emphasizing plant based foods and limiting trans fats and sugar in your diet. If cancer is in your family genetics, emphasize plant based foods, limit your sugar and avoid processed foods. When you acknowledge that your habits contribute to your disease, you have the option to change your habits and lower your risk for disease. That's when miracles happen. That's when real food becomes your very own life preserver.

The whole experience of getting healthy through food is about having a wide variety of plant based foods. We hear about "super foods" like kale and pomegranate and "bad foods" like gluten and carbs, but the truth is, the best way to be healthy is to eat a wide variety of real foods. Each plant based food has an array of nutrients specific to that food, and when you mix it with the nutrients of other plant based foods you will be covering most of the nutrition bases. I am not suggesting that you should never have meat or dairy, but researchers like Colin Campbell, MD have studied and supported the benefits of a plant based diet. My recommendation is that if you choose to have meat and dairy, choose organic to avoid Bovine growth hormones and antibiotics found in conventional meat and dairy.

Wanda and Heart Health

Wanda is a woman I began working with when she had some concerns about her heart health and cholesterol numbers. She is an active healthy woman and highly motivated to remain healthy in her later years. We looked at her diet and gradually increased vegetables and grains, while decreasing meat. In doing so, Wanda's energy increased as did her outlook on life. One day I asked her if anything she learned or experienced surprised her. She said " I'm learning to disregard everything I heard growing up about meat and dairy being good for you." She could see from her own experience that her health improved when she ate less meat and dairy and added more vegetables and grains.

John and Type II Diabetes

John's parents were both diabetic. He told me "Both of my parents have Type II diabetes so I will probably have it too." Because John saw his parents with the same illness, he didn't think he had any control over his future health. What he hadn't looked at was how his parents developed their disease. As John began to learn more about healthy foods, he realized that his parents had very poor eating habits that contributed to their illnesses. I asked John to look at his parents' habits as good information about what his own vulnerabilities might be and use that knowledge so he doesn't suffer the same fate. It would help if John learned about the glycemic index and how certain foods, lack of exercise and unmanaged stress can trigger elevated blood sugar. He would also do well to have whole foods based meals carefully spaced so as not to trigger dramatic spikes in his blood sugar. Removing excess sugar, soda and all the products made from white flour will give John tremendous protection from developing Type II diabetes.

Look at information about your own family's history to see what your possible disease sensitivity might be. Use that knowledge to adopt a lifestyle that gives you extra protection against that sensitivity.

Use this book as a tool to change your food for the better.

Think of your life right now as being at a crossroads. One path leads to a long and healthy life; the other to decline, medications and limitations. Look at each of these pathways and decide which one is for you.

highly processed foods - ➤ unmanaged stress - ➤ poor sleep - ➤ no exercise - ➤ overweight - ➤ chronic illness - ➤ medications - ➤ lifestyle limitations - ➤ death

quality food - ➤ managed stress - ➤ quality sleep - ➤ regular exercise - ➤ normal weight - ➤ minimal medication - ➤ active lifestyle - ➤ brief illness - ➤ death

Notice each path begins with food. Regardless of the path you choose, you will eventually die. The second path is far more pleasant than the first. For my part, I prefer to steer myself onto the second path. How about you?

A question for you

Think about a health issue you have today: gum disease, pre-diabetes, cataracts, acid reflux, gallstones, diverticulosis, osteoarthritis, osteoporosis or anything that is bothersome to you but not life-threatening. Each may be defined as a lifestyle disease.

Ask yourself if any of your eating habits may be contributing to the problem.

If the answer is yes, go straight to my Back to the Kitchen chapter and learn now how to eat well. It will change your life for the better.

5

Is It Too Late to Get Well?

"The middle season of life is a time to rejuvenate and reenergize your body and mind. "
Quotes-Motivational.com

Key points in this chapter
- Moving beyond medicine as a remedy
- Looking at the cause of your illness
- Developing a strategy for healing
- Carving out time for healing
- Eliminating certain foods while recovering
- Best place to eat

I see a lot of people who feel they are on a slippery medical slope, taking medications for multiple medical issues. It's easy to think that there's no turning back, that medicine is what will keep you alive going forward. Sometimes that is unequivocally true and in those cases we pay homage to all the amazing work the science of medicine can do.

But sometimes we can look at symptoms and step back and ask what caused those symptoms. You don't have to think that once a condition or "disease" is named that the only solution is medicine. Look for the cause. Are you eating late at night and suffering from acid? Are you dehydrated and might that be the cause of your constipation, or your migraines, or your cramps? Are you eating too many foods with sugar or white flour that might be the cause of your elevated triglycerides? Are you loading up on foods slathered with cheese that might be clogging your arteries? When you get to the cause you can begin to activate your own healing program. To me, it all begins with what you put in your body for fuel, because to heal you need high test fuel, not just anything that fills you up.

A Strategy for Healing

If you have ever consulted with a financial planner about debt, he or she will tell you that you should always pay down the debt with the highest interest rate first and continue working down to the debt with the lowest rate. With healing your body, the opposite is true. If you have a serious, chronic illness, you need to free yourself of the less serious conditions first. Then your body can give its full attention to your greatest challenge when everything else is healed.

Let's use Mary as an example. Mary was diagnosed with rheumatoid arthritis in her late thirties. This condition began after a traumatic birth and loss of a newborn. She has two children, one on the autism spectrum and the other healthy. When I first saw

Mary she was chronically stressed and was not eating well. She had some problems with indigestion.

Clearly for Mary, rheumatoid arthritis was her most serious condition. When we first met she was recovering from a scare she had with a potent medication. Her goal was to take a new look at healing instead of managing her condition only with medications. She knew food played a role but wasn't sure where to begin.

Improving her food was not the only factor in Mary's healing. She needed to overcome her stress. Unmanaged stress affects all aspects of health. It causes inflammation in the body. It activates hormones that put the immune system on high alert. It interferes with sleep. It clouds your thought process and can disrupt the digestive system. It is both a behavioral and a physiological condition. For Mary to heal herself, she needed to calm her response to her surroundings.

Mary began to look at the stressors in her life. She recognized that some of them could be eliminated, while others were simply a part of her life. She developed some self-care techniques. When she noticed she was getting worked up, she would place her hand on her heart and remind herself she that wanted to heal. She'd hold that thought until her breathing settled down. She developed some affirmations, simple statements, that quieted her mind. She'd say "I know my body feels best when I am calm."

Mary was taking prednisone for her rheumatoid inflammation and worried that she would develop osteoporosis from the drug. At the time, prednisone seemed necessary as she was no longer taking the high potency drug that affected her liver, but she knew that prednisone could compromise her bone health. She was surprised to learn of the calcium rich content of many green vegetables that she'd previously ignored and began eating them regularly. She eliminated sugar and ate mostly vegetarian. To lessen inflammation she avoided certain foods, including nightshades. She began taking a high potency liquid fish oil.

Two things happened since Mary addressed her stress and food issues. Mary's health has improved dramatically. But most importantly, Mary feels a sense of control over her body and learned that when she cares for it, she can heal it. All of her blood work numbers have improved and she continues to receive both medical and wellness care.

If you have been diagnosed with one or more conditions, have you thought about a plan for healing? Have you even thought about healing as a possibility for you? If you want to embark on a healing journey, here are some actions to get you started:

- make a list of your symptoms and diagnoses
- look back at when each symptom or diagnosis presented itself
- step even further back and see if you can identify the cause of each symptom or diagnosis
- write down your health goals going forward

Once you have this information in front of you, you will have a bigger picture of how you got to where you are. Then you can begin unravelling the events that led to your health challenges and start to address your goals. When you integrate simple whole foods into your healing plan, your recovery will accelerate.

Food is an amazing healer. If you look at symptoms rather than a diagnosis, you will often find that the symptoms are a result of poor eating habits. Eat a bagel and coffee for breakfast and what are you doing? Creating inflammation from the white flour that made the bagel and elevating your stress hormones by having caffeine. If you do this every day you will have symptoms. If you eat anything late at night and then lie down to sleep you might have acid. Acid is needed to digest food, but if you lie down while you're digesting it puts you at risk for having the acid come up into your esophagus. If you have heart disease, have you been eating too many fried foods, meat and poultry and sugar? Look at your food and it will give you many hints as to why things have gone wrong.

Remember that what's gone wrong can often be righted. It happens when you believe your actions influence your outcome. Once you're there it opens the door for amazing change and healing.

If you have an illness you may need to be very restrictive in what you eat when you first begin the healing process with food. The major food sources of inflammation are meat, dairy, wheat, white flour, gluten, sugar, alcohol and caffeine. When you are in recovery, you may need to abstain from all of these foods for a while to give your body a break. Once you are feeling better, you can slowly introduce these foods, one by one, into your diet. Ideally you will keep sugar, white flour and caffeine out of your life indefinitely except for an occasional special event. Sugar, white flour and caffeine are not quality foods for anyone, but it is especially best to avoid them when you are recovering from an illness.

In later chapters we will look at how to get your food right. The first and most important step you can take in getting your food right is to make it yourself. Mary affirmed to herself "I know my body feels best when I am calm" to manage her stress. She later added "Preparing healthy food for myself will heal my body."

Being in the kitchen, preparing your own food, is a statement that you care what you put in your body. You have no way of knowing what additives or preservatives are used in restaurant and takeaway food from the grocery store. It is not the same as food that you prepare yourself. When you prepare your own food, you are affirming that food matters and it will help you restore your health.

If you think you do not have time for preparing your food, ask yourself how much time you presently devote to social media and online communication. While it seems to have opened the door to a wider world, in some ways it has created more isolation and less time. Take some of that online time and transfer it to cooking for yourself. If you don't know how to cook, don't let that stop you. Simple cooking is all you need. Find an adult education class that teaches simple cooking skills. Take a few days at Kripalu or Canyon Ranch in the Berkshire Hills of Massachusetts to learn to cook healthy. Buy a book on cooking skills. Hire a nutrition coach. Do a Google search for a nutritionist who teaches the basics. It's not hard. Being in the kitchen will remind you that food matters. It is life-changing.

6

Crowd Out the Old

"Your diet is a bank account. Good food choices are good investments." Bethenny Frankel

Key points in this chapter
- Your ever changing body
- A morning with Jean and Maria
- A word about will power and weight
- Why people change their food

Why is the kind of food you eat so important? Every food has a measurable amount of nutrients. Some food, like kale, flaxseed, and pomegranate are powerhouses. These are foods in their whole form, completely unprocessed. When a food is in its purest form your body does a great job of absorbing its nutrients.

When you eat a highly processed food, your body has to hunt through all sorts of things to find the essential nutrients. I like the idea of being kind to my body and giving it what it needs without loading it up with additives and chemicals that need to be processed and filtered.

Your body needs a fresh supply of nutrients every day because your body is replacing itself constantly.

Consider this:

- every 35 days your skin completely replaces itself
- every month, your liver does the same
- every day the blood makes 200 million red cells, 10 million white cells per day

If you think about these simple but astonishing biological events, you can't help but realize how very important it is to choose food that supports these constant changes. Otherwise, what would be the quality of these newly created cells and tissues?

As a student of integrative nutrition, I learned about a healthy eating technique that really works, called "adding the good to crowd out the bad".

If you're in the habit of eating poor quality foods, as I once was, you kind of settle for that and don't think too much about it. This works until you switch to better quality foods. Then you might become less satisfied with the junk foods and turn away from them. Back in my sugar days, I was best friends with many of the candy bars sitting on the rack at the supermarket checkout line. Today I cannot imagine wanting these highly processed, bland tasting products. This change of taste did not come from discipline or will power. It came from noticing how I feel when I eat quality food, and how I feel when I eat those manufactured products. It becomes an easy choice. The only exception is when I find myself out of range of good food and I'm really hungry. That's why I do my best to always have a pack of raw almonds or a piece of fruit in my purse.

Eating well is also the best kept secret for weight loss. Let me explain. Your body relies on its central nervous system for information and signaling to the brain. When all systems are functioning well, the brain will only activate certain responses. If you are eating quality foods, your brain knows that and will turn off your hunger signals. How easy is that? On the other hand, if you're only counting calories and not focused on the quality of the food you are eating, your brain will keep calling for more. Our basic human nature does not like deprivation. Our brain is programmed to connect deprivation with hunting for food so we won't die. If you are not eating nutrient rich food, and are instead relying on low fat and "lite" foods to keep your calorie count down, your brain will alert your hunger signals and you will feel hungry.

The successful way to maintain a healthy weight is to always have an abundance of fresh vegetables and fruits nearby. These foods fill you up and have very low calorie counts, so they are good for both nutrition and for weight management. If you think about it you would never be hungry enough to eat a whole bag of apples. One, or maybe two apples, would be enough. Once you have enough to eat, it is much less likely that you will be looking for chips and cookies. You won't need them. Even better, if they are not in your cabinets, you won't even be thinking about them.

That is the essence of the crowding out theory. Eat quality foods so that you will have energy and you won't feel hungry.

A Morning with Jean and Maria

I'd like you to travel with me through Jean and Maria's morning.

Jean is 30 pounds over her ideal weight and has a Body Mass Index of 29. BMI is a measure of relative weight based on an individual's mass and height, demonstrating a rating from underweight to extremely obese. Jean grabs a low fat muffin at the coffee shop on her way to work. Maria is at a desirable weight and has a normal BMI of 24. She sautes fresh kale with an egg for breakfast and eats at home.

Who is eating the better breakfast? Who will have more energy through the morning? Who had lower out of pocket expense? Contrary to popular perception that eating well is expensive, Maria's breakfast costs less than Jean's.

Let's take this idea a step further. If Jean had a low fat muffin with barely any nutrients, what are the chances she will run out of gas by mid-morning? In her effort to control calories she chose a low fat muffin, but we know today that low fat foods, once very trendy for heart health, have excess sugar in them to offset the absence of more filling and flavorful fat. Sugar is burned very quickly so it does not give the staying power of fat. You get hungry faster with sugar. The only good news about Jean's choice is that she got lower trans fats in a low fat commercially baked muffin that she would have in a full fat muffin.

Maria's breakfast gave her quality nutrients, including protein, a little fat and complex carbohydrates. These are the very foods that are essential to good health and energy to carry Maria through the morning.

A Word about Will Power and Weight

A book about food would not be complete without some discussion about diet and weight loss. Being overweight brings more frustration and anxiety to more women than almost anything I can think of, even the threat of illness. I am here to tell you: stop blaming yourself if you are a dieter and are overweight. It is not you. If you want to blame someone, blame the food industry and the diet industry. Being overweight comes from eating highly processed foods that have few if any real nutrients. When you body doesn't get enough nutrients, the brain will send hunger signals to activate your appetite. We know now that many processed foods also contain additives that trigger appetite.

The diet industry takes it a step further and sets you up for deprivation with a big dose of their commercially made food products. These foods focus on calorie count, not nutrient value. They may include some nutrients but they are highly processed products fortified with synthetic nutrients. Please stop blaming yourself and start eating real food and everything will change. I want you to believe as strongly as I do that we all have the potential to be healthy and in a good weight range all the days of our lives. We simply have to eat well and build healthy lifestyle habits. It is your birthright to live a long healthy life but you need to do your part to make it happen for you.

What if you are a Baby Boomer and have already had a brush with cancer or heart disease? Like the old movie, it's never too late. If you are alive today and are reading this book, you have survived your health scare and have the potential to live a long life. You may have to change some of the lifestyle issues that led to your illness, but doesn't that seem like a good alternative to the other option? We will look now at a few examples of the effect real food can have on improving health, quality of life and weight.

Why People Change Their Food

Mary came to me after diagnosis and treatment for endometrial cancer. She was afraid of what the future had in store for her, but was willing to take a chance and see what a change in food might do for her. Mary is 62 and has a challenging and gratifying job, counseling victims of sexual abuse. When we first began working together Mary would go for long periods between eating. When she did eat it was often a rushed mouthful of something in between clients. As we worked together, she was able to step back and consider how little that kind of nourishment afforded her as opposed to a quiet 10 or 15 minutes of eating something nourishing in solitude. She adjusted her schedule and began eating a simple nourishing meal away from her desk. When we met again she said "I'm noticing I don't have a sense of bloating and stomach acid after I eat now. I always thought that was normal, but I don't have it anymore. Could it be the change in atmosphere?" You know, obviously it was the change in atmosphere and better food choices. Now take this story beyond the bloating and acid Mary used to have. Doesn't it make sense that with a better approach to eating Mary's cellular health will improve as well?

Kirstin Gillibrand is a US Senator from New York. In a story told to writer Margy Rocklin for Whole Living Magazine in 2012, Kirstin says she decided to put her health on track after gaining quite a bit of weight from 2 pregnancies. She describes her transformation, not in terms of the bathroom scale, but by how great she feels. "I don't frame it as losing weight...I would say focusing on my health. It gives you much more energy. You feel better about yourself and have a more positive outlook." Sounds like something we all want. Kirstin changed her food to lots of fruits, vegetables and lean meat and stopped eating refined and fried foods and has maintained a healthy weight ever since. This is quite different from dieting where you're counting miserable calories and waiting for it to be over.

Fashion designer Norma Kamali is admittedly a former New York party girl. Everything changed when she moved to the Meat Packaging District where the odor of beef carcasses wafted through the air. She became vegetarian. For years Norma has experimented with many ways to eat, always edging toward healthier choices. She switched her 10 cups of coffee a day habit to a couple of cups of green tea. She gave up smoking.

The transformation that occurs when you change your food can feel magical. It gives you clarity about all the ways you are living and the richness of your life because *IT FEELS GOOD*. Today Kamali is a vibrant 67 year old

Mary, Kirsten and Norma's experiences all highlight the way food changes you. Change your food and you change your very self.

7

Kitchen Talk - Success Stories

"We have far more control over our health and the condition of our bodies than we ever thought possible." Mike Rabe

Key points in this chapter

- Vegans do not eat meat, fish or poultry or any byproducts of these living beings.
- By becoming nearly all vegan, Bill Clinton lost 30 pounds and has kept it off
- See how everyday people and changed their lives with better food
- Your lifestyle and career choices impact your energy and food choices

In this chapter I'm going to whet your appetite for healthy eating by sharing a few stories with you. As an intelligent Baby Boomer, you may have read about the importance of healthy eating, or diet management many times, only to look at it as information.

It is sometimes difficult to find the motivation to change any habit with just information. I for one find stories of other people who changed their food for the better can be the most inspiring motivator of all. I hope that these stories inspire you as they have me.

A Famous One

Today former President Bill Clinton says we each have a responsibility to eat healthy, for ourselves, for our children and for the country. I believe that too. President Clinton is a living example of how food changes everything. He famously loved his burgers and fries and pulled pork and many of the dishes of his Southern heritage. He became overweight and developed heart disease, and in 2004 had quadruple bypass surgery. Despite these warning signals, Clinton resumed his old eating style with few modifications. It's magical thinking but not uncommon to assume that once you have bypass surgery you can resume your old eating habits. The trauma of surgery and replacement parts calls for some tender loving care of your heart going forward. Within 6 years Mr. Clinton learned that simply having bypass surgery would not protect his heart from future damage. In 2010 Clinton found himself pale and weak and required two stents to support a vein in his heart that had given out. At that point he took his diet seriously and transitioned to a nearly exclusive vegan way of eating.

Vegans do not eat meat, fish, or poultry. They do not eat other animal products like eggs, or dairy products including cheese and yogurt. They eat whole grains, nuts, seeds, fruits, vegetables and beans. Mr. Clinton adheres to and enjoys this way of eating but supplements once weekly with organic salmon or eggs to maintain muscle mass. This is not necessary if the vegan meal is carefully planned so all nutrients are included. An absolute vegan would not have salmon or eggs. Mr. Clinton chose to modify his diet from completely vegan to mostly vegan. This is a good example of a healthy way of personally modifying a way of eating to something that is satisfying and meets a person's individual needs and tastes.

What has this change in eating done for Mr. Clinton? He dropped 30 pounds in 2010 and has since kept it off. His staff, some of them 20 to 30 years younger, say he has so much energy they cannot keep up with him. His cravings for junk food have diminished almost entirely.

He says he enjoys the tastes and flavors of his food which, along with his improved health and waistline, are great motivators to keep doing what he's doing.

Meat, dairy and white foods like bread and pasta are such a part of our culture. They are not at all good choices when it comes to a quality diet. To get away from them, it helps to ask yourself how important these foods are to you in comparison to a healthy quality of life. You may be thinking that changing your diet from meat, dairy and white foods to healthier choices like lean meat, wild seafood and the components of vegan cuisine would be too boring, or too difficult, or too expensive. It is not. Look at Mr. Clinton's experience. His diet is distinctly different and better than the Standard American Diet. (SAD is the acronym for the Standard American Diet, and it truly is a sad one when it comes to outcome.)

The rest of this chapter is devoted to the many people who have changed their food, and subsequently their lives, for the better. They each had health issues at midlife and wanted to learn how food could change their health for the better.

Getting Better

Norma, 47, came to me with concerns about her digestive tract. She had acid reflux, was on medications and would frequently vomit whenever she was at her weekend Master's program. Her gastroenterologist discussed the possibility of surgery and was running a number of tests on her. We changed her food to a cleaner diet, eliminating processed foods and adding lots of fresh greens. We worked on her stress by talking about how she could best arrange her weekends. Some alone time was needed to unwind from the busy days of lectures and labs. She used guided imagery recordings to both relax her and to build her confidence. She is now off all digestive meds, has completed her degree and just started a new job.

Jane, 62 had elevated cholesterol and her doctor was advising her to take a statin medication, something she didn't want to do. We looked at her food intake and there was a fair amount of meat, dairy and refined sugar in it. We added some good fats like walnuts, fish oil and avocado and cut back on meat, dairy and sugar. Within 5 months her numbers dropped to normal levels. Her doctor was surprised and pleased. Jane said, "Why didn't anyone ever tell me those white flour and sugar foods could be at the heart of my problem? This is like a miracle." It's not really a miracle. It's just about figuring out the best and worst foods for your body, and a good place to start is by eliminating some likely culprits like meat, dairy and simple sugars.

Carol was 46, single, and had a high pressure job in human resources when I first met her. She lived in a townhouse with her cat and barely knew her neighbors. Her job was demanding and she had a substantial commute. When we first began working together she was about 30 pounds overweight and very tired. She had no interest in cooking when she got home and usually ate a bag of microwave popcorn and fell asleep watching television. Carol couldn't seem to get herself out of the rut she was in. As I got to know her I learned that one of her lost passions was performing. She was a trained singer and had not been involved in the field for some time. My daughter is a professionally trained singer so I had a fairly good understanding of how an artist's passion runs deep, and when not actualized in some way can lead to a sense of settling. You only need to see the many actors, singers and dancers in New York and Los Angeles who wait tables or drive cabs to pay the bills so they can create space for their passion. I knew for Carol to come alive again we needed to see how we might put some spice in her life in the limited free time she had.

I found a number of performing arts companies near where Carol lives, and a couple of others near her work. She read over the materials and decided to try one near her work. It was a chorale that met once a week for rehearsals and had a public performance twice yearly. Carol learned many of the members had been professionally trained and belonged to the group as an outlet for their talent and as a place to be with like-minded people. After Carol attended three rehearsals, I asked her how she felt at the end of such long days. She said, "Surprisingly, I feel more alive on the nights I have rehearsals than I do when I don't have rehearsals and get home earlier." After she said that, her face softened as she realized it wasn't about how long the day was. It was about how she spent it.

We continued to work together over the next six months. There was no disputing the fact that Carol's free time was limited, and for her to improve her food and lose unwanted weight, we had to do some strategic planning. We developed a whole foods menu plan that was easy for her to manage. You can find my formula for a specific whole foods menu plan in the appendix. It gives you basic suggestions for breakfast, lunch and dinner, all of which can be modified to comparable foods of your choice.

It was essential for Carol to continue to nourish herself through her food and her lifestyle. In addition to the chorale, I recommended the following to her, encouraging her to tackle one goal at a time:

1. Reach out to her neighbors to see whom she might enjoy getting to know
2. Make a weekly plan to do one thing that she thoroughly enjoys
3. Get to bed by 11 to allow for a minimum of 7 hours sleep
4. Incorporate some form of movement into her life that she enjoys - either alone or with others
5. Keep her resume up to date and be aware of new career opportunities
6. Plan her menus and prepare some of the basic dishes over the weekend
7. Eat 3 meals and bring a healthy snack (fruit or nuts) to work every day

As we continued to work together, we tweaked Carol's food so it was easy for her to focus on simple whole foods and eliminate the microwave popcorn altogether. Carol's energy increased, she lost weight and had a new spring in her step.

Carol's experience is an example of how poor food habits are often symptoms of life being out of balance. Has this ever been your life? Is it now? When you look at nourishment holistically, you see that your lifestyle, your friends and social connections and your degree of self-care all affect the way you eat and your zest for life.

Lynne is someone I loved working with. If you know someone who has been touched by cancer, you may have noticed that they have a very strong desire to recover and live a long life. In looking for ways to recover and remain healthy, women like Lynne are very motivated to boost their immune systems to stay well. The solution to that is a diet of nutrient and antioxidant rich foods.

Lynne is a Mom with 3 school aged children and is recovering from breast cancer. I call her a post-cancer thriver. I tend not to use the term survivor, and instead suggest that thriver might be a better term for someone who takes an active role in their recovery and joy in living. Lynne is one of those people. She told me she ate fairly well before she was diagnosed but had some concerns and wanted to know more about ingredients in packaged foods and how to choose the best meats and vegetables. We studied labels together and I encouraged Lynne to eat more fresh foods, especially vegetables and fruits. We examined the antioxidant benefits of the rainbow of colorful produce, as each color offers unique disease protection benefits. Lynne became much more conscious of what she was eating. She began buying much of her produce from a local organic farm in the warmer months. I gave her additional resources for buying meat and fish.

I gave Lynne tools to identify the fruits and vegetables that should always be purchased organically and those that are acceptable to buy conventionally. An excellent resource for this is the website www.ewg.org, managed by Environmental Working Group. This organization does extensive research into food safety. Its website is rich with content on food and household items like toiletries and cleaning products and lists them by degree of safety. When you have a diagnosis like Lynne's you want to do everything possible with your food to optimize your protection from a cancer recurrence. Knowing that what she eats ultimately becomes her cells was enough reason for Lynne to become a nutrition rock star.

Wendy, age 58, came to me shortly after receiving a diagnosis of leukemia. She had breast cancer 20 years earlier, and this second diagnosis was devastating and frightening to her. She had intense chemotherapy and the cancer went into remission. Wendy was looking for answers. She wanted to know more about the power of food and how to relieve her anxiety. It turned out she had been a lifelong member of a diet program and had based her food intake on calories, not quality. She loved her sugar and ate many processed foods.

Wendy has dramatically changed the way she eats. Her health is excellent and she feels confident that she is on the right path, with a much improved diet and a brighter mental outlook to match. No more packaged foods with calorie counts as the barometer. She looks at nutrient value and purity of the food. Today she is well steeped in knowledge about nutrition and has a growing confidence in her health and her future.

I do not know if a poor diet can cause cancer. What I do know is that a high nutrient diet, coupled with a balanced lifestyle, will never hurt you and probably offers a good deal of protection from any disease, including cancer.

The youngest of our Boomer generation turned 50 in 2014. Fifty is a particularly important milestone. If you've had a fairly poor lifestyle to this point, the jig is mostly up. It's time to get serious. It was at age 50 that I began to get real about my own diet and self-care because the diseases of lifestyle, not the diseases of aging, were creeping up on me. Simple but consistent changes and improvements in my food changed everything. It can for you too.

We all have our priorities. Yours may be to live large and throw caution to the wind, or you may have a focus on the future and are highly motivated to do whatever will give you the best chance for a long healthy life. Seventy-five percent of Medicare's costs are for chronic disease. With modern medicine, you can live a long time with chronic disease, but the question is, what is the quality of that long life if you are saddled with physical and emotional pain and other limitations? Chronic disease increases your chances of having many out of pocket medical expenses. I for one would prefer not to go that route. While not all chronic disease is avoidable, many can be if you practice healthy eating habits, manage your stress and move your body. Chronic disease can limit your opportunities for living an enjoyable life. For me, giving up junk food and frequent restaurant dining seems to be an easy trade-off for the benefits that come with eating well and having a balanced lifestyle.

What are your priorities? If a long healthy life is your priority, do you need to do what I did and change your food, or are you already there? It is not so hard because you'll not only be supporting your priority for a long healthy life, but you will find that good food really tastes good! It also makes you look good! Who doesn't want that?

If we were sitting around your kitchen table today, here's what I'd ask you to do:

Tell me how you'd like to feel in 6 months

Tell me how your life would be different when you feel that way

Look through your pantry and refrigerator and toss out the junk

Plan what you're going to eat for the next week

Make a shopping list of staples and the ingredients you need for your menu

Start every day complimenting yourself for something

Remind yourself how precious your life is

Start every day with an expression of gratitude

We all have good intentions but you need a plan to make them a reality. Think about what else you might need to do to realize your goals. If you need someone to hold you accountable, be very clear with them that you need someone to encourage you, not criticize you. We do that to ourselves very nicely and don't need anyone else adding to the pile of guilt and criticism.

8

Back to the Kitchen

"True health care reform starts in your kitchen,
not in Washington." Anonymous

Key points in this chapter
- How getting back to the kitchen will get you healthier
- The correlation between obesity and de-valuing home cooking
- Home cooking requires planning and organization
- Cooking and eating good food is a pleasurable experience
- Essential foods by category
- Start with simple menu planning

How did the people in our success stories change their food for the better? You guessed it: they went back to the kitchen. Allow me to share some meaningful data about the beloved kitchen and what has happened in our modern lives. From there I will take you step by step through all the food essentials that will get you feeling great again.

In 2011, 16 million Americans ordered a pre-cooked Thanksgiving dinner from their local supermarket or restaurant. How have so many people become too busy to prepare this annual feast? What has happened to home cooking and the traditions that we once honored? It's no accident that Americans have become increasingly overweight in the generation of take-out and restaurant dining. Is there a direct correlation? Perhaps so, or perhaps take-out and restaurant dining are two of the many factors that have led to our chubby nation. Additional causes may be overconsumption of processed foods that provide few nutrients and can trigger hunger. We have become a nation of grazers who seldom sit for a meal of real food. As a result, 33% of American adults are obese today, and fully 66% are overweight. While overweight is not a disease in itself, it lends itself to increased risk of many chronic diseases like high blood pressure, heart disease, joint pain, and Type II diabetes.

When is the last time you cooked a meal for yourself? Or your family? No blushing here if you can't remember - you are not alone. Our upwardly mobile Boomer culture has more spending power than our parents did. This unprecedented cash flow has led to suburban sprawl, long commutes, automobile transportation and to organized sports and other activities. In the midst of all these shifts, the home cooked meal that a family eats together around the table has slowly slipped away.

New homes grew from the old 1800 sq. ft. model to 4000+ sq. ft. To keep in scale with home size, kitchens had to grow too. Today's kitchens have expansive granite countertops and 6 burner stoves, but they are used less than ever before. Sadly, the take-out dinner sits on the counter while the unused stove stands shiny and new. Family members grab and go without ever sitting down at the table or joining other family members.

Let's look back at how you grew up and then at some of the ways you can get back to the kitchen and enjoy it.

Fast Food is Born

Early boomers like me got to try "modern" food and convenience when our Moms bought frozen TV dinners. These were a rare occurrence for us, but we five children thought they were very cool. This was our first exposure to ready made factory food. It was glamorized by the media and defined the "modern family". Slick advertising and marketing were effective enough to convince me and my siblings that fast food was even more delicious than a home cooked meal. Ah, the power of advertising. McDonalds came on the scene shortly thereafter and fast food moved from the freezer to the sterile restaurant and ultimately to the drive-thru with many of us eating in our cars, barely aware of the experience of eating.

Another factor in the shift to fast food was Title IX. Sports became gender neutral so girl boomers grew up on the soccer field or little league field along with the boys. Creative marketers seized on the upswing in sports participation to suggest a quick stop at McDonalds after the game would solve the hungry kids problem. Building on that idea they created the irresistible appeal of Ronald McDonald and the Happy Meal. Effective advertising made us all oblivious to the irony of wanting to be a good athlete and calling upon McDonald's for nourishment. Our Moms, the principal cooks then, welcomed the relief of a quick take out.

Fast food marked the beginning of our detachment from real food and where it came from.

The Degree of Disconnection to Cooking

A client of mine went to a healthy eating class at the Kripalu Retreat Center in the Berkshire Hills of Massachusetts. We had been working together on correcting her gastrointestinal and headache issues by changing her food. She was feeling much better and decided to take it up a notch and hone her cooking skills. "I found out how knowledgeable I already am," she said, "when I found some of my classmates literally did not know how to turn on a stove!"

It's ironic that cooking shows and celebrity chefs are hugely successful and widely viewed at a time when fewer and fewer people cook. There's a reason cooking shows dominate television - they are pleasure showcases. We innately want to experience the pleasure of cooking and eating good food. But healthy eating does not happen from watching someone on television. You need to actually eat quality food, and the best way you can do that is by preparing your own. Take the healthiest recipes the celebrity chefs offer, go to the kitchen and do some cooking. Alton Brown is one chef who offers many health conscious dishes.

We're too Busy to Cook? Really?

Marketing professionals have done a stellar job convincing us that we don't have time to cook. There is a principle in advertising that suggests that repeating the same statement multiple times will eventually convince listeners that the statement is true. Listen to the ads for take-out from major restaurant chains and they will tell you it is more convenient to buy from them than to cook. Cooking is described as an annoying chore that can easily be avoided. Nothing could be further from the truth. With the right attitude, cooking can be a creative experience filled with color, taste and aroma. Watch those celebrity chefs and you will see that cooking touches many of the senses in very positive ways. It's all about the know-how, and we'll cover all the basics in this chapter. What to buy, when to cook, and when to eat.

Finding time to cook on a regular basis is a matter of good planning and organization. Planning and organizing are not personal strengths of mine, but since eating quality food is a priority, I make it work. Our world has become a very busy place. Most of us work outside the home today. If kids are added to your mix, there are many commitments to their activities as well as to your own. The boundaries between work and home have narrowed because of technology, potentially adding more stress to your day. All the more reason to be well nourished.

Here's a question for you: are you too busy to shower or to get dressed in the morning? Of course not. Isn't getting nourishing food into your body just as important as a clean, clothed body? Give cooking your own food the same priority. Make it an essential part of your morning or some part of your day. It will change your health, adjust your weight, increase your energy, improve quality time and save you money. Studies have even found that family dinners improve academic performance in children. What else in your life can do all the things good nourishment can do for you? I don't think there's really anything equal to good nourishment.

It's Only Me/Us

Is this you? Have your kids grown and you are giddy with excitement that you no longer have to plan and prepare meals for your family? Don't let that be a reason to stop cooking for yourself.

The older we are the more we need the added oomph that comes from good food. Many people tell me they graze, rather than make meals. When I asked Joan to describe her grazing, which only began when her life circumstances changed and she was living alone for the first time in many years, she said: "well, I will grab a piece of a bagel and eat it going out the door. Then if there's food in my break room at work, I'll nibble on a few things. It might be someone's left over dessert, or a bag of chips, or an apple. It just is easier than thinking about what to eat." When I asked her if she ever feels full, she thought about it and realized she doesn't. I asked her if she ever feels hungry, and she said a little bit all the time. The bottom line is she never has the sensation of feeling satisfied that comes when you eat a meal. She's lost her hunger barometer. A good place for Joan to get back in touch with her nutritional needs would be right at her own kitchen table. If you want to stay healthy as you age, you need to see your own self as a very special person who truly deserves a good meal.

Preparing and eating your meals at home will boost your health. Your nutrition matters and you are as deserving of a good meal as any other member of your family. Sadly, we do not hear much about this from the media, or even from the medical community. Focus on food for older adults seems to be directed only at those with financial need, but every older adult should be counseled in the importance of eating real food.

Eating real food calls for creative cooking, just as it did when you were cooking for others. Make enough to give yourself a couple of good meals from a single time at the stove. If you want to be healthy as you age, you need to feed yourself. Let's move now to a discussion of food basics.

Food Basics 101

This section is devoted to getting you past any obstacles to making your own food. There is nothing embarrassing about not knowing how to do it. I promise you, I will give you all the basics that will make it easy for you to cook for yourself. When you prepare your own food, you will experience an awareness about food and your own body that is pleasurable and affirming. It will make you wonder why you waited so long.

The operative word is *simple* when it comes to healthy cooking. Simple herbs and spices and whole fresh foods are the ingredients for creating healthy delicious dishes.

But wait! Are you already feeling resistant? If so, start small. If you want to have a well-balanced way of eating, start with the basics. Think of a dehydrated sponge that expands when immersed in water. That can be your plan for cooking. Start really small and slowly expand your repertoire in the kitchen. Make the journey of getting well with food fun and pleasurable.

In planning your meals, I am not asking you to be perfect. That is no fun and can be stressful, which is never good for digestion. I am asking you to make a habit of eating quality foods consistently and to throw caution to the wind only occasionally. Use the 90-10 rule - 90% good choices and 10% anything goes. Doing this will demonstrate very quickly the way you feel when you eat well most of the time, and how you feel when you "celebrate". Trust me, I've had the experience on Thanksgiving and Christmas when I choose to sample too many of my family's yummy desserts as well as my own not-so-healthy but otherwise delicious holiday traditions. In the moment it is wonderful, but by the end of the day I don't feel so great. You can only notice the effect of these high fat high sugar foods when you eat them occasionally. If you eat them all the time, it's easy to think that the feelings of bloat and discomfort are normal.

The following section describes each of the basic food groups and how to choose them.

Meat and Fish

You need to decide if you want to include meat and fish in your diet. If you are someone who really likes meat or seems to need it to feel balanced, include it in your planning. Just make sure it is free of added hormones and antibiotics. That is the first step in eating clean. Step it up a notch and eat only organic meat and wild fish, i.e. not farm raised fish. If you choose not to include meat on your plate, don't worry when your meat-eating friends tell you that you need meat. Remind your friends that cows and horses are vegetarians and seem to have no trouble staying alive and thriving on grass.

Eat Your Vegetables

You may have heard your Mom say this many times as you made faces at the peas or spinach on the table. I hope today you know that vegetables truly are super-foods when it comes to nutrients. There may be many you still don't like, but the good news is there are literally hundreds of varieties of vegetables to choose from. Recently I worked with someone who only ate 5 vegetables and we were able to work that into several varied meals.

Vegetables can be eaten steamed, stewed, roasted, grilled or raw, so the possibilities are endless. The important thing is that you get them into your body several times a day. I will often saute kale to accompany my organic egg for breakfast, or I will add a handful of greens to a smoothie on a summer morning. A vegetable soup at lunchtime with some grated cheese or kidney beans will get more vegetables into you. Dinner usually is the easiest time to have vegetables but do not wait until the end of the day to start thinking of where you'll get your vegetables. Use them at all meals and for snacks if you eat between meals.

All About Grains

In my experience this is the most missing but important piece on your plate. It is a food that is packed with vitamins and minerals and the fiber you need for proper digestion. The problem is there is so much confusion and misleading information about what whole grains are. When the label says 100% whole wheat on the label that does not mean it is a whole grain. You need to read the ingredient list on the back panel and if the list says enriched flour, it is not whole grain. It must specifically say whole grain to be whole grain. The safest way to avoid confusion about what a quality grain is would be to change your "grains" from bread to actual grains like brown rice and quinoa. Grains are not difficult to cook and you can season them in all sorts of ways so you don't feel you are eating the same thing all the time.

How often have you heard that carbs are bad for you? That is a half-truth: simple carbs made of white flour and sugar are definitely of very limited nutritional value; complex carbs, including whole grains, offer many nutrients and are very good for nearly everyone. An exception is someone with Celiac intolerance, a condition caused by gluten causing harm to digestive villi in the small intestine.

Unlike whole grains, there is no digestive fiber in meat to move it through your digestive system, and that has a way of making us hang on to it. Lynda is a woman I worked with who ate a lot of meat and was trying to lose weight. Because of the fat content in meat, calories add up pretty quickly. I asked Lynda to add a cup of grains to her meal and see what happens. She did, and you might guess what happened. She said, "I'm eating much less meat because I feel fuller from the grains". She began to lose weight and felt much better.

Beans and Legumes

Beans and legumes (lentils, kidney beans and chick peas) have been around for centuries and are great foods for their nutrient content and for filling you up. There are many varieties of beans to choose from. Some will work really well for you, and others not so much. It takes some experimenting to find the right ones for you. I encourage you to try them all.

Beans have a reputation that in some ways is warranted, so experiment at home with them if you haven't eaten them in the past. The key to eating beans comfortably is to soak and rinse them before cooking, simmer to slow cook, and chew thoroughly. It may sound like work, but what you will find is this kind of eating slows you down, gives you a chance to experience your food, and makes friends with your digestive system. Another option with beans is to purchase already cooked beans. Always buy organic and compare the sodium content on the labels of what's available in your store. Also, studies show some beans effectively reduce belly fat. Who wouldn't like that?

Nuts and Seeds

Like beans and legumes, these power-packed foods slow you down because you really need to chew them before you swallow them. They are rich sources of the good fats you hear about but aren't quite sure where to find. I eat nearly 1/2 pound of walnuts every week and have connected that piece of my plate with my lessening need for meat. You get selenium from nuts and research is finding that selenium is an important nutrient in preventing dementia, a fear of many Boomers. As long as you do not have a nut allergy or some other dietary restriction, experiment with nuts and seeds. Add them to your salads, your cereal and on your vegetables. Chia, flax, sunflower and pumpkin seeds are a few of my favorites.

Herbs, Vinegars, Oils and Spices

These are what make food interesting. You can cook your basic vegetables and grains and completely change the taste of them with these magical add-ons. One meal may taste very Italian, while another leans toward the Middle East or Asian, and another All-American. It's all in the way you choose to flavor your foods with a combination of these beautiful add-ons.

Dairy - or Not

The National Dairy Council would have you believe that you are in a nutrient desert if you don't have milk and cheese every day. You only need to look at other cultures to find that many of the healthiest people in Japan, China, and Africa have no dairy and do very well. The key is to look at how your body tolerates dairy. If you have sinusitis, IBS, menstrual cramps, acne, or phlegm, stop all dairy for a month and see how you feel. If you tolerate dairy and really like it, buy organic to avoid bovine growth hormone and other additives.

The Icing on the Cake

This is where fruit comes in. Like vegetables, there are hundreds of fruits to choose from. Fruits provide you with water, fiber and nutrients and have a natural sugar that will satisfy your sweet cravings like nothing else. Choose the ones you like that are in season where you live and they will be the freshest. Have them plain or blend in a smoothie with some vegetables and yogurt or almond milk. Like vegetables, fruits may be eaten raw, baked, grilled or stewed. When you eat different colored fruits you will be getting a variety of protective anti-oxidants, so mix it up to get the best protection.

That sums up the food categories. You might want to focus on just one of them for starters. If you are a meat eater, I would start with choosing hormone and antibiotic free meats as your first change to healthier eating.

The rest of this chapter will be devoted to how you take these foods and make some easy meals.

Keeping It Simple

Here are the nuts and bolts of menu planning and eating that will make it easy for you to eat healthy most of the time so you can enjoy occasional guilt free indulgences. Imagine how cool it will be to dig into your favorite brownie sundae without one ounce of regret!

1,   Keep your pantry filled with staples that make it easy to put a meal together. These staples include a variety of vinegars, extra virgin olive oil, all the spices you like (organic preferred), jars or cans of tomatoes and tomato paste, cartons of chicken and vegetable broths, whole wheat pasta, brown rice, quinoa, couscous, whole oats, dry cereal, sea salt, pepper, a jar of artichoke hearts, a jar of capers, garlic and onions. Load your countertop and refrigerator with whatever vegetables and fruits you like.

2,   Do some general planning for the upcoming week and write a shopping list to include the items you don't have on hand but will need to make the meals you want.

3,   Get a good cookbook or two - several are listed in the appendix. Experiment a little with a cookbook you find appealing, but don't feel wedded to every ingredient in a recipe. If it calls for red wine vinegar and you only have apple cider vinegar at the moment, try the apple cider - the more you free yourself from the constraints of recipes, the more you'll enjoy cooking. Of course you need to have a well-stocked pantry to make this work.

4,   Share cooking and dining with others. I live by myself right now, and one of my favorite things is shared food prep and eating with someone else at the table. It just makes the experience more fun. Maybe it's a throw over to memories of The Big Chill, but wherever it comes from, I know for me shared dining is what I most like.

Including most of the food groups listed above in your meals will ensure a balanced diet that will keep you energized and satiated.

Turn to the appendix where you will find a sample menu for 7 days' worth of meals.

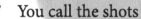

9

12 Week Plan for Optimum Health

"One cannot think well, love well, sleep well, if cne has not dined well."
Virginia Woolf

Key points in this chapter
You call the shots
One focus per week
Make each week stick as you build the next week

I'm going to give you another approach to eating well. You may be someone who has had the best intentions to eat well and engage in other healthy lifestyle practices. You may already know a lot about what you've read in the preceding pages, but have failed to make it a part of your life. Perhaps life keeps getting in the way.

With this in mind, this chapter will give you a very simple way to improve your food, one week at a time. Each week has a single goal. Here's how it works: you choose the order of the 12 weekly actions. Give each weekly goal your full attention so it will become a habit, not just a temporary experience. If you do this, by the end of the 12 weeks, you will have 12 lasting practices that are sure to make you a vibrant boomer. You will see how meeting each goal feeds the next, and good habits build more good habits. I suggest that you choose which week to focus on each goal because some will seem more difficult than others. There's a personality test called Myers Briggs that you can find online that helps define the way we look at life. One aspect is whether we prefer to choose difficult things first and easy things second (that would be a "J" in the Myers Briggs inventory; or the opposite, "P", choosing easy first and difficult second. I happen to be a P.

To be successful in developing lasting healthy habits, you need a plan. I've done the hard part for you and laid it all out in a simple program that will get your juices flowing and will move your ambitions and intentions out of park and into drive.

When you complete the entire plan in this chapter, you will be amazed at how much more energy you have and how much better you look than you have for a long time. Don't accept bloating, gas, headaches, grogginess, body aches or clogged arteries as just old age or your new normal. All of this can be relieved and even reversed through the power of nutrition and positive lifestyle practices.

Here we go:

1. Eat your veggies

This is the week when you put a laser beam on your vegetable intake. Dr. Walter Willett, a renowned nutrition researcher at

Harvard School of Public Health, said one study found that 4-5 servings of fruits and vegetables each day gives you the greatest benefit. If you're looking for ways to manage your weight you can eat even more until you're feeling full, as vegetables are very low in calories and high in nutrients.

Here's the plan: choose the vegetables you really like. Buy fresh and frozen so you have a good supply at home. Aim to eat 1/2 to 1 cup of vegetables 4-5 times every day. A big salad at lunch time could take care of it. Just don't forget to put some protein in your salad to help balance the meal. Vegetables can be part of any meal or you can have them for snacks. I often have my first serving at breakfast.

2. Breakfast time

Let's look at breakfast this week. The plan here is to have a good breakfast *with no refined sugar* every day of the week. Do you have a tendency to skip breakfast, or eat a sweet roll or bagel? These foods won't start your engine. They will set the stage for illnesses like unstable blood sugar. No skipping breakfast this week, and no sugar, just a good mix of protein, whole grain and fruit or vegetable. Commit to having a real breakfast every day for the week. Watch your energy and hunger through the morning. Watch your mood. Play with different foods for your breakfast. It might even include a vegetable or two. See how a good breakfast helps. Some examples include whole oats with cinnamon and walnuts, sauteed green vegetables with organic egg; grapefruit with a bowl of steamed quinoa and greens of your choice.

3. Reading time

This week is all about daily reading. Being a health and nutrition coach and writer, I am reading about nutrition all the time.

Whatever *you* put your attention to will reflect in your behavior. This week I'd like you to read something every day about healthy eating, or health in general, or aging, or cravings, or whatever your interest is. It's easy to find articles on health and wellness. One word of warning: do not read articles about rapid weight loss and perfect bodies. These are designed to make you feel like you can never measure up. Find a favorite website, or google a topic, or take a book out of the library that interests you. Keep reading. Notice what is relevant for you and read more on the topic. Soon you will be your own nutrition expert. There are MDs I like - Andrew Weil, Mark Hyman, Christiane Northrup, and other solid health sources like Michael Pollan, Andrea Beaman, Marc David and Annemarie Colbin. Google them and see what they have to say that relates to your life.

4. Great grains

Grains might be the biggest missing ingredient in the Standard American Diet. They are also a source of confusion because many bread items are described as whole wheat, which is not a whole grain. Grains in conventionally processed foods have been emulsified, purified and stripped of their nutrients, then shot up with synthetic vitamins and minerals for repackaging. Avoid these highly processed grains. Real grains haven't been torn apart, they are robust and full of nutrients, and they keep you full, just like vegetables. Some examples are brown rice, whole oats (not instant oats), quinoa, bulghur, amaranth, and barley. Some have gluten. Brown rice and quinoa are gluten free. Choose the ones you like. Find some easy recipes and cook up a batch. Replace your bread with portions of whole grains. One slice of whole grain toast in the morning should be enough bread for the day, at least for this grain-focused week. Get the rest of them from whole grains.

5. Desserts

Do you love the idea of dessert? At least occasionally? I am a P in the Myers Briggs profile, so I like a little treat sometimes. Choosing a dessert isn't always a poor decision. If you have visions of double fudge brownies piled high with whipped cream, that's not where I'm going. Some examples of healthy desserts include a bowl of berries, a sliced apple or pear with cinnamon and walnuts, baked until caramelized, a piece of high quality dark chocolate, a ripe fig, or a bowl of warm applesauce.

When you have dessert over this week ask yourself if you want one to complete your meal. If you have been accustomed since childhood to having dessert after your dinner, it may simply be a habit and not a necessity. But if the answer is yes, you really do want dessert, then choose one of the above, or some variation of these suggestions, and enjoy it. If the answer is no, have a cup of herbal tea or leave the table to carry on with your evening. You will discover that sometimes dessert has been a habit more than a need. This is an important piece of self-discovery when it comes to your eating habits.

Focus this week on modifying desserts by choosing both delicious *and* healthy with a focus on opting in or out of having dessert after your meals.

6. Move and stretch

Boomers need to move. Many people I work with first complain of body aches and pains. It's a common condition but not an inevitable one. Just watch a child for an hour or so and you will see how much they move, and they rarely if ever complain of aches and pains. If you have a dog or cat, you will see they stretch every time they stand up. Humans should too.

Ironically, the older you are, the more often you should be moving, but life often gets in the way of physical activity. Desk jobs, driving and sitting at meetings are just a few things that take up a lot of time for adults, and none of these activities provide opportunities for movement. You need to find time to move and stretch. Most aches and pains will go away when you eat well and move often.

Make a plan for this week to move for at least 30 minutes every day. You can do it all at once, or you can break it up each day if you don't have a 30 minute block of time. If your daily routine requires a lot of sitting, make a plan to get up and stretch several times each day. If you have a condition that doesn't allow for independent movement, have someone help you with some form of passive movement and stretching.

7. Commune with Nature

Find a way to get yourself outside every day to take in the beauty of nature. We often think of spirituality in relation to religion, but communing with nature is the simplest form of connecting with something greater than ourselves. Just read the work of Henry David Thoreau, or Robert Frost, or Mary Oliver to capture the deep meaning that this connection offers.

Dig your hands in the garden if the weather is good. Find an outdoor sanctuary, especially if you live in a busy city. The land around you may be beautiful too, but if it isn't, keep your eye on the ever changing sky. Being outdoors every day gives you a chance to recharge and move your body in ways you cannot inside a building. In planning this week of communing with nature, you might want to be outdoors at the same time of day, or you might want to explore the outdoors at different times. Whatever you choose, be mindful of what you experience outdoors. Begin by breathing deeply and relax into the sights, smells and sounds around you. Touch a flower, a tree, or a stone, as you move through the space. Plan to spend at least 15 minutes each day outdoors during this week. If it's winter, bundle up. If it's raining, put your boots on and splash through puddles. Have fun.

8. Get fruity

This should be an easy one. The hardest part of this is having a supply on hand. I recommend buying in season for many reasons. Buying in season increases the likelihood that your fruit is local and fresher than something that's been shipped from the other side of the world.

Buying in season gives you a nice variety if your climate and fruit production changes over the course of the year. In New England we have cranberries, apples, pears and dried fruits in autumn and winter, berries in late spring, and an abundance of choices all summer long. See what is seasonally available in your community and buy those fruits. Keep a few bags of frozen fruits in the freezer too. They are great for smoothies and fill-ins when you run out of fresh fruit.

Eating fruit is easy because it is so portable. You can tuck an apple in your briefcase or backpack. Three fruits every day for one week should get you in the habit, and remind you of just how delicious and filling a piece of fruit can be.

9. Take a refined sugar fast

Are you a sugar addict? If so, you are not alone. Sugar is the simplest and fastest way to access quick energy, and it tastes good.

Refined sugar is that white or brown kind of sugar that comes in a box. It is highly processed and too much of it leads to all sorts of inflammatory responses in your body. You may not be aware of how much sugar you eat because most of us don't dive into the sugar bowl and scoop out spoonfuls of sugar. The sugar bowl is not the source of most sugar consumption. The real source is any processed food - food that comes in a box: white bread, cereal, juice, and soda. Sugar is hidden in nearly every packaged food you can buy.

To be successfully sugar free this week, you will need to look carefully at any packaged foods you use to see if there is sugar on the ingredients label. It may be listed as sugar, corn syrup, cane syrup, high fructose corn syrup or fructose. To successfully complete this week, any food with more than 2g. per serving of any of these forms of sugar should not be eaten.

Because sugar is so ubiquitous, this week's challenge may prove difficult. I recommend that you wait until you have completed your fruit and vegetable weeks before you do your sugar fast. Eating fruits and vegetables will give you natural forms of sugar that will give you energy and a flavorful experience without the inflammatory effects of refined sugar. Sweet vegetables like squash, beets, sauteed onions, and sweet potatoes, along with an abundance of fresh fruit, will please your palate.

You may find that abstaining from refined sugar will improve your energy and your focus. If you've had an achy body, foggy thinking or fluctuating energy levels, abstaining from sugar can change all that for the better. Post on my Wellness and You Facebook page and tell me how it's going.

10. Eat at the table

This is a really important one if you want to fall in love with healthy eating. Today many families and individuals eat on the fly, and not together, due to schedules that give higher priority to things other than quality food and dining together. Eating at the table puts you directly in touch with your food and your immediate social circle. It gives you the opportunity to taste and enjoy your food, and the space to know when you have had enough.

Put the effort into buying and preparing healthy delicious food every day this week. Now you might be thinking that sitting at the table is too hard, but give it a try and see what happens. Follow this practice for at least one of your meals. Create a peaceful atmosphere at your table. Imagine you have a special guest joining you if you normally eat alone. If you have family with you, light a candle to create a welcoming table. Create a nice atmosphere for yourself.

As you eat, look at and taste your food. Chew it. Enjoy it. There's no need to rush. A surprising outcome of this practice is that when you fully focus on the experience of eating you just might eat a lot less. You may also digest in a completely different way than you do when you eat on the fly. Take note of all of this to fully appreciate the difference between eating mindfully and eating on the fly.

11. Express gratitude

This is one of my favorites. A client told me today how her Mom is on a negative jag. Every time she stops by to visit she feels drained and sorry she went there. This astute woman knows that an atmosphere of negativity makes it very difficult to appreciate all that is good in a person's life, even when it is right in front of them.

The expressing gratitude week is something that will get you out of the messiness of negative thinking and will give you an amazing burst of energy. Begin each day with a few moments of reflection on all that you have. It may be your health, your loved ones, a sunny day, or even having a chance to be alive again today. Make a mental note that you will be doing a gratitude reflection again at the end of the day. That will keep you more aware of the positive moments you experience throughout the day. Take time in the evening to remember and give thanks for all the things you were grateful for that occurred during the day. Include any difficult moments that taught you something, because learning from difficult experiences can be enormously helpful to our growth. When you catch yourself having a negative thought, see if you can switch it around to something positive. Lift yourself up.

These gratitude practices are a little like morning and evening prayers. The nature of these practices is spiritual. When we tap into gratitude, everything gets better.

12. Beans, nuts and seeds

Beans, nuts and seeds have a great number of nutrients and because they are packed with fiber, they fill you up and keep you from feeling hungry. If you include beans nuts and seeds in your diet every day for one week, I predict your meat consumption will drop without your even noticing it.

Nuts and seeds have good fats in them. These foods require a fair amount of chewing, and that always slows down the volume you consume. Mix these foods into any meal. Very often I have nuts or seeds as part of my breakfast, and if I'm snacking, they will be included. Beans are great in burritos, with rice, in soups and in cold bean salads. These are really good foods for you and will bring a good balance to your plate.

If beans, nuts and seeds are not foods you typically eat, start slowly, adding one food at a time. I know someone who feels ill from cashews but is fine with almonds and walnuts. We're all different. If you have diverticulosis you need to be cautious with these foods, and perhaps avoid seeds altogether. But if you have no digestive or allergy related sensitivities to these foods, make them a regular part of your plate over this week. If you find you enjoy them, continue eating them. I make a Tuscan bean soup in the winter that I just love. It's a great meatless meal. A three bean salad is refreshing and healthy as a summer dish. Explore ways to use these great foods.

Put it all together

So there you have it. Twelve weeks of change and improvement in your diet and lifestyle. When you take one bite of the lifestyle challenge each week you will see how manageable it is. It's been my experience that success comes most easily when you take the challenges in little steps rather than trying to do everything at once. With this plan, you also have control over the order in which you make the changes. You make the call on what comes first on your path to healthy eating and a balanced lifestyle. The balanced lifestyle you achieve from some of these steps is a significant piece on the path to true self-care and nourishment.

In each food category, mix up your selections so you are eating a variety of tastes and flavors. I like to put something on my list each week that is new to me or at least something I haven't had in a long time. Go organic whenever you can because you'll get the added benefit of plant food grown in mineral rich soil. Make a shopping list and get started.

10

Final Thoughts

"Whole foods give us all that we need to perfectly nourish ourselves." Pooja Mottl

Key points in this chapter
  What happens when you do the work of improving your food
Be your health record keeper
Put your mental focus on what works
Be aware of what you eat and where you eat it

Before you finish this book, I want to feel confident that somewhere between beginning and end you will find a technique to get you consistently eating well so you have the best chance of aging well. Perhaps you will be inspired by the thought that eating well will keep you from spending your retirement time and money on medical issues. Or maybe you saw yourself in one or more of the stories of other Baby Boomers included in these pages. Perhaps the detailed trip through the kitchen exploring all the food groups simplified the process for you. Or you may love the menu plan in the appendix. Whatever it is, I promise you that if you change your food for the better, you will feel better and build better protection from disease more than any supplement, diet or medication can do for you.

"I have now been working with Peg for five months. I have learned a great deal of how food affects the body, why chemicals in foods are so damaging and even how they affect our moods. I feel stronger, have more energy and am thoroughly enjoying cooking a variety of new foods."

"Working with Peg has greatly enhanced and solidified my foundation for life work and self care. Her knowledge of holistic health care wrapped a beautiful ribbon around all aspects of life and made me ever mindful of the whole."

"There isn't a quick fix. There's just a quiet, ongoing motion of my body always seeking to heal itself. I've learned it from you, and so appreciate your patience and kindness in teaching me to heal my life."

These are the words of three women, Maureen, Barbara and Wendy, who were self- motivated toward eating well and subsequently balancing their lifestyle. One was motivated because of two serious illnesses. All three were motivated by the vision they had for their older years. In all three cases, these women found that the power of food could change their lives for the better. You may have noticed in the second two quotes that food was not mentioned. That is because these women successfully incorporated food into the overall context of health and well-being. They didn't isolate their new food practices into a silo with no connection to the bigger picture. They viewed their new healthy eating practices as a foundation or springboard for all aspects self-care and healing.

In all three cases, the main focus was on food when we began working together. I guided each of them through the very same things you found in this book: recognizing that food changes everything; how to identify and eat real, not processed foods; having a ready supply of these real foods in their kitchens; tuning into appetite; crowding out poor quality foods for better ones; and recognizing that how they eat every day affects their health.

From there these women discovered that a healthy lifestyle with food would change their perspective on many other things. Wendy was overcoming the second of two serious illnesses in her life. She was fearful of the future, unsure if she had one. Changing her food changed her weight, her energy and her blood. It also changed her thinking. She has better checkups now and is growing confident that because of changes in her food she has increased her chances for a very bright future.

Because food becomes you, it affects the flow of blood to your brain and all of your organs. When you have a better flow of blood to your brain, you think more clearly and your emotions can be in better balance. When blood flows more freely to your heart, all of your systems function better and you have the energy to move on in your life and realize your dreams.

In this, the closing chapter of Food becomes You, I'd like to ask you to think carefully about your next steps. I hope that you believe, as I do, that food does become you, because whatever you eat changes your body's composition. You don't have to be perfect because no one is. You only have to be clear that you want to eat quality foods most of the time. If you have been changing your food for the better as you've been reading this book, you already know it can be a pleasant experience. Good food tastes good. Good food digests well. Good food gives you energy. Good food keeps you from feeling hungry. Good food lets you live your life without being distracted by hunger, low energy, high blood pressure, bloating, gas and the many other things caused by poor quality foods.

I hope you know now that this way of eating is quite different from being on a diet. Diets are designed to hold you to a restrictive protocol for a set period of time, usually with the goal of weight loss. Once you reach your goal, or give up, you are highly likely to regain the weight you lost in a very short time. Eighty-five percent of dieters do. It happens because diets have focus on calories, not on nutrients. Your body will be starved for nutrients and when you end the diet, unless you have been supported in eating healthy real foods, you will return to the Standard American Diet and gain your weight back. Sound familiar? It's not your fault and I only ask you not to do this to yourself again. You deserve better.

To be consistent in moving to a life of eating healthy, you need to have a plan. Food won't miraculously appear in your refrigerator. You need to grow it or buy it. You need to eat it regularly, and vary it so it is enjoyable. If you eat with the seasons you will always have a new food to look forward to.

Your attitude and perspective on aging is a very powerful indicator of your future. Keep a record of your health. Include details from your annual physical. Add some anecdotal information, like a rating scale of your energy, sleep and happiness. Sadly, the current medical model has a focus on what's wrong with you, not what's right, so what is right will need to be determined by you. Sometimes a client will complain to me about all over body pain. Then I ask them to mark the spots where they hurt on a drawing of the human body. When they show me, I ask them to look at all the places on their drawing that are not marked. They look at me, somewhat surprised, but also relieved to see they really don't hurt everywhere. It opens them to a different kind of thinking about pain, one that includes possibilities of having more spots that won't hurt if they take some pro-active nutrition steps to decrease inflammation. When you focus on your potential to heal through quality food, you will see vitality and lifelong health as a real possibility going forward.

Refer to your rating scale every few months and see how it changes. If things are improving, keep doing what you're doing. If things are sliding, look at what might be interfering with your goal to eat healthy. Are you still on the 90% healthy 10% less than ideal food spectrum, or have you slipped? If so, you know what to do - get back up to the 90%-10% model and you will feel better. Life is filled with change, and if you want to stay on track, you may need to make adjustments along the way. You may be in a cycle that requires you to eat in restaurants more than usual. If so, Google healthy restaurants for a listing of places that are more health-conscious. If you're in a steak house with 24 oz. steaks and fries on the menu, ask for a 4-6 oz. steak with steamed vegetables. Share a meal with your dinner mate. There are always ways to adjust and make things work a little better.

Have you ever noticed that who you are with can influence your food choices? If you want to eat well, hang out with people who have the same goal. Hang out with people who are not taking about "getting old". That's an excuse for poor lifestyle choices. Hang out with people to have an action plan for healthy living. It makes eating healthy easy because with like-minded people you will have a tendency to buy healthy foods and patronize quality restaurants.

Look at your workplace to see what's working and what is not with food offerings. Do you have a communal kitchen? What kinds of foods are there? I was asked to assess the kitchen of a pediatric medical practice in 2011and make recommendations for improving food offerings. The staff was motivated to get the junk out and replace it with foods that would carry them through their days in a very busy practice. A medical office is an environment that does not lend itself to quiet, restful dining. Creative planning for healthy snacks and flexible break times can make it work even in the busiest of practices.

The same goes for meetings at your workplace: what are the food offerings? Now that you are savvy about healthy foods, you might volunteer to order the food and make healthier choices. One school principal did this after we looked at the teachers' room. We replaced bagels and cream cheese with fresh fruit, Greek yogurt, sprouted wheat bread and almond butter. What's interesting to me is most people happily migrate to healthier choices when they are available. The bagel and cream cheese model is simply a habit, and habits can be changed when something better comes along.

Some final thoughts: those of us at midlife have been blessed with amazing opportunities and experiences we might not have thought possible as youngsters. The evolution of technology has brought the world to our desktop, and even to our pockets.

Information comes our way every day by the boatload. The challenge is to step back and think about what is relevant for you as an individual and for society as a whole. Health is something to be nurtured and treasured. Its existence influences our individual quality of life and the economy of the future. If you believe as I do that health comes from the quality of your food, you will be willing to use this book as your springboard to improved and lasting health. You will see from your own experience that when you eat simple real food on a consistent basis, you give yourself the best odds of living a long healthy life. No magic bullets. No counter full of supplements. No cabinet full of drugs. Just plain and simple real food that tastes good.

In her book If the Buddha Came to Dinner, author Hale Sophia Schatz says "I have found the discipline of nourishing our bodies to be an amazingly effective vehicle for spiritual development and transformation." As you continue to nourish yourself, you will see that Shatz's statement is true. A nourished body nourishes the mind and spirit as well. It is how we become whole and have the capacity to live a truly rich and blessed life.

Be well. And for you Trekkies, "Live long and prosper."

Appendix

When you make a commitment to eating healthy, you know there will be some items you won't want in your pantry. These include: artificial sweeteners, butter and egg substitutes, foods labeled "lite, fat free, zero calorie" energy drinks and diet and regular sodas. Limit your boxed and packaged items to spices and herbs, condiments, oils, vinegars, cereals, whole grain bread, broths, pasta and items for baking.

Setting your pantry and refrigerator up accomplishes 2 important steps in your path to wellness: 1. you have the supplies you need to put together a healthy meal in less than 30 minutes, and 2. you have eliminated easy access to junk food and given yourself a variety of healthy food choices.

Your Pantry and Refrigerator Supplies
To start, purge:
Foods with excess sugar, high fructose corn syrup, partially hydrogenated oils, artificial ingredients including dyes. Replace with brands that don't contain these things.
Watch salt and sugar content – salt = max 1500-2000 mg/day; sugar 4g = 1 tsp.

Add

Whole Grains – whole oats, brown rice, barley, etc. air tight containers; keep for <2 months

Whole grain crackers with *no partially-hydrogenated oils* (Kashi TLC, Newman's, 365)

Bread crumbs – look for Ian's or make your own in food processor with stale multigrain bread

Legumes: kidney, cannelini, black, garbanzo beans, rinse thoroughly; green, French and red lentils

Tomatoes – canned or bottled diced, whole, crushed

Extra virgin olive oil for tasting Olive oil for cooking low heat

Expeller pressed canola oil, coconut oil, unrefined sesame oil for cooking

Vinegars – Bragg's organic apple cider vinegar, balsamic, wine, rice

Broths for soup (watch sodium content) or make your own from chicken carcass or water from boiled vegetables

Spices and herbs – try Simply Organic, 365 or Frontier - all organic

Dressings – Drew's, Newman's or make your own

Peanut butter – Teddy, Roche Bros, Whole Foods fresh made

Almond butter

Cereals: buy cereals with no added sugar; sugar from raisins is ok. some brands to look at: Sam's, Barbara's, Post Shredded Wheat. Hot cereal: Bob's Red Mill Whole Oats

Dark chocolate (Green & Blacks, or others with 60% or more cacao)

Beverages: water is #1, then teas, sparkling water, occasional wine; no "energy drinks"

Milk: rice milk, soy milk, almond milk, organic dairy if desired and no sensitivity

Nuts – walnuts, almonds, Brazil nuts (refrigerate walnuts once opened)

Perishables for the refrigerator or freezer

Berries   Fruits   Fresh vegetables   Fish   Meat

Hummus Poultry   tofu   tempeh   organic eggs

Cheese (not lite)   Organic Butter (not margarine or butter substitutes)

Bread – Ezekiel sprouted wheat, Iggy's, When Pigs Fly (bread should be whole grain, not whole wheat; it will be chewy)

Frozen vegetables, plain, without sauces or butter

Frozen berries

Sauces – Bragg's liquid aminos (vegetable protein instead of soy sauce), sesame oil, tamari sauce, wasabi

Countertop

Fresh garlic, ginger, onions, seasonal fruit

Herb plants - basil, parsley, thyme, etc. – keep in sunny window

Recipes

Meals should have a combination of the 3 basics - protein, carbohydrate and fat. Fat should be lowest in proportion to the other nutrients. In most cases complex carbohydrates (grains, vegetables and fruits) should dominate your plate, with a variable portion of protein according to your needs (lean meat, poultry, fish, beans, lentils, nuts, seeds, tofu, tempeh).

Breakfast Recipes

A big glass of water in the morning is very cleansing to the kidneys – better than juice, which is high in sugar. Add fresh squeezed lemon for added benefits. If you start your day with a big glass or two of water, wait 30-45 minutes before you eat breakfast.

Breakfast Scramble with Baby Spinach

Whisk 3 egg whites and 1 egg yolk in a bowl; add pinch of sea salt. Add 1 T. olive oil to skillet and heat to medium; add spinach leaves and sauté, turning to coat with olive oil. Once the spinach reduces, add egg mixture, turning the pan to bring the uncooked part to the edges, gently moving the cooked part inward, until the eggs are cooked through. Turn onto a plate; serve with a wedge of orange or mango and a slice of whole grain bread.

Overnight Oats

Cook whole oats in a slow cooker set on low. Place 1 cup whole oats in cooker with 4 cups of water. Add a handful of chopped walnuts and 1 tsp. of cinnamon. Cover and let slow cook overnight. Wake up to the smell of cinnamon!

Steel Cut Oatmeal with Cinnamon, Nuts and Berries

2 servings

Bring 2 cups of water to a boil   Add ½ c. steel cut oatmeal
Handful of chopped walnuts,   ½ tsp. cinnamon
raisins and/or cranberries
Stir, reduce heat and simmer over very low heat for 15 minutes or until water is absorbed.
Remove from burner, stir and serve.

Variations:
Add chopped apples   Serve with fresh strawberries or
                            banana
Pour slight amount of warm milk or soymilk over oatmeal
Most important:
chew each bite thoroughly so you have a chance to taste and enjoy it, as well as begin the digestive process using your salivary glands.

If you choose commercial dry cereals, always check the sugar content – remember 4 grams = 1 tsp of sugar. Breakfast is the worst time of day to have refined sugar in your diet because it spikes up your blood sugar, setting off the spikes and dips in energy that trigger cravings.

Recommended cereals are unsweetened shredded wheat or whole oats. Add nuts and fruit to round out your nutritional needs. Use rice, soy, almond or 2% milk

Lunch Recipes

Black Bean Smothered Sweet Potatoes

2 medium sweet potatoes

1 can (15-ounce) black beans, rinsed

1 medium tomato, diced

2 teaspoon(s) extra-virgin olive oil

1/2 teaspoon(s) ground cumin

1/2 teaspoon(s) ground coriander

1/4 teaspoon(s) salt

2 tablespoons grated cheese

2 tablespoon(s) chopped fresh cilantro

1. Prick sweet potatoes with a fork in several places. Place in a baking dish and bake at 425 degrees until tender all the way to the center, about 1 hour.
2. Meanwhile, combine beans, tomato, oil, cumin, coriander and salt in a medium saucepan, cooking until just heated through.
3. When just cool enough to handle, slash each sweet potato lengthwise, press open to make a well in the center and spoon the bean mixture into the well. Top each with a dollop of Greek yogurt and a sprinkle of cilantro.

Quinoa Burgers

Makes 4 patties

1 cup cooked quinoa (about 1/2 cup uncooked quinoa)
1 cup cooked mashed beans (about 1/2 cup uncooked beans; use your favorite kind)
1/4 cup cooked brown rice or bulgur (about 1/8 uncooked)
1/3 cup ground flax seeds
2 eggs

1/4 cup tomato sauce	1 T. Dijon or spicy brown mustard
2 garlic cloves, minced	1/2 teaspoon onion powder
2 tablespoons prepared horseradish	1 cup whole wheat bread crumbs
3 tablespoons canned chopped green chiles	3 tablespoons vital wheat gluten (optional)
1/4 teaspoon ground cumin	salt, to taste
black pepper, to taste	cooking spray or oil, as needed

Mix all ingredients, except cooking spray or oil, in a large bowl until well blended.
Shape into patties. Chill for 20 minutes before cooking.
Lightly mist a skillet with cooking spray or oil. Brown each patty for 5 minutes on each side, until nicely browned. Let cool for 5 minutes—patties will firm up as they cool. These patties freeze well.

Portobello Burgers

fresh green lettuce leaves   roasted red peppers   portobello
mushrooms   olive oil
sea salt and pepper to taste   whole wheat bun

Take a large portobello mushroom, rinse and remove stem. Pat dry
Pour small amount of olive oil in sauté pan; place mushroom in
pan when heated. Cook on each side for about 5 minutes.
Place mushroom on paper towel to drain.
Layer the lettuce on the bun; place mushroom on top, along with
slices of roasted red pepper. Add salt and pepper to taste.

Corn Fritters

Servings: 4
Cook Time: 1-30 min

Chef Mary McCartney shares simple, vegetarian meals that the
whole family can enjoy in her new cookbook, "In Food: Vegetarian
Home Cooking." I liked this one a lot.

1 cup wheat or light spelt flour   1/2 teaspoon baking powder
2 large, free-range eggs, beaten   1/3 cup milk
2 cups corn kernels, cut fresh   1 clove garlic, finely chopped
(or frozen corn)
1 red chili, seeded and finely   2 scallions, finely chopped
chopped (optional)

1 tablespoon fresh parsley or sea salt and black pepper
cilantro, chopped
1 to 2 tablespoons light olive oil for frying the fritters
For the dipping sauce:
6 tablespoons plain yogurt ½ small red chili, finely chopped
1 tablespoon fresh parsley or cilantro, finely chopped ½ teaspoon
fresh lemon juice
1 tablespoon chili pepper jam or sweet chili sauce

In a medium mixing bowl stir the flour and baking powder together, then gradually stir in the beaten eggs and milk. Mix well to form a smooth batter.

Stir in the corn, garlic, chili, scallions and herbs, and mix the ingredients well so that they are coated in the batter. Season with salt and pepper.

Heat the oil in a large non-stick frying pan until it is hot but not smoking.

Spoon in a tablespoon of the mixture for each fritter. Cook until golden brown and turn it over to brown the other side. This should take about 2 minutes per side. Repeat this process until all the mixture has been cooked.

Serve immediately, or wrap the fritters in aluminum foil and keep in a warm oven until they're all cooked.

To make the dipping sauce, just mix all the ingredients together in a small bowl.

Makes about 12 3-inch fritters.

Dinner Recipes

Chicken Scallopine

4 skinless boneless
chicken breast halves
salt and black pepper
3 T unsalted butter
1/2 c. white wine
2 c. chicken stock
2 T salted capers, rinsed

whole wheat flour for dusting

3 T olive oil
8 cloves garlic, minced
juice of 2 lemons
2 plum tomatoes, diced
1/4 c. chopped parsley for garnish

Place the chicken breasts, two at a time, under plastic wrap and hit with a mallet until they are 1/2" thick

Arrange flour in a shallow bowl. Season chicken with a pinch of salt and pepper then dust generously with flour on both sides. Shake off excess

In a large skillet, heat the olive oil over medium high heat. Add 1 T. butter. When butter melts, place the chicken in the skillet. Cook 4 to 5 minutes, until golden brown on the bottom. Turn over and cook and 2 more minutes. Transfer chicken to a plate.

Add the garlic to the pan, cook, stirring for 30 seconds. Add white wine and lemon juice. Simmer, scraping up the browned bits on the bottom of the pan, for a few minutes, until most of the liquid is gone. Add the chicken stock, tomatoes and capers. Increase heat to high, and bring the liquid to a boil. Simmer for 6 minutes, or until the liquid is decreased by about one third.

Stir in the remaining 2 T. of butter. Return the chicken to the pan and simmer for 2 minutes, or until the sauce thickens slightly and the chicken is cooked through.
Season to taste with salt and pepper.

Garnish with parsley and serve immediately with broccoli rabe and carrots.

Adapted from a Sweet Basil Restaurant cookbook. David Becker, chef extraordinaire.
Note: the butter and olive oil in this dish makes for a rich meal. The key is to have a small portion and embrace the flavors and juices. Go heavy on the vegetables if you are hungry.

Rice and Lentil Salad with Spicy Broccoli

Serves 4

2 T. extra virgin olive oil
1/4 t. ground pepper
2 cups cooked brown rice
1 T. Dijon mustard
1 carrot, diced
1/2 t. paprika

1/4 t. salt
2 T. sherry or red wine vinegar
1 1/3 c. cooked lentils, any kind
1 T. finely chopped shallot
2 T. chopped fresh parsley

Whisk oil, vinegar, shallot, Dijon mustard salt and pepper together in a large bowl. Add rice, lentils, carrot and parsley. Stir gently to combine.
Refrigerate for 30 minutes. Serve warm or cold.

Spicy Broccoli

Serves 4

1 Bunch Of Broccoli (about 1 pound)
¼ cup Bragg's liquid aminos   2 T. rice vinegar
2 T. Sesame oil   1 T. Minced fresh ginger
1 T. Minced garlic   ¾ tsp. chile pepper flakes

Cut off florets and cut into small floret pieces. Cut tender parts of stalks on the diagonal into 1 inch pieces.
Heat a pot of water until boiling. Add broccoli and boil for 2-3 minutes, or until tender. Drain in colander, and refresh under cold running water. Drain and place in bowl.
Combine liquid aminos and rice vinegar in a small bowl
Heat a wok until hot, add sesame oil heat, add ginger, garlic and chile pepper flakes. Stir fry for about 10 seconds.
Add aminos and rice vinegar mix and stir fry for 30 seconds.
Pour over broccoli and toss to coat.
Before serving--Let sit at room temperature for 30 minutes or chill for several hours to blend.

Turkey Burgers with Grated Zucchini and Carrots

Serves 4

¾ pound ground turkey
1 medium carrot, grated
¾ t. dried thyme
¼ t., pepper
3 T. olive oil

1 medium zucchini, grated
2 cloves garlic, chopped
¾ t. salt
1 large egg
4 slices crusty bread (Sourdough or multigrain)

4 lettuce leaves

Heat the broiler. In a large bowl, combine turkey, zucchini, carrot, garlic, thyme, salt and pepper and egg. Form into 4 patties.
Heat 1 T oil in large skillet over medium heat. Cook patties, turning once, 4-5 minutes per side.
Meanwhile place bread on a baking sheet and brush with remaining oil. Broil until golden brown and crisp, about 1 ½ minutes. Transfer bread to plates, Top with lettuce and burgers.
Great way to get vegetables into the kids and adults who say they don't like them.
Serve with baby carrots or a side salad.

Steamed Halibut Filets

serves 4

4 halibut filets (4 oz each)
pinch paprika
2 tsp. dried parsley
1 clove garlic, minced

juice of 2 lemons
3 tsp. dried dill weed
2 T. finely chopped onion
s + p to taste

Heat oven to 375.

Cut 4 squares of foil or parchment paper and center one piece of halibut on each. Mix dry ingredients together and sprinkle over each piece. Drizzle lemon juice over all.

Allow fish to steam in the oven for 30 minutes. Serve with a generous portion of vegetables and grains.

Soups

Carrot Ginger Soup

(serves 4-6)

1 tablespoon olive oil	1 medium yellow onion, sliced
3 garlic cloves, finely chopped	2 teaspoon ground cumin seed
1 1/2 tsp ground coriander seed	1 Tbs grated fresh ginger
pinch cayenne pepper	1 lb. carrots, thinly sliced
1 large sweet potato, thinly sliced	1/2 cup fresh orange juice
5-6 cups water or vegetable stock	salt and pepper to taste

Heat the oil in a heavy soup pot. Add the onion and a pinch of salt. Cook over medium heat for about 5 minutes.

Add the garlic, cumin, coriander, ginger and cayenne. Cook for 8-10 minutes - until onions are very soft. Add a little water if it sticks to the pan.

Add the carrots, sweet potato, 1 teaspoon salt and 5 cups water or stock. Bring to a boil. Reduce the heat to medium and simmer until the carrots are very tender, about 20 minutes.

Puree the soup in a blender until smooth, using extra water if necessary.

Return soup to the pot. Add the orange juice and season to taste with salt, pepper and cayenne. Thin with more water until it reaches the desired consistency.

Immune Building Soup from Ming Tsai

Chef Ming Tsai makes this soup for his family in cold and flu season and swears by it for its immune building properties

chop one jalapeño pepper	heat grapeseed oil in stock pot
add pepper	1 T. chopped garlic
1 T. chopped ginger	bunch of chopped scallions
1 package of chopped mushroom caps	
cook down with 1 qt. low sodium chicken broth for about 20 minutes	
add 1 cup shredded carrots	juice of 1 lemon (for sour)
1/2 package sliced silken tofu	lemon zest
cook 1-2 minutes longer	

Pesto Minestrone Soup

serves 6

2 T. olive oil	1 c. diced onion
2 ½ c. water or stock	2 c. diced zucchini
1 -2 carrots	1 can 14.5 oz diced tomatoes
1 can cannelini beans, drained	¾ t. oregano
½ t. pepper	2 handfuls spinach
2 garlic cloves, minced	2 T. pesto

½ - 1 cup small dry pasta   grated pecorino cheése

Heat oil, add onion and sauté 4 minutes. Add water or stock and zucchini, carrots, tomatoes, oregano, pepper and garlic.

Bring to a boil, cover and reduce heat to a simmer for 5 minutes.

Lift cover and return to a boil, stir in pesto, pasta, beans and spinach cover and simmer additional 6 minutes.

Thai Chicken Soup

1 T. olive oil	1 clove garlic
1 small onion chopped	1 can coconut milk
2 c. water or broth	1/2 lb. boneless chicken breast
or tenders	
4 carrots. Julienned	1 c. frozen peas
Red pepper flakes	½ tsp. cumin
optional minced jalepeno pepper	

Heat olive oil to medium. Sauté onion 5 minutes, add chopped garlic clove. Pour ½ the coconut milk into the saucepan and slowly heat till steamy.

Meanwhile, gently sauté diced chicken pieces in a shallow pan, just till browned. Add to pan and pour remaining coconut milk, water and bring to a light simmer. Add carrots and peas, red pepper flakes. and cook over low simmer about 15 minutes.

If soup is too watery, remove ½ cup liquid and place in a glass cup, add 1 tsp corn starch and whisk until blended. Return to pot and simmer 5 minutes more.

Season to taste.

Tuscan Bean Soup

Serves 6-8

1 ½ c. diced onions	1 c. diced celery
1 c. diced carrots	3 diced garlic cloves
3 T. olive oil	1 can kidney beans (15 oz can)
1 can cannellini beans (15 oz can)	1 can diced tomatoes (14 oz can)
4-6 cups chicken stock	1 T. fresh rosemary or (2t. dried)
1 T. fresh thyme (1 tsp. dried)	2 T. fresh basil (3 tsp. dried)
8 oz baby spinach or chard	

Heat olive oil in a large soup pot. Saute the onions, celery, carrots and garlic for 3-4 minutes

Finely chop the fresh herbs and add them or dried herbs to the pot. Add diced tomatoes, beans and chicken stock.

Bring pot to a boil and reduce heat, cover and simmer 10-12 minutes until vegetables are tender.

Add spinach or chard, cover pot and simmer 2-3 minutes until greens are wilted.

If desired, stir in ¼ c. cream to slightly cooled soup.

Grain Dishes

Cooking Instructions for Grains

Grains can be cooked on their own or as a part of a more complex dish. If you want to prepare grains on their own and blend them into different dishes over the next few days, use this general rule of thumb for preparing them: 1 cup of grains to 2 cups of water or broth. Rinse grains, place in a pot with liquid and bring to a boil. Reduce heat and simmer, covered, on low until the liquid is absorbed. A see through cover is recommended so you can watch the absorption. Hint: quinoa, bulghur and quinoa cook in less than 20 minutes; brown rice and barley take about 50-60 minutes.

Brown Rice Pilaf

Makes 4 servings

8 ounces button or baby bella mushrooms, diced (about 2 1/2 cups)

1 onion, diced	1/4 cup water
2 garlic cloves, minced or pressed	1/2 teaspoon dried thyme
1 Tbsp. fresh thyme	1/2 cup dry white wine or vegetable broth
1 cup long-grain brown rice,	2 cups boiling water or vegetable broth
1/2 teaspoon salt	1/4 teaspoon ground black pepper

Heat 1/4 cup of water in a large saucepan with a see-through cover. Add the mushrooms, onion, and garlic. Cook and stir over medium heat for 5 to 10 minutes, until the mushrooms and onion are soft.

Add the thyme and cook and stir for 2 to 3 minutes. Add 2 table-spoons of the wine or vegetable broth and mix in well.

Stir in the rice and the 2 cups of boiling water. Add the remaining wine and the salt and pepper. Stir to mix well. Cover and cook over low heat for about 60 minutes, until the rice is tender and all the water has been absorbed. Check the saucepan occasionally to make sure the rice doesn't cook dry, and add a small amount of water as needed to prevent sticking.

RECIPES

Warm Bulghur Salad

Makes 4 servings

1 cup bulghur wheat	1 1/2 cups fresh broccoli florets
1/3 cup chopped fresh parsley	1/4 cup minced red onion
1/4 cup chopped fresh mint or cilantro	1 tsp. fresh lemon juice
1 Tbsp. extra virgin olive oil	Salt and black pepper, to taste

1 chicken breast 4 oz., cut into strips and sautéed in a pan with small amount of oil

In medium saucepan, bring 1 cup bulghur and 2 cups water to a boil, reduce heat, cover and simmer for 15 minutes.

Steam broccoli florets in a pan with a small amount of water until just barely tender, about 1 1/2 to 2 minutes. Carefully transfer broccoli to sieve or colander and let it drain.

In a small bowl, whisk together lemon juice and oil.

Place the cooked hot bulghur in a large bowl. Lightly toss with a fork to separate kernels. With a fork, mix in parsley, onion and mint (or other fresh herb). While tossing mixture lightly with fork, drizzle in juice/oil mixture. Add salt and pepper to taste. Top with the chicken slices.

Moroccan Couscous and Chickpea Salad

1 c. Israeli couscous	1/2 c. dried cherries or cranberries
1 c. boiling water	5 T olive oil, divided
1 lrg orange bell pepper, cut bite size	1 lrg onion, thin sliced

1 1/2 t. ground cumin
1/4 tsp. cinnamon
2 cups chick peas, drained
3 T rice wine vinegar

1/2 tsp. ground ginger
Salt +Pepper
1/4 c. fresh cilantro
3 T. frozen orange juice
concentrate

Place couscous and dried cherries or cranberries in medium bowl. Add boiling water; cover bowl with plastic wrap and let sit until water is absorbed, about 5 mins
Meanwhile, heat 2 T olive oil in large skillet, add pepper and onions and saute until tender, about 5 mins, and season with cumin, ginger cinnamon and S+P as they cook.
Add to couscous, along with chickpeas and cilantro.
Whisk remaining 3 T of olive oil with vinegar and orange juice concentrate. Pour over salad; toss to coat.
Cover and refrigerate until ready to serve.

Quinoa Tabouli

serves 4

1 cup uncooked quinoa, rinsed and drained

2 cups water

1/2 teaspoon sea salt and more to taste

2 lemons, juiced

4 tablespoons extra virgin olive oil

2 cloves garlic, minced

1/2 cup Italian parsley leaves, chopped

2 sprigs of mint leaves

1/2 teaspoon dry mint
1 medium cucumber,
chopped finely
Freshly ground black pepper to taste

1 large ripe tomato,
1/2 cup red onion, minced

Bring the quinoa, water and salt to a boil in a heavy saucepan.
Cover and turn to lowest heat. Cook undisturbed for 15 minutes or
until water is absorbed. Remove from heat and let quinoa steam for
5 more minutes. Fluff it with a fork. Transfer the hot quinoa into
the bowl.
In a bowl combine the rest of the ingredients and season with salt
and pepper. Gently mix the quinoa into the vegetables. Chill for 30
minutes.
Be sure to use fresh lemons. The fresh juice is what makes this dish
so flavorful.

Smoothies

Make your own with the following formula:
Choose 1 cup of either spinach, kale, chard, broccoli or parsley,
celery or cucumber
Choose 1 cup of two of the following choices: grapes, orange, pineapple, banana, kiwi, papaya, pear, apple, melon, strawberries, or
mango
Choose 1 cup organic soy milk, 1 cup Greek yogurt, 1 cup silken
tofu, 1 cup organic fruit juice, 1 cup water
Put ingredients in a blender and add 1 cup of chopped ice. Blend
until smooth.

Green lift smoothie

2 servings

1 bunch of kale, finely chopped   1-2 grated carrots
1 cup coconut milk   3 cups boiled water
Add kale, carrot and water in a blender and puree very well, about
2 minutes. Add coconut milk and blend for 10-15 seconds more.
Chill and serve.

Strawberry Smoothie

Wash and prepare 1 c. strawberries
Wash and prepare ½ c. any other fruit – peaches, pineapple, kiwi
Pour 1 c. crushed ice in blender
Add ½ c. non-fat yogurt
Add 2 T. ground flax or wheat germ
Blend and enjoy.

Simple Green Smoothie

1 apple, chopped
1 banana
1 scoop Greek yogurt
1 handful kale, chopped with stems removed
1 scoop whey protein

Green Drink – a favorite of Dr. Oz

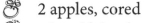 2 apples, cored
2 handfuls of spinach, chard or kale
½ cup of chopped parsley
1 celery stick, chopped
1 thumbnail length of ginger root, peeled
1 lemon - juice only
1 medium cucumber

Place ingredients in a blender, add 4 oz. spring water or a handful of ice cubes, then puree quickly for one minute. Makes two glasses. The green drink has a strong taste and if you are used to drinking soda or sweet tea, the taste will take some getting used to. Dr. Oz suggests adding other items at first to sweeten the green drink to your taste.

Green drink – Optional ingredients: 2nd cucumber, raw carrot, unsweetened fruit juice, banana

7 Day Menu Plan – putting it all together

While I've given you recipes, I also want to give you some additional menu ideas. Next is a 7 day menu plan for you to try. Modify each meal as you see fit if you have health conditions or allergies that preclude you from eating particular foods. If you find a food you do not like, replace it with another food from the same category. You can repeat any of the meals you like. Delete the meat and fish if you are vegetarian and replace with beans or organic soy foods. I only include this menu to give you a starting point. The best meals are the ones that come from a well stocked kitchen where you use your personal tastes and imagination to make meals you love.

It usually takes 21 days of repetition to replace one habit with another. To make this eating pattern stick, take the menus you enjoy and repeat them for two more weeks and you'll have healthy meal prep and eating down pat.

Make a shopping list of the menus you like to get you started.

Day 1
Breakfast

1 banana

1 oatmeal with cinnamon and raisins

1 glass water or tea or coffee

Lunch

soup of your choice with a slice of whole grain bread

1 piece of fruit

1 glass of water or tea

Dinner

salad with greens, avocado, slivered almonds and dressing

1 baked sweet potato

1 4oz breast of chicken

choice of steamed vegetables – beans, squash, spinach or carrots as much as you want – season with herbs and 1 t. olive oil

Day 2
Breakfast

Barbara's shredded wheat – 1 or 2 pieces

½ c. plain organic soy or rice milk

1 banana

1 T. ground flaxseeds

Lunch

Squash soup (can be served on day 4 as well)

1/2 teaspoon dried basil

1/2 teaspoon cumin

1 t. coriander

1/2 teaspoon cinnamon

1 large onion, quartered

1 peeled and chopped butternut squash

1 small sweet potato quartered

Sauté onion in olive oil, add other ingredients along with 4 cups vegetable or chicken broth, Bring to a boil and reduce heat to simmer for 20 minutes.

When cool enough, pour into blender or food processor to puree.

Slice of whole grain bread

Dinner

1 small sweet potato	½ small yellow onion
1 T. extra virgin olive oil	pinch sea salt
1 clove pressed	1 T. lemon juice
1 t. dry mustard	
1 T. chopped	¼ lb. fresh green beans, trimmed
fresh rosemary	
Lemon zest	
4 oz. wild salmon fillet	

Preheat over to 425. Slice potato and onions ¼ " thick. Put potato and onion on greased baking sheet (or on a sheet of parchment paper) in single layer. Drizzle with olive oil and sprinkle with salt. Bake 15 minutes.

Mix garlic, mustard, lemon juice and rosemary to make a paste and set aside.

Remove potatoes and onions. Place beans around potatoes and onion and lay salmon fillet on top. Spread mustard paste on top. Put back in over and bake for 12 more minutes.

Day 3
Breakfast

Omelet with vegetables

Whisk 2 eggs together with a pinch of sea salt and set aside. Heat sautee pan with 1 T. olive oil and place cut vegetables in pan to cook. (May be onion, broccoli, spinach, chard) Leave in pan and turn off heat when cooked.

Heat small omelet pan with 1 t. butter. As soon as butter starts to bubble, pour in egg mixture, moving uncooked egg to the side until all egg is cooked. Slide onto serving dish and place vegetable either inside the egg or on the side. Serve with 1 slice whole grain bread.

Lunch

Couscous and Vegetable Sauté

1/2 c, cooked couscous (1/2 c. couscous with 3/4 c. boiling water poured over it)

1 tsp olive oil

3/4 c. shredded zucchini (1 medium)

1 oz. chopped onion

3/4 c. summer squash

1/4 tsp salt

¼ tsp black pepper

Keep couscous warm.

Heat oil in a large skillet over med high heat. Add zucchini and onion, sauté 3 minutes or until tender. Stir in couscous and corn, cook 1 minute or until thoroughly heated. Stir in s + p. (This makes 3 servings and can be used for days 3, 4 and 5)

Apple for dessert

Dinner

Sole or Cod with Baby Bok choy and brown rice

Place 1 t. unrefined sesame oil in fry pan. Lightly coat fish with thin layer of sesame oil and then dip fish into a thin plate of sesame seeds to create a crust. Place fish in pan with heated oil and slowly cook 2-3 minutes, then gently turn over, cook 2-3 minutes and remove from pan.

Chop ½ lb. baby bok choy and add to pan with sliced ginger and 1 clove of garlic, pressed. Toss well in the pan to absorb flavors. Place on top of rice and serve fish on the side.

Day 4
Breakfast

(this makes 4 ¾ c. servings – can be used for remaining breakfasts if you like it)

pear quinoa with flax and nuts

1 c. dry quinoa, rinsed and drained

2 c. plain soy or rice milk

¼ t. allspice

2 medium pears, diced, or 2 medium nectarines, diced

2 T. flaxseeds, ground

2 T. chopped walnuts

Place quinoa, milk, spice and pears in medium saucepan. Bring to a boil, stirring frequently. Cover and simmer on low for about 20 minutes. Top with ground flaxseeds and walnuts.

Lunch

See squash soup day 2

Dinner

Stir fry of sliced chicken, carrots, onions and spinach
Brown rice
Bowl of berries with dollop of yogurt

Day 5
Breakfast (if you don't make the quinoa dish)

poached egg (choose free-range, omega-3 fortified eggs) to eat with whole grain toast. Peanut butter or small portion of butter on your toast

Lunch -

Sandwich
2 slices whole grain or sprouted wheat bread
Greens, sliced fresh tomato, sliced cucumber, Bermuda onion, hummus or avocado
Water or seltzer
Afternoon snack - carrots with hummus

Dinner

Roasted vegetables – sweet onions, sweet potatoes, butternut squash, beets, mushrooms.
3-4 oz baked chicken seasoned with Bragg's Liquid Aminos.
Dessert- baked apple or pear with cinnamon

Day 6
Breakfast

Quinoa and pears, tea or coffee

Lunch

2 slices whole grain bread
Coat bread with fresh avocado, layer lettuce, tomato Sliced cucumbers, tuna and Bermuda onion.
Bowl of melon

Dinner

brown rice and kidney beans with diced peppers
4 oz fish of your choice, baked with herb dressing
green beans and carrots
water

Day 7
Breakfast

1/2 cup shredded wheat
1 banana
1/4 cup walnuts
milk

Lunch

bowl of brown rice with black beans, steamed carrots and green beans
apple or other piece of fruit

Dinner

grilled polenta disks with tomato sauce and parmesan cheese
bunch of asparagus sautéed in olive oil
cup of lentil soup

Assorted Snacks:

Nuts – walnuts, almonds, pine nuts, soy nuts
Seeds – sesame, flaxseeds, sunflower seeds, fennel seeds
Fruits and veggies of all kinds
Herbal teas
4 oz Sparkling soda + 4 oz. 100% juice or sparkling raspberry soda

Recommended Cookbooks

These are some cookbooks I use and find easy to follow. If you find a recipe you like and don't have all the ingredients, substitute the missing ones with an equivalent that you do have on hand. As you become more comfortable with cooking, rely less on cookbooks and more on your creative flair.

For Meat and Fish Eaters:

Sweet Basil, by David Becker Garden Variety Publishing, 2008 Cambridge MA
ISBN 13-978-0-9818507-0-2

Lidia's Commonsense Italian Cooking. Lidia Matticchio Bastianich & Tania Bastianich Manuali. Alfred A. Knopf, 2013 New York ISBN 978-0-385-3944-4

Eat, Drink and Be Healthy. Walter Willett, M.D. Simon & Schuster Source New York 2001. ISBN 0-684-86337-5

Vegetarian

Greens Glorious Greens! Johnna Albi & Catherine Walthers St. Martin's Press, New York 1996 ISBN 0-312-14108-4

Healthy Eating for Women for Life. PCRM with Kristine Kieswer, foreword by Neal Barnard, M.D. John Wiley & Sons, Inc. 2002 ISBN 0-471-43596-1

Engine 2 Diet. Rip Esselstyn, hgbusa.com

Recommended Readings

Food Rules, Michael Pollan. Penguin Books, New York 2009 ISBN 978-0-14-311638-7

Ultraprevention, Mark Hyman MD & Mark Liponis MD Atria Books New York 2003 ISBN 0-7432-2711-5

Savor: Mindful Eating, Mindful Life Thich Nhat Hahn & Dr. Lillian Chung. Harper One, New York 2011 ISBN 978-0-06-168770-8

Nourishing Wisdom. Marc David. Bell Tower 1991

Recommended Websites on Food and Nutrition

eatwellguide.org Eat well guide, resource for sustainable stores, farms, restaurants

ewg.org Environmental Working Group information on clean food and environment

pcrm.org Information on vegetarian eating and the cancer project website

localharvest.org provides information on community supported agriculture, Farmer's Markets, etc. by zip code foodandhealing.com Website of nutrition expert Annemarie Colbin, Ph.D.

integrativenutrition.com Institute for Integrative Nutrition online program (If you enroll, use my name as a referral for mutual financial benefit)

wellnessandyou.com/localorganic author's site. A detailed listing of food sources in Greater Boston

wellnessandyou.com author's website. Information on health and wellness through nutrition ; Nutrition counseling for individuals and groups.

http://blog.zagat.com/2013/05/8-best-farm-to-table-restaurants-around.html farm to table restaurants in Boston

www.NOFA.org/NH; www.NOFA.org/MA Organic Farmers of NH and MA
www.mayflowerfg.org Mayflower Farm & Garden

www.westonaprice.org/ Info on healthy food - Weston Price Foundation

Center for Food Safety: www.truefoodnow.org/

Local farms and farmer's markets : www.localharvest.org/
Slow food movement: www.slowfoodusa.com/

Outfitting Your Kitchen

My Dad was a skilled craftsman. He could make almost anything. I remember clearly the many times he would say: "Having good tools makes all the difference when I'm building something." The same is true for cooking. You need to have some high quality tools to make it all work smoothly. Here are a few:

Knives - Wusthof is a good choice and should include:
>   a 7" santuko knife for cutting/chopping vegetables -
>   a sharp paring knife
>   a bread knife
>   a carving knife

cutting board
chopping board
blender
food processor
juicer
vegetable peeler
quality cookware, including a sauté pan, large skillet, soup pot, and sauce pans
serving bowls and utensils
baking sheet
roasting pan
thermometer
wooden spoons
wire whisk, egg beater and electric mixer
mortar and pestle

Take Action!

Now that you've seen the great potential of food to keep you/ get you healthy, enabling you to have a long healthy life, it's time to put a plan together that supports consistent action going forward.

To that end, refer to these options for connecting with me and building on what you have learned so far.

I wish you great health and much happiness with your beautiful gift called life.

Warmly

Peg Doyle

Register for my free newsletter

The best way to keep up with all future events and sources of support is by signing up for the Wellness and You newsletter. Visit www.wellnessandyou.com to register for the newsletter and you will receive a free bonus gift personally from Peg.

Three annual tele-seminars on nutritional cleansing.

Spring, Autumn and Post-Holiday cleansing programs are simple ways to recharge your body, mind and spirit. With 4 phone sessions from the comfort of your home, you will receive all the tools you need to adjust to a new season or recover from holiday indulgences. Every session is recorded for later access. Contact Peg at peg@wellnessandyou.com for details.

Ongoing nutrition counseling by phone

Do you feel like you have a lot of knowledge about food but can't seem to stay on track? Research shows that when you invest in your goals you are much more likely to achieve them. You hire advisers for your finances, your home decor, your exercise and your careers. Why not have the support and knowledge of someone who really cares about your health and your future who won't make you feel guilty about your habits but will guide you to positive changes? With carefully scheduled phone calls, you can live anywhere in the country and receive all the support you need to be successful. Contact Peg at peg@wellnessandyou.com for a complimentary consultation.

Learn to cook video series

This is all about the basics. Nothing fancy. Just enough to get your cooking to a healthy nutritious place. These sessions are different from celebrity coach sites in that they provide you with simple practical every day recipes that nourish you with real food.

Contact Peg at peg@wellnessandyou.com for details.

Need a Speaker for Your Company or Organization?

Peg Doyle is a popular speaker and program leader. Her presentations are perfect or corporate wellness programs, health care professionals, policy makers and over 50 organizations. See more at www.wellnessandyou.com/speaker

About the Author

Peg Doyle, EdM., CHHC, is a certified holistic health coach and educator who has been studying health and nutrition for over fifteen years. She firmly believes nutrition and lifestyle, not age, are the principle predictors of health later in life and, as a clinician and educator, is dedicated to helping her clients realize and appreciate the critical link between food and health.

Doyle is a member of the national gerontology society, Sigma Phi Omega, and holds a master's degree in education as well as numerous post-graduate certificates.

A popular keynote speaker and nutrition/lifestyle consultant, she has spoken and led workshops at Harvard School of Dental Medicine, Boston College, the National Millender Conference for Occupational Therapists and numerous business organizations. Her writing has appeared on various websites, including Gatehouse Media's Wicked Local, Spirit of Change Magazine and My Menopause Magazine.

Food Becomes You is Doyle's first book. Her previously released motivational work includes two highly acclaimed recordings Stress Management|Meditations and Affirmations and Beyond Cancer.

35057919R00083

Made in the USA
Middletown, DE
04 February 2019